Amrut Laya

The Stateless State

Shri Sadguru Siddharameshwar Maharaj

Amrut Laya
The Stateless State

Spiritual Discourses of His Holiness

Shri Sadguru Siddharameshwar Maharaj

Also included in this book is the spiritual text titled:

Master Key to Self-Realization

© 2023 Sadguru Publishing

2023, First International Edition

ISBN: **978-1-7376607-3-6**

No part of this book may be reproduced or utilized in any form or by any means, electronic or mechanical for commercial or social media usage without written permission from Sadguru Publishing.

Contact Information:
Email:
sadguru.publishing@gmail.com

This book was previously published in a different form and is a derivative work printed with Permission and Cooperation from Shri Sadguru Trust - Mumbai, India

A Sadguru Publishing Publication

SADGURU

Shri Nisargadatta Maharaj

Shri Ranjit Maharaj

Renowned Disciples of
Shri Sadguru Siddharameshwar Maharaj

A Brief Introduction from the Editor

It is a great joy to be making these newly revised editions of *Amrut Laya - Volumes I and II* available in print for English speaking readers. *Amrut Laya* is comprised of what were originally hand-written notes of talks given in the Marathi language by Shri Siddharameshwar Maharaj, taken down his devotees who were co-disciples of Shri Nisargadatta Maharaj. These talks were originally broken into four volumes of unedited and largely unorganized text. Heartfelt gratitude goes out to those original note-takers and translators who have worked on these texts. Only these two volumes have currently been edited and published in English and Marathi. The remaining two volumes will hopefully become available sometime in the future. It needs to be said here that what has come to be called *Amrut Laya II* in English was actually called *Amrut Laya III* in the rough unedited volumes. This is only being mentioned because *Amrut Laya II* that can be found in the French language is not the same as *Amrut Laya II* in English. The rough unedited text of volume II is so desperately in need of better translation from Marathi to English that it is nearly impossible to decipher the original meanings of the Marathi text without the assistance of a native Marathi speaking translator, which is not available at this time. Thus, it was decided to edit and publish what was previously being called *Amrut Laya III* as *Amrut Laya II* since it was the second volume to be printed in English. The editor of the French version of *Amrut Laya II* did have the assistance of a native Marathi speaking translator, so the quality of that text is greatly improved over the rough unedited version that is still the only version available in English at this time.

The main inspiration for publishing this text is twofold. First and foremost it is an offering and a service to my spiritual master, Shri Ranjit Maharaj, as well as to his master and the author Shri Siddharameshwar Maharaj. The second compelling reason to publish these texts is as an offering to sincere English speaking seekers of advaitic wisdom because of the great benefit received by myself, the editor, when having first read these words shortly after meeting Ranjit Maharaj in 1996. The book *Master Key to Self-Realization*, which comprises the first section of *Amrut Laya*, is one of the clearest expositions on many of the fundamental principles of Advaita Vedanta that I have ever come across in over thirty years of reading spiritual texts. Reading *Master Key* and *Amrut Laya* answered many lingering questions and cleared many doubts that I had as an aspirant, paving the way for being able to receive and understand the teachings of Shri Ranjit Maharaj. It is my sincere wish that these texts will be as beneficial to others as they have been to me in de-mystifying many of the fundamental principles of the teachings about non-duality and the direct path to Self-realization. It is still quite rare to come across such clear and comprehensive presentations of Advaita Vedanta teachings in the west. As *Amrut Laya* has been out of print since 2000 and *Amrut Laya* II since 2005, it seemed fitting that these texts should be made available again to spiritual seekers and aspirants.

This is the third book of the teachings of Shri Siddharameshwar Maharaj to be published by Sadguru Publishing. The first being *Master Key to Self-Realization*, and then *Master of Self-Realization*, which was in a much more polished original condition as the Marathi text *Adhyatma Jnanacha Yogeshwar* that had been meticulously edited and published by Shri Nisargadatta Maharaj himself with the aid of some of his fellow disciples in 1960 and 1961. That text coming to us from Nisargadatta Maharaj out of reverence for his master's teaching is truly a timeless spiritual masterpiece of the highest caliber which I strongly recommended to all aspirants seeking Self-realization. The timing now seems propitious after having published *Master of Self-Realization* to present these newly revised editions of the two volumes of *Amrut Laya* in a single volume. Most of the editing on these two volumes has been minor, but there has been some significant editing in places, as well as some reformatting, in an effort to make the experience of reading more enjoyable and beneficial for the readers. It is truly a great blessing to have been given the task of editing and publishing these timeless spiritual teachings of such a great Saint.

Rarely are the teachings of such great masters as those of this lineage found in this world appearance. For the most part, the teachings contained herein represent the teachings of pure Advaita Vedanta that have changed very little from how they have been presented for thousands of years. That being said, these teachings also have a timeless quality to them that stands outside of commonly found ritualistic and dogmatic teachings from India. These teachings are about waking up to one's Self, in the moment. You are what you seek, and these texts can be an invaluable aid in to discovering that for yourself without delay.

May the teachings of the Sadguru awaken you to the fact that you are and have always been the Eternal Reality.

Jai Sadguru Parabrahman!

David Moe
Editor and Publisher
July, 2023

Table of Contents

Chapter 1: The Importance of Self-Knowledge..........................1

Chapter 2: Investigation of the Four Bodies in Search of "I"............18
    The First Body - The Physical Gross Body..................................21
    The Second Body - The Subtle Body..27
    The Third Body - The Causal Body..31
    The Fourth Body - The Great-Causal Body (Turya)....................32
    Brahman...33

Chapter 3: Investigation of the Four Bodies in Detail........................34
    A Methodical Approach to Explanation....................................34
    The Investigation Commences...38

Chapter 4: The Great-Causal Body - "I Am"......................................55

Chapter 5: The Appearance of the World..59
    Experiencing the Castes in a Human Being.............................63
    The Three Worlds..64
    Understanding the Knowledge of Self......................................66

Chapter 6: Maya and Brahman..70
    Search for the Lost "I"..73

Chapter 7: Devotion and Devotion After Liberation..........................76

The Beginning of Amrut Laya

Lecture 1 – *Dasbodh* and The Qualities of Aspirants.........................84

Lecture 2 – Visible Appearances are Untrue..86

Lecture 3 – All is Brahman...87

Lecture 4 – Uproot the Sense of "I"..89

Lecture 5 – Mental Renunciation..90

Lecture 6 – Turn the Mind Away From Objects....................................92

Lecture 7 – The Dream Within a Dream...95

Lecture 8 – The Five Sheaths and the Eight Bodies............................96

Lecture 9 – Be Free of "I" and "You"	101
Lecture 10 – Erase the Ego	105
Lecture 11 – Know the One True God	107
Lecture 12 – The Search for God	110
Lecture 13 – Brahman is the Original Illusion	113
Lecture 14 – Illusion is Imagination	116
Lecture 15 – Knowledge is Illusion	117
Lecture 16 – Everything Occurs Only in Illusion	119
Lecture 17 – Practice What You Have Heard	123
Lecture 18 – Devotion to the Master	124
Lecture 19 – Utilize the Human Birth	126
Lecture 20 – God is All-Pervasive	128
Lecture 21 – Identify With Brahman	128
Lecture 22 – Qualities of Realization	130
Lecture 23 – Be Brahman	131
Lecture 24 – Remain Detached	132
Lecture 25 – Be Firm in Self-Knowledge	134
Lecture 26 – Life Fulfilled	137
Lecture 27 – Be Oneness and See Oneness	138
Lecture 28 – Outward Signs of Self-Knowledge	140
Lecture 29 – Words About the "Wordless"	144
Lecture 30 – Reality is Bodiless	145
Lecture 31 – True Renunciation	149
Lecture 32 – Like Reflects Like	150
Lecture 33 – Knowledge is the Primal Illusion	151
Lecture 34 – Drink the Nectar of Soham	154
Lecture 35 – Self-Knowledge is Liberation	156
Lecture 36 – Brahman is Unaffected by Maya	158

Lecture 37 – You Are That...159
Lecture 38 – Know the Self..162
Lecture 39 – The Inner-Mind of All is One.......................................163
Lecture 40 - Only the Self Remains..164
Lecture 41 – Know the Self..166
Lecture 42 – Relinquish Pride and Gain Self-Knowledge.................171
Lecture 43 – Only Brahman Exists...173
Lecture 44 – The Knowledge of Brahman.......................................175
Lecture 45 – Devotion to the Master...177
Lecture 46 – Saguna Worship..179
Lecture 47 – Desireless Worship...181
Lecture 48 – Knowledge is the Primal Illusion.................................182
Lecture 49 – Awareness is Illusion...186
Lecture 50 - "I Am" is the Original Illusion.....................................190
Lecture 1 - The Sadguru, the Greatest Illuminator..........................195
Lecture 2 - The Four Bodies and Five Sheaths................................196
Lecture 3 - Vidyamaya, Avidyamaya, and Moolamaya....................197
Lecture 4 - One's Primary Duty..198
Lecture 5 - The Consciousness of All is the Same...........................198
Lecture 6 - The 3 Gunas, the 4 Geneses, and 5 Dissolutions...........199
Lecture 7 - Elements of the Subtle Body...200
Lecture 8 - Discrimination Between True and Untrue.....................201
Lecture 9 - The Steady and the Unsteady..202
Lecture 10 - Keeping the Company of Saints..................................202
Lecture 11 - The Power of the Saint..203
Lecture 12 - Spiritual Practice and the Gunas.................................204
Lecture 13 - Renunciation of Pride and Desire................................204
Lecture 14 - Pride is Ego..205

Lecture 15 - The Self is Not the Body..206
Lecture 16 - The Inner-Mind, and the Five Elements......................207
Lecture 17 - Worship of the Master..208
Lecture 18 - How to Worship..210
Lecture 19 – Give Up Pride for the Body..211
Lecture 20 - Spiritual Science and Eliminating Pride....................212
Lecture 21 - Description of the Master..213
Lecture 22 - Four Types of Speech, and "Soham".........................215
Lecture 23 – The Three Gunas..215
Lecture 24 - The Mantra "I Am Brahman"....................................216
Lecture 25 - The Self Does Not Die..218
Lecture 26 - There is Only One Self...219
Lecture 27 - The Self is the Only Experiencer...............................220
Lecture 28 - Renunciation of Desires and Pride............................221
Lecture 29 - Abandoning Pride...223
Lecture 30 - The Self is not Affected by the Body.........................224
Lecture 31 - Renunciation of Passionate Attachment...................225
Lecture 32 - Relinquishing "I" and "Mine"...................................226
Lecture 33 - The Objective World is Like a Dream......................228
Lecture 34 - The Self is Consciousness..229
Lecture 35 - The Self is the Real "I"..231
Lecture 36 - The Knowledge "I Am Brahman".............................232
Lecture 37 - Non-Conceptual Knowledge......................................233
Lecture 38 - Attainment of Knowledge..235
Lecture 39 - The Pride of Ignorance and Knowledge...................237
Lecture 40 - Be God to Know God...239
Lecture 41 - Salutations to Ganesha..239
Lecture 42 - The Self is Beyond Concepts.....................................240

Lecture 43 - The Nature of the Mind..241
Lecture 44 - Giving up Body-Consciousness...................................242
Lecture 45 - Destroying Illusion with "Right Thought"..................244
Lecture 46 - Right Thinking Brings Liberation...............................245
Lecture 47 - Give up Body-Consciousness......................................248
Lecture 48 - Three Types of Differentiation....................................249
Lecture 49 - The Jnani is Beyond Karma and Death......................250
Lecture 50 - The Nature of the Body..251
Lecture 51 - The Jnani is Reality..252
Lecture 52 - Illusion is That Which is Not......................................253
Lecture 53 - Knowledge and Worship..254
Lecture 54 - Only Brahman Exists...256
Lecture 55 - Knowledge, or Jnana...257
Lecture 56 - Names Are Untrue...259
Lecture 57 - Renunciation is True Happiness.................................260
Lecture 58 - Ignorance Vanishes with "Right Thought"................262
Lecture 59 - Primal Illusion and Destruction..................................264
Lecture 60 - Brahman, Five Sheaths, Four Bodies of Ishwara.......270
Lecture 61 - The Secret Ganga Revealed..275
Lecture 62 - The Changeless and the Ever-Changing....................278
Lecture 63 - Prologue, Procedure, and Epilogue............................279
Lecture 64 - Paramatman alone Exists..281
Lecture 65 - The Self Functions in All..283
Lecture 66 - The Jnani is Beyond Actions, Bhajans.......................284
Lecture 67 - Spiritual Practices, Vegetarianism..............................286
Lecture 68 - Domestic Life and Being Alert...................................286
Lecture 69 - The Self Knows All...288
Lecture 70 - The Five Elements and the Mahavakyas....................289

Lecture 71 - Renunciation and Discrimination..................................292

Lecture 72 - Swaroopa and Self-Declaration.................................294

Lecture 73 - Primal Illusion and Death of the Ego........................296

Lecture 74 - The Knowledge of Brahman.......................................300

Lecture 75 - Bhajans and the Name of Rama.................................300

Lecture 76 - A Story..301

Lecture 77 - The Transient and the Eternal....................................303

Lecture 78 - The Self (Atman), Brahman, and Parabrahman............305

Lecture 79 - As You Conceive, So You Perceive.............................307

Lecture 80 - Knowledge and Universal Compassion.......................308

Lecture 81 – Kirtan Means "I Am He"...309

Lecture 82 - Cultivating Habits...310

Lecture 83 - Effort and Worship...310

Lecture 84 - The Human Body and Discrimination.......................315

Lecture 85 - Skillfully Eliminate Concepts....................................318

Lecture 86 - Parabrahman is "Seen" Through Merger...................321

Lecture 87 - Absorption of the Mind..322

Lecture 88 - Signs of a Sadguru and a Disciple.............................326

Master Key to Self-Realization

The Spiritual Science of Self-Knowledge
as Presented by His Holiness
Shri Siddharameshwar Maharaj

Chapter 1: The Importance of Self-Knowledge

At the beginning of this exposition reverential adoration is offered to Shri Ganesh first, then to Shri Saraswati, and finally to Shri Sadguru. What is the reason for offering salutations in this order? If someone were to ask, "If the sequence of this adoration is changed will there be confusion?" The answer has to be, yes, there will be confusion. This is because Shri Ganesh is the deity for meditation and contemplation, and Shri Saraswati is the deity for the exposition of the teaching through words. With the help of these two deities, the deity in the form of "The Light of the Self," that arises in the heart of the aspirant is none other than the Sadguru. Therefore, the Sadguru necessarily has to be adored after Shri Ganesh and Shri Saraswati. Only when the understanding of the subject becomes firm does "The Grace of the Sadguru" descend. Neither the exposition of this text, nor the contemplation on the contents of this text will by themselves lead the aspirant to the goal. Therefore, one should reverentially adore *both* Shri Ganesh and Shri Saraswati.

There is an ancient method of expounding the teaching of Vedanta that is commonly followed in this tradition (Sampradaya) when presenting the subject matter of this text to the aspirant. According to this method, first the manifest form of the Sadguru is seen by the eyes. Then the knowledge about the teachings of the Vedanta, and the value and significance of these precious teachings is extolled through the words of the Guru. Then, a Mantra (a subtle name of God, or a phrase) is given and the aspirant is instructed to practice meditation on the repetition of the Mantra for a short period of time (usually several weeks) to imprint its significance within. This provides a means for the aspirant to make the mind more subtle so that the teachings to follow can be more easily grasped and realized. This is the seekers initiation to the teaching and invitation to become an aspirant on the path to realization.

In accordance with the method of the Saints that has been outlined above, the Sadguru first explains about the subject that is to follow, then indicates its characteristics, and finally follows by imparting a detailed knowledge of the subject. In most schools of education, when teaching small children about any subject, the teacher first verbally informs the child about the subject matter that will be taught. This is called the kindergarten method of education. Similarly, initially the Sadguru verbally gives you a concept or idea of Reality (such as "You are He" or "Only Brahman Exists," or some other similar form of mantra) that is to be contemplated upon. Through repetition or churning, this idea will be indelibly imprinted on the mind. This is called "The Tradition (Sampradaya) of the Sadguru." Through this preliminary method the aspirant achieves results sooner. So be it.

Afterwards, the Guru expounds the Truth (the subject matter) to an ordinarily intelligent aspirant, and he understands what the Sadguru conveys, and about "That" which He is teaching. However, the main difficulty is in experientially realizing what has been intellectually understood. Through the exposition of the subject by the Sadguru, one understands what the Self (Atman) is. However, the ghost of doubt pops up in the mind of the aspirant in the form of the question "How am I the Self?" and the aspirant's mental attitude does not become free of doubt. There is an intellectual understanding, but no realization. The remedy for this is to study with determination and learn the teaching. Unless there is sustained and repeated study, it will not be fully understood and realized. For example, in the instructional handwriting book, the letters presented are very beautiful. We understand this, but initially we cannot write the letters in the same way. If however the same letters are written repeatedly, then by virtue of that practice or study, the letters are beautifully formed as soon as the pen touches the paper. Here someone might ask, "How much study or practice is required to learn the subject well?" The answer is, "The study and the practice, or effort, must continue relentlessly according to each one's capacity, until it is understood or realized."

A general example can be stated here to impress upon the mind of the aspirant the importance of repeated study. An ordinarily intelligent man can understand something if it is explained to him two or three times. If he repeats it ten or twenty times, it becomes a habit. If he repeats it a hundred times, it becomes like an addiction. Once he becomes familiar with it a thousand times, it becomes inherent nature for the one practicing it. If we look at the fibers of the jute plant, they are so delicate and fine that they become scattered in all directions when blown by the wind. However, when the same fibers are entwined together to form a rope, it is so strong that it can bind even a strong and violent elephant to a small peg. Similarly great is the power of the repetition of the study of this type of practice. It is indeed true that Parabrahman is All-Pervading and Eternally Free. However, the Wind in the form of mind has become so strong in us due to misdirected practice and study through birth after birth that it has imprisoned the eternally free Brahman in the thought of identification with the body. About the tremendous result of repeated practice Saint Tukaram has said, "Whatever is unachievable, becomes achievable only by virtue of repeated study and practice." Recognizing the importance of this study, the aspirant should adore the principles symbolized by Ganesh and Saraswati. This means that one should fulfill himself by continuous meditation, and learn through repeatedly hearing the exposition of Truth.

Now, before one begins this study it will be desirable for the aspirant to know many other things relevant to the subject. Why has the illusion "I am the body" arisen in a human being? What was the condition of the human being when he was born? How did he develop this idea of "me" and "mine"? Is his condition in the world free from fear? If so, by whom and how was he helped to be rid of that fear? All of these things must be taken into consideration.

First, the human being was lying twisted up in a small space inside the mother's womb. When he was born, he came into this boundless world and slightly opened his eyes and looked around. Upon seeing the immense space and tremendous light, he averted his eyes, and he was in shock. "Where is this that I have come alone? Who is going to give me support? What is going to be my fate?" These types of fear arose in his mind. Immediately after birth, with the first shock, he started to cry. After a little while he was given a drop of honey to lick. With this, he felt relieved thinking that all was well, and that he had someone's support. Thus, he pacified himself. However, that first shock of fear was so ingrained in his mind that he became startled at the slightest sound, and then again becomes quiet when given honey or his mother's breast. In this way, taking external support at every step, this human being became dependent on the support of his parents. As he grew older, his parents as well as those who looked after him as a child started giving him knowledge about the world. After that, his school teachers taught him the various physical sciences such as geography, geometry, geology, etc., which are valueless like dust.

As one enters the stage of youth, he again looks for additional props for his life. As it is determined in the world that support for life comes from money, wife, etc., he gathers wealth and takes on a wife. He takes it for granted that he can be sustained on this worldly support alone, and he squanders away his life. With fame, learning, power and authority, wealth, and wife, he gets added prosperity, and becomes entangled more and more. His principle possessions and his entire support, are his wife, wealth, status, youth, beauty, and authority. Taking special pride in all of this, and becoming intoxicated with worldliness, the human being misses knowing his "Real Nature." The pride about money, pride about authority, and pride about beauty absorb the man and he forgets his Real Nature. Eventually, the above possessions start dwindling one by one. When these possessions start to drop off according to the law of nature, the memory of the original shock that he received earlier shakes him to his very roots, and he becomes frustrated. Panicking, he inquires "What shall I do now? I am losing support from all sides. What will happen to me?" However, this ignorant man does not understand that all these possessions had only one solid support, which was his own Existence, or sense of "I Am." It is by that support alone, that money had its value, that his wife appeared charming, that honor received seemed worthwhile, his learning gave him wisdom, his form acquired beauty, and his authority wielded power. Oh, poor man, you yourself are the support of all the above described wealth! Can there be a greater paradox than to feel that wealth gave you support? In addition to this wealth, power, woman, youth, beauty of form, and honor, if one further receives ill-gotten fortune, how strange and perverted would one's actions become?

A poet once wrote (describing the pranks of the human mind), "It is primarily a monkey, in addition to that he gets drunk, and to top that, a scorpion bites him." Even such a poet would put his pen down seeing the ludicrous absurdities of this human being, and would bid goodbye to his poetic talents. The sort of man who considers his body as God, and is absorbed in its worship day and night should be considered to be like a shoemaker. There is an appropriate proverb that says that a chambhar's God should be worshipped only with shoes (in Marathi, the word chambhar means "the one who carries a hide on his back"). This tells us the way in which this "God" (the body) of such a man has to be adored. The devotion of an atheist is the feeding of his body, and his liberation is the death of the body. For such a man whose ultimate goal in life is feeding his body, and his liberation is death, there is no rising above the

"Gross Body" level. This is not surprising in his case. If due to some misfortune, he were to lose all his wealth, he would still borrow money to indulge in his habits of eating, drinking, and enjoying. If creditors were to hound him, he would declare insolvency to be rid of the whole issue. When death strikes him, ultimately he just lies dead. He passes away just as he had come. Could there be anything more tragic or wretched than this sort of life?

Why should the woman who showers praise on her husband for getting her a lovely nose ring think of the Lord who has provided her with a nose to put the nose ring on? In the same way, how can the animalistic human beings who only look to the body as the "be-all" and "end-all" of life, see God? The One whose power gives the Sun its existence as the Sun, the Moon its existence as the Moon, the Gods their existence as Gods, is the One Almighty God. It is He, who is the support of all, who is present in the hearts of all beings, and has become invisible to man. The one whose eyes are trained on external objects sees only that which is external. The word "Aksha" is a synonym for "eye" in Marathi. "A" is the very first letter of the alphabet, and "ksha" is one of the last consonants. It means that whatever the eye sees will lie within the range of these two letters of the alphabet. It will only bring information or knowledge of external objects. Gross objects will be visualized by the gross eye, and the subtle will be sensed by the senses, which are subtle. However, one letter of the alphabet that comes after 'ksha' in Marathi is "gnya." The letter "'gnya" indicates Knowledge that cannot be seen either by the gross external eye, or the subtle eye of the intellect. Therefore, the intellect and the senses together indicate the "eye" with the synonym "aksha." Like the eye, the other sense organs, the ear, nose, and tongue, are all pointing outwards, and continue to exist on the strength of external objects.

The "King of Knowledge" ("I Am") influences all of the senses, and seems to grant these senses the "lordship" over the sense objects. It is because of this externalization that the fact that He is present prior to the senses does not attract anyone's attention. Over many births, the mind and intellect have acquired the habit of only looking outwards. Therefore, to "turn within" has become a very difficult task. This is called "the reverse path" which the Saints follow when they turn in the opposite direction, and behold the mind completely giving up seeing all that is external. Where an ordinary man is asleep, the Saints are awake, and where an ordinary man is awake, the Saints dose off. All beings find themselves awakened to external objects, and have become extremely skillful in this type of awakening. The Saints however, have closed their eyes to external things, and it is the Self, to which other beings are asleep, that keeps the Saints wide awake.

One who gets a million rupees is worried about how to double it the next day. He pushes himself to acquire more and more. However, the Saints warn him, "Turn back, turn back, you may be caught in the whirlpool of Illusion (Maya). This Maya has come in like a full tide, and you might be carried away." The modern technological advances that come to this world with newer and newer innovations, as well as those yet to come, make up a cyclone of "Great Illusion" (Mahamaya). Be certain that you will be held captive by it. Who knows to where the one who is caught by this great cyclone will be carried off? When the Saints see one whose attention is taken up by these modern advances running here and there, struggling in his pursuits, they try their utmost to bring about an awakening of Self-Knowledge in him.

There is a story about when Saint Ramdas and Saint Tukaram met each other while standing on the opposite banks of a river. With a gesture of his hand, Samartha Ramdas asked Saint Tukaram "How much awakening have you brought about among the people?" Saint Tukaram replied with a gesture forming his right hand in a fist and putting the back of it to his lips to indicate that nowhere had he found anybody who cared for awakening to the Sel3f. Then Tukaram Maharaj put the same question back to Samartha Ramdas, who then indicated that there was no one awakening whatsoever. They then continued on their way. Saint Tukaram has said, "How can I describe the obligations of the Saints? They are continuously awakening me." Even though it is true that Saint Tukaram and Samartha Ramdas are no longer with us in bodily form, they have given us all that they wanted to teach in the books **Abhangagatha** and **Dasbodh**. The great wealth that they have handed over to us is the priceless legacy of these books. Whoever makes a claim that he is heir to their legacy will enjoy this priceless inheritance. However, the one who wants this wealth must give up the pride of mundane demonical wealth. In addition, whatever acts that one considers as meritorious, and dear to one's heart, must also be renounced. One must be prepared to take a step on the path that turns inward. These are the conditions for becoming a beneficiary of this legacy.

Man is fully immersed in the pride of his body, his caste, his family, his region, his country, and whatever good or bad is in his nature. All of these various types of pride have possessed him. Until he becomes completely free from these various types of pride, how can he claim to benefit from the legacy of this treasure that the Saints have left behind? Only the one whose heart sincerely relinquishes pride can become the beneficiary of this wealth. There is hope for the man who becomes aware of these various types of pride that he has acquired from birth after birth, which have become his second nature, if he sincerely relinquishes this pride. He need not be frustrated. If a slave is awakened to the knowledge that he is a slave, he instantly starts looking for a way to freedom. A slave who finds joy in his slavery, and makes every effort to continue in that condition, cannot even conceive that a highway to freedom exists, until such time that the knowledge of his slavery dawns on him. Similarly, a lucky man who feels that the ambition of getting ahead of others is actually taking him on a downward path, will get from that day onward a glimpse of the reverse direction shown by the Saints. Slowly, he automatically starts making the effort to step onto a new path.

The various types of pride may not leave one all at once. If the aspirant starts to become completely determined to be aware of the pride that he harbors, and begins to leave them one by one, the infinitely merciful Lord will not fail to give him a helping hand. If one takes pride in vicious or evil acts, this should be counteracted by increasing pride in good acts, thus eradicating all of his bad qualities. The good qualities should be nourished and developed. However, one should not be attached to them, and should slowly begin to abandon the pride arising from good actions. A doubt may arise here that although vices deserve to be left, "Why is it that you tell us to leave good qualities also? After all good qualities are always good." Dear aspirants, although the possession of good qualities in comparison wit3333333333333333333333333333h vices and bad qualities seems to be better with regard to the pursuit of attaining Self Knowledge, the possession of the good qualities which one holds dear to one's heart is really a hundred times worse, and truly needs to be thrown out. Look into this and see. An aspirant tries to leave his bad qualities on the advice of the Saints because of the sense of shame that is created by society or in one's mind, however, the one who possesses good qualities is always getting praise in the world, and is accordingly full of pride about these good qualities. It is very difficult for one to let go of the pride about good qualities.

The pride regarding negative qualities can be left fairly easily, but it is not so in the case of pride regarding good qualities. Nobody wants to admit that he has committed any error, but the pride that one harbors when he has given meals to thousands who have visited the four holy places, or opened lodging for holy people, or worshipped the deity millions of times, becomes so firm in him that it becomes almost impossible to give up. It is when one recognizes one's worldly ways and is ready to relinquish them that he soon finds a Sadguru. However, the one who is sought after by everyone for performing many good deeds, gets so deeply buried in the flattery that is showered upon him, that his way to the Sadguru becomes lost due to his pride. Realizing this, one must conclude that pride about bad qualities is tolerable, but the pride about good qualities is best to be avoided completely. Both the pride about one's good qualities and pride about one's bad qualities are thorns on the path to Self-Knowledge. When one thorn is pulled out with the help of another thorn, there still remains the second thorn (pride of good actions) that one carries around in the shirt pocket. Will this thorn not also prick the chest or rib? If a thief is shackled by iron handcuffs and a king by golden handcuffs, does that mean that the king is not bound?

Take it for granted that while the man in the iron cuffs will thank someone who frees him from them, the man with the golden cuffs will pounce on the throat of anyone who tries to free him. He will try his best to permanently keep the golden cuff on his hands. What is the force behind this? Who is this "friendly enemy" in this example who makes one feel so happy in his bondage? It is the pride one has in good deeds that is the real archenemy of the aspirant. This pride is the enemy who blocks the way to "Ultimate Truth" (Paramartha). Therefore, it is necessary to renounce any pride that one has about good deeds. This may require tremendous effort, but without renouncing all pride, the aspirant can never claim his legacy to the wealth of "Knowledge." It is believed by many that a man's worldly wealth such as money, a beautiful wife, status, etc. is the result of meritorious deeds done in previous births, but these very beliefs act as boulders obstructing the way to finding the "Ultimate Truth." Therefore, it may be said that these things are really the result of body identification (the definition of sin). When a person is infused with pride, he becomes possessed, and therefore becomes incapable of treading the path of Ultimate Truth.

Contrary to the wealthy man, there might be a man who does not have a penny, who is quite ugly, has no wife, no status, and is so poverty stricken that in order to fill his belly, he is willing to eat whatever food he could get from anyone. He may have lost his caste, family, friends, and all who were dear to him. This homeless wanderer may be naked on all fronts, and even believed to be wretched by the whole society, yet he truly may be more worthy of gaining Self-Knowledge, because he is naturally free of pride. The ears of someone like this poor naked man turn towards the Sadguru sooner than one whose ears are filled with flattery. The one who is puffed up with pride has no room for receiving the advice of the Sadguru. Such a person has no time to turn to the Sadguru's advice even for a minute.

The whole of humanity has become entangled in Illusion from birth, and lives in bondage. In addition to this, man creates many types of artificial bondage around him in the form of comforts and attachments resulting from ever newer inventions. If man has to live in modern society, he has to abide by and respect the norms of traditional social conventions, and governmental rules. For example, wearing a necktie in order for one to do one's daily work is supposed to be the proper social etiquette. In these types of ways, to be up to date in society makes one feel that he is getting more and more freedom. In modern society, if one does not indulge in drinking or drugs, or does not shave everyday, he is considered a social outcast. By diving into the bondage of such a society and holding such silly ideas dear to the heart, one only continues binding oneself, only further increasing the pride that one has about worthless things. Unless these types of social bondage and pride are completely thrown off, and unless one is considered to be a madman by the "socially wise" people, there is no hope that one will arrive at such a mental state that allows one to be free from pride, and such social bondage. The Sadguru's only aim is to help one to become completely free of all pride, and to eradicate the identification with the body. If the aspirant finds the renunciation of all pride and social bonds difficult to do, or is unwilling to formally renounce his wife, money, or estate, he can begin with inward renunciation. When this becomes successful, the formal renunciation slowly becomes possible.

Inward renunciation means renunciation that is undertaken with the mind. For example, there may be someone who has the habit of hurting others with harsh words. It does not cost the aspirant anything to replace that habit by saying only kind words to others. As another example, there may be some people who have the habit of telling lies unnecessarily, in their case, they should begin renunciation by stopping the telling of lies, at least until such time that an occasion arises where unless they tell a lie, some great calamity may occur. This type of mental renunciation will also not require any expenditure. While looking at a neighbor's prosperity, one should not be envious of his neighbor. Will making such a decision bring the aspirant any harm? In this way, when one begins to renounce negative qualities, he also begins to gain strength in renouncing external things. This world is like a dream, and in this dream-like world whatever is considered to be good or bad, merit or sin, or anything in the realm of dualistic morality is of no consequence in the process of awakening to the Self. Therefore, renunciation of both sides of duality such as good and bad, or auspicious and inauspicious, is necessary to gain Self-Knowledge. Even though this may be understood, it is still difficult to eradicate pride. No matter how often someone may repeat to himself to "renounce, renounce," it will not make even the slightest dent on pride. However, if the reason why this pride enters one is discovered, it can be eradicated, and renunciation automatically follows. The aspirant must come to understand that the reason why one harbors pride for objects is because he believes the objects to be true.

If one understands that objects are only a temporary appearance, and becomes convinced that objects cannot really provide true happiness, then the apparent reality of the objects automatically fades away. It then becomes possible for one to develop detachment for those objects that were previously held dear to one as true. A wooden toy in the shape of a tamarind pod is not a real tamarind pod. It is made of wood. However, unless one has the discriminative ability to be able to tell the difference, the sight of the wooden tamarind is sure to make one's mouth start watering. The reason for this is the conviction that the thing is real. Once one becomes aware that the tamarind is made of wood, he may appreciate the artistic or aesthetic lines of the toy, but it will not affect his salivary glands. This discriminative knowledge, or the recognition that it is not real, results in true detachment towards the object. This example shows us that the detachment towards objects is brought about by understanding their true nature. Unless the futility of acquiring objects in this world is impressed irrevocably upon the mind, Self-Knowledge is difficult to attain. Unless one understands the false nature of objects, one will never aspire for the "Real Thing." There can be no renunciation of the false as long as the intellect believes it to be true. The day that the wrong knowledge regarding the world is eliminated by virtue of the Sadguru's advice, one becomes convinced that this entire world is only a temporary appearance. When this happens, one becomes able to look at the world and appreciate it as if it were a cinema, or a source of entertainment, and with the detachment that has been achieved, one remains unaffected.

Detachment without Self-Knowledge is like what is experienced when one is watching the activities going on at the cremation grounds. Without Self-Knowledge, there can be no real renunciation, and without renunciation, there can be no Self-Knowledge. This is the paradox. The Saints have given us various methods of getting out of this situation through such means as devotion to the Guru and God, singing the praises of the Guru and God (Bhajans), visiting holy places, giving in charity, etc. In this way, the Saints have given an infinite number of means of salvation to humanity. Human nature is such that if a man is forcibly robbed of a thing, he suffers immensely. He will make persistent efforts to regain that thing. Yet, if he were to part with the same thing out of his own free will, that sacrifice would bring him immense joy. A man who is normally unwilling to spend a dime under compulsion, would out of his own free choice spend thousands in order to feed the people at a religious gathering. However, there are countless examples of how after mixing with Saints, and chanting bhajans, even very proud people have changed. One whose pride previously would not have allowed him to submit to another person's will is now willing to bow in submission to someone even of a much lower standing in society. By his keeping the company of Saints, he naturally and easily completely forgets his pride of caste or social status. That important man who was filled with pride, and felt ashamed to even apply sandalwood paste to his forehead in his own house, now allows Bhuki (a black powder) to be smeared on his face, indicating a total lack of pride. The same person who previously considered singing and dancing obscene, forgets himself and his body, and starts dancing in ecstatic joy with a partner, while chanting the name of God. Understanding how aspirants sacrifice pride in this way, the Saints have given mankind the teachings prescribing Bhajans and Worship (Puja) for daily practice. With this teaching, they have pointed out a progressive step on the path of Self-Knowledge. In this way, they impress upon the aspirant how easy it is to renounce the objects of the world, and how to clear one's mental attitude from pride.

Self-Knowledge is the Knowledge about one's Self. Once we recognize who we really are, then automatically the determination is made regarding what is permanent and what is transient. Then, very naturally the renunciation of the impermanent, and the acceptance of the permanent follows. Because of the transient nature of things, the fear of dissolution is inevitable. The one who is overpowered by this fear of dissolution, or death, continuously strives to see that some particular thing is not taken from him. He takes every precaution to preserve his money, tries hard to see that his wife's youth and beauty does not deteriorate, and struggles to keep his status and authority. However, try as he may, nothing ever happens according to his wishes or desires. No one can escape their destiny, and because death is all-consuming, everything will eventually get crushed in its jaws. Even Gods like Brahma are not free from the fear of death.

Even if such a fear-ridden man were given everything he desired, could he avoid being afraid? If he needs anything at all, it is the gift of fearlessness. The aspirant must find that which will free him from fear permanently. This beggar called man, who has lost his own treasure of the Self, continuously chants "I am the body, I am the body." He is forever discontent saying "I want this, I want that," and wanders around always begging for something in the world. He can only truly be pacified with the gift of the Self. The man who chants "What will happen to me, my wife and children, and the money that I consider to be mine?" is always disturbed and upset. This sort of man needs to be given the gift of fearlessness, and thus be made fearless. Only the Sadguru is generous enough, and capable of bestowing the gift of fearlessness, which is the noblest of all the gifts. Kings and emperors, and even gods are incapable of granting this gift of fearlessness. Although all earthly wealth is at the feet of an emperor, he is restless with fear at the very thought of an enemy attack. Even Lord Indra is anxious day and night with the thought that his status as "King of the Gods" might be shaken by the austerities and practices performed by some sage. Think deeply on this. Can those who have not freed themselves of fear give the gift of fearlessness to others? Only those Great Saints, the "Mahatmas," who have uprooted fear from its very depths by establishing themselves in the Self and destroying the identification with the body are capable of granting the gift of fearlessness. Except for these Mahatmas, the hosts of gods, demons and men are like penniless beggars. They can never get the gift of fearlessness unless they take shelter with a Sadguru. If they are gods, they entertain the pride of godly wealth, if they are demons, they carry the pride of their own vicious wealth on their heads, and human beings are crushed under their own burdens. Gods are no better than servants who carry other people's burdens on their heads. What is the lowly status then of the human beggar? It is only the Sadguru who extends his hand to lift their burden, and blesses them at the same time with the gift of fearlessness.

Out of all the various types of knowledge, Self-Knowledge is the greatest, and of all the paths, or dharmas (dharma is one's religion, or one's nature), Swadharma is the most noble. The Mahatmas spread the "Knowledge of the Self" among mankind and teach them the meaning of Swadharma. In this world, the knowledge of astrology, black magic, public relations, the fourteen types of sciences, and the sixty-four arts are taught. However, all that knowledge except for "Knowledge of the Self" is false knowledge. Saints refuse to recognize these other types of knowledge, and spread only the "Knowledge of the Self." Many missionaries who are competing with one another assert their opinions and start giving advice saying, "My religion is the noblest, and all others will only lead one to ruin." Not only do they just give advice, but also they fulfill their sacred duty of conversion, sometimes through bribes, or threats of burning people's houses, or sometimes even by killing people. Without much change from days of old, this kind of propagation of religion is going on even today. This piracy of religion full of compulsion and tyranny is not useful for accomplishing the well-being of anyone.

Saint Ramdas said, "If there is any one religion in the world that is noblest of all, it is Swadharma." Swadharma means to live in one's "True Nature." To live in one's innate nature is Swadharma even though one may belong to any caste, religion, or nation. To understand Swadharma, one should realize that it is existent in all forms of life, be it an ant, or an insect. One's "True Nature" alone is Swadharma and all other paths or cults parading as religions are "paradharma," meaning that they are religions pertaining to something that is other than the Self. These various cults and religions put down certain rules and methods which are alien to our real nature. This is how we can define Swadharma and paradharma. If we take for granted the currently accepted meaning of Swadharma, it can be considered absurdity. Suppose there is a prostitute. She also has a relevant dharma, her nature, which she follows diligently believing that it is her swadharma, or her true nature, her true religion.

She teaches the same to her daughter from the time she is in the cradle, and in the end she dies following her own religion. Who can say, perhaps some "Streetwhore Swami" (a lover of women) may even come forward to include that woman's life story in some book about religious saints.

The Lord has cautioned us in the **Bhagavad Gita**, "It is best to die in Swadharma (the death of body identification, which brings one into the Self). Dharma that is alien, is full of danger. While trying to achieve this, if death comes, it is to be preferred over following some other dharma which is alien to the Self." The aspirant should recognize the importance of the caution that is being imparted in the Lord's words. Eradicating the idea of identification with the body is the sign of the "Knowledge of the Self." Mahatmas experience this type of death while living. This type of death is to be preferred over the death that occurs when following someone else's religion. Saint Tukaram said, "I have seen my own death, how shall I describe that process which is unique?" How can those who live in a religion that is not of the Self, and who die a corpse's death, understand this process of death while living? The unfortunate one only thinks of death in terms of various customs and rites according to one's religion. Those dharmas built on the strong basis of body identification contain the dualities of temptation and fear, heaven and hell, merit and sin, and bondage and liberation. Every human being has the right of following Swadharma, one's own nature where there is no temptation of heavenly enjoyments and no fear of pain in purgatory, and where bondage and liberation have no meaning. There is a cruel but true maxim that states, "Whatever comes has to go." All of the recent "pseudo-religions" are spreading because of their newness, and in some cases even with government patronization. They will definitely sink to the bottom, and there will be nothing but glory and victory to Swadharma alone. (Note - During Shri Siddharameshwar Maharaj's time, the Government in India was in many cases helping to fund religious schools and even missionaries. In this paragraph all religions that are not of the Self are being called "pseudo-religions," not being of our "True Nature," or "Swadharma," and ultimately they will not last)

Lord Krishna advised Arjuna on this. He said, "Leave aside all religions and come seek refuge in Me. Come to Me, and leave off all of those religions which create hindrances on the path to reaching Me. Seek refuge in Paramatman who is of the nature of Self-Knowledge. You will have realized your Self when you attain Me, and there will be nothing more for you to do. All karma (actions) gets exhausted in Self-Knowledge." On the pretext of advising Arjuna, Lord Krishna has given this advice to all human beings that they should fulfill themselves by accepting this advice that he has given. There is nothing in the whole world as sacred as Self-Knowledge. All other work or action is meaningless. In this context one should not think that all other types of knowledge or actions except Self-Knowledge are useless, meaning that they are of no value, or without any result. However, they are of no help in achieving Swadharma. It is not that getting results such as a son, or heaven by means of performing sacrifices. By studying scriptures one becomes proficient, and it is possible for one to appease various deities by worshipping them. Even if this is so, and even if all these actions are supposed to be meritorious in this mundane world, they are still hindrances as long as the Self is not pleased, and does not shower His Grace. The qualities valued as best in the practical world only count as disqualification, and all remedies only turn into obstacles in pursuit of Self-Knowledge. The sages know this well and do not even care in the slightest if they are able to conquer all of the three worlds. They consider Lord Indra's status, that is ridden with jealousies, to be as useless as the droppings of a crow. The Saints harbor only one desire in their hearts, and that is the desire of achieving "Oneness with Brahman." With regard to everything else, they are desireless. Those Saints who are represented by statues of auspiciousness became one with Brahman when their Consciousness became dis-identified from their body. In ordinary cases, the body is viewed only as a corpse, while in the case of those Mahatmas, they became worthy of worship, and they receive adoration from people. Not only this, but also many temples were built around their shrines. Thus, they became immortal by becoming the object of worship and adoration by the whole world.

Rama, Krishna, Siddhartha, Hanuman, Malhari, Jagadamba, were all Mahatmas in the form of Gurus. While they were alive, they did the work of spreading Knowledge and they became gods when they left the body. All the temples on earth belong to these very gods who grant the wishes of devotees according to their vows and desires. They lift the aspirant to their own level and bring them to the achievement of Self-fulfillment. Many people think that the God that one worships meets him (when he sees a vision) and gets his work done, but God is not limited to one point or place as the devotee imagines. He resides in the devotee's heart as well as in every heart, and it is He who inspires one to get one's work done.

Nobody should ever entertain the wrong idea that after the Mahatma leaves his body, he assumes the same body again and comes out of his Samadhi (comes back from the dead) and then gets his devotee's work done.

When you wish that a certain person should get ten rupees at Pune (a city in Maharashtra State in India), you give a ten rupee note in cash to the main Post Office at Sholapur. On the second or third day, you get the receipt indicating that the intended person has received the amount that you have sent. Have you ever made inquiries to the effect that the same note, or the same coins that you handed over to the Post Office have reached the intended person? No, this type of question never even arises in your mind. Your attention is centered not on that exact note, but on the value of the note. When the amount sent has reached the person, you do not have any complaints. In the same way, these past Saints and Mahatmas who have turned into gods get the devotees work accomplished through the Mahatmas that are living today, and who are of the same caliber. This is the way their devotees' wishes are fulfilled.

What magical skill did these persons possess who were honored in their lifetime and became immortal, thereby retaining their fame even after their bodily death? What special learning did they have that they should be adored by people even after death? In this world, there are many arts and sciences. Many discoverers and many adventurous heroes are praised during their lifetime. These heroes are congratulated and covered with garlands of flowers, and bouquets. The people even express their admiration for the heroes by carrying them on their shoulders. However, in due time, a hero who had been an object of people's adoration soon becomes a subject of their abuses. Soon people who were pampered as heroes for a few days, are condemned in an assembly. Sometimes, even resolutions condemning them are carried out. It is clear that the greatness of these heroes is artificial and not everlasting because their "greatness" is based on transient learning or adventures. Their greatness is not based on the sacred learning that gives everlasting peace like the "Knowledge of the Self." It is based on some science such as politics with some practical motive. In politics names and faces continue changing with time, and in the physical sciences new discoveries follow one after another. A person who was once proclaimed as great is found to be of no importance and in some other corner of the world some other person starts shining on the horizon. The greatness that is achieved through any learning other than Self-Knowledge eventually takes an opposite direction. Because of this, these "great ones" have to suffer the sweet and sour experiences associated with honor and insult. It is no wonder that no one goes to the trouble of thinking about these "great men" after they are dead.

Out of all the types of Knowledge (Vidya), Self-Knowledge (Atma Vidya) is the only Knowledge that grants everlasting peace. One Saint asked, "What is the use of any knowledge that does not grant peace of mind?" There are many types of courses of learning that are available in the world. Why is there such a proliferation of courses? The reason is that no one has found peace of mind. The struggles in the world have not stopped even a little because the restlessness of the mind has not ceased. Why is this? It is because all of these sciences and arts are centered in Ignorance, and they are useful only for increasing the agitation and restlessness of the human mind. There is no relationship of cause and effect relating learning to peace. The one who evaluates various kinds of gems, and one who examines various sciences and arts, or aesthetics, has lost the happiness that comes from peace of mind because they have no ability to examine themselves.

Why should one search another man's house when he has not searched his own house for something that he lost while he was at home? The man who boldly asserts "This man is like this, and the other man is 'Mr. A' or 'Mr. B,'" while he does not know who he is himself, is never free from restlessness. It would be futile to discover what thing could be extracted from where, or to know many addresses, if one does not know one's own address.

Chapter 2: Investigation of the Four Bodies in Search of "I"

Who is this "I"? Once upon a time, there lived a man named "Gomaji Ganesh" who lived in a town called Andheri. At one point in time, this man established a custom in the Courts of Law that no order or document could be accepted as legal unless it bore a stamp with his name on it, along with the words "The Brass Door." From that point on, all of the officials of that town only accepted a document as being legal if it bore the stamp of **"Gomaji Ganesh, The Brass Door."** This procedure for making documents legal continued for a long time until eventually the stamp officially became part of the legal system of the city of Andheri, and no one ever enquired as to just whom this "Gomaji Ganesh" was. As time passed, it happened that one day an important document that did not bear the official stamp of "Gomaji Ganesh, The Brass Door" was cited as evidence in a case filed in the Court of Law. Except for the fact that this document did not have the official stamp, it was otherwise completely legal according to all other points of law and ordinary procedure. At one point in the case, an objection was raised that the document should not be accepted as evidence because it did not bear the official stamp of "Gomaji Ganesh, The Brass Door."

At that point, a courageous man who was a party to the lawsuit argued before the judge that the document was perfectly valid because it bore all of the relevant signatures of the current government officials. He argued "Why should the document not be admissible if it is otherwise perfectly legal except that it does not bear the stamp of Mr. Gomaji Ganesh? Thus, he questioned the legality of the stamp itself. Consequently, the legality of the stamp was made an issue of contention. Until that day, no one had ventured to bring this issue before a Court of Law. Since it had now arisen for the first time, it was decided that a decision should be made regarding the legality of this stamp. Out of curiosity about how the procedure of the stamp of "The Brass Door" came to be put in place, the judge himself took the matter in hand for inquiry. When his inquiry was completed, he discovered that many years in the past, a man of no particular status, a Mr. Gomaji Ganesh, had taken advantage of the badly administered government of his day, and put his own name on a stamp that was to be used for all official documents. From that time onward, all government officials simply continued following the tradition blindly. In fact, the judge discovered that Mr. Gomaji Ganesh was a man of no importance whatsoever, who had no authority of any kind. When the judge made this discovery, a decision was made by the Court that the stamp was no longer necessary for legal documents. Since that day, the stamp was looked upon with ridicule. In the same way, we should inquire about the sense of "I," and how it dominates everything with the stamp of "I," and "mine," just like the stamp of Mr. Gomaji Ganesh described in the above story. It is a general rule or principle in nature that if two things are combined, some new third thing is produced.

For example by the contact of a piece of thread with flowers, a garland is produced that did not previously exist. Even the names of the parent objects whose contact was responsible for producing the garland disappear as soon as the garland comes into existence. The garland then comes to be known by its own label. The labels of "flowers" and "thread" become extinct, and the new name of "garland" is used, and with that new name, further action takes place. With the contact of earth and water, mud arises as the labels "earth" and "water" become extinct. In much the same way, stones, bricks, mud, and mason come together, and a third thing called a "wall" stands before our eyes, while the stones, bricks, mud, and the mason simply vanish from our sight. It is by the coming together of Knowledge and Ignorance that a peculiar thing called the "intellect" comes into existence, and it is through this "intellect" that the contact with the world emerges. Gold and goldsmith come together and produce a third thing that appears before our eyes as an ornament. The ornament is seen, and the gold and the goldsmith are forgotten. As a matter of fact, if anyone was to try to find out if there is any such thing as an "ornament" inside the gold, one would see nothing but gold. If we tell someone to bring an ornament without touching the gold, what could he bring? The thing we call an ornament would simply vanish. In the same way, out of the union of Brahman and Maya (Illusion), the thief called "I" has come along proudly saying "I," and raising its head proclaiming sovereignty over both Brahman and Maya. This "I," or ego, is a barren woman's (Maya's) son who tries to establish unlimited sovereignty over the entire universe. If we observe the parents of this "I," it is clear that it is impossible for them to give birth to such a child. The mother of the child is Maya, who does not exist. From the womb of this Maya, the "I" has come forth. It is supposed to have been produced by the "Life-Energy." Yet, this Life-Energy (Brahman) has no gender, and does not even claim to possess "doership," so the readers can imagine what kind of an "I" this is.

As described above, the existence of "I" is only in name. Yet, like Mr. Gomaji Ganesh, he announces his name everywhere as "I." He goes around saying "I am wise, I am great, I am small," all the while having forgotten from where he came. Instead, he starts glorifying himself as "I," like the cat who laps up milk with its eyes closed, not aware of the stick that is ready to strike him from the rear. As soon as he accepts a right, or a privilege, he must also accept the responsibility that goes along with it. As soon as one says, "I am the doer of a certain act," that "I" must enjoy the fruits of such action. Enjoyment and suffering of the fruits or the results of action are tied to the action itself, and to the identification as the doer. Actually, no such thing as an "I" exists. The entire doership that is the motivating force behind the "I" is contained solely in Brahman. However, Brahman is so brilliant, the moment that he finds someone who takes pride in "doership," he leaves all responsibility for the actions on the head of that "I" and remains unattached. Consequently, the poor "I" is destined to revolve on the wheel of birth and death. In the example of the garland mentioned above, the name "garland" came forward after the names "flowers" and "thread" were forgotten. When the garland dries up, nobody says that the flowers have dried up, they say the garland has dried up, or if the thread snaps, they say the garland has snapped. This indicates that the "doership" of the original object is imposed upon the third object due to the pride, or identification with the object. In the same way, a series of miseries strike the non-existent "I." If one wants to get free from this misery, he must leave the "I." However, before it is left off, one has to find out exactly where this "I" resides. It is only when we find the "I," that we can talk about leaving it off. The aspirant should begin the search for this "I" at his or her own center. It will never be found outside of us. In every human being this sense of "I" or ego, and "mine," the feeling of possession, is filling one up to the brim. All the actions in the world are carried out by the force of this ego, and the sense of "mine." The assumption of "I" is taken for granted by all human beings. However, all actions can be carried out without this ego, or the sense of "mine." How this can be done shall be seen later. Presently we will discuss only this sense of "I" and "mine."In order to trace this "I" let us first examine our own Physical Gross Body that seems so close to us. After analyzing it, let us see if this "I" can be found anywhere in this body.

The First Body - The Physical Gross Body

What is a body? It is a collective assembly of parts (limbs and organs) such as hands, feet, mouth, nose, ears, eyes, etc. The assembly of all these parts is called the "body." Out of these various parts, let us find out which one is "I." We can say that the hand is "I," but if the hand is cut off, nobody says "I have been cut off," or "I have been discarded." Suppose the eyes go blind. No one says, "I am gone," or if the stomach is bloated, no one says, "I am inflated." No, instead one says "my hand is cut off," or "my eyes have gone blind," or "my stomach is expanded." All of these parts are spoken of as "mine." Not only that, but the body itself that is an assembly of all these parts, is also spoken of as "my body." By looking in this way, it can easily be seen that the one who asserts ownership of all the limbs, and even of the body itself, is really someone who is quite different from the body that he calls his own.

We have stated above that the "I" is not any part, or any of the limbs of the Gross Body, and that all the limbs are considered as "mine." There is an established general truth, or maxim, that says, "Where the 'I' does not exist, there cannot exist anything that can be called as 'mine'." From this maxim, it follows that the body and limbs actually do not belong to "me," as there is not any "I" residing there. The same maxim applies if "I" do not reside in the neighbor's house, can the neighbor's house, or its contents or associated parts belong to me? If one wants to verify the truth of the maxim "Where there is no I, there can be nothing of mine," one only has to go to a neighbor's house and say "I am master here, and the wife of this household is also mine." If you try to show your sense of "mine" to the wife in that house, and start making advances towards her, you will quickly see what kind of an experience you will get. The true master of the house would hit you so hard that you would quickly realize "I am not the master here, and she is not mine." In the same way, when the "I" cannot be traced anywhere in the body then how can it be said that the limbs of the body and its tendencies belong to "me". If you still insist upon calling it your own, find out why, and also look closely at the condition of all human beings who look upon their bodies as their own and act accordingly.

The human being forgets his True Self, and does not understand who he really is. Therefore, he has to take many births in numerous species. Sometimes he becomes a worm and passes out in a stool. Sometimes he becomes a bullock and gets yoked, turning around and around in a mill. Sometimes he becomes a donkey and works hard wallowing in a heap of garbage. How many such miseries one has to suffer is almost impossible to describe. After suffering births in all the other species, finally one gets the good fortune to be born as a human being. This birth in the human body is unique as it has the capacity for higher intellect and discrimination so that we can know God, the "Supreme Self." If we look at the body of the human species, it can be compared to a dressed-up character in a vulgar play during the period of the *Shimga* festival. This character can be described thus: The character's face is smeared with black paint, the body is dressed up in rags with a garland of shoes around his neck, and an umbrella made of shoes is held over his head. Then, this character is seated on a donkey and taken in a procession through the streets accompanied by various strange noises. Ironically, this character takes pride in being the center of such a demeaning show, and salutes people on the street. In the same way, one's body is also a peculiar part of this passing show. All the beauty of the face is supposed to be concentrated in the nose and eyes. We say that a man is handsome or a woman is beautiful if they have a good nose and good eyes. However, what is the nose except a tube for nasal discharge?

The mouth is like a spittoon full of saliva and phlegm. The stomach resembles a sewage plant of some city. The body is given some respectable name, but it is only an accumulation of bones, flesh, and blood. It is the intention of the Supreme Self, to awaken the human being by demeaning him and making him miserable with the body. He then makes the human being cry aloud for happiness, and wander about in all directions in search of it. In spite of this, the human being considers the body to be a great gift, and with joy he describes it with flowery language. The nose, which is a tube of mucus, is compared to the bud of some beautiful flower. The eyes, which are the places of abundant discharge are called lotus eyes. The face, with a mouth like a spittoon full of saliva, is called a moon face, and the arms and legs which are like crooked branches of a tree, are referred to as lotus hands and lotus feet! The human being looks upon this type of behavior as normal, and exhibits his foolishness shamelessly.

However, the Great Lord grants a wonderful thing called the "higher intellect" even to this "Shimga" character of a human being that He has not given to any other species. The purpose of that gift of higher intellect is for the human being to be able to realize the "Divine Nature of the Self" and put an end to this demeaning show. However, the human being misuses this great gift of the intellect. He looks upon a gutter as the Ganges, and the body as God, and only spoils it further. The human being spends a lot of his time adorning the Physical Body. Taking this body as "I," he then comes into contact with a female body and begins calling that person as his own. He then begins to place the sense of "mine" or possession on that female body. By virtue of the contact of this "I," with that which is "mine," many children are born and a whole household is brought into existence. The household eventually gets shattered, and the poor man suffers ridicule. This story has been described in great detail in the book **Dasbodh** by Shri Samartha Ramdas. It is recommended that the knowledge in this book be studied and understood.

We have determined that the "I" cannot be traced anywhere in the body. It is also a fact that the body is not "mine." Then to whom does the body belong? Who is the "owner" of the body? The five elements (Earth, Water, Light or Fire, Air or Wind, and Space or Sky) have the right of ownership to this body. After the body falls, each of these elements takes away their own share, thereby destroying the body. The body is a bundle of these five elements. By analogy, it's like clothes that were tied up in a bundle and have now been taken away by their respective owners, and even the cloth in which the bundle was wrapped up has also been taken away. How then, can anything called a "bundle" remain? There is not even anything left that can be seen.

In the same way, once the body that is composed of the five elements is unbundled and dispersed back into those five respective elements, there remains no object such as the body. Examining in this way, we can see that "I" am not in the body, nor does the body belong to me. This type of body consisting of a bundle of the five elements cannot support any pride of "I" or an "ego." Nor can it sustain the relationships that existed due to the identification with the body, such as birth and death, or the six passions (greed, anger, desire, hatred, craving, and pride) that affect the body. These cannot be related to any "me," as being "mine." The body may be in a state of childhood, or youth, or old age, or the body may be dark, fair, beautiful, or ugly. It may be infested with disease, it may be wandering aimlessly, going to holy places for pilgrimages, or it may be motionless in samadhi. All of these attitudes, properties and modifications belong to the body, but the "I" is separate from all of these.

From the analysis of the Physical Body, we have learned that the "I" is separate from all of its qualities. Additionally we can easily see that someone else's beautiful cute bonnie baby is of no value to us, compared to our own dark stocky boy who has pockmarks and a flowing dirty nose. We do not suffer if someone else's sweet child dies as much as we suffer if our worn old shoe gets lost. The reason for this is that we do not have the same sense of "possession" or "mine" for the other person. Once one understands that some particular thing is not "mine," and that it belongs to someone else, he becomes indifferent about that thing. He even gradually starts disliking that thing which belongs to "someone else," or "another," and then it is easily renounced. Understand clearly that the body is not "mine," it belongs to the five elements, and that it is someone else's property. When you understand this, whatever kind of properties the body may possess, how does it affect you? So, let us leave the Physical Body, and let us proceed ahead. However, to leave the body does not mean that it should be pushed into a well, or be hung with a noose around the neck. We leave it by understanding it, and by gaining the factual knowledge about it. When the body is known for what it really is, the obsessive interest in it subsides, we can step beyond it, and it is automatically renounced. If the body is purposefully destroyed physically, then one definitely gets reborn again and again. Complete renunciation of the body is achieved only through discrimination of the Real from the unreal. By using discrimination while one has the human body, one naturally arrives at a state of renunciation, and instead the body becoming a reason for rebirth, it has the capacity to liberate one from the cycle of birth and death altogether.

There are five types of dissolution. Two are at the level of the body, two at the level of the universe, and one through discrimination. They are:
1) **Daily dissolution, or the Dissolution of Deep Sleep**
2) **Dissolution through Death**
3) **Dissolution of the Creator and Creation (Brahma Pralaya)**
4) **Dissolution at the time of many Ages or Kalpas (Kalpa Pralaya)**
5) **Dissolution by Thought, or Discrimination**

Out of these five types of dissolution, everyone is familiar with the two types of dissolution associated with the body, or daily dissolution, which are Deep Sleep and the dissolution of Death. In Deep Sleep, the whole world, including our body is dissolved. However, upon awakening, the body and the world are present just as they were before going to sleep, and all actions start again, just as they did before. The dissolution through Death is the same as the dissolution through Deep Sleep, however, after Death, in the absence of Self-Knowledge, the being has to take a new body in accordance with one's actions (karma) and mental disposition. In the new body, the actions such as eating, sleeping, mating, and fear happen according to the impressions remaining from previous lives.

Above the bodily level at the universal level there are two other cosmic types of dissolution. The first is the dissolution at the end of the life of the Creator and his Creation (Brahma Pralaya). The second is the dissolution that takes place at the end of an age or "Kalpa" after many such Creators and their Creations have come and gone (Kalpa Pralaya). With these two types of dissolution, a new "Creator," or a new "Kalpa" starts, and "Creation," which was latent for some time, rises with renewed vigor and activity, and starts all over again. In this way, the wheel continues to revolve, rising and setting at fixed periods. One can see from the descriptions given so far of these four types of dissolutions, that bodies cannot be dissolved finally in all of them. However, the result of the dissolution by discrimination, or thought, is very powerful and unique. In this type of dissolution, the body not only is dissolved while living but also after death, and when it gets finally dissolved it will not rise again.

Suppose there is a toy snake lying around that is made out of rubber. It is only until such time that one understands that it is only made of rubber, that the fear of the snake will completely disappear. Otherwise, by closing ones eyes, or putting the snake away in a basket, the fear subsides. However, in that case, as soon as the eyes open, or the basket is opened again, the fear returns. Suppose someone throws the rubber snake away and some mischievous person again throws it in front of the fearful one. He will again be shaken. In order to escape the snake, the man goes into Deep Sleep, however he will see the snake again as soon as he wakes up. Suppose he gets intoxicated with drink, or is made unconscious by chloroform in order to make the snake go away. Again, as soon as the effect of the drink or anesthesia wears off, the snake is there once again. This shows that the eradication of the fear of the snake by any of the means described is only temporary and not lasting. How is it then that he can be freed from the fear of the snake? The only remedy to be rid of the fear of the snake, is to know for certain that it is only made of rubber.

Once this knowledge dawns, then even if his eyes see the snake, or if somebody wants to frighten him with it, there is no cause for fear. In the same way, when one knows correctly as to exactly what this body is, the pride for it and the sense of "mine" about it vanishes, and it is automatically renounced. This is what is called the "dissolution by thought." One who dies with this certainty of thought is free from the cycle of births and deaths. However, it should be taken for granted that one who dies "thoughtlessly," dies only in order to be reborn. By virtue of the "dissolution by thought," the thing is seen as if it were immaterial, whether it is or is not there. With the other types of dissolution, even if the thing is hidden from sight, it is just as if it still exists. Samartha Ramdas therefore asserts that it is only "thoughtfulness" (Vichara) that makes a human being complete, and brings one to fulfillment in life. After thorough investigation, the "I" could not be found when the Physical Body was dissected with the procedure of "dissolution by thought."

The Second Body - The Subtle Body

Now we will use the same process of "dissolution by thought" in trying to trace the "I" in the Subtle Body. Let us investigate and see if this thief called "I" can be found anywhere in the Subtle Body. First, let us find out what the Subtle Body is.

The Subtle Body is comprised of a committee of seventeen members. These are:

1. The Five Senses of Action (hands, feet, mouth, genitals, and anus),
2. The Five Senses of Knowledge (eyes, ears, nose, tongue, and skin),
3. The Five Pranas or vital breaths (vyana vayu which supplies liquid food materials throughout the body, samana vayu which is found in the navel, udana vayu which is found in the throat, apana vayu which is found in the bowels, and prana vayu which is what we breath in and out),
4. The Mind (Manas), and
5. The Intellect (Buddhi)

Whatever orders that this committee of the Subtle Body puts forth are carried out by the Gross Body. The Subtle Body's "field of authority" is very vast, so in conducting a thorough investigation, it may be possible to find that elusive "I" here because he has a strong passion for asserting authority. When we begin our investigation of the Subtle Body, we find that the "I" puts his stamp of "mine" here also. Whatever is found here is labeled as "my senses," "my pranas," "my mind," "my intellect." However, upon closer examination, no such sound as "I am the intellect" is ever heard. That "I" parades around as the "owner" here in the Subtle Body also, but is nowhere to be found. Thus, according to the same reasoning used previously that "There can be nothing which I can call 'mine' where 'I' am not present," the Subtle Body, nor any of its collective members (the senses, the Pranas, the mind, or the intellect) can be "me."

There is an objection that can be raised to this logic of "Where I am not, there can be nothing which I can call my own." For example, King George the 5th is not present in Sholapur. Does it then follow that

Sholapur is not under his ownership? The answer to this objection is thus: At least there is an individual who is called George the 5th, and even if he is living elsewhere, he can have ownership in Sholapur even though he is presently not there. However, this "I" is a "non-entity," and like "Mr. Gomaji Ganesh" from the example earlier, the proliferation of its arrogance and ignorance has remained unexamined, and this "I" is claiming authority here in the Subtle Body as well. When the "I" cannot be traced, how can there be anything there that can be claimed as "mine" to be sustained by the Subtle Body?

The Subtle Body is like a subtle silk bundle. Even though it is more difficult to untie the subtle silk knot with thought than it was with the Gross Body, it is still necessary for the aspirant to put forth the effort to untie it. Once the bundle is untied and left open for thorough examination, the Subtle Body is automatically renounced. It is important to recognize that the Subtle Body is itself the seed of birth and death, which is of the nature of desire. If that seed is roasted just once in the "Fire of Knowledge," it may appear unchanged, but even if it were ever to be sown, there is no hope of it sprouting.

A doubt may arise here that if both the gross and subtle bodies are renounced, and the attitude of pride such as "I" and "mine" also disappears, is it not possible that the actions of the body may either come to a halt, or might not be executed efficiently? The doubt may be removed thus: Suppose someone keeps a thing in a locker because he is under the impression that it is made of gold. However, at some point, he finds out that instead of gold, it is really made of brass. With that recognition, he can choose to either leave it in the locker or remove it and keep it outside. His attachment to it will either vanish or become greatly diminished, and this is a fact. In the same way, if the pride of possession of the body as "mine" is ignored, nothing of value will be lost.

Saint Tukaram said, "Let the body live or die, I have complete faith in my Self Nature." If an aspirant reaches this level of conviction, the attitude arises, "When one experiences the 'Bliss of Brahman' (Brahmananda) who cares for the body?" When this attitude arises, it is truly praiseworthy. A dog once bit off a piece of flesh from Saint Kabir's calf muscle. Saint Kabir simply said, "Either the dog knows, or the flesh knows. Anything is possible." What could have been the feeling of the people around upon hearing this from Saint Kabir, who was a great devotee? The aspirant can easily see the degree of renunciation that Saint Kabir had reached. He fully understood that it was the flesh that was affected and not his True Nature.

Although this understanding that the Self remains unaffected was experienced by Saint Kabir, and also by Saint Tukaram when he lost his whole household, the aspirant might not get the same sense of unshaken ecstasy within oneself in the beginning when one initially undertakes the search for the "I." If by God's Grace, such bliss does overwhelm you, you might say, "What are all these worldly possessions worth after all?," and you will never feel the need to ask such pointless questions as "Will my house be run properly?" At that point, you will have developed such an indifferent attitude that you will say, "Let whatever is to happen, happen, and let whatever has to go, go."

However, if the aspirant understands intellectually, which is easier than experiencing the Self, he raises the question "After the Knowledge of the Self is attained, and the possessive pride of the body and the mind is left behind, can one's worldly duties still be performed?" To console him, the Sadguru answers "Dear one, of course, even after realizing the utter uselessness of the body and mind one can establish a household and have children without bringing in the pride of the body and the mind. In fact, these things can be looked after very well. All of the relevant duties one did earlier can still be diligently performed."

How is this possible, you may ask? Understand by this example: Look at the behavior of the nurse of a motherless infant. She nurses the child, carries it around, consoles it if he cries, and nurses it back to health if he gets sick, just as she would if she were the child's actual mother. If she likes the child, she even kisses it lovingly. While doing all of this work, she does not even have the feeling that the child is her own! In spite of all that she does for the child, if the father of the child dismisses her, she at once picks up her things and gets out of the house. At the time of quitting her position, she is neither happy if the child was to put on weight, nor sad if the child were to die. The reason for this attitude is that she does not have a sense of "mine" regarding the child. However, it cannot be said that she has not performed her duty properly due to the absence of this sense of "mine."

Let us look at another example. Take the case of a trustee who manages a minor's estate worth many millions of rupees. His lack of the sense of "mine" does not hinder him in his duty, and he has been managing the estate of the minor very efficiently. If the duty is not discharged properly, the trustee is liable, and will surely suffer the consequences. The trustee does not have the feeling that the estate is "mine" and accordingly, is not affected if the estate increases in value, or even if it is decided in a legal suit that the estate does not really even belong to the minor. His duty is to look after the estate carefully as long as it is under his management. In short, in order for one's duties to be performed properly, it is not necessary that one must have the sense of "I" or "mine" while performing them. In exactly the same way, the gross and the subtle bodies form a bundle that is rooted in the five elements, and is given as a "keepsake" which is entrusted to the human being.

As a trustee, you must look after the bundle in the best possible way. If you neglect this responsibility, you will surely suffer consequences in the form of the loss of health of both body and mind. If the trustee manages the minor's estate efficiently, and the nurse looks after the child very well, they are awarded their salaries in return. Likewise, if you look after your body and mind well, and keep them in a healthy condition, you also get a return, in a form of joy. A healthy body is definitely useful in the search for the Ultimate Truth.

All of this carrying out of one's responsibilities has to be achieved without the sense of "mine." With this attitude, even if the body becomes fat or thin, or lives or dies, there is no elation or lament. If a trustee of a minor's estate is led astray by a sense of "mine" and claims ownership and embezzles from that estate, he will be jailed. In the case of spiritual practice, the identification with the body means forgetting the Self, or killing the Self. The hope of liberation recedes for the one who is bound by the idea of being a body, even though in truth, he is only nothing but the Self.

From the above discussion, it can be understood that the usual obligations and actions of the body and mind should be fulfilled in a proper manner, and that it is not necessary to establish a sense of "ownership," or a concept of "mine" in relation to them. The obligations of the trustee and the nurse while carrying out their responsibilities do not require them to have any sense of possession, and their duties are performed quite normally. In the same manner, the duties of a human being can be performed without entertaining the sense of possession, or any concept of "mine" in relation to the Physical or Subtle Bodies

The Third Body - The Causal Body

Suppose we lose the concept of possession for the Gross Body, as well as the Subtle Body, and admit to the fact that the bundle belongs to a stranger. Still, we must find the answer to the question "Who am I?" or, "Where am I?" Let us now go over the definition of the Causal Body. What is the Causal Body? As soon as we step in here, there is pitch darkness everywhere. Is it possible that this dark Ignorance is the place of residence for this "I"? It surely seems this is his main headquarters. Ignorance seems to be the main property or quality that belongs to him. There is certainly some hope of finding the elusive "I" here. Let us see.

Here we move about as if blindfolded searching for it, and the "I" is not to be found anywhere in Causal Body. Here the "I" seems to have even given up his sense of "mine." There seems nothing that can be called "mine" in this place. Everything seems to be absolutely quiet. That "I" who loudly proclaims "I, I" so arrogantly in the gross and subtle bodies, seems to be totally silent here. The "I" seems to be playing hide and seek so that he does not get caught by the one who searches for it. In the Causal Body, the "I" seems to have dug itself into a trench of darkness so that the one making the search might fall in, being forced to end his search.

Dear aspirants, do not be concerned. The Sadguru is standing behind you as well as in front of you, and He will take you safely across this trench of darkness. Many scholars and learned persons have turned their backs at this point and abandoned their search failing to have faith in the guidance of the Sadguru. For you however, there is no reason to abandon your search like them. You have a guide who is a very capable Master, a Samartha Sadguru. (Samartha means "The Powerful One" who knows his own significance, in the highest sense.)

After stabilizing in this darkness of the Causal Body, and firmly planting one's feet therein for some period of time, a voice is softly heard that says, "I am the witness of this Ignorance." With this, there arises some courage offering the hope of catching the thief called "I." With the recognition of this voice who says it is the witness of the Ignorance, there also comes the thought, "This thief is here somewhere. He may be near, or a little further ahead, but he is witnessing the Ignorance from somewhere nearby." Here the searching takes the form of watching persistently. How this is done will be discussed in the next chapter. The witnessing that is going on is happening from beyond the emptiness of the Causal Body, from the position in the Great-Causal Body (Mahakarana Body), or Turya State. When this is understood, the "I" is quickly overjoyed in finding himself. Who can describe that Joy? In that Joy, the "I" cries out "I am Brahman, I am Self-Knowledge."

The Fourth Body - The Great-Causal Body (Turya)

The one who says "I" is really the all-witnessing Brahman. It is He, who is of the nature of Knowledge, the sense of "I Am." When this certainty is established, there arises wave after wave of Bliss. Afterwards, when this bliss ebbs away, look at the miracle that happens. After enquiry and deep thought (Vichara), one arrives at the recognition that, "I am not even of the nature of 'Knowledge,' for just as I am covered with Ignorance, in the same way, I am covered with Knowledge. I was not originally having any Ignorance or Knowledge. Ignorance and Knowledge were born out of 'me,' and were mistakenly taken to be me. With the aid of such deep thought, it can be seen that the arising of both Ignorance and Knowledge within me, points to me as their creator. Therefore Knowledge is my child, and I am its father, and as its father, I am prior to, and different from, that Knowledge."

Brahman

When this sequence of deep discriminative thought dawns within, the sense that "I am Brahman," (Aham Brahmasmi) that is the Self-Knowledge in the Great-Causal Body, or Turya State, also starts ebbing away, only to finally be fully eradicated. Then "I" am absolutely naked, without any covering whatsoever. Arriving here in this nakedness, it cannot be described as to who or what this "I," is. If you want a description of the "I" who is found here, you may utter any word found in any dictionary, but that is not "I." This "I" here, can only be expressed as "Not this, not this." It is the one who throws light on anything called "this." You may utter words and sentences to try to describe it, but those are not it. Whatever meanings come forth, you take those to be the description of "I," but those are not it. If you do not understand what is being told now, you must leave off the words and concepts, and merge in Deep Silence, and see who "I" am.

Chapter 3: Investigation of the Four Bodies in Detail

A Methodical Approach to Explanation

So far, during the search for the "I," we turned the four bodies inside-out and could not find a trace of it. It is true that the "I" disappeared without words beyond the four bodies, where even the ideas of "I" and "you" do not exist. However, it will not do to just keep quiet, and mistake this for Deep Silence. In the exposition thus far, the Gross, the Subtle, the Causal, and the Great-Causal bodies have been superficially described. It is necessary to examine in detail all aspects of the four bodies. Unless these are fully understood correctly and this understanding is made a part of one's nature, an aspirant will not be able to arrive at this Deep Silence, which is Reality. We will therefore examine in detail what the aspects of the four bodies are.

It is necessary to understand that these four bodies are the four steps that one must ascend in order to proceed on to the fifth rung of Deep Silence which is "Nihshabda," where the "word" becomes silent. Going step by step, one can surely reach the end of the journey. However, if some steps are missed, and one puts one's foot on the next step prematurely, there is a likelihood of losing one's balance, and falling back. Therefore it is only when one body is fully understood that the aspirant should continue on to the next body. Without using this methodical approach, if one starts stepping up the steps too hastily, there will be confusion. In this confusion, true understanding will not be gained, and the aspirant will likely misunderstand the subtle differences between Deep Sleep and Samadhi, as well as mistake Ignorance for Knowledge.

By way of comparison, consider the difference between a toy top that is still when it is not moving and when it appears to be still due to intense speed, or the difference between total darkness and the blackout that is caused by intense light. Although these things appear similar from a casual glance or superficial perspective, there is a vast difference between the two states, and their usefulness or capacity is also different. If one works methodically step by step to gain understanding, there will be no confusion as to the subtle differences that are being indicated. Here it is prudent to bring to the attention of the reader the method of exposition of a subject that is provided in the ancient scriptures. This will convince the aspirant that there is no basis for any doubts to arise regarding any apparent contradictions in the method adopted for the exposition of some particular point in the scriptures. Therefore, we must first describe the method of expounding the teaching that has been adopted by the ancient scriptures (This is often referred to as the "primary premise" presented in the Vedas).

When a subject is to be explained to an aspirant, there is first a description of the subject matter, showing its great importance. It is then explained that a great reward will follow if the subject matter is correctly understood. Once the aspirant understands the subject completely, before moving on and explaining the next subject, the instructor using the scriptural method is to first impress upon the aspirant the uselessness of the subject that has already been understood. Only after that can the importance of the subject to be taught next be impressed upon him. The reason for this method is that there is no inclination for one to strive to understand a subject unless its importance is first brought out, with a promise of some reward as a motivation. Next, the uselessness of the subject matter just learned is brought home to the aspirant so that the subject is automatically renounced, and the aspirant becomes eager to understand what is to be presented as the next topic.

The Mother Shruti (the Vedas) takes into consideration the psychological background of an aspirant, and then inspires him to work for food, first telling him that the food is Brahman. She then gives him time to fondle the Gross Body, telling him that the Gross Body is Brahman. Then it is explained that all experiences of joy that come to the Gross Body are actually enjoyed by the Subtle Body. The Gross Body is shown to be merely a corpse, and it is told how the corpse could in no way enjoy anything if it were not for the Subtle Body. Thus, the uselessness of the Gross Body is demonstrated.

Next, the mind, intellect, senses, and the sheath that makes up the Pranas (vital breaths) are described, and this Subtle Body is said to be Brahman. It is shown to be bigger or more expansive than the Gross Body. In this way, the Vedas give importance to the Subtle Body. After that, comes the description of the Causal Body, which is still and even more expansive than the Subtle Body. It swallows the Subtle Body. The Causal Body is then proclaimed to be Brahman and the advice is given to the aspirant that "You yourself have become the expansive Causal Body." However, since the Causal Body is considered to be Ignorance and in total darkness, the final claim of it being the Self cannot really be made here. Accordingly, the aspirant is therefore compelled to investigate further, into the Great-Causal Body. This Great-Causal Body is still more expansive, and it is from here that the voice saying "I am the witness" emanates. Upon arriving here, the Great-Causal Body, or Turya State, is investigated and examined thoroughly.

In this way, the Mother Vedas dismiss each body after having asserted that it was Brahman. When she is finally confronted with the problem of explaining the changeless, attributeless Brahman (Nirguna Brahman) she claims an inability to describe it, and only keeps repeating the sentence, "Not this, Not this. That which is not Ignorance, and that which is not Knowledge is Brahman, and that which you call Brahman, is not Brahman." In such a negative way, Mother Shruti describes Brahman as "That" which is beyond all of the four bodies.

The principle of what has just been described is as follows: When it said that one body is bigger than the previous body it does not mean that it is higher in relation to it, etc. In a comparison of needles for example, the needle used for stitching jute bags is bigger than one used for cotton, but it is not bigger than an iron rod that is used for digging. This indicates that qualities like "bigger" and "smaller" are not inherent in a thing, but are imposed upon it by relating it to or comparing it with some other thing. The same rule applies here. After listing in sequence first food as Brahman, then Gross Body as Brahman, then Subtle Body as Brahman, then the Causal, and finally the Great-Causal Body as Brahman, and in each case, the latter being greater than the former, the intention is to give the instruction and demonstrate the principle that out of all these, ultimately none can be said to be Brahman. Although it is shown that in each case that the latter state is relatively higher or more expansive than the previous one, it is still not Brahman, and moreover, this Parabrahman is absolutely unique and beyond all of these four bodies.

While utilizing the above-mentioned method of explaining a point, it is necessary to understand clearly just what it is that is being described as Brahman. Why is it that it should be described in this way? How far can one go to describe it as being with some particular qualities? Moreover, why is it that what was once called Brahman, is then negated as not being Brahman in the same breath? It is important to understand this correctly. For example, in giving instruction on how to cook rice to a person who is not a proper cook, the person is told to first light a fire under the utensil in which the rice is being cooked. After some time, another instruction is given to the same person to put the fire out now. It is natural that the person may wonder about the contradictory instructions. His teacher explains to him, "Dear one, it is necessary to keep a fire under the utensil until the rice is cooked, but later, the fire has to be put out, otherwise we would get coals instead of rice."

This is the reason why any method to be practiced is necessary only until its goal is achieved. Otherwise, it will only bring on exhaustion and nothing further beneficial will be achieved. Thus, when the Subtle Body being called as Brahman is thoroughly examined and understood, the merit of calling the Subtle Body as Brahman loses its value, and it becomes necessary to move on, and continue the search for "I" by examining the next thing. This demonstrates that sometimes when we offer a price for something, or place some value on it in order to achieve some particular results, that value that we have placed on it may not necessarily be the real value of that thing. For example, some occasion may arise in one's life where you might have to address even a donkey as uncle. In this example, the honor that is given to the donkey is due to some consequence you must endure for some action done.

In the same way, some great calamity that someone may be facing is because he has forgotten his real nature. It is therefore necessary to become liberated from the calamity or obstruction, which is like being caught in the jaws of a crocodile. If you free yourself from the crocodile by flattery saying that her back is very smooth, does it really mean that her back is as soft as a feather mattress? This question should be asked of the man who gets released from the crocodile's jaws. To rid oneself of the crocodile like grip of the four bodies, they are called Brahman for some short period of time. Taking into account that this is the method of explanation that will be used, we will now turn our attention to the actual explanation and description of the four bodies.

The Investigation Commences

The nature of the Gross Body is quite well known. It is a mass of flesh and blood that can be touched with the hand, and all are quite familiar with it. Not only that, but everyone uses it fully. The Gross Body is "I" and therefore all the passions and desires that happen to the body are "mine." Accordingly, the dark or fair complexion of the body, and the stages of childhood, youth, and old age, belong to "me." The relationship of the body to caste, religion, house, land, and wealth, are all "mine." This is a lesson that every human being has learned through many births, and he has learned it very well. In fact, it is so well learned that even while dreaming, someone will tell you that he is "So-and-so." It is therefore not necessary to teach anyone this lesson that has been repeatedly learned over and over, and has been so firmly implanted in one's psyche. The feet of all human beings are resting steadily on the step of this Gross Body. The state of this Gross Body is that of "wakefulness" and in this body, there is partial forgetfulness and partial remembrance. The quality of worldly action, or "Rajoguna," is predominant in the Gross Body. This basic explanation is enough for one to understand the Gross Body. We will now turn to the next step, that of the Subtle Body.

As has been previously stated, the Subtle Body is a committee. It is a collection of the senses, the Pranas, the mind, the intellect, seated on the "Inner-mind" (Antahkarana), which collectively create a type of mental world or "dream world" that is seen when the visible world becomes invisible when closing the eyes. After some thought and investigation, it can be noticed that the Subtle Body is really a very peculiar thing. Upon examination, it can be seen that all of the movements of the Gross Body are according to the dictates of this Subtle Body. The assertion of a concept, such as "something is like this," is called "Sankalpa," and a doubt, or the notion that "something is not like this" is called "Vikalpa." This Subtle Body is such that it is always presenting this perverse type of knowledge of contradictory thoughts, and its state is that of "dreaming." Continuous memory is the indicative quality of the Subtle Body, and the quality of "awareness" or "Sattvaguna" is the quality that is predominant here.

After being introduced to the Subtle Body in this way, the aspirant becomes that body. When one foot is planted firmly on the next step, the other foot is lifted from the previous step, and placed beside the first foot. In this way, one leaves the first step completely. When one crosses the boundaries of a village and puts his foot within the limits of the next village, the first village is left behind, and one becomes a traveler to the next village. Similarly, in order to understand properly the step of the Subtle Body described above, when the aspirant plants his foot firmly on this step he has to lift his foot from the Gross Body in order to bring this understanding into practice. When the Gross Body is left behind, the aspirant then has to sever all connections with it.

However, this work is not so easily done, as it seems that for crossing over these steps, every human being has only two legs. One leg is the leg of learning, and the other is the leg of putting into practice what one has learned. Taking both feet away from the step of the Gross Body and planting them on the step of the Subtle Body means that one has to transcend the Physical Body. When one leaves behind the sense of pride and possession of the Gross Body and takes up the pride of possession in the Subtle Body, he has to say, "I am only the Subtle Body." Only when this is experienced does it mean that the Gross Body has been renounced and the Subtle Body is now accepted as "I." When the aspirant comes to this second step, then the lower step is left behind and one now accepts that the Gross Body is not "I." The "I" has no relationship with the Gross Body. The changes that happen to the Gross Body and its qualities, such as having a dark or fair complexion are no longer considered as "mine." No qualities of the Gross Body belong to me, as I am only the Subtle Body. This means that the qualities of the Subtle Body such as the senses, the Pranas, the mind, the intellect, the sense of "I am," etc. are not endowed with gross physical qualities such as fat or thin, dark or fair, young or old, etc. It is clear that "I" am only the mind and the intellect, etc., with subtle qualities. If the aspirant studies this diligently, then both feet become firmly planted on the second step and he loses the sense of pride in, and identification with, the Gross Body. He becomes indifferent to all qualities and conditions of the Gross Body.

The third step is above and beyond the Subtle Body, and is the Causal Body, or "Ignorance." The Causal Body is a state of "pure forgetfulness" where the quality of Ignorance or "Tamoguna" is predominant. Here in the Causal Body, there is no thought as to the well being of, or any relationship with, either the Gross or the Subtle Bodies. The Causal Body means that there is no knowledge of anything. It is like the state of Deep

Sleep, but it is not Deep Sleep. The Causal Body is difficult to understand, however it is very important to understand this state. Those who proclaim to understand the principle of zero (nothingness; the void) came to this state and turned back saying that there was nothing ahead.

The Causal Body is the state of the "unknowable" or "the void" which is presented in the point of view of western philosophers. This state which is devoid of all thoughts, imagination, and doubts, is often mistakenly taken by aspirants to be Samadhi, and thought to be the same as Brahman without concepts or qualities (Nirvikalpa Brahman). When this void or state of emptiness is reached, one is likely to get a false satisfaction and say, "Today I saw Brahman." The interval or pause between where one modification of the mind disappears, and another one does not arise (such as the space between two thoughts, or the intervening pause between when sleep sets in and the waking state disappears) is a state of pure forgetfulness. This is what is described as the "Covering of Bliss" (Anandamaya Kosha) in the scriptures. In the Causal Body all chaos, struggle, and the infinite number of waves of thought have ceased. Therefore, there is a sense of peace in this third body that is not found in the other two bodies. It is true that the aspirant experiences a certain joy, but this is not Ultimate Peace, or even true Bliss. One must understand this point very well. This Causal Body is the natural state of all the gods, demons, and every human being. The state of the Causal Body is the state of "Forgetfulness."

The chief sign or indication of the Causal Body is to forget everything. For example, unless one forgets everything he cannot get Deep Sleep. To say "I was asleep, but I remembered something," is to really say, "I never slept." To really have Deep Sleep means not to remember a single thing. Similarly, to forget everything while in an awakened state, is to enter the Causal Body. To be in a state where you do not know anything, is to also come to this state. As previously mentioned, this is the natural state of a human being. Even the most learned scholars do not understand the nature of a human being, let alone the nature of Shiva. In order for one to fully understand this state of human forgetfulness, the method of studying the pause is prescribed. If anything is very difficult, it is to be completely stabilized in the state of forgetfulness, and to know it thoroughly. To achieve this is important in one's spiritual progress, and takes considerable effort on the part of the aspirant. The Saints have put particular emphasis on this point.

The pause between two states is nothing but Pure Consciousness. The state of the "mouni" (a silent one) is such that he does not allow a single word to rise, or even if it did rise, he does not allow its meaning to rise, but simply lets it slip by. When the word rises, and is allowed to impress its meaning on the inner-mind, the world is born. Ignoring the word, and not allowing it to carry any meaning for the mind, is the eradication of the world. When the word does not energize the mind, what remains is the "Pure Energy of Consciousness." To experience this state continuously is called "The State of Silence."

The aspirant who is about to put his foot on the third step after climbing the first and second, is told that this step is the state of Pure Consciousness. He is under the impression that this state is the Pure Void, and taking this void to be Brahman, he is unable to witness the void. However, when the aspirant proceeds to the fourth step, he begins to look back at the third step. Being unable to see anything in the void of the Causal Body he wonders why the Guru has instructed him to put his foot on this step of nothingness which doesn't exist at all. The reason is, that once Pure Consciousness is known, there can be no trace of anything that is called "Ignorance," so one does not come to understand what the state of "Forgetfulness" is. Once known, there does not arise any modification in the aspirant's mind except that of Pure Consciousness.

Knowledge, or Consciousness presents itself to the aspirant in two ways:
1. When there is an object in Consciousness it becomes "Objective Knowledge" and one will experience it as knowledge of objects.
2. When there is no object, it is experienced as objectless Knowledge, or "Pure Consciousness."

When there is an object, that is called "Objective Knowledge." When there is no object, that is simply "Knowledge," which is Pure Awareness, or Consciousness. With the exception of these two (Objective Knowledge and Pure Knowledge), no other modifications are present in the aspirant's mind. In Pure Consciousness, the word "Ignorance" is meaningless from the aspirant's point of view. It is not possible for Forgetfulness to exist in his case. Whatever is experienced will either be Objective Knowledge, or Pure Consciousness that is without any objects.

Presenting the state of the Causal Body to the aspirant that it is just Ignorance, a void, a state of Forgetfulness, or something where there is nothing to bring home to him, is to lead him to the above fact of Pure Consciousness. By analogy, a teacher will draw on the blackboard a point of great length and breadth in order to teach the student about a point that has neither length nor breadth. Similarly, this is how the point is being illustrated here. If it is not done in this manner, the next step cannot be explained. The aspirant should therefore have full faith in the Sadguru without further argument and take it for granted that there is a state of Forgetfulness. He should thus commence practicing what is being told, and begin the process of forgetting each and every thing. It must be understood that the casual body is the cause of the two previous bodies. Hence the label "Causal Body."

Here the example is given of the side curtain on a theater stage, which is called the wing, from which the actors emerge and where they again disappear back into. The Causal Body, which is the natural state of a human being, is like this wing on the stage, and exists in the state of the form of "Forgetfulness." From behind this curtain, all memories appear and then disappear. When we say that we have forgotten a thing before remembering it, this means that the thing was abiding there in that state of Forgetfulness, and it is proved that it has emerged from that state alone. In opposition to this, when we say that we forgot a certain thing, this means that the thing that was in memory has disappeared behind this curtain of Forgetfulness. A memory before it is forgotten, and something forgotten after it is remembered, are companions in this arena of Forgetfulness. The rising and setting of all ideas are in the womb of this one "Forgetfulness," which is the common ground for all human beings. It is by reason of this Forgetfulness that each human being feels he is ignorant and strives to obtain knowledge. During this struggle, the majority unfortunately only gain worldly knowledge, thus missing the Knowledge of their "True Nature."

When introducing the Causal Body in the manner described above, the Sadguru tells the disciple, "Dear one, you are not the Gross Physical Body, and you are not the Subtle Body, so you should identify yourself with the Causal Body." For an aspirant to be in the state of "Forgetfulness," it means that he should have the feeling that "I am definitely not the Gross Body, and I am not the Subtle Body. Therefore, all of the dreams and doubts that arise in the Subtle Body, do not reside in me. I am complete 'Forgetfulness,' empty of all concepts and imaginings. The birth and death of the body, the miseries and temptations, the pain and pleasure, as well as the hunger and thirst that arise in the Pranas, cannot touch me. Honor and dishonor are only notions in the mind, and qualities such as fair or dark complexion belong to the Physical Body, but I am none of these. Nothing can attach itself to me. I am Forgetfulness."

Committing oneself to this lesson again and again and becoming firmly established in the state of Forgetfulness without any idea or attachment, it becomes our own nature. In this way, one experiences oneself as being completely empty of all of the qualities of the Gross and the Subtle Bodies. When this practice of experiencing oneself as Forgetfulness is firmly established the aspirant definitely rises to the third step. Becoming steady in this Forgetfulness, the aspirant is worthy of proceeding to the next step, to the Great-Causal Body (Mahakarana Body), the Turya State.

However, before going to the next step, it is necessary to mention that the Causal Body although similar to Deep Sleep, is a state quite distinct from sleep. In Deep Sleep, all of the senses are in complete repose with the complete absence of any activity, and consequently any perception of sense objects. In Deep Sleep, all beings enjoy the bliss of being in their own nature, yet do not really know their True Nature. Upon awakening from Deep Sleep, everyone will say these two sentences: "I slept happily," and "I did not know anything." Like this, everyone conveys the contentment and bliss of their own nature, as well as their ignorance regarding it. In this manner, although one unknowingly conveys their awareness of Ignorance, it also proves the existence of a deeper Awareness. However, this does not mean that one was aware of their true Self, even though they were experiencing it during Deep Sleep. During Deep Sleep, one does not experience the Awareness that is present there. For example, suppose that there is a person who is unknowingly an heir to a treasure of buried gold coins. Everyday he goes to sleep on the ground and does his normal begging in the morning for his livelihood. For him, the treasure is as good as not being there at all. Similarly, each human being goes into and comes out of their true nature, diving deep and experiencing bliss. However the deep ignorance about one's real nature is there as part of that experience. It is for this reason that Deep Sleep cannot be the means of gaining "Self-Knowledge," the Knowledge of one's "True Nature." In Deep Sleep, the aspirant has no ability to study that state. However, this is not the case with regard to the state of "Forgetfulness."

To study Forgetfulness is to enjoy the state of Deep Sleep while being fully awake. The manner in which to enjoy this wakeful Deep Sleep is taught by the Sadguru. How does a fish sleep while living in water? One can only understand this if you get a birth in that species. How can the sleep of a fish not be disturbed by the water entering into its eyes? This secret is known only when one is born as a fish. In the same way, how can one experience and understand this Deep Sleep state while one is fully awake? One can only understand this by becoming a true Son of the Sadguru, a "Guruputra."

The Causal Body, which is of the nature of Forgetfulness is nothing but a very deep sleep. However, that which is described above, is the silence within that is experienced knowingly, or consciously, during the Waking State. It is not the Deep Sleep state that comes "unknowingly," without conscious awareness. Nothing is known in the state of Deep Sleep which comes "unknowingly." However, the nature of the Self can be known by means of employing the method of knowing "Forgetfulness" which is experienced while awake. This is the difference between "Deep Sleep," and Samadhi.

Although it is known that "Forgetfulness" is a state where nothing is known, the fact is, that after everything is forgotten "Knowledge" remains. This "Knowledge" can only be understood through the study of Forgetfulness.

This state of Forgetfulness exists, and must be understood. Deep Sleep and Forgetfulness are both the result of "Tamoguna." By way of analogy, an analysis of coal and diamond shows that both are made of carbon. This means that the coal and the diamond are but two aspects of carbon. Although this is the case, there is a vast difference in their respective values. When the ingredient of carbon is the same in both, how is it that the diamond shines and the coal is black and lusterless? The reason is that the proportion of the same component is different in the two. Likewise, Deep Sleep and Forgetfulness share different proportions of Ignorance, which explains why in Deep Sleep the immense density of Ignorance is felt, while in Forgetfulness the flimsiness of Ignorance is realized.

As the depth of Deep Sleep decreases, the onset of wakefulness arises. The man who wakes up from Deep Sleep is at first slightly under the fuzzy influence of sleep, and then awakens slowly. This state is the result of the depth of sleep becoming thinner, or more flimsy, as the state of full wakefulness emerges and sleep ends. Deep Sleep is like a pitch black curtain which covers the lamp of the Self, while the Causal Body or the state of Forgetfulness that is being examined is like a thin transparent velvet curtain. This means that the enjoyment of bliss is the same in both Deep Sleep and the Causal Body (Forgetfulness). However, from the point of view of achieving the knowledge of one's True Nature, Deep Sleep is useless. It is like attempting to procreate by having sexual intercourse with a barren woman. The study of this "Sheath of Bliss," (Anandamaya Kosha) in the form of the state of Forgetfulness provides one with joy and is a necessary step in reaching the goal of knowing one's "True Nature."

Having said all of this, we will now observe the Great-Causal Body, or the Turya State, which is endowed with the "Knowledge" that comes after the study of Forgetfulness. Here, let us digress a little. Those aspirants who have taken the traditional Mantra, according to the tradition of Shri Sadguru Bhausaheb Maharaj may have doubts at this point. The study of the Causal Body means that one should learn to forget everything. Does this also mean that repeating the Mantra given by the Guru, and the color or forms that stand before one's half-closed eyes should also be forgotten? The answer is Yes! You have to do this. Before doing this, while repeating the Mantra the colors and whatever forms are present, so the aspirant must check for oneself that the mental noises and chatter cease and die out completely.

When concentrating on the tip of the nose with half-closed eyes in a relaxed manner, with the exception of the repetition of the Mantra and the color form, there should not arise any other word or form. This having been done, even that has to be forgotten. The broom in one's hand that is used to sweep out the rubbish in the house should not be kept in the hand after the rubbish has been cleaned out from every corner of the house. The broom also has to be thrown out in the end. The Sadguru imparts the Mantra to the aspirant as a discipline. He gives a tool in the form of the Mantra which sweeps clean all rubbish in the form of doubts, fears, imaginings, and concepts that have been accumulated over the infinite number of births. This tool of the Mantra helps the aspirant learn how to concentrate, or focus his attention, and enables the mind to become subtle. How the tool should be utilized, and when it should be left alone has now been clearly explained.

Now, we will see what the fourth body, the Great-Causal Body is. (The Great-Causal Body is also known in the teachings of Vedanta as the Turya State, or SatChitAnanda. It is called Great-Causal because it is above, or beyond the limits of the Causal Body.) It is the father of the other three bodies. In Hindu mythology, King Janaka (Janaka means Creator, or Producer) was one without a body (Videhi). He had a daughter named Janaki (Janaki means Awareness). This mythological story tells us that King Janaka is the same as the fourth body, the Great-Causal Body. This indicates a state of Consciousness that is without a body in spite of the fact that the body still exists. That is the state of "Knowledge" in the fourth body. This is King Janaka. Out of him, the daughter Janaki (Awareness) is created. Compared with the previous three bodies, the fourth body is a state that is without a body, and without any conditions, in the form of "Knowledge." However, this does not mean that there is an absence of Knowledge found in the previous three bodies.

Knowledge is the same whether it is in an agitated condition or in equanimity. It is clean and pure in the state of equanimity as well as in the disturbed condition, even when immersed in the flood of objective knowledge. In all states, Knowledge is One, and the same. However, the knowledge in the first three bodies is adulterated knowledge, or conditional objective knowledge. The Knowledge in the state of the Great-Causal Body is balanced with an intermingling of the three gunas (Rajas, Tamas, and Sattva), and can be experienced as "Pure Knowledge."

Whether Knowledge is in a balanced or an unbalanced state, Knowledge is always Knowledge. However, it is different with respect to its conditioning. Because of the identification with particular conditionings of Knowledge, a human being sees differences, and creates distinctions and separateness in the "One Knowledge." For example, the sweetness that one tastes in the various sweets called laddoos, or jilebis, or basundis, is all sugar. However, because it is in these particular forms we say that the laddoo is sweet, the jilebi is sweet, or the basundi is sweet. If we taste some sugar that is not mixed with any other ingredients, we will say that sugar is sweet. If someone is given a description of what sugar is like, and is given a laddoo and told that the sweetness in the laddoo is sugar, he will never get the knowledge of the true nature of sugar. However, if he is given pure sugar unmixed with any other ingredients he will know exactly what sugar is.

This example illustrates why Knowledge cannot be experienced in its primal state in the first three bodies because it is always in some form of conditioning. In the first three bodies it will always be experienced only as objective knowledge. In the Fourth Body, that Knowledge that is non-objective and Pure, and which is not apparent (visible) in the other three bodies, shines in its "Pure Nature." This is the reason why aspirants have to be taken to the Great-Causal Body. When Pure Knowledge, or Consciousness, is known, then even if it is mixed with objective knowledge, or is in any other state, the aspirant will understand correctly that the entity that is called "the world," is not separate, or different from that which is called "The Knowledge of the Self" (Self-Knowledge).

Even when each state comes and goes, the witness of these states does not come or go anywhere. The one who sees the dark and fair complexion, as well as childhood, youth, and old age, of the Physical Body, is also the one who sees all concepts, imaginings, dreams, and doubts in the Subtle Body. The same witness also sees the Causal Body where there is a complete absence of concepts, imagination, and doubts. The one who witnesses all three of these bodies is forever awake.

There is a story of a woman with a peculiar characteristic who delivered a child. The child died before it knew its mother, and never saw the faces of its brother or sister that were also dead. This woman had many such children who died. The woman however remained where she was after burying all of the children. Not one child saw the face of another child, but the woman had seen all of the faces of the children, and had within her a recognition of all those children. This is exactly like the three bodies that were born of the Great-Causal Body, which is in the form of the Primal Illusion (MoolaMaya). However, none of these three bodies ever had the chance of seeing the face of each other, or the face of their mother.

Even while one state penetrates into the other, the Knowledge present in all these states is never adulterated. Just as in the example of the thread which supports all beads equally where one bead does not penetrate into the other, the Great-Causal Body is like that, as it pervades all the other states like Deep Sleep, Dream, and the Waking State. The state of Awareness, or Consciousness in the Great-Causal Body is the "Self-Luminous Flame" which becomes naked without any covering whatsoever, by making Ignorance forget itself.

Once the nature of the "Witnessing Knowledge" is known, the state of Ignorance vanishes completely. Though it is true that Ignorance vanishes, it is not true that the appearance of "the seen," or "manifestation," also vanishes. It is only the attitude, or the understanding of the aspirant that changes. By virtue of the intensity of the study, we will experience that all that is seen and appears, is in the form of "Knowledge." As soon one gains the understanding that it is only "gold" that is perceived in a piece of jewelry, the piece of jewelry itself is not destroyed. Similarly, when it is known that everything that exists is only "The Lord of the Universe" the visible universe is not destroyed, just as when the light of a lamp destroys darkness, the objects that become known do not vanish. At first there was no light, and nothing was known beyond the fact that there were some objective forms. The nature of the objects simply became clearly known in the light. In the same way, when we were looking at and feeling the world with blind eyes in the darkness of Ignorance, the Sadguru's advice brings correct vision to our sight.

When the Flame of Knowledge is lit in the "Inner-Consciousness," it spreads light all around and the darkness of Ignorance is destroyed, yet the world appearance remains, as its True Nature is uncovered and revealed. In this way, the point of view from which one was viewing the world changes after one acquires "True Knowledge." A mirage is viewed differently from the perspective of a man and that of a deer. The object is the same, but the seeing of it is different in each case. When sand in the desert, or a road stretching out into the distance becomes hot from the sun's rays, the heat waves that rise will appear to be a body of water to someone standing far away. This appearance is called a mirage. In Marathi language, the mirage is called Mrugjala. The meaning of this is "an appearance of water at a distance that entices a deer." The reason for this name is that the deer is deceived by the mirage, and imagines it to really be water, and runs towards it to quench its thirst. Upon realizing the absence of water, the deer becomes disillusioned. It is the limited capacity of the deer's intellect that leads it to believe the appearance of water is true, and although it looks like water, a thirsty man will not run towards it to quench his thirst. The reason for this is that the mirage is not what it appears to be, and the man understands this. He is not deceived into believing that there is the presence of water there. This is the capacity of the human intellect for discerning the True from the untrue. From the point of view of the sun, there is nothing like a mirage. From where does the appearance of a mirage arise? It is similar to this that the attitude of an aspirant who is ignorant and therefore bound, and the attitude of a Siddha, or a "Liberated Man," are different. The one who is bound is driving the cart of practical duties taking it for granted that the world is true. When an aspirant gains the "Knowledge of the Self," he looks at the world with the attitude that it is just a temporary appearance or an illusion. However, the Siddha is one who has become "The Self of All," and does not see the world at all.

At this point, the first part of the exposition of the teaching, and everything regarding the Physical Gross Body up through the Great-Causal Body has been included. The next part of the teaching that is given after the explanation of the Great-Causal Body, is the teaching of the Final Reality. A person cannot be called a Siddha even if he gains Self-Knowledge by becoming identified with the Great-Causal Body (SatChitAnanda) and has realized that state. Even though he is accomplished, he is still looked upon only as an aspirant (sadhaka). The field where the Siddhas rest is in that field of "Supreme Knowledge," or Vijnana (Thoughtless Reality). However, we will not discuss that yet at this point.

At this stage in the exposition, the step under our feet is the Great-Causal Body (Mahakarana Body), also known as the Turya State. First, we must discuss the Great-Causal Body in more detail. We have said that the Great-Causal Body is the state of the annihilation of Ignorance. However, it should be understood that Ignorance, the state of Forgetfulness, comes into consideration only in relation to the Gross and the Subtle Bodies. Actually, it has no real existence that has to be annihilated by acquiring "Knowledge."

It is ridiculous to say that Ignorance, or "that which is not," has to be annihilated. For example, Rama has a ring and Govinda does not have a ring. Does the absence of a ring indicate the state of existence of a certain thing called a ring? No it does not. It is in exactly the same way that the state of 'Forgetfulness," that is non-existent and appears only in relationship to the Gross and Subtle Bodies, is an imagined state. It truly does not exist. Samartha Ramdas points out in his book **Dasbodh** that this state of Ignorance in the form of Forgetfulness is the state in which that which was "not" becomes non-existent. It is natural at this point that the question might arise, "Does the state of Self-Knowledge really exist?" The one who saw the absence of dreams, imaginings, and doubts, in the state of Forgetfulness, and knew of their absence or non-existence, is "The God of Knowledge" (Jnanadeva). It is He who witnesses the dissolution of all the modifications of Knowledge and is the one who presides over the Great-Causal Body. However, it should be clearly understood that this "Witnessing Knowledge" is also a parasite (an unwanted presence) on the "Pure Nature of the Self." This "Witnessing Knowledge" is only needed to be used to annihilate the "Ignorance" of the Causal Body which means having "no knowledge." When the "Witnessing Knowledge" of the Fourth Body is left behind, the state of Forgetfulness is forgotten, and "Knowledge" sees only at itself. Observation of one's Self cannot be called "witnessing." The seer is called a witness when he forgets the Self and sees something objective or different from the Self. When seeing only Himself, he abides in this "Supreme Knowledge," Vijnana, which is of the nature of the "Absolute."

In that "Aloneness" one likes humming to himself "Aham Brahmasmi, I am Brahman." With that sound arising from within, even this "Knowledge" is limited, or bound, and is still caught in the Great-Causal Body. This hum is the Primal Illusion, the original Illusion that is of the nature of the "Three Gunas" (GunaMaya). If one wants to be rid of this Illusion, even this humming sound has to stop for that rumbling Primal Illusion (MoolaMaya) to be permanently left behind. "I am Brahman" is a very subtle sense of "I Am" that is imposed on the Self, which is actually the absence of the ego or a sense of separate self. However, even this subtle type of "I Am" is like a molecule of salt in milk, and therefore has to be eradicated. To take the false as true, is a mistaken concept, but to take the True as True is the absence of any such concept. By virtue of this statement, in the absence of all concepts, the Gross Body is "I," the Subtle Body is "I," and the Causal Body is also "I." However, as long as one continues to assert oneself to be any of these three bodies, it is certainly a mistaken concept, and a type of pride.

This having been said, the Consciousness that says "I," as "I am Brahman," can be called egolessness, or having no pride, because this "I" is upholding the Truth. Where is the falsehood in it? Actually there is nothing untrue or false in this, yet, if that "True One" goes on announcing, "I am True," or "I am Brahman," there arises a doubt about this truth. If a Brahmin (someone of the priest caste) goes on telling everybody he meets "I am a Brahmin, I am a Brahmin," the listener will say, "If this man is a Brahmin why is he repeating this? He must really be of some lower caste." In the same way, the repeated assertion of the concept "I am Brahman, I am Brahman," shows that this Consciousness, this Knowledge in the Great-Causal Body is not free from doubt about its Real Nature. From this point of view, even the memory of the concept "I am Brahman" that reminds one of the Self, has to be erased. The Consciousness (SatChitAnanda) that is of the Great-Causal Body should be stabilized to such an extent that it is of neither memory, nor forgetfulness. Only then does the aspirant become "The Nature of Pure Knowledge and Bliss."

Even when we consider our usual daily gross experiences, we are in a natural state that is without any remembrance or forgetfulness. Does anyone have an experience like "I have forgotten myself," or "I was remembering myself"? Has anyone ever tried to prove his existence by making such efforts? We do not ever forget ourselves, nor is it necessary to remember ourselves. We are always naturally in a state that is beyond the state of remembrance or forgetfulness. That is really our True Nature. Remembrance or forgetfulness is always of something "else" that is separate from ourselves. From the basis of this truth, one should make a firm mental decision that whatever is remembered or whatever is forgotten is not "I." It should be your firm conviction that whatever is remembered or forgotten is definitely not you. When there is no memory of Self or forgetfulness of Self, there is just being one's Self, which can be recognized as "Self-Illumination." Therefore, know that the Gross Body is not you, the Subtle Body is not you, and the Causal Body is not you. You are of the nature of Self-Knowledge, the Awareness that "I am the SatChitAnanda of the Great-Causal Body." You must constantly remain the same.

Going by the theory of progressive elimination according to the instruction given above, once the conviction of one's True Nature as "Pure Knowledge, or "I Am" is realized, the four bodies have been collectively considered using the ancient method of investigation and deductive elimination. Up until now, it has been explained that you are not the three bodies. At this point, the Vedas again turn back and now announce that all of the visible appearance of the world is the sport or play (Lila) of your own Consciousness. There is a maxim, or statement, that goes like this: "A thing that is produced is like the thing from which it was produced." For example, when water is turned into ice it is still water. For the one who only sees superficially, water has a flowing tendency while ice is solid. Water has no shape and ice has shape. However, when the substance is known, they are known to be one and the same. According to this maxim it can be understood that the world, and its Lord (Brahman), are the same. This is the teaching in the Vedas.

From the gross point of view, Earth, Water, Light (Fire), Wind (Air), and Sky (Space) appear different, but the difference is only in quality. Ice becomes Water after melting, just as the Earth gets dissolved in Water, and Water dries up by the heat of Fire. Fire, or Light, is contained in the Wind, and Wind gets diffused and simply disappears in the Space. Because the Self is the womb of all these five elements, they all disappear in the Self. If these principles were absolutely different from one another, they would never have dissolved into each other as one, without any remnant of difference. Consequently, the five elements, this gross world, and the subtle world, are only the Self. The Self appears as all of the different characters and species. When a painter paints a tree, a stone, cows, buffaloes, a river, the sky, gods, demons, and human beings, they are all painted with a single thing called paint. In the same way, this spectacle appearing as the world in an infinite number of forms, is nothing but Pure Knowledge. This is the bold and convincing deduction that one must conclude.

One thing has to be mentioned at this point. It must be said that the method itself is of secondary importance, whether it is the method of deductive elimination, or some different or contradictory method, the main purpose of a particular method is to impart the Knowledge of the Self. When an example in math is solved by several different boys, using various methods, and their answer is the same, it becomes compulsory to accept the answer as being right. The answer is what is important, and the method of arriving at the answer is of secondary importance. That is how the Vedas view the methods being used to explain to the aspirant the nature of one's True Self. There is a snag in proving the identity of water and ice, the world and God, and gold and jewelry as being the same. Even if the gold and the ornaments are the same, the ornament could not be manufactured unless the goldsmith puts his skill to work on the gold, and water could only turn into ice by virtue of intense cold. Similarly, although the world and God are the same, the rationale still presents itself that this means that some transformation must have occurred in God. He solidified as Earth, or melted and became Water, then He dried up and became Fire, etc. In this argument, first God became the five elements, and then the world was formed out of the five elements. This is a flaw in the method of deduction, and an objection can be raised in this manner. However, Samartha Ramdas has eradicated even this objection by the sentence, "Oh Man why are you asking about a thing which does not exist at all? The world has not come into existence. The Absolute Parabrahman alone exists."

To forget one's Self is the birth of Illusion, or Maya (Ma means "is not," and Ya means "which"). Maya is that "which is not," which means that she is "that which does not exist." How can one describe this non-existent woman? Is the barren woman's son fair or dark? What is his age, his height, his breadth, his caste? How can we answer these questions about that which has not come into being? To keep a child quiet from crying, he is told "the scarecrow has come." He is quieted by the creation of the tale of a scarecrow that is not really there. After the child becomes quiet, he asks his father "Daddy, what did the scarecrow look like? How long was his beard and how long was his mustache? How big were his nose, eyes, and teeth?" What answer can the father give? Until he responds the child is not going to keep quiet. At such time, the father has to stretch the nose of the scarecrow as far as Rameshwara, and his feet up to the Netherworld, and his head has to reach the sky. Thus, saying whatever he likes, he draws a frightening picture of the scarecrow saying, "he is like this, and like that, etc., so do not cry again." This kind of description alone will match the description of Maya.

The non-existent Maya exists, and she has created this world. The Vedas tried to explain to the Jivas, the human beings, how this world was created according to the capacity of their understanding. The Vedas somehow trace the source of Maya and the world. "This is just the way it happened." It can be seen that the reasoning used in the deductive elimination method at times contradicts some other theory or method. Yet, instead of accusing the Vedas that since they tell one thing to A, and another to B, that they are deceptive and telling wrong things, it must be said that the Vedas have explained the "Knowledge of the Self" to all. By using different methods according to the capacity of the aspirant's intellect, the Vedas have eradicated their Illusion, and as to who was deceptive, the aspirants were deceiving themselves as to the real nature of this world. The mother gives wheat porridge to one child and gives roti (a type of flat bread) to another child who is suffering from indigestion. Can you call this mother partial? That mother knows which food is beneficial according to the capacity of each child's digestion. Similarly, with regard to the Vedas, different methods are used for the different types of aspirants. They differ in intellect but they are suffering from the same disease of Samsara (belief in mundane objective existence).

"Bhava Roga" means the disease that created the idea that the world has been created. To treat this disease, the Vedas and various scriptures had to give explanation in different ways according to the aspirant's capability of understanding. Even if a fever is only one symptom, a clever doctor will give different medications according to the physical condition of the patient. The doctor's goal is only the restoration of good health. There might be different medications but there is no difference in the ideology. One medicine suiting one patient may not suit another patient who has a different physical condition. Similarly, spiritual instructions given to one aspirant may not appeal to another. The knowledge or advice given to an aspirant who has a certain background may not be suitable for who another who has a different background. There is no fault regarding the methods that Mother Shruti (the Vedas) gives. The faults are in the mental disposition of the aspirants at the time the exposition is made. Mother Shruti's final goal is to make all children attain Self-Knowledge. Therefore the aspirant should abandon the faultfinding attitude, and fulfill oneself by achieving the goal of acquiring Self-Knowledge.

Chapter 4: The Great-Causal Body - "I Am"

Up to this point in the text, the explanation has focused on the definition of the four bodies. Now we will see how "Knowledge" arises in these four bodies. To gain the knowledge of objects with sight through the Gross Body, it is necessarily implied that all of the four bodies are instrumental in bringing this about. If we take into consideration a pair of eyes that are drawn in a picture, it is obvious to us that those eyes cannot see an object. In the same way, the physical eyes alone cannot see an object without the help of the subtle eye of the intellect. For example, we see a mango, or have the knowledge that "this is a mango," but what would happen if we were only to just see what the physical eyes alone see? Of course, the physical eye should also see the object as a mango. However, it does not happen like that. Behind the physical eye is the subtle eye of the intellect whose help is sought to know the "mango."

However, even this combination of the physical eye and the subtle intellect is not sufficient. If these two do not have the support of the Causal Body, the intellect is dead. The Causal Body functions in various ways, like space, sky, the void, distance, etc. The intellect needs the background of space in order to function. So, now there is the eye, the intellect, and space in the form of the Causal Body, but if there is no witness, in the form of the Great-Causal body (Consciousness; "I Am") to connect these three, there is no knowledge of anything.

Thus, in order to get the knowledge of objects, it is necessary for all four of these bodies to be present. However, if we look progressively from one body to the next, it needs to be pointed out that in order to know the activity or changes in the Subtle Body, the Physical Body is not necessary. Additionally, the activity or changes that occur in the Subtle Body such as attraction and repulsion, thirst and hunger, and pleasure and pain, can be known only with the aid of the Causal and Great-Causal Bodies. However, looking in the other direction, in order for knowledge to arise in the Causal Body, the help of the Gross and the Subtle Bodies is not required. At this stage in the explanation, it must be made clear that knowledge on any level is always dependent upon the Great-Causal Body.

For gaining knowledge in the Causal Body, the elements of the Subtle Body (mind, intellect, thinking, prana, and the senses) are of absolutely no use. The elements of the Subtle Body only have influence over the Gross and Subtle Bodies. The field of the Causal Body is entirely different from the Gross and Subtle Bodies, and nothing from them can ever step into it. The question naturally arises at this point, "If this is the case, how then, can one enter into the Great-Causal Body?" It is a fact that the scope of the mind and intellect is limited only to the Subtle Body and they do not have the capacity to enter the further two bodies, the Causal Body, and the Great-Causal Body.

At this point, it must be stated that the "Knowledge" of the Great-Causal Body (Turya) is absolutely "Self-Sufficient." It stands on its own, and has no dependency or expectation of help from the previous three bodies mentioned earlier. This Knowledge is "Self-Luminous." By way of analogy, even though the eye sees all objects, no object can see the eye. No one feels the need of the light of a lamp to see the sun. Similarly, nobody is capable of seeing this "King of Knowledge," which is the eye of the eye.

This "Knowledge" proves its own existence by its own luminosity. Even though the eye cannot see itself, anyone who has eyes never has doubts as to whether he has eyes or not. He can see because he has eyes. This type of certainty naturally abides in him. Similarly, one has knowledge of oneself while witnessing someone or something other than oneself. In order to see our eyes, we need a mirror in order to see the reflection of the eyes. That objective knowledge is only the "reflected knowledge" of the eyes. However, the "Knowledge" of the Great-Causal Body proves its own existence by witnessing everything other than itself. For its proof of existence, no other evidence is required.

This Knowledge of the Great-Causal Body is "all-pervading," and yet, it is as if it were invisible from the ignorant being's point of view. Instead of seeing the "Knowledge" of the Great-Causal Body, for him the Gross Body, which in proportion is like a poppy seed in the ocean, has become the biggest thing of all. The ways of this world are indeed perverse. It has become our habit that when looking at a smaller thing, that which is objective, we forget the bigger thing, that which is subjective. We abandon that which is "Self-Proving," and "Self-Sufficient," and praise artificial things. It is like when words of praise are given to beautiful electric lights, yet we fail to give the same praise to the light of the sun, or when we look at the pictures painted on a wall and forget the wall itself. The process is such that even when we look at a wall, we forget the house itself, and when we discover objects in the light, we forget about the light, and when we are reading letters written on a piece of paper, we are not conscious of the paper at all.

What actually happens in this process is that in spite of the fact that the pervading substance is infinitely bigger, when we pay attention to the pervaded object we forget the pervading substance. (The examples of gold and the ornaments, or earth and the wall are commonly used to illustrate this point.) The Gross is pervaded by the Subtle, the Subtle is pervaded by the Causal, and the Causal is pervaded by the Great-Causal (Consciousness, or Knowledge). However, even with this being the case, the "Knowledge" of the Great-Causal Body cannot be seen because everyone's attention is focused on the Gross, and that which is objective. When the narrow focus of the aspirant widens, becoming that which is all-pervading, then one will have the vision of Truth, the "Infinite Knowledge" that covers and envelopes the vastness of Space.

Although the Knowledge that abides in the Great-Causal Body is the destroyer of the Causal Body (Ignorance), it cannot destroy the Gross and Subtle Bodies. The ordinary and superficial objective knowledge that is gained through the Gross and Subtle Bodies is not the destroyer of Ignorance. Only that extraordinary unique "Knowledge" of the Great-Causal Body is the opponent of Ignorance. Ignorance is actually sustained by ordinary objective knowledge. It is only after achieving that Knowledge which is original, that Ignorance vanishes. However, at the same time, the functioning of the Gross and Subtle Bodies does not stop.

Just as the Gross and Subtle Body's inherent activities function for an ignorant man, these activities also continue to function for the Jnani after he has gained "Self-Knowledge." It is similar to the analogy of how the objects that are invisible in darkness are seen when the darkness is destroyed by the light of a lamp. The light destroys the darkness, but not the objects themselves. It is by the power of the light that the objects become known. It is only the darkness that is destroyed while the objects are illuminated. In the same way, when one gains Self-Knowledge, the darkness of Ignorance is completely eradicated, yet the Gross and Subtle Bodies continue functioning.

In the natural progression of this exposition, the question arises, "In the Light of the Knowledge of the Great-Causal Body, and with the destruction of Ignorance, will the Causal Body cease functioning? Let us give this point some thought. Ignorance has many forms such as sky, space, point of contact, distance, etc. After gaining Self-Knowledge it is true that Ignorance is destroyed. In this Self-Knowledge, all impulses or activity (movement) appear in space as either subtle or gross desires. These impulses will not arise at all unless the space is first created.

So what happens is this: When one looks at these bodies after gaining Self-Knowledge, the four bodies appear, or are viewed, in reverse order from the sequence that was used when each body was being transcended in the process of arriving at "Self-Knowledge." First Self-Knowledge ("I Am"), then the Causal Body in the form of space, then the Subtle Body, and after that, the Gross Body, all readily appear and take form. However, before the activities and functioning of the Gross and Subtle Bodies become apparent, although the Ignorance in the Causal Body has been destroyed, out of necessity the Causal Body establishes a "step of space" between the Subtle Body, and the Great-Causal Body.

Chapter 5: The Appearance of the World

When "Knowledge" begins to stir, activity or motion arises, and the Causal Body in the form of the "Space of Consciousness," or Chidakash, is simultaneously created. Then in sequence comes the Subtle Body, and then, the Gross Body appears. In the method of gaining Self-Knowledge that has been expounded previously, the four steps that are ascended in sequence are:

1) The Gross Physical Body
2) The Subtle Body
3) The Causal Body
4) The Great-Causal Body

Now the same sequence is reversed:

1) The Great-Causal Body
2) The Causal Body
3) The Subtle Body
4) The Gross Physical Body

Instead of Knowledge abiding peacefully within itself, it begins to stir and begins its downward descent. The last two steps, those of the Subtle Body and the Gross Body, cannot be stepped upon unless the third step, the "Causal Body" is first stepped upon. Stepping down from this "Causal State," the last two steps, the Subtle and Gross Bodies arise, and it is on these steps alone that the appearance of the world is felt.

Ultimately what happens is this: The Knowledge that contains the appearance of the world has not been able to completely destroy Ignorance. Think about how light destroys darkness, thus giving us the knowledge of objects which were previously unknown because of the darkness. Similarly, the world appears only because the Causal Body has sustained it, or preserved it, in Space. As long as the appearance of the world is felt by either the Jnani (one who has realized "I Am"), or an ignorant one, it must be understood that Ignorance is still lurking in one form or another. The difference being that Ignorance does not appear to a Jnani in that particular form (The Jnani experiences Ignorance as

Knowledge). Unless Knowledge dies, Ignorance does not die. Knowledge and Ignorance are Siamese twins born of Illusion (Maya). They are both born, and both die, at the same time. If one is there, the other lives on, and when one dies the other is no more. Since this is the Truth, we will see how Knowledge itself dies. Before the Knowledge in the Great-Causal Body dies, the bodies that are below it must all die. These four bodies die in sequence. When looking at a dying man, we do nothing but look at him. We do not die with him. In the same way, we can calmly look within ourselves at how these four bodies die.

One principle that can be easily noticed about death, is that when growth stops, dissolution begins. The meaning of this statement is that whenever something stops growing, it starts disintegrating and follows the path of death. It is unnecessary to do any work for death. Destruction is inherent in growth. In birth, there is death, and in death, there is birth. This is the tradition of birth and death. An object that is born dies its own death, even though there may apparently be some other reason. The root cause of death is nothing other than birth. These four bodies have come upon the "Pure Nature" and they have to die. How do they die? We shall see. The death of the Physical Gross Body according to the principle of "where there is growth, there is destruction" can never be avoided. If not today, at least after one hundred years, or some length of time, whatever it may be. The Gross Body grows until the age of twenty-five or so, and after that, the body begins disintegrating and slowly walks along the "Highway of Death," until one day it becomes a victim of death. As the Gross Body is only the physical form of the Subtle Body, it can be said that it has no separate independent existence. A tree in its gross form is nothing but the result of its seed, which is the subtle form. Both forms of this tree automatically die off.

The Subtle Body is the seed of birth and death. This seed does not get destroyed as easily as a tree. Its growth is so enormous that if it is not sought out and destroyed by man's effort, it will keep on growing indefinitely. This growth becomes the cause of an infinite number of gross bodies. This is what puts a being through births in 8.4 million species. When the growth of the Physical Body naturally stops, the Subtle Body does not stop growing. It is here, that one feels the need for a Sadguru in order to understand how to stop the growth of the Subtle Body. Arresting the growth of the Subtle Body of imagination and doubts means giving up dreams and desires. Desires, dreams, worries, imagination, etc. are the products of the mind. The task of breaking them can be done only with one's own mind. Whatever is created by the mind cannot be destroyed by the hand, and conversely whatever is created by the hand cannot be destroyed by the mind. Whenever we try to forcefully break up these dreams and desires, their number only seems to grow. The mind is frivolously disrespectful. When we try to curb it, it becomes more agitated. Therefore, to stop the growth of the mind, the Sadguru gives us the remedy. "If you try to keep quiet, gradually the imagination and doubts dissolve." When a small infant is sleeping, if you observe its eyes for some time you can easily learn a lesson from him how to stay quiet. When going to sleep, you will see how easily the infant slips into sleep, forgetting himself. While you are looking at the baby, you can also slip into the state of forgetfulness devoid of imaginings, dreams, desires, worries, and doubts.

While a thorn can be taken out by the trick of using another thorn, the mind can only be broken with the mind. Birth and death, or appearing and disappearing, are the two opposite sides of the same state of Consciousness. When one comes, the other goes, and conversely when one goes, the other comes. Death dies its own death like the demon Bhasmasura who put his hand on his own head thereby destroying himself. Thus, when the mind is broken the state that is the Causal Body in the form of Forgetfulness gets completely exposed, and the aspirant gets the Knowledge of that state called "Forgetfulness." The remedy is to diligently practice remembering the instruction, or the repetition of the mantra given by the Guru. Once one begins to stop the growth of the mind, the mind slowly goes along the path of death, and can gradually be completely annihilated. Moreover, one's study and putting into practice the teaching learned from the Sadguru have to be persistent. For example, once a tree starts drying up, even if one tries to keep it green, it will in due time start breaking up, then become uprooted, and eventually fall. Even if one puts plasters on the top of it, paints it, and tries to repair it again and again, a time will come when it comes crumbling down. In the same way, if the mind is constantly stopped from growing, one day it will automatically become tired and break up. However, the aspirant should not become tired of practicing.

In this way, by persistent practice, the next body, the Causal Body, becomes exposed after the death of the Subtle Body. Once the curtain of the Subtle Body is destroyed, it ceases functioning as a covering over the

Causal Body, and the Causal Body automatically becomes exposed. Now let us see how the Causal Body dies. The Causal Body is the producer, or the father, of the Subtle Body. Whenever any state comes uninvited (the Causal Body is not invited) it is experienced for a short time, and once the flood of it recedes it is not remembered. The state of it while it is coming is forceful and growing, yet once the flood ebbs away, it is not even remembered. After having submerged everything for a short period of time, it begins to dissipate, and at last it becomes as if it were not there at all and completely disappears. When a human being is getting roasted in the hot sun and then moves under the cool shade of a tree, at that very moment the flood of cool peace comes to him with such force that he lets out "laugh" as an expression of joy. This shows that the flood of peace is overflowing from the inside as well as outside of him. However, after some time, that "laugh" automatically passes and he lies quietly unaware of his surroundings. Similarly, when the subtle qualities of the Subtle Body such as its hurry and its struggle, becomes comparatively less, forgetfulness in the form of the peaceful void of the Causal Body is automatically forgotten. When this negative state is negated, it results only in negation. To kill it does not require a sword of a positive statement of the "I Am." Shri Samartha Ramdas made this clear by the statement, "The negative is negated by its own negation."

When the state of forgetfulness is dissolved, the Fourth Body, the state of Knowledge that is the Turya State becomes exposed automatically (Turyasvastha - consciousness of "Consciousness"). This state of Knowledge comes to a being with the help of what? It comes in relationship with the state of Ignorance. But even this state of Knowledge, although very powerful, also dissolves eventually. When one attains Knowledge, it is necessary that the Knowledge also must be dissolved. That which comes, has to go. As Ignorance comes, likewise, Knowledge comes. Thus when the Knowledge that is the Great-Causal Body dies, Parabrahman, which is inherent in all of the four bodies, is exposed. This Parabrahman, is "That" which is never born, and never ever dies. After each respective body dies, "That One" who sees the death of all of these bodies, yet remains, is your Real Nature.

Experiencing the Castes in a Human Being

Lord Krishna said in the Bhagavad Gita, "I have created four types of castes." This can be a subject of experience for any human being in his own self. "My creation is divided into four parts and these parts are divided according to their quality and Karma (activity). The four castes are Brahmana (Brahmin; Priest), Kshatriya (Warrior), Vaishya (Merchant), and Shudra (Laborer)." The four bodies can be viewed along the same lines. The Great-Causal Body is of the Brahmin Caste, the Causal Body is of the Warrior Caste, the Subtle Body is of the Merchant Caste, and the Gross Body is of the Laborer Caste. In this way, Paramatman was dispersed into these parts within Himself. The Gross Body is heavy and is an instrument used for service and labor, and therefore it is the Shudra (laborer) Caste. Sitting on a mattress in the Gross Body, taking a balance in hand, and managing the business of the whole world, is the intellect (Buddhi) who compares things as good and bad, big and small, and employs the "laborer" (Gross Body) as a servant to gets things done as he likes, because he is the master. For this reason, this Subtle Body is the Vaishya (merchant) Caste. Now look at the brave actions of the Causal Body. The Causal Body establishes his kingdom by swallowing up the entire wealth in the form of the world that was accumulated on the strength of the capital of desires, imagination, dreams, and doubts. It also swallows up the servants in the form of the Gross and Subtle Bodies. This causality which is one of total destruction is the attitude of a warrior, and therefore the state of the Causal Body is that of the Kshatriya (warrior) Caste.

Now, what remains is only the Great-Causal Body (Brahmin caste). In this body, there is a complete neglect of all the other three bodies. "I have nothing to do with the Gross Body, which puts in hard labor and dies. Neither do I have anything to do with that merchant in the form of intellect, who trades in ideas and dreams, and spreads the vast panorama of the world. I have also nothing to do with the warrior in the form of the Causal Body who sits quietly as if nothing has happened after killing both the subtle and gross bodies. They all may do nothing, or let the Gross Body groan under hard labor, and let the Subtle Body do business with the world, and let the Causal Body wage war against these two. What have I do to with any of these?" There is a saying, "Think of the Self (Rama) and let the world fight." Knowing this very well, the Great-Causal

Body went on announcing the Vedic words "I am Brahman, Aham Brahmasmi," and sat quietly on his own ground, reaching the high stage of Brahmanhood. This Brahmana (Brahmin) is very orthodox about the touch of another caste and cannot tolerate the touch of another body. The other bodies hold the Great-Causal Body in high esteem and smear their heads with the dust of his feet. From the point of view of Vijnana (Supreme Knowledge, or Final Reality), even if this Great-Causal Body becomes polluted by being in contact with the other bodies, it is still the most sacred and highest in all the three worlds (the three bodies, the states of Waking, Deep Sleep, and Ignorance).

The Three Worlds

The Gross Body is the "Material World" (Swarga Loka), the Subtle Body is the "World of Birth and Death" (Mrityu Loka), and the Causal Body is the "Nether World" (Patala Loka). The Great-Causal Body is Brahman. These bodies are divided according to their qualities and these worlds are known by these qualities. The Gross Body is the Swarga Loka and sits on top of, or covers the other worlds. All sorts of external enjoyments and activities are experienced in this world. The wonderful gardens, and the beautiful forests, are created for this world only, and the presiding deity here is Brahma Deva, the Creator, whose main quality is activity, or the Rajas guna. The world below this is the world of death and birth, called Mrityu Loka. In this Loka is a big factory of birth and death where the qualities of appearing and disappearing are continuously being processed. This continuous process is nothing but the rising (birth) and setting (death) of mental modifications. In this way, one is born many times and dies many times during the same day. Everyone should keep for himself an account of his births and rebirths. Every idea produces a visible appearance, and when that idea sets, the appearance also sets. In this way when ideas stop, it is the end of and era, or Kalpanta (the final dissolution of concepts). This is experienced continuously in the Subtle Body. The scriptural writers have accepted the principle of creation and appearance. They stated that as soon as an idea rises, the world rises, and when the idea sets, the world sets. Unless the Subtle Body in the form of Mrityu loka is permanently destroyed and buried, hundreds of eras are sure to rise and set. Therefore, one should die such a death that eliminates the further necessity of being born at all, and live in one's "True Nature" in such a way that there is no fear of any further experience of dying. Let this be so. Whatever has to happen will happen, but until then, it is certain that this Mrityu Loka keeps its mouth wide open for entry. The abode of the Subtle Body is the "Inner-Mind," which is known as the "Antahkarana," or Consciousness. The presiding deity here is Vishnu, and He nourishes the world. (Note - Antahkarana is a word that has no English equivalent, and is difficult to define. Shri Siddharameshwar used this word frequently in many of his talks, so it warrants some basic explanation. It is generally considered to be the "Seat of Consciousness" that is the spark, or genesis of subtle manifestation arising out of Formless Existence. It is characterized by the motion of the attributes arising out of the objectless Consciousness. One could say it is the source of the mind, or one's innermost mind, or innermost heart. It is the origin of the assertion of objectivity. It is the mind at its most subtle. Shri Siddharameshwar Maharaj has said about it, "The Inner-Mind of all is the same, while their minds are different." Throughout this text it is translated as "Inner-Mind" for consistency)

The world below that Knowledge of the Inner-Mind is Patala Loka (The Nether World), which is the Causal Body in the form of forgetfulness. In Patala Loka, there is the pitch darkness of Ignorance. The destroyer, "Rudra" (Shiva) who is of the quality of Ignorance, or Tamas, is the presiding deity here. Above these three is the Great-Causal Body, which is the highest body and is therefore higher than these three worlds. The presiding deity here is "Pure Knowledge." That Knowledge rules here and is the God of all gods. From this God, all the worlds are produced, and He is called "The Lord of the three worlds," (Trailokyanath). The Brahmana (Knower of Brahman; Brahmin caste) is the Guru of all the castes and therefore is placed most highly among them. This gives him the status of a Master. This Brahmana does not allow even the shadow of Ignorance to fall on Him. What's more is that he refuses to even become polluted by the mind and intellect. So, give up the idea that He will ever embrace the corpse of the Gross Body. This orthodox clean Brahmin in the form of "Pure Consciousness," or "Universal Cosmic Consciousness" does not allow even a single entrant into his Great-Causal Body. Therefore, it should be understood that none of these bodies, or castes (Warrior/Causal Body; Trader/Subtle Body; Laborer/Gross Body), can ever enter into His abode. This means that the Gross and Subtle Bodies can never enter the Great-Causal Body. These bodies (castes) cannot do anything without the help of this Brahmana, the Primal Knowledge "I Am." All of their good and bad actions or works only go on the support and strength of this Brahmana.

At this time, the Brahmana comes out of his dwelling and accomplishes the work of these three castes. As soon as the work is done, he cleans himself of any traces of them right in front of their doorstep, and only then enters back into His "Own Abode."

Understanding the Knowledge of Self

Brahman is rich with Knowledge. That is why he is called Vedo Narayana (Knowledge that is God residing in All). He knows all the three times (the beginning, the middle, and the end), and He has a characteristic of Sandhya, which is the space between any two thoughts. He is worshipped by all people and therefore is also called the Lord of the World. The people of all castes and creeds worship this God whether they are aware of it or not. The worshipper may be a Hindu, a Muslim, a Christian, a Jain, a Parsee, or a Buddhist. He may be from any country such as Iran, Turkey, etc., yet he only worships this One God, whoever he may be. He cannot help it. When this God is hungry, all types of food and drink are offered to Him. There are mattresses with cushions made into beds ready for Him to sleep upon. If He feels like traveling, there are cars, airplanes, and many other types of transportation ready for him. To supply Him with fragrant garlands, there are many trees and vines that blossom forth laden with flowers. All servants and attendants are ready to obey Him with folded hands. The wife, children, and palaces are for His entertainment, and they are also His dwelling place. God is dwelling in the innermost heart of all beings, and receiving all of the different kinds of service that are rendered unto Himself. Yet, in spite of His greatness and omnipresence, we consider the body as God, and offer all kinds of services to it. The ignorant people have accepted this wrong idea, and have misunderstood the whole affair. It is this idea that has separated God from His devotee. What is there to be amazed about?

Those who are doing any actions are doing it for no other reason than out of worship rendered to Him. This Great God (Mahadeva) is constantly enjoying the shower of all the objects of the senses in the form of sound, forms, touch, taste, and smell. He receives everything that is of the nature the five instruments of senses of action and the five instruments of knowledge. That devotee is indeed glorious who understands the secret of this Great God, Mahadeva. All acts of such a devotee are naturally dedicated to Brahman. The bees, birds, insects, and even the ants, are performing worship to this God. However, they don't have the intellect to understand this so they cannot be blamed for their ignorance. However, it is unfortunate indeed that the intelligent human being does not understand that all of his daily and occasional actions, are but for the sake of this One God, alone. How very unfortunate this is.

This God is the same as the "King of Knowledge" who while swallowing a mouthful of food, tastes and enjoys it. It is He, who discriminates between fragrance and stench. It is He, who understands which sound is pleasant to the ear and which sound is harsh. It is He who observes the difference between a beautiful, or a fierce and ugly form. It is He who understands the soft or hard touch. He is always present, reigning supreme in every being's heart. How utterly misguided is the idea that we worship any other God than this One. Just think of which God is worshipped when the Christians worship Christ, the Hindus worship Vishnu or Shiva, the Parsees worship their Zoroaster, or the Buddhists their Buddha? Are they not merely worshipping the corpses of these mentioned Gods? However, what is the feeling of the devotee who is worshipping? Ask anyone from any religion "Describe your God," and they will answer "My God is Conscious, Luminous, Solid, Omniscient, Omnipresent, and Omnipotent. He animates all, and owns all. He is without birth, and without death." Will anyone say that his God is a stone, or a rock, or mud, or metal, or heavy, dull, and vacant without Consciousness, or that he is weak, blind, or deaf?

From this, it is clear that whether it is Christ, Vishnu, Buddha, Zoroaster, or whatever God it may be, His nature will be full of Consciousness, and He is full of the "Qualities of God." If anyone possesses all of these qualities, then the indication is that He is the Absolute Paramatman. He is God in the form of "Knowledge" that is present in everyone's heart. This God alone dwelled in Mohammed, and Christ's heart was pervaded by this One God as well. It is only by this God that the quality of Vishnu (The Protector) has been sustained, and not by any other God. For any devotee whomever he may be that worships any God, that worship is the worship of this "One Inner-Self." The obeisance made to any other gods, go to this One God, (Our Own Self Nature), alone. This is the "Absolute Truth."

The forms of all the above-mentioned Gods, are only temples of this "One God." All the names belong to His temples (bodies). He is present in the innermost region of all these forms. He sits in all of the forms of all beings and accepts all of their worship. Whatever actions are done by the Gross Body, and whatever imagination or desires, or concepts and doubts that have crossed the mind happen for the sake of this God, in order to please Him. If you recognize this much, your work is done. All of you are doing something through your body or mind. If you say, "We do not want to do it," you cannot stop from doing it. However, whatever you do, the doer, and enjoyer of your deeds is only God (The Self). This fact alone must be recognized in every movement. All auspicious and inauspicious acts thus become dedicated to Brahman, and the aspirant remains absolutely free. This is what is called the "Sacrifice through Knowledge" (Jnana Yadnya).

When you come and go, speak or swallow, when you give or take, stand or sit, do any action at home or outside, or are in bed enjoying sex, leave off all sense of shame or doership, and think only of God. It is the "One Knowledge" alone is playing at each point. To contemplate on this, means contemplating on God. The body-consciousness has to be turned into Self-Consciousness. The decision that the Self alone is doing all, is itself the state of Liberation. This is the advice given by Samartha Ramdas. Even Saint Tukaram asked for this gift from God. "May I never, never, forget you." Likewise, we also must never forget the Self. Then surely salvation is at your feet. As this rope, in the form of the mind, was twisted in the direction of body-consciousness, it now has to be twisted in the opposite direction of Self-Consciousness. When the rope gets untwisted, the strings will be blown about in the wind, and there will be nothing left to call "rope."

When a screw is screwed in, it has to be turned in the opposite direction to come out. Similarly, with regard to body-consciousness, if the mind which is guided by the intellect is directed towards the Self, it becomes absorbed in the Self. As the mind is directed towards the One God, Lord Rama, it gets absorbed in Rama. The mind itself becomes Rama, and there is nothing left in the form of the mind, inside or out, or anywhere, and it becomes one with the form of Rama. Take this advice, and you will see this for yourself. To better understand just how the "One Pure Knowledge" is playing about, you have only to come out of the house, and look at the moon. With what speed does the Pure Consciousness rush towards the moon out from the window of your mind? See how it pervades the whole sky in a fraction of a second. Try this.

Does the mind have this much speed? The mind received the speed of awareness of the moon, only through the help of this "Knowledge." Wherever the mind goes, Consciousness is already there. What a wonder it is then that the movement of the mind seems stuck in this Consciousness. You only have to open the eyelids, and the "Knowledge" (Consciousness) simultaneously pervades the entire sky, the vastness that contains the multitude of stars, and the moon. Instead of saying that it pervades, it is better to say that it has already pervaded the whole, which is now experienced.

When Consciousness travels from the eye to the moon and one recognizes it to be the moon, this is the objective knowledge. In this example, the moon is the object, and the Consciousness takes its shape immediately upon knowing that it is the moon. If there is a cloud in front of the moon, the Consciousness takes the shape of the cloud, and is viewed as that object. Thus, Consciousness pervades the cloud and knows the cloud to be an object.

Chapter 6: Maya and Brahman

Now, try to notice the "crust" of Consciousness that is without an object, the "Pure Knowledge" without the mixture of any objects. That space, which is lying between the eye and the moon, had not come to your notice, yet still it was there pervading, existing in its own nature. That is the pure form of Knowledge. When empty space that is not noticed previously, is purposefully made an object of attention, it becomes the object of attention, as "Space." What can be noticed is Maya, and whatever cannot be seen is "Brahman." While looking at the moon, the space in between did not come to your attention. Therefore, it is Consciousness without an object. If this space is separated, and is made an object of sight this Pure Knowledge is transformed into a zero, because if Space is seen separately, the modification of the mind becomes a void. If there is any difference between Space and Pure Knowledge it is this: To separately look at one's own nature is Space, and when the "looking" is abandoned, it is "Pure Knowledge." Once Pure Knowledge is recognized properly in this manner, even when mixed with any object, it can be selected and recognized. Once pure water is known, even when it is mixed with something else, its existence can be recognized within that mixture. Water is a fluid that can become condensed into ice. Even when water gives up its fluidity and assumes the density of ice, it is still recognized as water in the form of ice. It is not difficult to recognize the wetness in mud as water. Similarly, once Pure Knowledge is known, its steady existence in this moving world in the form of Sat-Chit-Ananda (Being, Consciousness, and Bliss) can also be recognized.

Pure water is devoid of any color, form, taste, or smell. Once this is properly understood, even when water is condensed to assume a dense form, or takes on a hot flavor by adding chilies, or a sweet flavor by adding sugar, or if it becomes fragrant, or takes on a color such as rose, or is used as water in paint, it is quite unmistakably still recognized as pure water, or water minus the form, the taste, the smell, and the color. Thus, by the same method of elimination, even when this Pure Knowledge is conditioned, by subtracting the conditioning and by dividing the form into its respective elements, it will be recognized as absolutely Pure Knowledge alone that fills all form everywhere to the brim. However, before attaining this Pure Knowledge by the method of elimination, if someone accepts the method of enumeration (listing the qualities of God), and goes on chattering about how God alone pervades all beings, and all forms, and that there is nothing else but Rama, and that "the world, and the Lord of the world, are but one," etc., etc., then such babble can never be useful. In contrast to this type of chatter, if one speaks only empty words without having the experience behind them, such as, "I am Brahman," or "the senses do their job, yet I am not the doer," or "there is no sin or virtue at my doorstep," etc., instead of gaining the Self, he will only deceive the Self. In this way, these so-called "Self-discoverers" lose the joy of this world, as well as that of the other world. Saint Kabir said; "He went away as he came." This means that these people die in the same state of consciousness as that in which they were born. They get no benefit from life other than this.

Such worldly scholars take words to be true Self-Knowledge, but has that Truth which is beyond speech ever dawned on an ignorant man? Anyone can say "The senses do the work of the senses, but I am not the senses," or "The mind's qualities are with the mind, and body's qualities are with the body, but what have I to do with them? I am different from these." What is untrue about these utterances? Who is it that understands the Truth? Who is it that has the experience of Truth? Only the one who knows who he is. Of what use are such statements to another? Each one enjoys his own pleasures and bliss. Tukaram said "Each one for himself." Even a parrot can be taught to repeatedly say the words "Brahman is Truth, the world is only an appearance." However, one cannot say that the parrot has understood the Truth of what Brahman is, or what the world is, or even what a statement of Truth is. Where there is no understanding there cannot be the "Bliss of Self-Knowledge."

Let that be as it is. However, an aspirant should not follow the example of one who is an expert with words, yet is a hypocrite. With persistent study, and by applying the method of elimination, one must first come to know what Pure Knowledge is. Knowledge is of different types, such as general, particular, objective knowledge of imagination and doubts, and the Knowledge that is without any thought. The particular, objective, imagining, and doubting types of knowledge are contradictory to Pure Knowledge. When the Pure Consciousness through process of sight takes the shape of an object, one gets objective knowledge, or knowledge which can be of a particular type, or an imagination type, or of a doubt type of knowledge. If the object is gross, it is objective knowledge. If it is only an idea that is subtle, it is idea knowledge, or Savikalpa. This means that when Pure Knowledge takes the shape of an object, an idea, or a thought, it then becomes categorized as particular knowledge. Particular knowledge, being artificial, is by nature transient and lasts only for a very short period of time. It is inherently transient and of an unsteady nature. However, the rule is that particular knowledge must return back into general knowledge, the knowledge that "I Am."

As an example, when we walk, this is considered the common or general speed, and when we increase the speed and start running, it becomes a particular speed. Yet, how long can we run? After sometime the running stops, and soon one assumes the natural speed again. Similar to this, we are naturally very loving and blissful within, and this love within oneself is the general type of love common to all. However, when love is for a son, a friend, or a house, etc., it is an objective and a particular kind of love. Thus, a love that comes, must also go. The love that comes, is of a particular kind which is transient and destructible. The happiness that one gets from objects, also falls into the category of being of a "particular" kind of happiness which only lasts for a very short period of time. A small thing brings in an experience of "particular" type, but while our attention is focused on that, the "One Thing" that pervades it cannot be experienced. The reason is, is that the pervading thing is big and infinite, and in reality we are that same "All-Pervading Brahman." The particular thing is Maya, and the general or common thing is Brahman, and we are "That." When we are focused on the experience of a "particular type" we do not experience the "Love of Our Own Self," nor do we enjoy the "Happiness of the Bliss of the Self."

We will now observe what is called "general knowledge" which is devoid of an object or an idea. There is a slight distance between an outside gross object and the eye, or the mind. That void or space although unknowingly observed, is as if it were not seen, and therefore we have no knowledge or acknowledgment of that space. This intervening knowledge (the space) being "Knowledge" itself, cannot become the object of its own knowledge. How can sugar taste its own sweetness? In the same way, Knowledge does not experience itself as an object. This Knowledge is naturally spread out between the eye and the object, as well as between the intellect and an idea or thought. One should repeatedly take notice of how this general "Pure Knowledge" naturally pervades everywhere before it acknowledges or recognizes an object. This noticing, or "seeing," is not the same as seeing an object such as, "I am the seer of an object," or "I am the thinker, of an idea." It is only seen when one gives up both the seeing as well as the thought that "I am the seer." The instrument of seeing is the eye, and the instrument of knowing a thought is the intellect. "Knowledge" itself can only be seen by setting aside both of these instruments. The instruments of sight and the intellect are of no value here. Any attempt to know Pure Knowledge by means of the eye or intellect is to forget that Pure Knowledge (the unadulterated sense of "I Am) by allowing these instruments to step in. To know Pure Knowledge really means not to know it, and once "known" in this way, the "knower" himself becomes Pure Knowledge.

Samartha Ramdas has said "In trying to meet Pure Knowledge one becomes separated from it. But there is always union with it without trying to meet it." This puzzle is very difficult. Wise men, yogis, and renunciates make a mistake and misinterpret the seen as the seer, when saying "Paramatman is like 'this.' He has four hands. He is like the light of a million suns. He is lustrous. He is dark complexioned. He is like a point, and He is like this and He is like that." etc. They say whatever they like, but by whose knowledge is it that it is stated that "This one is like this, and the other is like that"? That "One" is forgotten completely while they talk of the great things of Realization. However, when the seer is forgotten whatever is seen is "I," which is Brahman. One does not know what to say of this. The brave one sets out to find Brahman but the obstacle in the form of the seen gets in his way. This is the state of the majority of seekers.

Search for the Lost "I"

In a crowd during a pilgrimage, I lost myself and could not find myself even when I tried searching within. Then, I went to the police station and gave them the information that I was lost. At that time a constable came and slapped my cheeks hard until they were red and asked me, "Who is this fellow?" Only then did I become conscious of myself, and was very happy that I was found. This is the very condition of the one that is himself Brahman and yet is in search of Brahman. Where and how can He find Himself? His exact position is such that He is the one who knows everyone but is not known by anyone. The one who tries to know Him does not know that his own true nature is "Pure Consciousness" so he wanders about in the forest and jungle (searching for that which has never been lost). How amazing this is! How can He, the one who is known only after "the capacity of knowing" has been transcended, be known? Unless one becomes steady within oneself, leaving behind having the desire to know, one cannot have the "Knowledge of Brahman.

There is a story of one foolish fellow who wanted to know what sleep was. Whenever he would start to doze off, he immediately would remember "Aha, now I will catch sleep." With that thought, he would clap his hands and suddenly become completely awake. Repeatedly doing this, the poor fellow became tired and entirely gave up his efforts of trying to catch sleep. Similarly, trying to know Brahman is the same thing. When one gives up trying to "know" Brahman, one becomes Brahman itself. When the Gross and Subtle Bodies are negated the instruments of the mind and intellect are broken up. The aspirant then goes to the state of the Causal Body which is the state of "Forgetfulness." This itself is the Ignorance of the human being. To eradicate this Ignorance, it is necessary to acquire the "Knowledge of Brahman." Therefore, the aspirant tries to get the Knowledge of Brahman with the help of the subtle intellect and that part of Consciousness that is "Pure Knowledge." Saint Shankaracharya (Shri Shankara) has called such a man a great fool. If one tries to know Brahman in this manner with the subtle intellect the Subtle Body will only go on increasing.

When the Subtle Body gets destroyed and one comes to the Causal Body, the one who is trying to know Brahman with the subtle intellect does not become steadied in the Causal Body. Instead he gets pushed back to the Subtle Body with force from the Causal Body and once again comes under the sway of imaginings, concepts, desires, and doubts. If an aspirant dreams, employing the use of words or the mind, he will never progress to where speech and mind cannot enter. Instead, he will go to a lower plane. The aspirant cannot remain as an aspirant, but has to become "One who is Accomplished" (a Siddha). For this, one has to cross over the steps of all of the four bodies. By constant study, one has to enter on the platforms of the four bodies, and clean and clarify them through thorough investigation and deduction. Only then can "The Truth of the Self" be invoked and become fully established. Once this is done, it is certain that the aspirant will become a Siddha.

Up to this point in the text, the exposition regarding the four bodies and the method of study has been explained. The aspirants must also have understood what has been presented. By way of analogy, if a wooden stool with four legs made in the form of the bodies has been constructed, it still is very crude. In order to make it shine properly, more effort has to be made. It is necessary to polish it in order to make it shine so that it can throw off its own light. The procedure for making something is quite different from the procedure of scrubbing and cleaning thereby making it absolutely smooth and appealing. Unless it has been manufactured in that finished condition, it will be not considered finished, nor will it return a fair price. Therefore, before becoming a Siddha, we must be aspirants for some time, persistently polishing the "Pure Knowledge" of the Great-Causal Body. It must be made completely clean.

Chapter 7: Devotion and Devotion After Liberation

We know that the Pure Knowledge in the form of Paramatman pervades every form. After knowing the Self intellectually, the best way of studying it and realizing it fully, is to try to make everyone happy. It is with this practice alone that the Self is seen to be pervading in everything. The whole world is only "Knowledge." Since everything is the Self, by making everyone happy the Self is pleased. In this way, the Truth of the Vedas will be proven and experienced, and Self-Knowledge will become firmly established. The worship of Paramatman with form (Saguna) is the worship of the manifest. Brahmananda (The Bliss of Brahman) manifests in all forms such as that of an insect, ant, dog, or pig. It is the "Supreme Self," Paramatman alone, that pervades everything. Paramatman, which is formless, without any attributes, and not manifest, has become manifest with qualities in the form of the Universe. He is present in those things that are inert, but is experienced clearly in all moving beings. Instead of worshipping lifeless gross objects such as stone and metal idols, it is better to worship the moving, walking, talking God in whom the quality of "Knowledge" is clearly experienced. This is Saguna worship, or worship of the manifest God. What are the qualities in a stone idol? Out of the three qualities, Sattva, Rajas, and Tamas, none of these qualities is found in inert inanimate idols made of stone or metal. However, there is one or more of these qualities found in those manifestations of God who are moving. Therefore, all beings are forms of God.

If one prays sincerely to the Saints or to a good man who is full of Sattva Guna (Knowledge and an inclination towards spiritual understanding), he becomes pleased and grants us our wishes. Yet, if we censure his Tamo Guna, he slaps our face and gives us an experience of a jolt. Therefore, worship the God who is walking and talking. For gaining Knowledge, a stone is of no use. Saint Kabir gave this warning in clear words. He advised all to worship a walking talking God, alone. As soon as the word "worship" is uttered, sandalwood paste, incense, flowers, kumkum, and other various articles of worship come to mind. However, to really worship God means to please and make every being happy. Although Paramatman is "One," existing everywhere, the methods used by devotees to worship Him are different according to their conditioning and how they conceive of Him. A donkey also has God in it, yet if you fold your hands before it in obeisance, it would be like a joke or mischief played on Paramatman. Does it get pleased if you fold your hands before him? If not, then according to what is said above about worship, the worship that is pleasing to another form of God, would not really be the appropriate worship of the donkey. If the donkey were given green grass and clean water to drink, that would be proper worship to God in the form of the donkey. However, worshipping the God who has taken a human form is not just offering it food with the hands, but by pleasing him in a manner that suits him. This would be the proper worship of Paramatman. By giving someone whatever he wants, his heart is pleased, and he feels blessed.

The snake and a scorpion are also forms of God (Narayana), but to worship them consists of making obeisance to them from a distance. This means that they should be left alone to live their own lives. Instead of doing this, if you start embracing them out of devotion, that serpent God will bite you and prove to you that embracing him is not worshipping him. Here someone may raise a doubt, "How could allowing the snake and scorpion to escape alive mean that you are worshipping them? Those beings are wicked and they must be killed." I would say to them that snakes or scorpions do not bite unnecessarily unless they are touched or hurt. However, man is always ready to kill them even if they are off at a considerable distance. Is not the nature of man more wicked than the nature of a snake or a scorpion? Yes, it is, because man has the desire to kill them needlessly. Let the feeling of "The snake and scorpion are of my own nature" be firm, and then see the miracle that happens. The "Self" of a snake or a scorpion is not a stone. When your understanding becomes firm that your Self is the same as the Self in a snake or a scorpion, you will see the Self of the snake is truly one with your own Self, and there will arise no desire in the snake or scorpion to bite you. If one sees a snake as a snake, it also sees an embodied man as an enemy. You will see the same facial expression in the mirror as you have on your face. If you see a bad expression in the reflection in the mirror, is it the fault of the mirror? If you make a smiling face and look in the mirror, you do not need to order the mirror to make a smiling face. Why does the thief rob our house? It is because we also have a continuous desire to rob people in many ways and fill our house. As we develop the feeling of complete renunciation, then that feeling will be reflected in whatever comes before us. Even if you refuse to ask for anything, people are prepared to give up heaps of whatever they have for you. But the one who begs for it, does not get it.

From this discussion a reader may get confused and say, "Maharaj your way of thinking does not seem right. To leave a snake alone after sighting it, or to accept as God the one who pickpockets a bundle of notes and do nothing is something we can never do." Agreed! I would say agreed, a hundred times! Oh aspirant, this cannot be possible because of the habit of many, many, births. This type of worship cannot be achieved all at once. Yet, a beginning can be made in small steps, for example, from the small bugs in the house, instead of the scorpions and snakes. From a petty action like not killing the bugs in the house, one should study the "Oneness of All." See the "Oneness of the Self" in every thing, and every being, and then see what a wondrous experience that you will get. You will then come to have the feeling of the Oneness in all beings, even with those who are more troublesome than the bugs, and gradually "Self-Confidence" and "Self-Experience" increase. This means that one should not proceed with the feeling, "Bugs should not be killed, they should be left alone," but instead the feeling should be that "They are of my own nature, and they are my own forms. Their happiness is my happiness." A mother experiences the feeling of joy by pleasing her child when it suckles at her breast. With that same attitude, one should experience the feeling of satisfaction by allowing the bugs to suck the blood from one's own body. This idea may be difficult to accept, but it is the beginning, or the first lesson on feeling Oneness with all beings.

Gradually and persistently studying this, the earth will be without an enemy, and fearlessness will come your way. In this way, you shall be free from all fear. When an aspirant is free from all doubts and achieves "The Knowledge of the Self," he becomes free. Although this is true, he still cannot experience the "Full Glory of Real Liberation." For example, the achieving of wealth is one thing, while enjoying the status after becoming wealthy, is quite another thing. In the same way, unless a feeling of "The Oneness with All" comes to the Jnani, his Self-Knowledge does not develop or spread. He is like a stingy rich man with his wealth, and he cannot get the "Complete Bliss of Liberation" while alive. Even if one achieves Self-Knowledge, unless he experiences a feeling of "Oneness with All," fearlessness does not come his way. "Complete Bliss" is Fearlessness. Fear is an indication of duality. Fear is a very great impediment in the way of Bliss arising out of Liberation. After achieving

Self-Knowledge, the aspirant should worship Paramatman in the method explained previously. In this manner, dry Self-Knowledge will be moistened with Devotion. A jalebi, which is a kind of sweet that has been fried in ghee, becomes juicy and sweet only after it is fried and then put into syrup. In the same way, the Jnani gets the "Fullness of Life" through "Devotion after Self-Knowledge."

In the game called "Surfati" a player slides first from the lower to the higher house, and then brings back home all that he gets from the other houses. Only then is the game over. By gaining the knowledge all the way from the Gross to the Great-Causal Body, one has to bring this gift of Self-Knowledge back to the lower body in the same way. The factual experience that "The world is nothing but Knowledge" is itself Knowledge becoming the "Final Reality" (Vijnana). It is because of the feeling that there is someone else in the world who is not "I," that we go around night and day with a feeling of anxiety that we should protect our wife, our wealth, and our belongings from the clutches of someone else. In this way, we turn into a "Gasti" or watchman due to the feeling of possessiveness and ownership. However, when one realizes a feeling of "Oneness with Everyone," and the feeling that "I am present everywhere, I am pervading everything." On that day, the "Gasti" becomes "Agasti," the sage who drank the ocean in one sip. This ocean, which is the five elements that make up the entire universe, may not even be enough for one sip.

This is the way in which the devotee who knows the Self becomes fearless while in the body, and enjoys the "Full Celebration" of what is called "Liberation." Now, at this point, we have given the exposition about Self-Knowledge and the "Devotion after Self-Knowledge." We have reached a stage where an aspirant has become the "Self-Knowing Jnani." The end of all of the Knowledge of the Great-Causal Body bears fruit in the seeing of the whole world as oneself. This being true, Saint Ramdas still has called this Knowledge of the Great-Causal Body as being unsteady Brahman when compared with that of Paramatman (that is Parabrahman). Parabrahman is steady. It is different from the "Manifest Brahman" (Saguna Brahman), and the "Invisible Brahman" (Nirguna Brahman) associated with the four bodies, and therefore it is "No-Knowledge." So finally the Vedas have said, "Neti, Neti," meaning "not this, not this." "Not this" means it is neither Knowledge nor Ignorance. Unmoving Paramatman is the "Only Truth," it is the

"Essence." Nothing else is true. Saint Samartha Ramdas has expounded upon this conclusion very nicely in **Dasbodh**.

Why is this Knowledge unsteady? Because it is given many names and attributes of masculine, feminine, and neuter gender. It is called Satchitananda, Ishwara, Omkara, Shesha, Narayana, the Primordial Being, and Shiva, etc. These are some of the masculine names. It is called Shakti, Prakriti, Shruti, Shambhavi, Chitkakla, Narayani, etc., and these are some of the feminine names. It is called Nija Rupam (one's own nature), the Great-Causal Body, Pure Knowledge, Brahman, the Empire of Bliss (Anandayatnam), etc., and these are names of the neuter gender. These neuter gender names have come to be known as this "Self-Knowledge." The One who is not any of these, is the Steady, the Immovable, the Essence, the "Real Brahman." The great quality of the Knowledge of the Great-Causal Body is much greater in comparison than the Knowledge in the Gross Body, and by the process of elimination it can be gleaned, and after having been deduced, it can once again be mixed with (as it is all-permeating). However, it cannot be interpreted that the aspirant has achieved the Parabrahman stage by virtue of expertise with the process of elimination, and once again is consciously permeating everything.

Parabrahman is "That" from where no one can return. Knowledge has been labeled as "Knowledge," but Brahman really has no name. In the Knowledge of "I Am," there is the mixture of activity or changes in the form of the world. As the mind, called "chitta," undergoes this modification, Knowledge also undergoes modification. Modifications (changes) are a state, or stage. Parabrahman is beyond all modifications. Thus, there is as much difference between "Self-Knowledge," or "I Am" (Jnana), and the Absolute (Vijnana; Parabrahman), as there is a difference between darkness and light. "Where there is a contact between the steady and the unsteady, the intellect is confused," says Shri Samartha Ramdas. According to this statement, the last misunderstanding comes in here. (Contact between the steady and unsteady indicates the presence of a very subtle duality still intact.)

Before the Knowledge ("I Am") dawns, "Forgetfulness" is misunderstood as Knowledge. In the same way, when Jnana, or Knowledge, is under-developed it is misunderstood as Vijnana which is the last stage of the "Absence of modifications" of Parabrahman. When the aspirant mistakes Self-Knowledge, or "I Am" (Jnana) for Vijnana, his progress is arrested there. Samartha Ramdas has compared this type of an undeveloped Jnani to a man who is awakened in a dream, and thinks he is awake. Yet, he is still snoring! "You think that this is wakefulness, but your Illusion has not gone," is the warning given by Shri Samartha to this type of Jnani. That Great-Causal Body, or Turya state in which the Gross and Subtle Bodies are like a dream, is itself like a dream in Vijnana. There is bondage in Ignorance, and liberation in Knowledge, but when both Ignorance and Knowledge are not there, how could the idea of bondage or liberation exist?

The Vedas and scriptures talk up to the point of the Great-Causal Body. Until then, it is the primary premise, or the theory. In the field of Knowledge beyond the Great-Causal Body is the proven final conclusion, or Siddhanta, and the canceling of all that has been laid down is right there. When all phenomena is destroyed, or annihilated, whatever remains is your "Real Nature." It is impossible to describe it in words. Where "the knowledge of words" proves to be Ignorance, where Consciousness becomes non-Consciousness, and where all remedies recommended by the scriptures are only hindrances, you will see for yourself how you reach that highest point. The Sadguru brought you to the threshold and pushed you inside, but the Sadguru cannot show you the beauty, or the panorama within. You have to seize the treasure, the trophy, yourself. Now, after all this has been said, there remains nothing that can be conveyed through words. Words were used for whatever had to be told. That which cannot be conveyed by words has now been entrusted to you. We can only inspire you to be an aspirant, but you have to become a Siddha by yourself. We have reached the end of the book. Words are redundant. One thing is clearly enunciated here, and that is Sadguru Bhajana (All Praises to the Sadguru).

Hari Om Tat Sat.

The End

of

Master Key to Self-Realization

Shri Sadguru Siddharameshwar Maharaj

Amrut Laya
The Stateless State

Spiritual Discourses of His Holiness

Shri Sadguru Siddharameshwar Maharaj

Lecture 1 – *Dasbodh* and The Qualities of Aspirants

"One can certainly reach God through devotion to the Self. This is the meaning of the scriptural book *Dasbodh*." (From *Dasbodh* - Chapter 1, Sub-chapter 1)

Dasbodh tells us what one achieves by listening to and studying spiritual discourse, as well as how to practice devotion. It has been explained there how man becomes God after having developed detachment from the gross body, the mind, and the ego through spiritual knowledge. To be one with God is called single-pointed devotion, devotion through oneness, and non-differentiation.

The following topics have been explained there: Pure Knowledge, the Self, the Master's teachings, the means to achieve liberation through oneness after understanding, the answer to "Who am I?," and the means to achieve godliness after having understood one's "Self Nature."

The answers to common queries such as; Who is God?, Who is a devotee?, When does the Self become an individual (jiva) and, When does it become God (Shiva)?, are also found there. The way to realize Absolute Reality (Parabrahman), how people of different sects and opinions in fact all worship the same one God (although through various ways), and the method of worshipping Absolute Reality. All of these topics have been authoritatively discussed there.

Dasbodh also discusses its target readers, the people for whom the spiritual exposition is intended, its contents, the indication of true wisdom what the Primal Illusion (Moolamaya) is and how we are separate from it, and the nature of the five elements. All of this has been explained. Finally, *Dasbodh* also explains who the actual doer is.

Dasbodh dispels all doubts and resolves all problems related to this worldly life and spiritual life. The main topics of other related scriptures have been also carefully considered. One who understands *Dasbodh* certainly reaches Absolute Reality, also known as Thoughtless Reality, or Parabrahman. This is my experience. Additionally, through an exposition of Upanishadic and Vedic thought, it describes the means to become God. *Dasbodh* emphasizes that the objective of all the schools of learning and of all the holy scriptures is to gain Self-Knowledge.

To properly study *Dasbodh* aspirants should have the following qualities:

1. Auspicious aspiration - For one's own well-being, one should first have a strong desire for liberation. This is the primary requisite required for true spiritual knowledge.

2. Thoughtfulness and discrimination (Vichara and Viveka) - Motivated by the auspicious aspiration, one must think about Self-Knowledge. For this one must ceaselessly discriminate between the Self and non-self. The desire for liberation is itself the precursor of right thinking or discrimination.

3. Practice - Constant practice of behavior that is guided by thoughtfulness and discrimination.

4. Detachment - The absence of any attachment. This means not to get involved with anything objective, and to abide in one's own Self.

One who has the strong desire for his own well-being acquires Self-Knowledge sooner or later. Attaining what is "best" means to avoid birth and death. To walk with one's feet means to follow what the Master (Guru) has prescribed, while to walk with one's head means to argue or speculate. When you have the above qualities, the Guru leaves you on the sixth rung of the ladder (in Indian philosophy there are seven stages to Absolute Reality. If all of the above requirements are met, the Guru takes the disciple to the next to the last stage. After this, he imparts the knowledge of Absolute Reality which must be experienced by the seeker for oneself.) You have been able to eat all kinds of fruits from all kinds of trees, but you cannot eat the fruit of this tree, which is only found in the form of the human being. Very rare is the one who tastes this fruit. This fruit is called the "Nectar of Knowledge," or the fruit of liberation. Man alone has the ability to discriminate between the Real and unreal, and if he earnestly tries to understand his true nature, he realizes that he is God.

To attain this knowledge is to fulfill one's duty. The human body is a wish-fulfilling tree. If you ask for Knowledge (Jnana), it gives Knowledge, if you ask for liberation, it gives liberation, which means living as God even while in human form

Lecture 2 – Visible Appearances are Untrue

"The listeners had asked previously, "If the universe (all that is visible) is untrue then how can it be seen?" The answer is given now. Please listen carefully." (*Dasbodh* - Chapter 6, Sub-chapter 8)

All appearance is Illusion (Maya) and the witness is Brahman. The seen, the appearance, is false and the seer is Brahman. There is a declaration in the Vedas that there are only two entities, which are 1.) that which is seen, and 2.) the one who sees it. Vedanta declares this repeatedly.

There is nothing apart from the seer and the seen in this world. The One who resides in the hearts of all is Brahman, and He is "Real." One who takes refuge in the seen perishes, and one who takes refuge in Brahman attains That status. He becomes Brahman. Whoever worships, will attain the object of worship. If you concentrate your attention on the seen (objective world), you will be destroyed along with the seen. However, the question remains, if the seen is untrue, why is it visible at all?

The seen is false *because* it is visible. Whatever is seen is the magic created by the eye. Hence, it is untrue. In the mirror, a face is seen. This implies that two faces seem to exist, but does it mean that there are two of "you"? The fact is that you are only one, but two of you seem to exist nevertheless."

A painter draws pictures with paint and says, "This is a mountain, this is Lord Vishnu, this is Goddess Laxmi." Do you accept it as real? You are the creator. What is actually wood you accept as a chair. This is all the miracle of the eye.

One who worships the Self will become the Self. This mortal world is made of earth. It will eventually all be reduced to dust. The human body comes from a womb and goes to the grave. One should eat the kernel of a coconut and throw away the shell. One who eats the shell only succeeds in knocking out his teeth.

Lecture 3 – All is Brahman

"When objective knowledge comes to an end, the seer does not survive as a seer. At that moment, the pride of "I" (ego) melts away." (*Dasbodh*, Chapter 6, Sub-chapter 10)

The seer remains only as long as the objects that are seen are considered to be real. The ego is conceptual, and so is the seer. If you call this city as "Bombay," then it appears as Bombay. If you call it "earth," it will appear as earth. It all depends upon the seer's concept. If you call a thing "a chair," it is perceived as a chair, and if you call it wood, it is perceived as wood. If you say that "all is Brahman," then everything is perceived as Brahman. If you call it the world, it is perceived as the world. Perception of objects depends on the concept of the seer. Brahman is beyond concept. It cannot be captured by any concept.

There is a woman who one man calls wife, another calls sister, and a third calls daughter, while she is actually nothing but an animated lump of flesh and bones. Whatever you say happens. All is conceptual and depends upon the concept of the seer. The world and the being are conceptual. The "seer" who says that manifestation (the world) is true is the ego. This ego has to be eradicated. If the ego vanishes, only Brahman remains. King Dhrutarashtra of the Mahabharata was blind. He gave birth to a hundred Kauravas and took pride in them. One who conceives of the body as being oneself is the blind Dhrutarashtra. He is also the one who is called Ravanna in the Ramayana. All objects are demons and because you give them that status, you are their king, Ravanna. Ravanna is not the rightful king. He is not the Lord. Because you consider objects to be true, you become Ravanna. Rid yourself of this Ravanna.

The "I" does not exist. Getting rid of the sense of "I" can be called a "wishful death." In the Ramayana, it is said that Ravanna was a great devotee of Lord Shiva, and upon the request of Ravanna, Shiva gave him the boon of "wishful death." This Ravanna rules over the fourteen regencies (sometimes referred to as fourteen senses; five of knowledge, five of action, and the mind, the intellect, the thoughts, and the ego). When gods start to rule the earth, demons go to the nether world and when demons rule the earth, gods go away to perform penance. If objects are taken as true, it means that demons are ruling and God is absent. There is no trace of Him. However, when God becomes victorious (when the conviction that all objects are false becomes firm), the demon "I" also disappears. When the ego is destroyed, everything is seen as only Brahman. Spiritual practice means seeing that the "I," and all objects seen, are untrue. For the realized person, all is Brahman. Food, the wooden plank on which he sits while taking meals, wife, and water are all manifestations of Brahman. All are Brahman. Study and practice this, and then God will rule.

Brahman is without attributes. It is not music, it is not color, such as yellow, or black, etc. The ghee that is liquid and the ghee that is solid is the same, just as water is the same as ice. When a seed (form of earth) meets earth, there is a rise of consciousness. If matter is increasingly divided in to infinitesimally smaller parts, ultimately it is seen to be only Pure Energy (Chaitanya), or Consciousness. All that you see and perceive is nothing but Brahman. The "seen" is only qualified Consciousness, just as bracelets are made only of gold.

You must stop insisting that only good should happen to the body. You conceive that you have become the gross body because only this one body that you are holding is the main object of your concepts. Servants and attendants should be considered as God. There is nothing other than Brahman. With or without attributes, all is God. Because we categorize objects, there is ego (jiva). You perceive wife, daughter, horse or dog as separate, but they are all nothing but God. One need not change the form of the objects, only the attitude of the seer must change. Brahman is the same even when it is in a state with attributes. You should see Brahman in whatever state that He exists. Even the atoms and molecules of a chair are all only God. Once this attitude is adopted, then one is Brahman oneself. Then, even though the body may be sleeping, awake, or eating, you have never taken a meal. When all is Brahman what is eating and sleeping? The one who is without attributes and the one who speaks (with attributes) are both God. Whether a king sits on a throne or goes hunting, he is always the king. One is a devotee when he gives various names to objects and sees them as separate from himself. One is a sadhu (saint) or Paramatman, when one looks upon all creation as Brahman. To forget Brahman and eat food is to just turn it into feces. Silkworms are better off than those who forget Brahman, as the silk from their cocoons is used by priests while worshipping God.

Those who desire hell can digest hell. Gods and demons are right here. Gods and demons together churned the ocean of the world and got nectar and wine. Lord Vishnu gave nectar to the gods and wine to the demons. Saying that "Vishnu did this," means that the Inner-Consciousness did this. Nectar and wine are right here. It is in your own hands to drink the nectar and become immortal. One who "wakes up" will achieve Reality. Say that "All are God. May all be happy." If you practice this and take it to heart, then all is Brahman. One has to water a plant until it develops roots. Then it grows by itself. You should persist in your practice until you realize Brahman.

Lecture 4 – Uproot the Sense of "I"

"When objective knowledge ends, the seer does not survive as a seer. At that time the pride of "I" disappears." (*Dasbodh* - Chapter 6, Sub-chapter 10)

Brahman is one and only one, without any duality. Brahman is only one. Besides Brahman, nothing else exists. Why then does it appear as a universe? There is only gold in various ornaments, nothing else. It is only later that they are named as bracelets, bangles, necklaces etc. They are all different, but their substance is only gold and nothing else. What is one thing appears to be something else. Even if many different shapes are given to gold by bending and twisting it, it is still nothing but gold. The name and the form are nothing, and are untrue. Why is one boy named Hiralal (diamond)? Only to be able to identify him. He does not excrete diamonds. The world of name and form is untrue. Consciousness alone is true.

If it is gold, the color and the appearance are the same. Even if a camel is made of gold, it is only gold. Even if an image of Lord Vishnu is made out from it, it is still only gold. In all of those things only the gold exists. Existence is all-pervading, even in inanimate objects such as chairs. In the chair what is really there is wood. Similarly, in this world everything else other than Brahman is conceptual. There is nothing else. One should see without categorizing, then the "seer" is no more. The "I" must be uprooted. This is the purpose of the entire teaching of Vedanta. The "I" is like Rahu and Ketu, the two demons who swallow the sun. (In India when a solar eclipse occurs people say that the sun is swallowed by the demons Rahu and Ketu). Fire never makes a distinction and says that it is from the house of an untouchable. Even though you are effulgent like the sun, the demon "I" has come to obstruct you. The Self is forever shining but it is swallowed by the sense of "I."

When the ego disappears, that is the sign of the "ultimate experience." Ego is not the Reality, but appears as such. Everything is Consciousness. It is not necessary to say, "I am Brahman." Birth and death belong only to this "I." The five elements and Consciousness remain as they are, but the subtle body which calls itself "I," and which is full of desire, eventually succumbs to death. When someone tells us, "Wamanrao has passed away," it only means that the name is dead. He came therefore he died. Eradicate from your mind that you are some particular "I." That is the sign of Knowledge (Jnana). He who says, "I am the one who experiences," is swallowed by the demon of "I" (remains in the Illusion).

It is the hand that lifts, yet one says, "I lift." The eyes see, but one says, "I see." The nose smells, but one says, "I smell." All this is the power of the Self and one says, "I did it." That power belongs to God. Who is this ego that is asserting "I, I"? He had no place in the palace, but once admitted inside, he overruled the king and affirmed his own existence. However, when with the aid of scriptures he conducted a search, his existence was disproved. Then the king once again affirmed "I am Brahman." There is one quality about this condition, that is Bliss. If there are two, then there is pain. Where there is only One, there is bliss.

Lecture 5 – Mental Renunciation

"When objective knowledge ends, the seer does not survive as a seer. At that time the pride of "I" disappears." (*Dasbodh* - Chapter 6, Sub-chapter 10)

An aspirant inevitably faces the question, "Should we continue our worldly affairs or should we renounce the world altogether?" There is no sense in wearing a Tulsi (a holy plant) garland around the neck and at the same time having a rush of anger in the heart. What is the use of the saffron robes of a renunciate if one is not attentive to one's "Inner-Self"? Moreover, the trees, the tigers, and the beasts and birds do not run a household, so does this mean that they have become saints? One should be alert within oneself. Objective knowledge should be proven to be untrue. All of the affairs we conduct should be proven to be untrue and "That" which has been taken until now to be untrue should be proven True. Life is useless if one is not detached. It is one's attitude that must be changed. To remain in the world with the clear understanding that "All of this is false," is an act of great courage. In this way, remain detached mentally.

Once one learns how not to get involved, or how to renounce, then one gets the "ultimate experience." No matter what circumstances the body is in, you should be detached. Live as you like, but internally be unattached. Objects are untrue. You must turn your mind's attention away from them and cultivate the attitude that the Self (Atman) is Brahman. Even if we consider the five elements as benign, still we know that they are dangerous. Even when one thinks that it is only the Self that can bring happiness, the great Illusion (Maya) tempts him and drags him back to the former condition.

Only when one becomes steady in Brahman with all three, namely, the body, speech, and mind, can one achieve this Knowledge. One can do anything, such as adorn the body with gold or wear expensive garments, but the Guru's grace comes only to the one who considers all this to be untrue. If one does not renounce the objects of the world, one does one thing, but the result is quite different. One may wear gold, silver, a wire of brass, or very expensive garments, but there is no hope of getting joy from this life. A human being can never get peace. One who only speaks of the Truth behaves accordingly with body, speech and mind. If one thinks "I am the body," he will only speak of the body. As is the flower, so is it's fragrance.

Even when you are in the world, you should be as if you are not there. For Brahman, all are equal, whether it is a "worldly life," or a life in the forest. When you are not, how can the mundane existence be there? Live as you please, but you must change your attitude. Then all is over. Chokamela, was a true devotee, and a butcher, who used to live with a bone in his hand. You may eat good purified food, but what are you going to do about your mental modifications? Once it is realized that everything, including the "I" is false, only your true Self (Brahman) remains. There is nothing other than Brahman, so only your attitude has to change. This is the true sign of renunciation. In sleep when there is no world, a king and a pauper are equal.

When you leave the world at night and go to sleep, you feel so happy! There you do not need a world, a house, a job or a wife. When He is alone, He is only Bliss. Because you think that you have to do a lot of things, you become miserable. As we (realized ones) have to do nothing, what is there to worry about? That is why we are always happy. One who has a duty to perform, whether he is a king or a god, he is a laborer.

Saints must show compassion. One who is desireless is the God of all gods. At least once, try to be desireless mentally. This can happen only when you feel that the world is untrue. Take your mind off the world and fix it on the Self. Objects are untrue and Brahman is the Truth. When you make this attitude your own, you are through. Then, live as you will. One who cannot dance finds the ground uneven, but one who wants Self-Knowledge will find how to get it.

Prahlad (a devotee of Vishnu) was ordered by his father not to repeat the name of God. Prahlad told his father, "You may be the owner of my body, but you have no control over my mind." Even if you are very busy, identify your mind with Brahman. The intellect has to be transformed. Mentally say, "I am Ram (Brahman)." Then whatever you do becomes Brahman. Discard the idea "I am so-and-so," and pervade the entire universe.

Lecture 6 – Turn the Mind Away From Objects

"When objective knowledge ends, the seer does not survive as a seer. At that time the pride of "I" disappears." (*Dasbodh* - Chapter 6, Sub-chapter 10)

Your mind is engrossed in the objects created by Illusion (Maya). This includes even the body. As long as your mind is involved in Maya you have the concepts of "you" and "I." The whole struggle in Illusion is because you want the body only to get what the mind considers to be "good." Because you devote your mind to this struggle, the world exists. Because there are students, there are teachers. If the students go away, for whom is the teacher? Because there is objective knowledge, "you" exist. How can the Lord pervade the body in which "you" (the ego) have taken residence? How can one sheath contain two swords?

How can God occupy that place where the "I" is? To those who aspire to attain Brahman, can worthless objects be useful? So, you must understand that all this is untrue. Those who want Brahmanhood should get a dose of Lord Vitthal (should verify one's True Self). On one side there is the Self, and on the other side is an army, the world, and the domains of fourteen kingdoms, which includes the knowledge of spiritual powers (siddhis).

In the Mahabharata, Duryodhana (the eldest of the Kauravas) chose the armies. There are two alternate "realities," Illusion and Brahman. You should not even think of Illusion as being good or bad. This is what is called detachment. When everything from an atom up to Lord Brahma, and all wealth and prosperity is false, how can it be good or bad? When the mental inclination turns away from worldly desires, it naturally turns towards the Self. How can one who only thinks of objects all the time get the "Knowledge of Brahman"? When the objective knowledge ends, the seer does not survive as a seer. At night, in deep-sleep, objective knowledge fades away, the ego disappears, and only the quiescent Self remains. Whether one is a king or a beggar, all are equally happy during sleep. One who survives as "I" has all the troubles (of thinking about) of various gods, penance, money, heaven, and hell. This means that all of these miseries affect the mind. When the mind is erased, only the Absolute Reality remains.

Do not talk about objects of the world. Do not even talk of an atom or Brahman. Even if the mind enjoys worldly pleasures for millions of years, it will never be satiated. However, since the mind is "created" by saying something (if a concept arises), when you stop saying it, the mind vanishes. Ego is made up of only the mind, intellect, and the sense of "I" and "you." All talk except about ones own Self, is false.

The secret of the *Vedas* lies in the tenet that when objective knowledge ends, the seer does not survive as seer. What is the use of the great achievements of those who go to the grave in ignorance, just as they came from the womb, wasting their life in vain? Many aspirants who come here talk of nothing other than the objective world. What is important is that the "I" should be destroyed. The jiva enjoys eating the fruit of the tree of life in the form of worldly existence, but Shiva, the bird that is sitting at the top of the tree, does not care for it, even if he is sitting on the fruit. When the fruit is renounced, he becomes Narayana, the Reality, and when he looks towards objects he becomes a man. In order to transform an ordinary man into a realized man (Jnani), it is not necessary to physically renounce the world. Only a change of mental attitude is necessary.

One should have the attitude, "Let the objects come and go, it is all the same to me." Day and night the conviction "I am Brahman" should be sustained. Then there is no more concern about the body. One who censures oneself, does not censure another. One who does not get puffed up with pride by prosperity, does not become miserable by poverty. If a man has this attitude, he becomes God. Maya is like an untouchable woman. Unless you renounce her, whatever you have has no value. All those who ask (for material satisfaction) are of the "mang" caste (beggars). The saint asked for only one gift. "Give me just one thing, that I may never forget you." One should censure Maya and praise Brahman. To attain the "Absolute Truth" is very easy. The interested one, instead of looking at "here" (the world), should turn to "there" (the Self). You worship Ganapati and give him sweets, but you miss what is shown by one of his hands, the blessing that all is One.

In the epic Mahabharata, there is a story of the demon Jarasandha who had a boon that even if his body was cut in two, the halves would join again and he would live. He owed allegiance to the Kauravas, so the Pandavas could not kill him. When Bhima (one of the Pandavas) cut him in two in a mace duel, Lord Krishna made a gesture to Bhima to throw the body's left side to the right and the right side to the left. Thus thrown, he could not live again. In the same way, to attain the Absolute Truth, one should change the focus of one's thoughts, from Illusion to Reality. You have forgotten Paramartha, the Absolute Truth. You should turn your mind towards it. Forget Illusion. One has only to understand that the world is untrue. It should be seen as a kingdom in a dream world. Even if you get the status of Indra, the lord of heaven and prosperity, it is still false.

These breads (objects) are all baked in Illusion. They are to be prepared, baked, eaten and excreted. The excretion is then used as fertilizer to grow crop to make more bread. It should be indelibly impressed upon the mind that this world is untrue and that Brahman is the Truth. Once the knowledge of objects is put out of your mind, you are naturally the self-evident Brahman. Then peace, rest, and liberation stand before you with folded hands. When Bali gave everything in charity, God became the doorkeeper. Laxmi walks up to the one who makes Lord Narayana (her spouse) one's own. Those who are after Laxmi (wealth) get neither Laxmi nor Lord Narayana. Concentrating one's attention on objects is what is called the impurity of the mind. To be carefree about objects is purity of mind. When the mind is turned towards the Self, the Absolute Reality is attained.

Lecture 7 – The Dream Within a Dream

"Understand that the worldly Illusion is a dream within a dream. Having come here, you have given thought to what is Eternal and what is ephemeral."(*Dasbodh* - Chapter 6, Sub-chapter 10)

The One who is without birth went to sleep. He has no old age. He is One, who has no death. How is it that a dream was seen during a dream? "He slept and dreamt" means He is deluded. "He slept" means he has become a jiva (individual) and thinks, "I am the body. I am so-and-so." The state of Brahman was covered with ignorance and in that delusion there is again more delusion, which is this mundane existence. It is a dream within a dream. The worldly Illusion only appears true. He was all-pervasive, and then He became small when he considered the worldly existence as true. In that very dream, he discriminated between Guru and disciple, virtue and sin, and what is true and what is untrue. Other people pass away in this dream. It is a piece of great fortune for one to think of what is Eternal and what is ephemeral during this long dream.

It's said that "Even a dog does not eat a thing that belongs to a sinner." Renunciation of wealth, the feeling of detachment, and respect for a saint is the result of former merit and good fortune. Only such a one starts thinking of the saint. It is extraordinary to have an aspiration for realization in the dream within a dream. It is like being alert and fully in control of one's senses despite taking a shot of brandy, or despite possessing enormous wealth that ordinarily brings demonic pride. This is his good fortune. Such a person is in a dream within a dream. But on account of his virtuous intellect he went to a Guru and discriminated between the Eternal and the ephemeral. He got the experience that everything else is false and "I am Brahman." This means that he has awakened from one dream. Then in this dream he deliberated again he came to the further conclusion that even saying "I am Brahman" is false. The whole world and all words are only Illusion. As a result he became tranquil by staying in his own blissful state. Truth was revealed. He fully realized "I am Brahman." This condition means that one is fully awake. Not only the delusion, but also the feeling "I have experienced" vanished. For if one says that he has experienced the Self, it implies that he has taken himself to be different from the Self. The real test is when one has no sense of oneself. If the mango says, "I found myself sweet," then it is not a mango. If you say "I have experienced," that means your "I," the ego, is still there. The idea "I got an experience" is a delusion. The "I" in "I have become knowledgeable" or "I have become Brahman" is ego. The former "I" should disappear. Whatever was before, naturally is Brahman. The thorn of "I" has to be extracted. Then you are through. When you become all-pervading, you become Brahman. The ego "I am Brahman" comes at first, but it also disappears afterwards. It is One only, and there is nothing else other than That. To go beyond nothing is to be in Thoughtless Reality, Parabrahman.

Lecture 8 – The Five Sheaths and the Eight Bodies

"Brahman is without attributes and without form. Brahman is unattached, and without change. It has no limits, that is what the sages say." (*Dasbodh* - Chapter 7, Sub-chapter 2)

How is Brahman? It has no shape. It is the natural state that remains when all of the four bodies, the physical, the subtle, the causal (ignorance), and the great-causal, (Knowledge, or "I am") are set aside. One who knows his true "Being" is called "Ishwara," or God. Whatever remains prior to Being, or Knowledge, is Reality. After transcending these four bodies whatever remains is formless, immutable, in its own natural state and steady. It never goes anywhere nor does it come from anywhere. This is the Absolute Reality, Parabrahman, while the Inner-Self (Antaratman) is the "I," the most subtle form of ego.

The seer, the witness, the one who sees, and the one who sleeps is "Ishwara," God. He is a concept conceived through intelligence. When he sleeps, he is quiet. The One who experiences the state of wakefulness does not disappear when experiencing the state of unconsciousness or sleep. Why can't we express joy in sleep? Because the mind and the intellect are in abeyance. Only when one wakes up, can one express the experience.

A woman's nose-ring fell into the water. She asked a man to find it and inform her as soon as it was found. The man found the ring deep below the surface of the water but obviously could not inform her at the moment he spotted the ring, as he was completely under water. As water and fire are antagonistic, the power of the deity of fire (which enables speech) was absent when he was submerged. Thus he could inform the lady that the nose-ring was found only after he came out of the water. Similarly, one cannot express anything in deep-sleep because the instruments that are required for expression are unavailable. The mind is not involved during sleep, hence it cannot say anything. A man climbed up some stairs. If his mind was not focused on the number of stairs he climbed, then he would not be able to tell the exact number. But the Self knows that he has climbed the stairs.

The Self exists during sleep, during wakefulness, and during samadhi (conscious absorption in the Self). Who experiences sleep and samadhi? The Self alone. If the Self were not there, who would be there to experience sleep? So, Self is Consciousness, the essence of Awareness, and prior to that is Parabrahman. The Inner-Self (Antaratman) is the "I." He is God, and Consciousness is his eternal nature. He resides in the hearts of all beasts, birds, deities, demons, Ram, Krishna, etc. If He is not there, the living being becomes dead like a log of wood. When He disappears, the ears, eyes, nose etc. are all useless. When He disappears, all objects become inanimate. All grandeur is because of this Inner-Self. If He vanishes, then all perishes. It is due to Him that there is worldly activity as well as spiritual understanding. All this is due to His Existence.

During the time that the Inner-Self exists, (in association with the body) Gods, demons, customs, etc. also exist. But if He leaves, people will not touch the dead body. It is the Inner-Self that imbues the body with godliness. One who calls this body as God is none other than this Self. The one who writes the *Vedas* is also the Inner-Self. As long as this Inner-Self retains interest in worldly ideas, he is the jiva (the individual). If he starts talking about Knowledge, he is Shiva. When jiva and Shiva both disappear, what remains is Parabrahman. A man who engages in manual labor is a laborer. If he works as an officer, he is an officer, if he works as a judge, he is a judge. But when he retires from everything he is Parabrahman. There is a void that is emptiness, or ignorance, and beyond that is the fourth body which is of the nature of God. When a man worships a multitude of gods and goddesses like Keshava (a form of Vishnu), that worship goes only straight to the Inner-Self, because this Keshava (Ke means Knowledge and shava means corpse) is in the form of Knowledge in the body (which is but a corpse without the Knowledge). After worship, the offerings to that god are consumed only by the worshippers. If this Lord, the Inner-Self, makes that god (an idol of God) worthy of belief, he appears real for a lifetime. Each being, knowingly or unknowingly, worships the Inner-Self alone. But he does so without understanding. Therefore he is a jiva, or ignorant being. If he worships with the full understanding that he is God, he becomes Shiva, and is one with Knowledge (Jnana).

All gross bodies are actually living temples. Due to ignorance, children enjoy themselves by building a make-believe house out of stones. They take a small rock which serves as a utensil for drinking water, another stone may serve as a bowl, and then another stone is put up as God. In the same way ignorant people worship God by creating idols. The real God has Consciousness, or Awareness. The idol has no Consciousness. Only a fool worships an idol. Fool means an ignorant person. Those who have no "Knowledge of Self" (Atmajnana) have to worship an idol. But if they were to recognize just who those idols represent, how wonderful it would be! The one who recognizes this is the "Knowledgeable One," a Jnani. The ignorant man creates a make-believe God and worships him, the Jnani recognizes the "God of Gods" (that is his own Self) and then offers his worship. Shankaracharya called the Inner-Self, that is the fourth body, the "Original Illusion." God may have infinite number of names, yet Truth is only One. For example, if a child calls his own father "uncle," does it mean that the man loses his fatherhood?

Through the medium of this God (the Self), one will realize the natural state of the Supreme God, Parameshwara. If the abidance in this God becomes steady, one will realize Parabrahman. This God (Consciousness) is in the form of the power of knowing, will-power, and the power of matter. This means that he is constantly moving. If this mundane existence is ignored, then one will remain in this "natural state." The statement that Lord Vishnu (Consciousness) incarnated ten times implies that he began playing through all of the ten senses. To do something means to incarnate. When he becomes God, he realizes his ignorance. God is unsteady while Parabrahman is steady. To know the nature of both the steady and the unsteady is Knowledge. The followers of Vedanta get completely confused when they try to think about this subject.

The Inner-Self is the base of the entire universe, yet the true origin of everything is the original impulse of "Pure Awareness," that has no beginning or end. On one side the world is created, and on the other everything vanishes. If one's true nature is known, the Inner-Self disappears. The steady always exists and the unsteady perishes. The steady is immutable while the unsteady is forever changing. The Self, which is unsteady, has passions, changes, desire, anger, greed, pride, etc.

If someone calls him (the Inner-Self) good, he swells with pride, and if another calls him bad, he becomes sad. This indicates that the Inner-Self is subject to change. One who considers the changeless and the changing as the same, is but a beggar. Such a person is caught in the realm of the five elements.

The essence of the *Vedas* is "You Are That." The Supreme Self (Paramatman) is beyond the four bodies. There are various methods for explaining the *Vedas*. Brahman and Parabrahman are proved after debating and battling a billion times. "Yoga" means union.
Paramatman is covered by the five sheaths, or koshas.

1. The sheath of food: The physical covering, which is like a coat. It is worn on the outside to protect the Self. This is the body consisting of blood, flesh, bones, hair etc. produced out of food.
2. The sheath of vital airs: The Self is covered with five vital airs, or pranas.
3. The sheath of the mind: This is the cover of mind, the accumulated concepts.
4. The sheath of the intellect: This is the cover of intellect which discriminates based on concepts such as good and bad, or that one is of a certain caste (Brahmana, Kshatriya, etc.).
5. The sheath of bliss: This is the cover of rest, or deep-sleep, when one forgets oneself. One is happy when one has forgotten everything that produces unhappiness.

If one forgets everything, then there is bliss. One is happy because one has forgotten all sorrows. Where does the jiva (ego) find happiness? The answer is, in forgetfulness. Unknowingly, he enjoys happiness in sleep. Narada (a saint in Indian mythology) is our mind. He goes around in all of the three worlds namely the gross, the subtle, and the causal worlds. This mind sings the praises of the Lord, but also enters into arguments and quarrels. He always has a begging bowl under his arm. The begging bowl is his stomach. Whether one goes to the office or to a place where devotional songs are being sung, it is sure that "Mr. Mind" will take the begging bowl along with him.

The Self is beyond all states. Recognize the five sheaths explained above. It is said that three hundred and thirty-million deities reside in the body. All of those are for the sake of the body. Twenty five elements making up the subtle body, the five sheaths of the Self, and the three attributes (rajas, tamas, and sattva) make up these three hundred and thirty million deities who live in the city of Kashi (the body). Only after transcending the five sheaths, does one reach Vishwanath, the ruling deity of this city. Then the body itself is Kashi (a holy place) for you. Whatever is in the microcosm (jiva) is also in the macrocosm (God). Thus we employ countless ruses to prove that your true nature is Parabrahman. The jiva appears only within the realm of words, therefore whatever is expressed in words can only serve as a pointer to Reality (as words can never truly convey Reality).

What is the nature of God? God also has four bodies. The first, or gross body (Virat) is huge and made up of the five elements. The subtle body is the three hundred and thirty million gods, and Brahma, Vishnu, and Shiva. This subtle body of God, is called HiranyaGarbha (the Golden Womb), and the causal body of God is the Avyakrut (Unmanifest). The great-causal body of God is the Primordial Illusion (Moolamaya). This is Sat-Chit-Ananda (Existence, Consciousness, and Bliss), which is the highest attribute of God.

The jiva likewise has four bodies namely the gross, the subtle, the causal and the great-causal body. The first three can be described. The great-causal body cannot. From the earth comes the gross body. You may say the body is a part of the Virat. The air that is outside and inside the body is one and the same. So how can this air belong to you or me. It belongs to everyone.

Desire and the senses make up the mind. The deity is the Moon. Mind (moon) is treacherous to the Guru (sun). It does not go to Him. The moon is accused of treachery to the Guru, that is, it does not want to get Self-Knowledge from the sun because it will die in the process.

The senses may be termed as Lord Indra. Rain means the desire to drink. To perform a sacrifice means to prepare a good meal and eat it, and then it rains, that is, one has a desire to drink. Then man is nourished, as his senses are appeased, like how the earth grows when it rains. Saint Gautam means the best among the senses (Gau - senses, Uttam - best). Ahilya (his wife) is the body which nurtures the senses. Both have the same expression and also the same goal. Therefore, the jiva and Shiva are one. The jiva is really none other than Brahman. Jiva has four bodies, Shiva has four bodies. The eighth body, or the Primal Illusion is steady. This is his "primordial nature." Parabrahman is that which cannot be expressed in words. The God of the transitory is Ishwara, and that God's devotee is also transitory. Both of them are perishable, and hence false. Therefore, both jiva and Shiva are ignorance. Do not get tempted by them. All of these eight bodies are perishable and false. One who realizes this and discards both jiva and Shiva is the Knowledgeable One, the Jnani.

Lecture 9 – Be Free of "I" and "You"

"The thoughts of liberation and bondage are present only during the state of ignorance. The Original Nature is self-evident. It is neither bound nor liberated." (*Dasbodh* - Chapter 7, Sub-chapter 6)

The thoughts of liberation and bondage are present only during the state of ignorance. Our "True Nature" (Swarupa) is self-evident. It is neither bound nor liberated. The problem of bondage and liberation arises only because man, enveloped in ignorance, takes the body to be himself and assumes "doership" of all his actions. Does Self-realization mean inactivity? If that were the case, when King Janaka ruled over a kingdom even after Self-realization, was everything lost? Shuka (a great saint) and others had also realized the Self. How did they then write philosophical books? Suppose we accept that being a "mukta" or "being free" means remaining motionless. If remaining motionless like a log of wood means being Brahman, then Shuka and Vamadeva and other saints would have been like dead bodies. How then would it have been possible for Shuka to teach the Bhagwat to King Parikshita? It is necessary for the Master to put forward various arguments and provide a clear explanation when he gives sermons. If this is so, then how can any work be done if one is motionless. Because one gives sermons does it mean that he is not realized? How can you say he has not reached Absolute Reality? A motionless person is not automatically Self-realized. The "Knowledge of Absolute Reality" is obtained through the teaching of the Master. If a realized person becomes motionless, then who will impart this Knowledge? The realized ones have taken utmost efforts in order to uplift the world.

In the categories of liberation, there are three categories, namely: (1) jivan Mukta (2) Videha Mukta (3) Nitya Mukta. jivan Mukta refers to those who are fully conscious as to who they are and yet perform their worldly duties. Videha Mukta (Videha means separated from the body) means those that have understood and have identified with Brahman and just remain as they are. They do not care about what they eat or drink. Apart from these two, there are the Nitya Muktas (Nitya means eternal), those who have become the Absolute Reality (Parabrahman).

If someone gets the "experience" all of a sudden he becomes quiet. To be motionless or to be unconscious has to do with the body. It has nothing to do with Brahman. When the consciousness stirs up, he again regains body-consciousness. He understands, "This is all the Self, but I am Brahman," and stays thus. The Self is beyond bondage or liberation. If one continues to remain in body-consciousness, one will never be liberated. Even Lord Brahma and other gods will never become liberated if they remain in the body-consciousness. "He is free for a moment, and gets bound the next moment," such is the state of the one who has not understood Brahman.

Those who talk about bondage and liberation are only talking about Prakriti (what is manifest in Illusion). The Truth, which is of the nature of the Self, is self-evident. Bondage and liberation have no meaning there. One who says he is bound, is a fish in the ocean of this worldly existence, and one who says he is liberated, is a crocodile. One who has bound himself with a stone in the form of the idea that he is liberated, will go to Patala (the netherworld). One who says, "Until now, I have committed a number of sins and actions, and therefore I was bound, but now I am free," goes to the very depths of the ocean of worldly existence. He is in great danger. The ones with real "Knowledge," the Jnanis consider such people fools. Even at the time of committing a sin, he was the Self, but he was not aware of it. What is so great if someone says that he now knows the Self? He is still as ignorant as he always was, because the duality still exists.

Only one who is free of the concepts of "I" and "you" is truly liberated. Rahu and Ketu (the eclipses) mean "I" and "you." If such concepts remain intact, one's true Self is still eclipsed. Those knowing their own nature are the ones who know that they are beyond the body. The rest retain their identification with the body. That which gets into bondage is the body. Where is there any bondage if one knows that he is not the body?

One who has realized the Pure Knowledge of the Truth thinks that being bound or free is all a joke. Where Prakriti (Illusion) falls away, or when names and forms end, there all words become silent. How then can there be anything like liberation? What is the meaning of "liberated"? It is only a manner of speaking. All the bondage is for the one who says that he is the body. One who is a Jnani (Self-realized) is free from the sense of "I." For him, either being bound or liberated is only delusion. Bound and liberated are only concepts. A concept is never true. One who has understood Illusion is free from all fear. The one who says, "I will practice yoga after I become Brahman, then I will do something," is like the one going in search of water in a mirage. Such people are simply going back and forth in a mirage. One who considers the mirage as true, gets bound by it. For the one who is awakened, the dream disappears. In the same way, a Jnani finds that this mirage which is in the form of Illusion, disappears.

As far as one's True Nature is concerned, one's relationship with the body is untrue. Trying to contemplate on the One that is beyond contemplation is not possible. As far as Brahman is concerned, no contemplation is possible. However, one has the habit of seeing and contemplating on something. If one cannot see or think about the Self, then what can one do? If one contemplates on a thing, then that thing can be known. The very nature of the Self is such that even if you want to pull it down to the level of your mind, it is not possible. It is also not possible to discard the nature of Consciousness. It cannot be understood through the senses either. So, what can one do?

Brahman transcends concepts. When one starts meditating, the trinity of seer, seen, and seeing is produced. All objects and the senses are objective to us, but because we are Truth itself, contemplation on ourself is not possible. However, if contemplation is given up, great doubts overpower us. Only if one thinks and deliberates upon what is Eternal and what is transient, and what is the Self and what is not Self, is Truth revealed. We are not any of the things that exist in this world, and we are also not the body. We are not the *Vedas*, the ancient scriptures (*Shastras*), the moon, or the sun. We are none of these. We must sincerely find out who we are.

"You are That." So you must understand who you are. The word "I" comes from within, so you must be somewhere within. Where there is nothing, that is called the causal body. It is also called "ignorance." There is more happiness in the subtle body than in the gross body, and there is of course even more happiness in the causal body. If everything is left off, then only the One who leaves off everything remains. One who leaves off everything is the Witness. This means that only Knowledge (Jnana) remains, just an idol of Absolute Knowledge (Vijnana).

This is "Existence-Knowledge-Bliss" (Sat-Chit-Ananda). Who was the One that experienced or saw during sleep, that there is nothing? The answer is "I." So, "you" had the experience that there was nothing during sleep. Existence-Knowledge-Bliss is the fourth body. He is God. That there is "nothing" during sleep, is known without the help of the mind. Leave off even that "I am," then the modification of the mind which says "I am" also remains at rest. It is not even necessary to see how that modification is. Only if one forgets the great-causal body, does one then have to remember it. It is not possible to forget it, so no contemplation is to be practiced. One should meditate as advised, without any concept. Nothing is to be brought to the mind, and there is nothing to be known there, because at that point there appear two, one the mind, and the other, the thing which is brought to mind. So there at that point duality appears. If one tries to understand without discrimination, then duality ensues. The sense of being, meaning "I am the one remaining," also has to be discarded.

There is really no such thing as non-self, but there is talk of non-self to enable understanding. Unless the "I" is extinguished, heaven can not be seen. To say that Parabrahman is non-dual means we are "That." Therefore, we have to be That in order to know That. This does not require any other means or instrument. If we are to experience some other object, we have to see it. But because we are "That," we are by nature That alone. If we give up consciousness of "all the rest," we are as we are. We have never forgotten our nature. So accordingly, it is not necessary to remember it. Only if it is forgotten, does it have to be remembered. Therefore, our True Nature is beyond remembrance and forgetfulness. What is death? It is just like sleep at night. Whatever comes to your memory upon remembrance, is prone to death, meaning that it is bound to be forgotten.

By virtue of this body and Knowledge, the ocean (of existence) has been churned and this fourteenth jewel, the Vedanta has been extracted. This is the true nectar. Parabrahman is the natural state. It exists right from the beginning without doing or thinking anything. This is self-evident. In that natural state, there is neither happiness nor misery. Happiness and misery are coexistent, like two sides of a coin. As soon as a concept arises, there is duality. Because we are already "That," we become split as soon as we imagine something. When you were playing marbles in childhood, the Knowledge that you had then is the same as you have now. You do not have to remember (or think of) how it is. To forget everything is the only way to remember it. It is excellent if you also forget "I am Brahman." Experience it without experiencing. During sleep we have an experience of ourselves. But if we try to acquire such an experience, it cannot be had with effort. If one tries to see it, it recedes. We have to fall asleep to know sleep. And to not make any effort is to know Him.

If you say that you must do something to get to your existence, it means to try modify the mind in order to bring about your existence. This is ruinous. If mind tries to grasp it, it disappears. You have to leave the "I-ness" after knowing the "I am-ness." Until now, you were told that the origin of knowledge is "I." But now, you must discard this belief. One who uses the method of "I am not, you are not, nothing exists," is indeed fortunate. Nothing is to be done. Listen, reflect on what is being heard, and verify for yourself in your own experience (shRavanna, manana, nididhyasana), and then the True Nature of the Self is exposed. This Knowledge of one's own True Nature has to be continuous, otherwise, the concept of Maya presents itself. "I am Brahman" is also a concept. You are not the one that imagines or conceives. This means that you should not take yourself to be what is conceived. The knower should merge into Absolute Reality, Parabrahman.

This is the basis of the "Knowledge of Brahman." You become the stage. Do not become the scene, or the sets of the scene. This is done without moving away from your Self. Then, do your sadhana (efforts), deliberation, contemplation, worship, etc., or whatever you feel inclined to do. You become the goal and then if you deem it fit, do some sadhana.

Lecture 10 – Erase the Ego

"If one tries to conceive of Reality, it cannot be done, as Reality is by nature beyond any concept or imagination. There is no imagination in Parabrahman." (*Dasbodh* - Chapter 7, Sub-chapter 7)

The Self (Atman) is beyond concept (Nirvikalpa) and hence the Self is where imagination fails. As Self cannot be found by thoughts, one cannot think about it. The Self is not visible and not felt. It has no form and no color. Then how to "know" that which has no quality? If you cultivate a habit, you acquire it. If you form a habit of thinking, "The Self knows all, but none knows the Self," then you attain Truth. One remains ignorant without thoughtfulness, so think. Seek the company of the holy. Live in this world of five elements with awareness. The five elements (space, air, fire, water and earth) are dictating to you. You should slowly separate that elemental world from yourself with

Knowledge. This means that the world should be left aside. When I am not the body, then how can this elemental world be mine? You can have either God or the world.

Before the Mahabharata war, Lord Krishna said to the Kauravas "I am on one side, my army will be on the other. Take whichever you want." The Kauravas took the army, which means that they took the world, and the Pandavas took God on their side. Lord Krishna said, "I am without quality, and without shape, and I shall hold no weapon in my hand." The elemental world should be set aside with the help of Knowledge. The ego, or "Aham," should be allowed to ebb away, yet it does not subside. Those people to whom no good comes, despite listening continuously to the Jnani, are considered as fallen.

If one has understood that the body is of a low caste, yet continues on only with body-consciousness, know that he is but a dead body, a corpse. Consider them as fallen if they have heard words of wisdom, yet feel no devotion. Ego should ebb away, yet it does not vanish. This condition is called the state of the jiva. The notions of "I" and "mine" are the reason that one has become a jiva. These concepts should be removed. Absolute Reality is what it is. The feeling of "I" should vanish, yet it does not leave. "Aham" (the subtlest form of "I") is in the form of a feeling of ignorance. The scriptures have enunciated many methods for effacing the ego. "Aham" is the most crooked of letters in Sanskrit. One who has seen the death of his own ego is very fortunate. "I saw my death with my own eyes, the ritual was indeed without a parallel," says Saint Tukaram.

The effort of the jiva is directed towards increasing the ego, "I am an aspirant, I am a realized person. I am like this, and I am like that." You nourish the one who should be killed by your efforts. If you erase the ego, you are the Reality. I am narrating to you how one nourishes the ego. All the visible manifest world is perishable and is not true. As it is perishable, it is seen. If it were not perishable, there would not have been a seer. Because there is the seer, there is the seen.

Whatever is done in this world is the deed of the mind, intellect, etc. Whatever you see or say, you do so because mind and intellect exist. Therefore, as long as "you" are, the ego is susceptible to praise and abuse. Whatever action is done, is done by the senses. Whatever is done by the senses is done by the ego. You should surrender completely to the Sadguru saying "My brain is not working at all." The more you make use of your intellect, the more it grows. If you act depending upon the

Guru's intellect, your involvement with this world will cease. Then alone are "you" destroyed. Only then does one understand his own death.

"Take refuge in me, renouncing all of your duties and responsibilities," says Lord Krishna. Only thus will your ego leave you. We are all Parabrahman if you take refuge in the Sadguru. For this you have to leave your old ways. The one who wants to realize has to break this ego. If you are saying "I am Brahman," then note that you are calling that "I" as Brahman. So, it cannot be understood through meditation, concentration, incantation or penance. It is only attainable through the company of the realized, with devotion to the Self, singing God's praises (bhajan), and by understanding the knowledge imparted by the Master. This conviction that "I am Brahman," is important, yet Saint Tukaram's devotion made him understand that the Supreme Self exists without attributes, as well as with attributes. "Chant the name of God with fervor. This container (the body) cannot be relied upon, and death comes in the blink of an eye."

Lecture 11 – Know the One True God

"Let the audience remain attentive to this conversation between the Guru and disciple in which Pure Knowledge is made very simple to understand by way of listening." (*Dasbodh* - Chapter 8, Sub-chapter 1)

Even a lifetime will not be enough, if you conduct a search for Pure Knowledge in various scriptures. You will only find that they disagree with each other. Some advocate karma (worldly and religious action), some yoga, some the worship of a deity, and some advocate worship of a whole host of gods. Then, there will be someone who says that Goddess Amba is greater, or Khandoba is greater, etc. This cannot be known unless a wrestling match or some contest is arranged between them. When even philosophical scriptures and mythological books do not agree, it is very difficult to arrive at a conclusion. Doubts only go on increasing as to which god is greater, or which place is holier, such as Kashi, Pandharpur, Dwarka, or Rameshwar (all holy cities). There is no satisfactory answer, so how can one lifetime be sufficient to decide all this?

Saint Tukaram said, "Your whole family will go to hell if you do not visit Pandharpur." If one visits the temple of a particular deity, the other deities will surely get angry. Is there anyone in this world who can visit all the holy places? All holy places are there only to understand the one God. The various cults, vows, opinions, etc., exist only so that people can realize Him. In this world, there are many gods. Actually there is a chaos of gods in our (Indian) culture. Whom can we call the real God? The methods of worship are so many that men have lost count. Whichever deity fulfills a man's wish becomes God for him. He takes it for granted that his is the real God. What sort of devotion is this? Some people worship numerous gods because they are useful for appeasing their hunger, or for daily needs. The wife falls at the feet of her husband because he feeds her. He is the "husband god." These are all false gods. Then along come the "true" gods, Satyanarayan, Lord Ganapati, etc. Even sages are also considered gods, so there is no firm decision as to who the real God is. There were quarrels amongst scriptures (*Shastras*), mythological books (*Puranas*), the *Vedas*, and pundits, yet there is no unanimous decision regarding the real God. Wherever you look, there are different gods in each house.

After consuming a ton of food, he (the realized one) observes the Ekadashi fast. (The realized one may eat as much as he wants and yet for him every day is the Ekadashi fast. This is a pun on the word Ekadashi. "Eka" meaning one and "dasha" meaning state). In the Mahabharata, Lord Krishna says that even if he has 16,000 queens, he is still a celibate. Lord Hanuman is an eternal celibate. In one incarnation, Rama's wife was kidnapped, and in another incarnation, Krishna kidnapped women.(Rama and Krishna are both said to be incarnations of Lord Vishnu). If one does not steal, and behaves like Rama in his life, then Krishna will be angry. Because of a need to call others names (give abuse) a Vaishnava does good when he censures Shiva's devotee. So be it. In short, a household may have just two people, but in the "gods' temple" (a small temple of worship in a traditional Indian house) there are a number of gods such as Ganapati, Shankara, Amba, a bison, a tiger, a dog, etc. All of the gods have to eat from the same plate. This is a chaotic condition.

Thus, many people get engrossed with gods, but only one in a thousand thinks of the real God. Are all of these gods going to help the world function? They are a product of our imagination. Even if one starts thinking about God, God still eludes him. Generally speaking, every person has a concept that "God cannot be known," and this idea creates pride in him. Some people wonder at the need for the methods of yoga, or any such efforts. Therefore, a problem arises as to how God can be attained.

This is why it is necessary to first know what or who God is. Static and dynamic activities continue incessantly in this world. There must be someone who is the doer. Someone moves the feet, moves the eyelids, and works day and night. He works, he walks, and he sits, so why should there be any objection in calling him God? It is God who says "I am born, I am dead." The one to whom the sun owes its brilliance, is God. If the sun is shown to a chair, will that chair see the radiance of the sun, or give radiance to the sun? Will a dead body bring luster to the sun? No. So, if God is absent, who will talk of the sweetness or bitterness of food. Only if He is present is there joy or sorrow. Misery, heaven and hell are all due to His presence. He is the Self, He is Lord Brahma, the creator. All glory is due to His presence. Even the word God exists because of Him. Because He exists, the wife embraces the husband. If He leaves the body, no one wants a corpse, even if a request is made to keep it. When He leaves, people are afraid to see the face of the corpse. If a dead person is seen in a dream, people call an exorcist. Because this body is perishable (nashwar in Marathi), it is non-God (A play on the word Na-Ishwara; Na means no and Ishwara is God).

Where the sun cannot reach, God reaches. This body is perishable, but the one who resides in the body is God. There is no consciousness of the world when the mind rests at night. Even if the wife is close by, there is no thought of her. God (as the worshipper) bathes God and offers Him food, and then eats it himself. Even if God (the worshipper) says to Him, "I offer you clothes," it will suffice. But this God (worshipper) must have real clothes, oil, soap, etc. This God (worshipper) needs to shave. Is there anyone who shaves Him? What can the God who is perishable give the worshipper? If this God (worshipper) is ill, He will not get food to eat. The omnipotent is God. If one goes to see God, he has no limbs, no hands, no feet, no eyes. If there is a pain in the stomach, who experiences it? He is God not because he has no limbs, he is God because he knows that there is a pain in the body.

He has no limbs, no mouth, no stomach, he is not a hunchback, he is not the Void. He has no form. His true nature is known only to those who know. Brahman is not Lord Brahma, nor any other gods. The intellect is Lord Brahma, The "inner-mind" (Antahkarana) is the inner consciousness that is Vishnu. And ignorance is Shiva. When we say that the mind and intellect cannot know him, it means we cannot know him through mind or intellect.

Lecture 12 – The Search for God

"Let the audience remain attentive to this conversation between the Guru and disciple in which Pure Knowledge is made very simple to understand by way of listening." (*Dasbodh* - Chapter 8, Sub-chapter 1)

An entire lifetime will not suffice for a search for God in the scriptures. Whatever the sages and saints have expounded I shall tell you now in brief. Please listen attentively. If you want to investigate about who is the greatest God, you will have to meet that God. It is not possible to come to a decision only on the strength of your opinion. It is also not possible to come to a decision after reading all of the scriptures. By trying to make a determination this way, only doubts arise as to which holy place is the holiest. In the eulogy of the deity Jagannath, it is said that if one does not go to get a glimpse of Jagannath, one's life is an utter waste. What to do in such a situation? Is there a single human being who has visited all the holy places in the world?

All the various holy places, penances, charities, etc., are for the sake of only knowing the one God. These are all strenuous efforts to know God. There are many "isms" and various opinions about this God. Who is this God and how to find him? There are many methods of worship prevalent in this world. A man keeps his mind steady on the method he likes. There are numerous gods, and devotees have stuck to their god in accordance with their own will. When one takes into consideration all of this, one cannot decide who the "real" God is.

Lord Krishna has said in chapter 10 of the Bhagavadgita, that those who do not deliberate on this (situation) are but beasts. Scriptures and learned men have not come to a decision as to who the real God is. There are contradictory statements in all of the various traditions, and whichever tradition is acceptable to people, they hold on to that with pride. People get involved with many gods because of this sort of situation. According to them, the greatness of God lies in the fact that God cannot be found. There are many who have resolved that they will never find God, and hence for them, God has remained aloof. Then for what purpose are all one's efforts, yoga and sacrifices?

If one can find God, then the problem arises as to what one should do in order to find him. But before a question like this arises, one should at least know whom to call God. In everyday life one must first identify an object and then ask for details about it. The same is also true in the case of God. We must ask how to know Him. I will now tell you whom we should call God. God is not the idol in the temple, but the one who manages the affairs of the whole world. The One who sustains the activity of the whole world, the One who is the "doer" of all, and who is omnipotent is named as God. He performs all actions, like moving the eyelids, seeing through the eyes, etc. The "moving" is that through which He moves, and the "inanimate" is that in which He lies dormant. The Moon owes its coolness, and the Sun its radiance only to Him. It is only Him who enjoys all grandeur.

This body is perishable, so that means that it is non-God, even though He resides in the body. Only as long as God is in the body, is there glory. When He sleeps, it means that He rests, and the whole world disappears. When consciousness stirs, the Wind (Vayu) is produced. When Wind undergoes friction, light and fire are formed. All of these elements originate in Him, and it is only later on that they get various names such as the Sun, air, etc. This means that it is we who have given nature its various names. In fact, there is no east, no west, and no above nor below. These are all names (concepts) which we have conceived for our convenience. He is God who has created the gross, the subtle and the causal.

It is said that a tree on which Brahma was seated came out of Lord Vishnu's navel, and afterwards Vishnu started walking. This symbolizes that the "inner-mind" (antahkarana), or consciousness, that is the Self sprouted, and afterwards Brahma (the intellect) was born. Even after doing all of this, He is without limbs or parts. This means that He is doing everything even though He has no limbs. For example, in the dream, you can go on walking for hundreds of miles. Do you walk in the dream with the feet you have in the waking state? Even Brahma and the other gods do not know this God. This means that neither consciousness, nor intellect, nor ignorance know this one God. It also means that they can never know Him. However, the saints know how He works. Thus, by taking refuge in saints, one can know Him.

There is the vital Life-Energy of Consciousness (Chaitanya), and when it flows wind is created. Wind or vayu is Consciousness. All the elements are born from the form of Existence, Consciousness, and Bliss. The friction energy of wind has become the Sun (fire) and the coolness of vayu has become water. But all is Consciousness. This earth has come into being with the help of fire and water, and it is from the earth that all beings are born.

People build a temple, and in that temple they install an idol representing God, and they believe that the idol has some power. Therefore, they bow down to that god. Actually, God resides in the temple which is in the form of the body. That Life-Energy of Consciousness which exists in the body is God. In the Bhagavadgita, Krishna says to Arjuna, "I live in every being's heart. That which every being calls 'I,' that 'I Am,' is Me. Give up all other duties and take refuge in Me who resides in the hearts of all. I am not this gross body." He also tells Arjuna, "If you go to those who know Me, or those who are taken to be of My Nature, you will meet Me. Chaitanya is God. For one who worships it, God is easily found."

This earth is God's creation. But people who have not received any knowledge from the Sadguru worship things such as wood, stone, etc., which are created from the womb of this earth. God is imperishable and yet people take perishable things to be God. People are immersed in ignorance, yet when they bow, they bow only to themselves. While permeating everything, the creator is different from what is created.

Saint Tukaram has said that even a learned man who expounds upon mythological books and scriptures does not know about himself, about who he is. That which makes known whatever is unknown is called knowledge. If one carries out an introspective search, one will understand oneself and all creation. But one never bothers to search. Since one has not tried to understand God, one cannot find him. Avidya means literally "not knowledge," or ignorance. It is a perverse thought to accept this world as true, and then to think of God. This is due to ignorance (avidya). A wise man thinks differently. The seer and the seen are two entities. Hence, the *Vedas* say that the seen is Illusion, that the seer is the Self, that the "Supreme Self," Paramatman, is beyond concepts of the real and the unreal. Paramatman is Parameshwara, the Supreme Lord, who is beyond the perishable god. The world is untrue, and the Self is true. The One prior to both of these is Paramatman. He alone is to be called "God." Earth, water, fire, wind, and space (the five elements) are not God. People who say, "God came and went away, He was born and then died," are deluded, and their delusion has no limit. How is it possible for God who has neither birth nor death, nor the knowledge of it, and who is beyond birth and death, be born or die? Birth and death are characteristics of the body, hunger and thirst are characteristics of prana (breath), and pain and pleasure are characteristics of the mind. You are Shiva (God) and beyond these six characteristics. The body will perish, and the gross world is also perishable. All that is imagined is found only in the world appearance.

When there is not even the slightest feeling of separation between you and God, then you are That. Here there is no imagination whatsoever. There is no sense that "I am God," nor is there a feeling like "I am Shiva." Some say that as the doer can be found in action, the Self can also be found in this world. Dualists make the assertion that this world has come out of Brahman and lives by virtue of it alone, so it must be residing only in Brahman. This is the reason that the dualistic notions of Brahman and Maya came to stay. Neither Brahman nor Maya have any beginning. Maya has been created out of Brahman. Yet as soon as Maya approaches Brahman, Maya disappears. If one says that the world enters or disappears into Brahman, then Brahman will have a hole in it. But it is not so, nor is there any burden of the world on Brahman.

This Maya (Illusion) appears in Brahman, but it is not in Brahman. It is like the appearance of a reflection in a mirror. You can say your clothes are dried by the sun, yet the sun did not come and dry them for you. There are a hundred pitchers full of water on a terrace and there are a hundred reflections of the sun. Does it mean that there are a hundred suns? So, even when the sun, in the form of hundreds of rays, dries your clothes, it will never get caught up in the clothes. In the same way even though the Self is in the body and is doing all actions, He is not in the actions. If you look into your Inner-Self, you will find Him in your own heart. Hrishikesha means One who stays in the heart. Realize Him, then you will reach the highest God. To know Him is the state of liberation.

Lecture 13 – Brahman is the Original Illusion

"The listeners had previously asked the question as to how the One who is without attributes could become that which is moving and that which is inanimate. This must be explained now." (*Dasbodh* - Chapter 8, Sub-chapter 2)

One should realize first, and then speak. The body is bound by its own karma (action). Devotion is like a farm and Knowledge is like a fruit. The listener has asked that since Brahman is without attributes, how did it contain Maya inside? Brahman is eternal, and Maya is an appearance. Vedanta has two theories, Vivarta (no cause) and Upadana (cause). Vivarta theory says that where there is nothing, for no reason one feels that there is something. Upadana theory says that the cause can be seen directly or evidently. For example the product is a pitcher and the cause (or base) is clay.

If Brahman is the direct cause of Illusion, then something would be subtracted from Brahman in the creation of Illusion. Consciousness, or "the power to know," has become Illusion. God is the cause, and Illusion is the effect. There is another theory called the "theory of cause and effect" (Parinamavada) put forth by dualists. They consider this objective world to be true. But this is because they have become a part of the world. They have forgotten the True Self and have accepted the world to be true due to ignorance.

According to Vivarta theory, Illusion which is not really existent appears in Consciousness. This Illusion has appeared on Brahman. "I am awake," means I am in all. Even if Maya appears, Brahman is unaffected. When sugar is mixed with water, it disappears, yet it is there in the form of sweetness. Similarly, Maya exists in Brahman in a hidden form. Has this world come out from Brahman in some other way? If it were from Brahman, there would be a loss to that extent of Brahman. It has come from Parabrahman. Just as sugar put in water gets lost, the world gets lost in Brahman. Once you approach your own nature, Illusion disappears.

If one separates Brahman from Parabrahman, then the former is called the Primordial Illusion (Moolamaya). Power and Pure Knowledge (Prakriti and Purusha, also Shakti and Shiva) are one and the same. Pure Knowledge is a very subtle concept or thought. It is true that God has created this world, but the world exists only as long as the perishable body exists. God exists only as long as the devotee exists and vice versa. As long as the dream lasts, the dreamer is present. However the base of all this is Parabrahman, where there is nothing. God has intense fear of getting destroyed. That which is without fear is Parabrahman. In this "stateless state," there is no God, no man or woman, and no Ignorance or Knowledge. If Brahman (God) and Parabrahman were the same, there would have been no need at all for the prefix "Para" (beyond).

Vivarta means feeling that there is something when there is nothing. We feel that there is something because of imagination. The world appears because of the awakening of concepts and hence does not require a place to reside. The concept is the cause and the world is the effect. God and the devotee coexist, meaning that one cannot exist without the other. God exists only when a devotee imagines him, and without God there is no devotee. To realize Truth, both Knowledge and Ignorance have to be eradicated.

In Vedanta it is told that there are five sheaths, or covers, on the Self. The Self is different from the four bodies. Beyond the Self is Parabrahman. The gross body is made up of food so it is called the cover of food. The ten senses, the five vital airs (pranas), and the mind and intellect together form the covers of the subtle. Thus, there are three sheaths in the subtle body. When everything is forgotten, nothing remains and there is ignorance. This is the cover of bliss (anandamaya kosha). In this cover made up of forgetfulness there is neither happiness nor sorrow. To enable the experience of joy, day and night have been created. If one does not get any rest in deep-sleep, one does not get any joy at all. Rest is joy. During deep-sleep, a beggar gets the same happiness as a king.

The jiva (the individual consciousness) gets entangled in the five covers but the true owner is beyond them. Going beyond nothingness is going to Knowledge. This means that Pure Consciousness, or Knowledge remains. The satisfaction one gets in the state of forgetfulness is hidden, while the satisfaction one gets in the state of Consciousness is full of joy. This state of Pure Awareness is called by various names like Sat-Chit-Ananda, Om, Narayana, "Brahman of Profound Knowledge" (Prajnana Brahman), etc. When this state is also left behind, only Thoughtless Reality (Vijnana) remains. In this "stateless state," even the sense of "I Am" is absent. There is no scope for giving any name to this "stateless state," so it is termed as Parabrahman or "beyond Brahman." We are in fact Parabrahman.

If Parabrahman had become the world then it would have undergone some distortion or change, and also it would be known even during deep-sleep. But this does not happen. Prior to all, is Parabrahman. Then comes Knowledge, forgetfulness, the intellect, the mind, and the body (in a downward progression). That which is original, is Parabrahman. In Parabrahman, arose the "I Am." In Parabrahman we do not remember ourself, nor do we forget ourself. Where there is the arising of Knowledge, the universe exists (in subtle form). Hence, Knowledge can be likened to a pregnant woman.

It is true that God has created this Illusion because it has been created by Knowledge ("I Am"). It is God's will and hence it so happened. In the state of Knowledge, Illusion is untrue. This means that Illusion is present in the "Nirguna Brahman," or Brahman without attributes, right from the beginning. All this is so because of the will of

God. As long as Knowledge exists, Illusion appears to be true. If in a dream you see a big elephant in a small vessel, you would say that it is not true. How then, can this world be true despite the fact that you see the whole of it inside your little eyes? This is why whatever you see is not true, but absolutely false.

Lecture 14 – Illusion is Imagination

"The listeners had previously asked the question as to how the One who is without attributes could become that which is moving and that which is inanimate. This must be explained now." (*Dasbodh* - Chapter 8, Sub-chapter 2)

Chitragupta in Hindu mythology is the one who keeps account of the sins and merits of everyone during their life for God's judgment later. Actually Chitragupta means one who is secretly (gupta) residing in the heart of everyone, as the inner-consciousness. Earlier, the listeners had a doubt as to how the formless Brahman without attributes has become Illusion. What is the meaning of "earlier"? Actually, time itself is an Illusion. Due to this Illusion we feel that it is a particular day or month. Light and darkness occur in sequence on earth. It is for the sake of convenience that days, months, etc. are fixed. There are thousands of such waves that appear on the Self.

The primary "thing" is the natural Parabrahman and Illusion appears on Him. Parabrahman is free and does not do anything, and on That background appears the non-existent Illusion. Actually, the world does not exist at all, so its burden is never felt by Parabrahman. In the same way, a concept arises in us, and because the concept is firmly held, we believe it is true. An object seen in a dream is not real, yet it appears to be real. Similar to one's reflection in a mirror, Maya (Illusion) appears to be true. Practice the thought, "All appears on my Self." Even if you do it sincerely for only eight days you will experience Reality. Brahman is the embodiment of Knowledge.

The *Vedas* have said that Pure Knowledge is Brahman. The great statement of another *Veda* is "I am Brahman." As you conceive, so will you become. You, the Self, are the king, and Illusion is your servant. Illusion is as per your perception. The king experiences as he imagines.

Illusion means our idea. As are a person's concepts, accordingly does Maya bind him. One may ask that if Illusion is untrue why is it visible? I ask in return if all of what is seen is true? Where are the objects seen in a dream? If you arrange a number of mirrors in one place, the same scene will be visible in all the mirrors. Is it all true? The knowledgeable one does not consider this world appearance as true. Hence, the Vedas say that whatever is seen gets destroyed. Whatever is seen are mere distortions of the mind.

Lecture 15 – Knowledge is Illusion

"Why do you ask about that which has never happened? Yet, I shall tell you something so that there is no room for doubt." (*Dasbodh* - Chapter 8, Sub-chapter 3)

Why do you ask about that which has never existed at all? As you think about the world, so will you see it. According to Pure Knowledge, this universe does not exist at all. This worldly manifestation is the doing of the Self. This is all imagination. This is a phase of Knowledge that is a peculiar spectacle. The Self is the king. When he gets seated in a body, he holds onto various concepts. The thought of the Self keeps changing constantly. Nothing of this world actually exists in the Self. Whatever this "I" has imagined, has appeared. We experience an infinite number of universes because the Self imagines that they exist.

The Self is the doer of all. He is God, Ishwara. God, or Bhagavanta, means the Self. This universe has arisen from the Self, from Knowledge. The Self is the doer. This entire panorama is due to him. When the Self knows himself, he is called God or Ishwara. When he forgets his own nature, he is called "ignorance," or Rudra. When he is not aware of either his own Self or the world, he is called the state of the void.

When the Self looks at his True Nature, there is empty sky (space). That is called the Inner-Self. When he looks away from his True Nature, he is called the jiva, or individual being. When he forgets his own nature, he is called ignorance or Rudra (the ignorant aspect of Shiva). The Self, which is Knowledge incarnate is Ishwara, God, who has created this world. From him, from Knowledge, this elaborate panorama has come into being. He is called Purusha/Prakriti. He has many names. In him appears the power of action, the power of will, the power of proliferation, etc.. All of these are born out of Knowledge. This Knowledge is called Primordial Prakriti (Moola Prakriti), or Moolamaya, in the scriptures. It's primordial nature is the reason that people traditionally worship this Ishwara. Accordingly, they also worship the other "so-called" gods that come later.

The holy place called Prabhasa means the "Place of Light." There, all the Yadavas perished. The Yadavas, being relatives of Lord Krishna (Knowledge) had to be destroyed by Him (Knowledge) since they became egoistic. The power of all action has come due to this Knowledge. That God is Knowledge cannot be talked about openly, because all devotees feel good when it is said that "God has made everything," but they do not know who God is. The aspirant, due to ignorance, does not believe that Knowledge is the true "doer."

One who says that he accrues merit or sin, has birth and death, happiness and misery, takes rebirth, etc. is called the jiva, or ignorant one. When the ignorant one understands through the advice of the Sadguru (Master) that "I am not the mind, intellect, senses or body," he becomes Shiva (Pure Consciousness; Pure Knowledge). The cause of all this universe is the Primordial Illusion (Moolamaya). There is bondage for the jiva (ignorant one), and liberation for Shiva (God). Bondage and liberation are mutually dependent. One who has bondage alone will have liberation. One who is beyond both Knowledge and Ignorance has neither bondage nor liberation.

The nature of Parabrahman is beyond both bondage and liberation. Saint Tukaram said, "In this body, and by these very eyes, see the celebration of liberation." Bondage is nothing but ignorance and liberation is nothing but a higher degree of ignorance. One who achieves Self-Knowledge after erasing the conditioning of both jiva and Shiva, attains the greatest good. The one who experiences Reality knows that bondage and liberation are both delusion.

The Self in its purest form of Self-Knowledge is called Moolamaya, while the ignorance which results from the state of no-knowledge is called Maya. Only as long as this Jagadeesha, the "Lord of the World," is present in the hearts of all, does this Maya last. Once He disappears there is no Maya. Moola Purusha, the Primordial Being (Knowledge), is Illusion, and ignorance (Avidya) is also Illusion. It must be analyzed just how this Illusion has appeared on that which has no form. For example, just as the magician performs many tricks through his will or sleight of hand, the drama of this world appears through the will of the Self. If one starts thinking of the origin of this drama, there is nothing. As is your thinking, so will be the result. Through the grace of the Master you get the knowledge that all of this is nothing. Mind, intellect, ego, the senses, etc., are visible to you, and they are all perishable. You are neither the body, nor the senses, nor the pranas, nor the mind, nor the intellect. Bondage and liberation are the nature and the play of Illusion.

Moolamaya arose as a state of Pure Awareness in Parabrahman. When the gunas (attributes) arose in that, it became what is called Gunakshobhini, that is, the stirring or arousal of the gunas. When wind flows in the sky, it does not distort the sky in any way. Similarly, when Gunamaya (Illusion with attributes) arose in Parabrahman, there was no change or distortion in Parabrahman. Bhoota (the five elements) means "that which happened." Movement and speech are the attributes of the sky. This creation is created out of the five elements, so what you see in the world is all false and imaginary. As is enunciated in the Bhagavadgita, "Whatever is, never perishes, and whatever is not, never comes into existence." This body is born of the five elements. The mountains, and rocks, are all of the nature of the earth.

Lecture 16 – Everything Occurs Only in Illusion

"Why do you ask about that which has never happened? Yet, I shall tell you something so that there is no room for doubt." (*Dasbodh* - Chapter 8, Sub-chapter 3)

Many people feel that they should do something to acquire true "Spiritual Knowledge." But what remedy does the Master prescribe for the disciple to acquire Knowledge? A man is healthy and he asks the doctor how his disease can be cured. What can be said about that? Then he asks the same to the chief of the village, to the lawyer, etc., and all of them say, "You have become stout." Then he thinks "What could be the reason that I have become stout?" He asks the doctor. The doctor feels his pulse and thinks, "What can I say to him, he has no disease, so it cannot be diagnosed." Then he meets someone wise like me, who tells him, "You are affected by a terrible disease!" What else can I say?

Pursuing Paramartha (Supreme Truth) is similar to the example given above. People started doing something because they must act.

People also say, "You have become a jiva, an individual being." So, just brush it off saying, "Nothing has happened." Truly, nothing has happened. Let your understanding be like this and become absolutely free. Can there be any talk of that which never existed? You all say "I," and it is this very thing that creates your idea of "mine."

There is one and only one Truth. See, when you say "My hand is hurting," that you are not your hand. Knowledge is for learning what you have heard. One should know God as he is, then there is nothing left to achieve. When you understand the true meaning, then nothing is left to be done. So, to understand Truth, Illusion (Maya) has to be destroyed. People start making efforts to conquer her, but she has many tricks." She resides in one who says he has conquered her. How should she be tackled? And, what has to be done after one becomes a Jnani, a realized one? If you ask this, the answer is "You have to do nothing regarding the body, your household, etc. Let them be as they are." Suppose that while you were asleep, you had a dream where you met a bear while walking on a road. You wrestled with it, and you sat on its chest, and even killed it. The moment you awoke there was no bear, there was nothing. Similarly, to feel "I am a Jnani, I am a Saint, I am an aspirant, or I am after Spiritual Knowledge," is all delusion. To feel that God comes and God goes away is only Illusion. Our concept is the bear in the form of Maya. Sometimes, it makes you fall and at other times, you make it fall. The Master's advice is, "Why do you meddle in this? All this chaos is the chaos of Illusion. So let the objects be wherever they are." If you try to manage affairs, you forget the Moola Purusha (Primordial Being). Doership rests in Maya and non-doership in Brahman.

The aspirants always think of that which is untrue. "What shall I do, Maharaj?" The Guru tells him not to sniff tobacco, and so the disciple's reaction is to put his nose into the box containing tobacco. You say that all this is false, yet you indulge in it. There are only two things in the world, worldly existence and Brahman. To take interest in what has happened is to get involved in worldly affairs. If you abandon all of these things, True Knowledge will dawn. This is why a man gets caught in bondage. Jivahood is to involve the mind in the objective world, and Godhood is to do nothing. God is in the temple, and lying outside are rocks. Why should the God inside value the rocks (the objective world)? For God (the Self) to live among stones is called jivahood.

Saint Tukaram says, "This God is most ancient." The Self is first, prior to all. He who has understood that the Supreme Being, Paramatman who is prior to all, while sitting in this body is a Jnani.

Leaving this God alone, people think of doing good or bad. That is Illusion for the jiva. Maya makes man knowledgeable and a narrator of the *Vedas*, and makes him play this worldly game. If a thing is good, it is good, if it is bad, it is bad. If one is wealthy, he is wealthy, and if one is poor, he is poor. Who is the real aspirant? One who has understood that Illusion is nothing. However much you may have wrestled with the bear in the dream, it is all still false. But Illusion does not want the aspirant to be victorious.

"The concept of "I" and "you" is delusion, as is the concept of the "aspirant." Even the idea that "I am God" is a delusion. This world itself is rooted in delusion. "I am God" is a delusion. If "I" and "you" are gods, then why should there be any supposition or assertion? As told before, abandon everything! Ignorant people start beating cymbals for worship. This knowledge is actually ignorance. Hence, even this knowledge is not of true value. Knowledge destroys ignorance. The jiva is the one who dabbles in Illusion. So, just do nothing. The aspirant is tortured. "You must do this, you must do that" All this is only to fool him. "Maya has long horns on her head. If one supersedes her, she gores him, and if one falls behind, she kicks him.

Thus, the key to transcending Illusion lies in just doing nothing (not becoming involved in objectivity). All happiness, misery, worry and anxiety appear only in Illusion. You have to do nothing, you have to abandon nothing. All this action and non-action is Illusion. This is what Saint Ramdas has said in *Dasbodh*. So, those who have not understood this Illusion may dance wildly. Maya is dreamlike. If you wrestle with a bear in the dream, your victory or defeat is irrelevant. So it is said, that Maya is unconquerable, even for Brahma, Vishnu, Shiva, etc., (since they take it to be true).

Vishnu said, "I shall protect them," so he became a four-handed God. This is Illusion. All are engrossed in this Illusion. A barren woman's son said that he held a torch at Maruti's (Hanuman, who is celibate) wedding. This world in the form of Maya is just as fictitious. Those who say that they have conquered Illusion are thoroughly deceived. The devotees of God do not experience the happiness or misery arising from Maya. His aspirant's glory is small, but it is higher than that of the gods Vishnu and Shiva. The reason is that he has understood all to be untrue. There is no action, cause or doership. Wherever there is a feeling of cause and effect it is due to the feeling "I am Brahman." This feeling is the effect, and the jiva, ignorance, is the cause. When you feel you are not Brahman you become a jiva. When you feel you are neither jiva nor Shiva you become the Absolute Reality, Parabrahman. jiva, good, bad, etc., are all signs of delusion of the nature of Prakriti, or the manifest world. All this is a game of blind man's buff. He is the one who covers the player's eyes, hence he is not part of the play. And he blindfolds the participants but once.

Both knowledge, and ignorance are of the nature of Prakriti. This itself is called delusion. Who expounds the scriptures and who gives knowledge? Chanting, penance, various practices, study, etc. are all the mesmeric activities of Maya. You cross over Prakriti, the manifest world, only when you are free from all duties. These are all matters at the initial stage. As long as there is Knowledge, there is delusion. Leave off whatever you suppose you are. "Leave off" means do not dabble in anything. Continue your worship. "I am the Self, I am Brahman, I am not the body, I am not so-and-so." The one who is speaking inside is "I," he is God. Just be convinced of that.

There was a princess who wanted to marry a lazy man. Accordingly, an announcement was made in every village. Prospective suitors claiming to be lazy soon arrived. The princess wanted to ascertain the validity of their claims. Some people pretended laziness by arriving to the town seated on other people's shoulders. Others feigned silence in support of their claim. Yet others decided not to use their hands for eating food. There were as many pretensions of laziness as there were suitors. The princess rejected them all. But there was one shrewd fellow. He simply informed the princess that he had come to get married to her. The princess asked, "How can you prove that you are lazy?" He replied that he had come to get married only because he was lazy. He said, "All the others are merely pretending. They are only actors, they aren't really lazy." Maintaining silence, not to walk, not to eat with one's hands, etc., are all only external actions meant to deceive. The really lazy person cannot be traced through such pretension. The really lazy person is lazy by nature. Similarly, for the Jnani, it is absolutely self-evident that he is Brahman.

The true mark of a saint is taking the world to be untrue. Maya is also untrue. If it is not understood that all is of the nature of Prakriti (Illusion), then one cannot get married to the princess. Lazy does not mean one who abandons outward actions, but one who is genuinely lazy (not becoming involved with objectivity). The jiva has the habit of engaging in some activity all the time. What has to be done and for whose sake? To do something is of the nature of body-consciousness. Illusion means our ideas or concepts. There is a proverb that says, "He started worshipping God when he was tired of doing things."

If you reject all that is untrue, then you become God. To say that "I ought to do this or that, and manage this or that. I will become rich, and then I will become a saint and start acting differently," is all an indication of Illusion. So, leave things as they are. If you meddle, your body-consciousness only gets increased. You always feel that you ought to do something. This is the obstruction for attaining the state of the Siddha (Absolute Reality). When you are not the body, then why all of this useless thinking about wealth or poverty? All is untrue. Then why this unnecessary query about what has not happened? To not do anything is Godhood. We say, "Remain quiet like God," but what is actually done is that we indulge our body-consciousness. To not worry about anything and to be at peace is called Om Shanti. This is my blessing to you all.

Lecture 17 – Practice What You Have Heard

"When one chooses to be with a sage, how much time does it take to become liberated? Oh merciful one, give this humble aspirant a definite answer." (*Dasbodh* - Chapter 8, Sub-chapter 6)

The aspirant asks, "When one is in the company of a sage, within how many days will one attain liberation?" After listening to spiritual discourse, and after implementing the advice, when one starts getting experiences, he will immediately be liberated. Faith in the teachings means that whatever the Master says must be brought into practice. When one takes this world as untrue, then one is content. As we honor the Master, so should we honor all. All have the Atman, the Self, present in them, so all should be treated with respect and dignity. The teachings of the Master must be brought into practice. Then one gets rest. There is no escape unless you separate the body from the Self. If there is pain, keep silent, knowing it is the nature of the body. Remain with the awareness that you are beyond the body. If this is not put into practice it is harmful. "Suchitpane dushchita" means that even if you think it is quite correct, it does not get put into practice.

Therefore, be generous. Try to bring the Inner-Self which is distracted (duschita) to awareness (suchita). Live with awareness and put this birth to good use. You are very fortunate because all in your family have got knowledge. You must make all of them knowledgeable. A man understands this knowledge more easily, while women and children find it easier to put it into practice. (Women and children are known for their stubbornness and strong willed nature, this is essential to bring about renunciation as advised by the Master. – translator's note)

Man dies only once. Always be fearless. Man has become a slave due to fear. You must become fearlessness. Faced with either happiness or misery, why should we not think that everything might be occurring for the good? Keep your faith in the unseen, adrishta. Adrishta, the unseen, means that which is beyond the realm of reason. Jnanis, the "knowledgeable ones," understand this and go their own way. Wherever God has put us, live there happily. We should keep to the path of virtue. The sign of a saint is that he does not act according to what comes to his mind. If someone is harassing you, bear it, knowing that he is talking to the mind. An aspirant should make his life meaningful in this manner.

If Brahmavidya, the "Knowledge of Reality," is imbibed, it gives a twofold result. This means that we understand Knowledge better, and that life becomes meaningful. Think about how you get up in the morning. Give up worldly thoughts and try to entertain lofty thoughts. Try to always go to sleep only after becoming free of all doubt. Get up in the same way, and then go about your duties. Do not entertain a bad thought about anyone. Whoever he may be, always take into consideration his better nature. Do not pay attention to what is bad. All this advice is for your satisfaction. This advice is to be brought into practice relentlessly as was done by Arjuna, the disciple of Krishna. Do not let the message of Reality stop at the portals of the ear, as it did for Karna (the rival of Arjuna; Karna also means ear).

Lecture 18 – Devotion to the Master

"Living beings are only bound by desires and the concept of being a limited individual jiva. One becomes liberated by the sages through the power of discrimination." (*Dasbodh* - Chapter 8, Sub-chapter 7)

Earlier, an aspirant inquired about the time needed for attaining liberation in the company of a sage. The answer to that is, as soon as one takes refuge in a sage and surrenders his ego, he will be liberated. As it is, it is very difficult to even have the inclination to take refuge at the feet of a Master. The arising of such a desire is itself a great blessing. By complete surrender to the Master, the heart becomes pure. The Sadguru is Parabrahman, Thoughtless Reality, itself. It is indeed a great fortune to have faith in the Master. By the grace of Saint Vasishtha, Lord Rama understood the essential quality of being Rama. Worldly existence and striving for Spiritual Knowledge are the two wheels of the grinding stone. All the grain put into the millstone gets crushed, but that grain which sticks to the central pivot is not crushed. Similarly, those who live in accordance with the guidance of a Master are saved from the travails of this mundane existence. Brahma, Vishnu, and Shiva have also become God through the Guru's grace.

When one speaks of Truth, he forgets it. When one says OM (the first word), he forgets "Soham" (I am That). If one takes himself to to be awakened he forgets wakefulness. Only the Master is the one who is capable of putting you in touch with Reality. When one is tired of incantation, penance, charity, virtuous deeds, etc., he finally gets convinced that nothing is possible without the Master. The scriptures say that one must obtain proof of Reality by experiencing it. Even to arrive at an understanding that it is not possible to obtain salvation without a Master might take millions of years. The Master is necessary beyond the gross, subtle and causal bodies. One who understands that there is no salvation without a Master, surrenders to the Master. To bow one's head means to surrender one's intellect. Whatever had to be done through the intellect has been done, but there is no fruition.

For a long time the seeker has traveled without a Guru in search of Truth. But there is no one to show him the destination. Aeons pass this way in fruitless travel, meanwhile Truth is close at hand. Man takes many days to achieve liberation. The reason is that the mind is not pure. This is why one gets liberated after going to a Master. In the beginning, no one knows what liberation is. Someone says, "You must do virtuous deeds." Being greedy, man starts engaging in virtuous acts. If you truly believe that you get back whatever you give in charity, why don't you give away your limbs in charity, one after the other? But because of greed, man takes himself as a body and starts engaging in charity (with the hope of reward). One does good deeds and eagerly awaits the fruit (reward). But is anyone ready to accept the fruit of a sinful act? There is no one capable of giving this "Knowledge of the Self" except the Master. He frees you from all karma (action). Lord Krishna told Arjuna to just leave off all actions and only surrender to him, because he was the Guru.

All karmas, or "spiritual" actions, have as their purpose the purification of the mind. Only the Master bestows Knowledge. So, surrender to Me (the Master) because all your actions and religious duties are intended to achieve Me. Without the Master you cannot get "True Knowledge." When the Master promises to give you liberation, at that very moment you get liberated. There is no doubt about it. He has the capacity of bestowing liberation. The Master explains this knowledge to you in countless ways. He proves it until it becomes crystal clear to the aspirant. The Master has a monopoly over liberation. Take it for granted that devotion is the mother of Knowledge, and the travails of the world and God that give you stress go away. Devotion means faith in the Master. There is no difference between your Self and the Self of the Master.

It is not really possible to worship the Self. Worship Knowledge, or worship the inner-mind (Consciousness). The Master gives without expecting anything in return. It is impossible to repay what He has given by any means. Therefore, each devotee should express devotion to his Master. Any spiritual life that has no support of saguna worship (with attributes) is baseless. The day you leave off worship there is no relation between you and Me (the Master, the Reality). Saguna worship (devotion to Master with form) is for the enjoyment of the devotee. One who has both Knowledge and Devotion is like a king. I am telling you the secret of secrets. Do not abandon saguna worship. Devotion is like nourishment. I have presented you with this fifteenth gem, "Devotion after Liberation."

The Master's feet are worthy of the greatest worship. Do your utmost to imbibe devotion. In the ocean of this existence you have the great support of devotion to the Master. He is the Self who grants the intellect the ability to be able to discriminate. He is pleased by devotion. Devotion to the Master corrects all mistakes and is the remedy for all your mistakes, or "misdeeds." So, be devoted with fervor, then the good that follows from devotion will be yours. Do not create any obstacles. The Master is the "wish-fulfilling cow" (Kamadhenu). In order that knowledge should remain steady, devotion is imperative.

Lecture 19 – Utilize the Human Birth

"Previously it was explained that you and you alone are the Supreme Self, Paramatman. The signs of that Paramatman will be told now." (*Dasbodh* - Chapter 8, Sub-chapter 8)

We come to know who we are only by thinking about it (vichara). What is our duty when we have taken birth as human beings? This human birth is not for just doing household and worldly duties like the bull that works the oil mill (ever engaged in mechanically repetitive activities). Carry on your duties in such a manner that you become immortal. Do not live to do worldly duties only to then die. Do not live thus. Live for attaining the state of immortality. One day you will surely die, and what will remain then? The bones are burnt like a bundle of firewood. Will it be like Shimga (an Indian festival when people disguise themselves as different animals and enjoy themselves. In the same way, once you die you have to undergo births in the 8.4 million species of beings as per Hindu mythology), a wasted life and endless births? "If a man (works) acts truly, he can become Narayana, God." A jiva is resigned to births in the 8.4 million different species. No one will come to rescue you if you choose to remain a jiva. When the hook is swallowed, it tastes sweet, but when death comes, the throat is torn. You will see how futile worldly life is as the days pass.

Therefore, try to take advantage of this human birth. Do not waste it. A beast's hide can be used for making shoes, but a human hide is of no use after his death. Yet, if a man makes an effort towards understanding Reality, he will become God. This body has absolutely no use after death. "I lived only to die in the end." Do not lead such a life, live to be immortal. Your birth will be in vain if you do not utilize it for understanding Reality. "One should have such a son whose banner flies high in all the three worlds." You must think of why you were born. "He came from a womb and entered a grave, unnecessarily wasting his birth." Do not let this be your condition. Men eat, excrete, and finally die. Then they have to pass through births in the 8.4 million species, thereby becoming miserable. The purpose of human birth is to obtain ultimate bliss by realizing God. Instead, people involve themselves in various things, and waste this priceless human body. Everyone must prove that he is Brahman to obtain the ultimate peace. This is called Purushartha, the goal of man.

Only the banner of such people as this flies high in all the three worlds. If we are God we should behave accordingly. We are all-pervading, without quality and without shape. How then, can Brahman be entangled in worldly life? If the devotee searches for God, He is found. The devotee is in fact himself God. When he goes to look for God, he finds that he himself is God. You worship Shiva by becoming Shiva, and further, you must remain stable in the state of Shiva. Acquire

Shiva's state. Saint Ramdas says, "God is quite near in the heart, but the meeting does not take place for an entire lifetime."

Lecture 20 – God is All-Pervasive

"In the recognition of God there is oneness with Him. There is no separation between God and devotee at all." (*Dasbodh* - Chapter 8, Sub-chapter 8)

That "God should be worshipped with clean hands" implies that God is to be worshipped without letting in any dirt (Illusion and ego). God should be worshipped by abandoning contact with the body or worldly affairs. Saying that you must understand God first implies that you should make your vision all pervasive. Just as the sky pervades all, so also does God pervade all. Bear in mind that God is in all. The sunlight and the moonlight are the light of the Self. The God that pervades the world also resides inside us. Just as the sky fills a pot, the Self also fills us. When the pot breaks, the embodied portion of the sky merges with the sky at large, likewise, the light of the Self merges in Brahman.

How is the Self? The answer is that it is thinner than water, lighter than a flower, and yet heavy like a mountain. It is very delicate and very peaceful. Whenever you look at others, always look upon them as the Self, do not focus on their bodies. "The crown jewel of spiritual study is that the mind should stabilize in the One without qualities."

Lecture 21 – Identify With Brahman

"The sign of Atma-nivedan (self-surrender) is to find out 'Who am I?' With that comes the recognition of the attributeless Self that is Paramatman." (*Dasbodh* - Chapter 8, Sub-chapter 8)

The meaning of self-surrender is to first investigate "Who am I?" Self-Knowledge is quite easy. There is a difference in one's inner attitude when attention is turned away from the objects of the senses. Then it is all over. Then it is "I am Brahman." The Self is One, but he becomes a mere soldier (instead of the king) when he is attracted towards the external side. What is the sign of knowing the Self? It is the understanding that "I am Brahman." The sign of the one who does not know this is the sense of being an individual, a jiva. It is an Indian custom that one should rise upon seeing the face of a good person. Start with the feeling "I am Paramatman." That's all. If you rise as a beggar then you remain a beggar, saying "I want this, I want that," and you worry while going about your duties. We must identify the signs of knowing the Self. It depends on your wish, whether to be the king or a beggar.

"What shall I do, where shall I go?" When Paramatman, the Supreme Self, becomes a jiva (the individual), the mistress of the house, the body, always says "Bring this, bring that." The husband (the Self) is not allowed to sit quietly. Laxmi is the one who bestows the highest bliss. So it is up to you, whom you choose, the body or Laxmi (bliss). If you are the jiva, the body, then worries will never cease. You are really without qualities, so you have no worries. The Master merely shows the way. Ultimately, you are your own Master. This world is involved only with itself. It will talk only of worldly things.

If you cultivate your mind to identify with Brahman, it will do so. The mind will do what you contemplate upon. Never come down to identify with the body. One who achieves this, does not care for wealth or worldly pleasures. All of this is untrue. Of what use are gold, silver, diamonds and rubies? One who has understood the path of no-mind has no cares. He is always immersed in his own Self. True devotees may be humble, but they are actually greater than worldly gods. Those who are true followers of a Master achieve the status of Brahman and get liberated from this mundane existence. A true aspirant is one who has destroyed the idea that "I am the body." When you surrender the god-given body to God, the Master (Reality) is all yours. This conviction will arise within you.

Once an aspirant said, "I have come, Maharaj." Who are "you"? "I am Brahman." If you are Brahman, be Brahman and live thus. Then your glory will be the glory of Brahman, eternal, pure, free, without beginning, without quality, without shape and omnipresent. Abandon the attachment to the body, and you become God. Become Shiva and worship Shiva. Saint Ramdas says, "If you identify with the body, you will have to suffer misery. As soon as you go beyond the body, you are the Absolute Reality (Parabrahman)."

Lecture 22 – Qualities of Realization

"Now let this be enough of this talk. See God through the eyes of the devotee and immediately see the glory of God." (*Dasbodh* - Chapter 8, Sub-chapter 8)

The devotee is God. Being God, one enjoys godhood. The concept that God is some other entity is false. Your actions are according to your concepts. If you imagine that realization will be achieved by a specific method, you are wrong. Never imagine that someone else will grant you the status of Brahman. If someone grants it to you, then the one who grants it is naturally greater than you. By his own will, He became a jiva (an individual), and by his own will, He becomes Shiva (God). It lies in your hands to be God, if you so desire. When you feel ashamed of the status of being a human being you will become God. You will gain the status of God only if your delusion is removed completely. Then you will have the feeling, "Why do I want this mundane life, wife, house, money, etc.?" To be ashamed of jivahood is itself the sign of gaining Brahmanhood. I am forever free, why do I need worldly pleasures?

Ask yourself, "What thoughts come to my mind, what does my desire prompt me to do?" The quality of the concepts that continually arise in your mind are an indication of your inclination towards Brahmanhood. Are the ideas that arise, connected to this world or are they about Absolute Reality? Do the ideas of your True Self arise at all? The one who is steady in the Self, says that "I am all-pervading, complete, and inherently present in every heart."

The qualities associated the attainment of Absolute Reality are:

1. **Detachment**: Absence of desire to acquire things (or people).
2. **Generosity**: There is nothing that belongs to me in this world. Let things come and go. I am free from all things. Severance from everything, including the body is okay. No motivation to protect worldly things.
3. **Knowledge**: I am Brahman. Success is certain.
4. **Success**: To be rid of Maya. Good riddance to rubbish (Illusion)!

The "God of Death" (Yama) is sitting on one side of the balance (the body) and casts nets in the form of sensual pleasures. To release oneself from them, you should be ready to give them up, then the

Master helps you. He is the true guide. If you get released from the bonds of death (transient appearances) there is success.

5. **Liberation**: Liberation from all karmas (actions). If you want sainthood, meditate on the teachings of the Master. If you only meditate on wife and worldly affairs, you will only be miserable.

Shri means the "Divine Wealth" that pervades all hearts, without pride, without concepts, beyond duality, dreamless, egoless, etc. Such is the nature of Brahmanhood. If one is committed to Brahmanhood, he acquires all of the qualifications mentioned above. If there is a lamp that is lit in the house, light will stream out through the window. When one gets the "Knowledge of Brahman," higher glory follows automatically. It becomes evident in one's speech, hearing, and in all the senses. Let one who has to die, die happily, and let one who is going to live, live. The Master easily helps the earnest seeker become free from the trappings of this world. We have to release ourselves. Let us not talk of others, such as how much detachment do other people have, and how much discrimination? Let us not get involved in the motivations of others. We must focus on releasing ourselves from the ego. Illusion comes dressed in many forms. She may come in a good form or a bad form. We must become free of this ghost of the ego. Exorcise the ego. Purge all these extraneous objects from your mind, and exorcise this ghost by the mantra, "I am Brahman." Then comes success, fame, and valor. We need only abide in the "Knowledge of the Self."

Lecture 23 – Be Brahman

"Now let this be enough of this talk. See God through the eyes of the devotee and immediately see the glory of God." (*Dasbodh* - Chapter 8, Sub-chapter 8)

Did a devotee become God or did God become the devotee? There is no difference between a devotee and God. If God becomes a devotee, ego goes away. If a devotee becomes God, the pride of "I" arises. The "I" is false. The world has only two types of entities, the five elements and the Self. It is God that is a dog, a cat, a human being, etc. Indeed, all is only Brahman. Then where is the "I"? All of the five elements and everything in the universe is God. To know this is the sign of Paramartha (Ultimate Truth). The glory of God is imbibed after one becomes God. Undoubtedly then, freedom from worry, success, and fame, are all attained. In Maya (Illusion) one becomes grief-stricken with failure, and one become her slave. You feel happy if something is given to you. But that is all false. It is like being served bread in a prison.

To be victorious implies freedom from everything. When the lamp is lit in the house, light streams through the windows. Similarly, when the light of realization dawns, the highest bliss, freedom from all worry, and glory are yours. One who is Brahman, abides as That. One who lives believing that he is a body, has to suffer the miseries of the body. The body is a storehouse of worries. Desire, anger, birth and death are all attributes of the body. To become an individual after understanding that one is Brahman is ridiculous. What is the sense of one who is a king taking a position as a sweeper who cleans gutters? He brings himself down. He becomes his own enemy. Who has claimed the delusion? We ourselves. It is an old habit to say "I am an individual." When the glory of Brahman can be attained, why become miserable with the false belief that one is a jiva? Stay in prison (the body) by all means, but stay with the knowledge that "I am not a criminal." Stay as a man lives in a guest house.

It is by being Brahman that the knowledge of Brahman comes to you. How suicidal it is to live as jiva, when one is Brahman. It is indeed ridiculous to take pride in "mine" even after knowing that we are not the gross body. So, one must not stubbornly revel in the pride of the body. You are Brahman, so enjoy the glory of Brahman.

Lecture 24 – Remain Detached

"This type of glory is acquired only after the body-consciousness is relinquished. Taking the body as "I" is the cause of downfall." (*Dasbodh* - Chapter 8, Sub-chapter 8)

It is only when you realize "I am Brahman," that the jiva acquires the glory of God. He becomes Paramatman, the Supreme Self. His glory is pure, knowledgeable, and ever free. When the jiva (individual) abandons body-consciousness, he becomes Shiva (God). Otherwise he faces a fall.

Nothing is impossible to achieve. Do not feel that you are being held back by others. The human birth is a wish-fulfilling tree. If one makes the effort, man becomes God. Even a stone can be turned into God (an idol), so why can't a man? You are the owner of the world, but you are deluded by worldly objects. You fall in love and become a husband (Pati), and you have fallen (Patan means to fall). You have fallen due to your obsession with the mundane existence, and gradually you started sinking deeper. Who knows how many births you may have to undergo? "This is my Pati" (husband) means "He is the one who falls due to me."

One who takes the (medicinal) dose of the Master's teachings should observe abstinence. Abstinence means to not accept the world. Be detached, and always fix your attention on the Self. We do not belong to this world. We belong to the world beyond. What have I to gain by accepting all this? What use does a widow have of kumkum (In India a woman applies red kumkum powder on her head as long as her husband is alive).

There is a principle that states, "While the world is awake, the Saint sleeps. While the world is asleep, the Saint is wide awake." This means that the Saints are asleep to the world of Maya (appearances) and awake in relation to Brahman. One who sleeps here, awakens to the Self. Do not crave for publicity or respect from others. So what if one has all of that? When they sit down for meals, more is given to the one who says, "I do not need, I do not want." The one who has really gained is the one who refuses even a kingdom. What are Lord Vishnu and Mahadev (Shiva) going to give? Who is really rich? Only the one who needs nothing from this world is really rich. Money is for beggars. One should be firmly established in the conviction that "I do not have any desire for objects." This must be the attitude of one who wants Paramartha, Supreme Truth. He must feel that he is a Jnani (a realized one), and not someone who is fond of domestic life. When you are a Jnani, regardless of whether you eat, drink or sleep, you still remain a Jnani. In the spiritual world one has to confer a degree upon oneself (while in the mundane world, someone else confers it on you – figuratively speaking).

Do not be concerned about anything. One has to act without the pride of Knowledge. Then he becomes Paramatman. These are the teachings of the Master. It is degrading to say that you are the body. Leave off the feeling of body-identification. Do not doubt what the saint says. If you do not behave according to what the saint says, you only invite your own downfall. You are the Self, full of bliss, immortal, eternal and pure, and you can create a hundred kinds of wealth. Do not be obsessed with the body, and then you will understand what "Soham" (I am That) means. This is the only advice of saints, and if you take it to heart, you become That. Keeping the company of saints implies that one must study one's Self, leaving the company of the mundane existence. Each one should quietly follow his own path, just as the thief leaves the scene of the crime after he has finished stealing. The Master likes when one has experienced the path by experiencing the Self. "A mute person eats jaggery but cannot express its sweetness." If you spit at this Illusion, Reality is attained. You must eat the fruit that the Master has granted you in the form of Ultimate Reality. Saint Tukaram says, "Everyday is a fast for me." You have to accept the "one state" that is the Ekadashi. (It is Indian custom to fast on the eleventh day of the lunar cycle which occurs twice a month. Eka means one, and dasha means state). Keep away from the objects of the world. Do not even touch them. Then, even though you may eat a mound of food, you still observe a fast.

"Laxmi (wealth) becomes the slave of one who does not beg (ask for anything)." Paramatman is attained if one asks for Him, and Maya (Illusion) always comes unasked. You may have tea, good sweets, good clothes, etc., but still observe a fast. The true Ekadashi (fasting) is "I am Brahman." Meditate on Him who is inherent in all hearts. One should only be proud of one's True Self. One should take oneself as Paramatman, the Supreme Self, and not as a householder (worldly person). What is mundane existence for a Jnani? The truly great ones outsmart Illusion. It is essential to remove impurities from the mind. Only then is one worthy of attaining Paramatman. If you consider Reality as nothing, or if you belittle Him, then so be it. If you think small, there is degeneration. Lift yourself up with your own hands. The more you neglect the world (Illusion) the braver you are. The greater the degree of detachment, the greater the bliss obtained.

Lecture 25 – Be Firm in Self-Knowledge

"The One devoid of attributes has become attributeless, the meaningful has become meaningful, and after a long time, One has met oneself." (*Dasbodh* - Chapter 8, Sub-chapter 8)

He was Paramatman, without attributes. Upon acquiring attributes, he had become miserable. He was released from birth and death after reaching his "original state." Thus, he reverted back to his original state to honor that Paramatman for whom all effort, scriptures, and spiritual life acquired true meaning. God's grace grants human birth. If one acts in accordance with Truth, one becomes God, one's own Self is attained, and a "Golden Day" dawns. Satiated with the nectar of immortality, I have found my home. All efforts were successful. I have met myself after many years. I had made a mistake. I was serving someone else (the body) taking him to be myself. For millions of births I had mistaken the body to be myself. I was deluded. This delusion has vanished and I have become Paramatman.

Assuming oneself to be the body, he was behaving like a donkey, ever-burdened, and likewise was his attitude towards his wife. Taking the body as the Self he nursed it. In this way, he wasted his whole life. This is "night" in the form of ignorance, where one has to labor for the donkey (body) for a lifetime only to be reborn. Ignorance itself is at fault for not permitting the understanding that the human birth is meant for the very purpose of being rid of birth. Ignorance is itself the source of all misery.

An illustration is given about how a foolish man's friends once made him drink a lot of liquor, and after he was completely intoxicated, they began crying and said to him, "We really pity your sad state. Just a few minutes ago we visited your house where we saw that your wife has become a widow." As soon as he heard this, the drunken man started howling and crying, and when some onlookers asked him the cause of his grief, he replied that his wife had become a widow." A mountain of misery has come down crushing me." The onlookers then knocked some sense into him saying, "How can your wife become a widow when you are alive? Are not these two things, your being alive, and your wife becoming a widow, contradictory?" The drunken man persisted however, saying "No, you people do not understand anything. My friends have only just visited my house, and they have seen with their very own eyes that my wife has become a widow." His friends all had a good laugh at his absurd behavior.

The above illustration is not only indicative of the state of the drunken man, but also of every human being. Without proper understanding, everyone is accustomed to looking at the world through other people's eyes. Let others say anything. My Self is pure and changeless. It is the light of all lights. It is impossible that it will ever perish. I am the embodiment of Existence, Consciousness, Bliss, and the

Witness of all. Such should be your understanding. Yet, even though this is so, we say, "How can we achieve happiness?," in such a pitiable way! People pray for God's mercy and throw themselves before God thinking that they are caught up in a big calamity.

Such a situation is not at all proper. Try to experience your Self. Do not believe you are mortal. Cast off this self-created ignorance and abide with confidence in the Self. Turn within. Do not entertain any fears. Erase the belief that external objects are true. Actually, if one inquires into one's nature ("Who am I?"), there is no one as great as you. Have Self-confidence. Make the understanding, "I am Paramatman," steady within yourself. You will not fail to cross over the ocean of this mundane existence. See only through the sight of the Self. Do not look through other people's eyes. All of your relations are ready to fool you. Nevermind the body while practicing this. One should be prepared to die with the conviction that "I am a witness of this body. Let the body stay or go, my heart rests at the feet of the Master."

Continue contemplating on this, and intuitive perception is sure to come. When one is practicing this, one may encounter many obstacles. This world is full of ignorant corpses. Life in ignorance is like death. Who is eating? For whom is all of this service? You do not know. The ignorant one serves six ghosts (greed, anger, desire, hatred, craving, and pride). If all that is done during one's life is pampering the body, one's entire life is wasted. After death (as per Hindu custom), the body and bones burn like a bundle of wood, and the hair burns like a clump of grass while onlookers weep. The dead man asks the onlookers, "Are you free from this fate? You seem to behave as I did." Even if a toilet is cleaned thoroughly, it is still a toilet. The world is full of living corpses that give no thought as to one's True Self. The ignorant ones serve only the body, and take along with them a bundle of sins and virtues. Such is the worldly existence of an ignorant person. But when one knows oneself, and leaves off the pride for the body, immediately he meets himself. Then all his actions have borne fruit. It is impossible to describe the glory of Self-Knowledge. Human life is meaningful because it is given with the purpose of achieving Self-Knowledge. When that has been achieved, life has indeed become fully meaningful. Its purpose has been served. For example, there may be nine hundred thousand stars, but it is the moon that shines the brightest. The rising of the sun and the falling of rain is all due to the one who knows Truth. There is no limit to His greatness. He is immortal and "almighty" in the truest sense.

Whatever happens, let it happen. Let whatever has to go, go. Erase all doubts. We have but a few days to live. Let us pass those days playfully with joy. Do not be too mindful of this body. A diamond is sure to shine regardless of where it is placed, whether it be in a crown placed upon the head, or around the neck, or on the ground. This Supreme Self, Paramatman, in the form of Brahman will likewise remain happy whatever the situation. This conviction should take firm root. "If the conviction of Truth is steadfast, strength can be gained on the path of Knowledge." That body which has Self-Knowledge in it, will naturally emit light (Knowledge). When there is the strong conviction, "I am the Lord who is existence, I am the Lord who pervades all," one has achieved all that needs to be achieved.

Lecture 26 – Life Fulfilled

"The One devoid of attributes has become attributeless, the meaningful has become meaningful, and after a long time, One has met oneself." (*Dasbodh* - Chapter 8, Sub-chapter 8)

One devoid of attributes recognizes his real nature which is without attributes. The real purpose of life is found. Whatever needed to be achieved is achieved. For achieving this, seekers have struggled relentlessly. Sage Vishwamitra performed austerities for sixty-thousand years but was unable to realize the Absolute Reality. Praise be to the one who attains the status of realizing Brahman. Such a person's parents also deserve to be praised because one's entire family is saved when such a one is born. What is the use of children like the hundred Kauravas described in the Mahabharata? There are many people who have studied the various sciences and have numerous degrees conferred upon them, but all of this is only for one's livelihood. Even dogs and cats can manage to feed themselves. Many living beings have come and learned the fourteen types of knowledge, and sixty-four arts, but this should all be understood to be worldly knowledge.

People are born, they pine for worldly objects, become miserable, and finally die. Only those who discover the real purpose of life, the real meaning of life, deserve praise. Such people are a beacon for future generations. After millions of years you met yourself. The curtain in the form of duality is taken away. The curtain of countless number of births vanishes at last. That sight which saw all as Oneness became divine. All is Lord Krishna. He alone, the "One Form, has all these myriad faces of all beings, and a countless number of hands, feet, etc. This is called Jnana Drishti, "the Vision of Knowledge, that sees that I reside everywhere (in all). This is also called the "Eye of Knowledge," the "Third Eye of Lord Shiva." To see everyone as part of the one Reality is the characteristic of such a Jnani. There is nothing except Consciousness. He is One. There is no duality. The jiva has gone back to its True Nature, from where it had arisen, and it now has no consciousness of being either limited or separate. One who has consciousness of the body is bound. When duality ends, there is no sin or merit. Nobody thinks that there is a problem with the saliva in our own mouth. It is not considered bad if we swallow it, because it is our own. No one calls their own saliva dirty or unhygienic. Whatever belongs to us we call good. There is no notion of sin nor virtue about what we call our own. In the same way, we are ourselves all of this creation, so why should we hold any notions of sin or virtue, or heaven or hell? No impurity can accrue to one who has understood Brahman thoroughly. All differences and dualities vanish. The Master dispels all of the six ghosts (greed, anger, desire, hatred, craving, and pride).

Lecture 27 – Be Oneness and See Oneness

"The One devoid of attributes has become attributeless, the meaningful has become meaningful, and after a long time, One has met oneself." (*Dasbodh* - Chapter 8, Sub-chapter 8)

I am always without attributes. Attributes are not my true nature. Upon realizing this, I truly become attributeless. The real purpose of life is found. I have come face to face with Myself after many years. All these days, I suffered many miseries because of having believed the outer actor to be myself. Thus I suffered bondage, believing the external world to be full of pleasures. I was like a king who took pleasure in begging. He thought that he served his own self while he actually served a stranger. He did not know that he was Paramatman, the Supreme Self, and that he should serve himself.

People worship other men because the world is materialistic. After one meets Oneself, the body is realized to be untrue. All forms in this world appear on the one Self. He is Paramatman. He is innate in all, so he does not have any idea of differentiation. The curtain of duality (objectivity) is pulled away. Once one seeks the Master's refuge, the world appears as "Soham" (I am That). But to all others it appears as "Koham"(Who am I?). The world appears the way one perceives it. One who identifies himself with Brahman sees all as Brahman. If one becomes a jiva (an individual), he finds the world as mundane. "For one who is good, the world is good." The ignorant find the world full of different entities (forms). For the realized one, it is all One. There is no duality.

Duality is due to two entities, the seer, and the seen. The disciples of the Master see everything as One. The Master gives the gift of the third eye, "The Eye of Knowledge," and duality flees away. The veil of Maya (Illusion) is removed. The state of "being" becomes undifferentiated. Truth is without any distinctions. The five elements vanish. Their influence is exorcised. The bad period of seven and a half years (considered a negative aspect of the position of Saturn in the natal chart) has passed away. All the nine planets have also gone on their own way. Mr. jiva, the ignorant one, has vanished. A layer of dirt had come over him due to the delusion, "I am the body, I am of an upper caste," etc. These ideas had deluded him, and then he realized himself as Paramatman, the Supreme Self.

This monkey (the whimsical mind) was eating fruits and flowers in the jungle (of the world). But when he met Rama (the Master), the mind became Hanuman (God's servant). He got That which was his own (the Self) due to the Master's instructions. "All is Brahman." For the one who sees Oneself, birth and death are eradicated. The one who pervades all the senses is Rama. Concentrate on Rama, the Pure Consciousness. If Rama had always known who Rama was (the Self), there would have been no need for him to seek the Sage Vasishtha's (Rama's Master) guidance. To see God in all beings is bhajan (worship of God). The one who resides in the hearts of all is God. Without the advice of a true Master, people get caught up in rituals of purity and impurity, or of turning the beads of a rosary, or chanting mantras, etc. Lord Rama's brother, Laxman, drew a line on the ground for Rama's wife Sita, and told her not to cross over that line, otherwise she would be taken away by the ten-headed demon Ravanna. The mind threw away the mountains of ignorance. The grossness of the mind vanished when the mind turned its thoughts towards Reality, and even the body became "I am That." Due to ignorance, the living being had become the gross body. By crossing over the line of ignorance, he became one with Paramatman.

Lecture 28 – Outward Signs of Self-Knowledge

"When nectar is imbibed, the body glows on the outside. What are the signs of a Saint who has acquired Self-Knowledge?" (*Dasbodh* - Chapter 8, Sub-chapter 9)

When nectar is imbibed, the body starts glowing. Similarly, what are the signs of one who is established in Self-Knowledge? The signs of identifying a saint are indicative of his attitude. The liberated one abides in the Self. "Self-existent" or "Swayam Siddha" means That which already exists without someone ever having created it. Such is the description of one's Self. The sun, moon, water, heat, light, earth, and even Brahma, Vishnu, and Shiva, are all subsequent creations.

"Swarupa" means your own Self. This is eternally present, so it is "siddha" (ever existing). When we are the Self, what objection should there be if we call ourselves "Siddha" (accomplished). So far, because of ignorance, we did not realize that we are "Siddha." Your true being is what is called "Siddha." There is no separateness or difference in that state. "Siddha" is the one who abides in the Self. When you know your own nature, all mental turmoil ceases.

In nature there are not two ideas such as capability or incapability. Capability or incapability is in the realm of Illusion (Maya). Your own good and bad ideas or thoughts give you good or bad results. God gives you nothing, nor does he do anything. Your inner sense, that is, your conscience is a very valuable testimonial. Your face reflects your inner conscience. Chitragupta (the one who records your innermost thoughts) is your Consciousness. It records everything secretly. You cannot do anything which your Consciousness does not know. The joy one feels by giving a penny to a beggar cannot be surpassed by eating something. For the benefit of the aspirant, I shall now tell you the outward signs of a Siddha (realized person). Actually, there are no specific signs. The realized one is beyond any rules or regulations. He has no worldly existence, neither happiness nor misery, neither wealth nor poverty. He takes all these as a dream. That "the worry for the mundane ceases," implies that he just stops worrying about this mundane life. Some seekers on the spiritual path go about naked, but this is only useful up to a point for destroying body-consciousness. There is nothing more to it than that. Such behavior has no direct bearing on Self-Knowledge.

The signs of an aspirant are, dedicated attention towards the expositions (of spiritual topics), and an absence of worry for the mundane life. The realized person is outwardly similar to an aspirant, yet inwardly he abides in his own Self. Nothing worries him, this is the sign of a realized one. After having overcome all doubts, just to listen, contemplate, meditate, etc. are the signs of a realized one. Outwardly and inwardly, there is complete unshakable contentment. Once this state becomes steady and the mind is directed towards one's own nature, one becomes the Self. For example, if the name of a particular village was previously not known, then once it is known, it is permanently known. Similar to this is the state when one's "Self Nature" (Swarupa) is known. Then, physical movement does not affect one's abidance in the Self. All this depends upon the inner-state, or Consciousness. Even if a brahmin were to grow a beard, can he rightly be called a Muslim?

It is enough if one knows that the inner-consciousness, the Self, is Brahman. Without knowing the Self even if one performs great acts, they will be in vain. Once the Self is known, there is no restriction on your action. The inner-state should turn into Brahman. Renunciation or detachment should take firm root in your Consciousness. Once one's Consciousness has turned towards God, one's outward appearance does not matter at all. When you are attracted towards your innate nature, the signs of a saint get rooted in you. Without this, even if you study to the best of your ability you cannot achieve that status. Therefore, abide in your "Being" or Self Nature, and if you want to study, just remember that you are already Brahman. This means you remain steady and at peace. Listening to spiritual sermons ensures this steady attitude. Realize that you are the Self and behave accordingly. Even realized ones can, upon abandonment of the Self, become bewildered. I am telling you the outward signs of a realized person who is totally unaffected by worldly joys and sorrows. To end misery or to remain blissful, listen to these ten outward signs of a realized person.

1. **Absence of anger:** One should not get angry. If someone insults you, you should take it as an insult to the body. Keep your mind (attitude) completely free of anger. To merely repress an impulse of anger (and keep quiet) is not an indication of absence of anger. Absence of anger

implies absence of any reaction to an anger-provoking stimulus. If anything happens against your mind's liking and there is a surge of anger, it indicates a habit of wanting to dictate to others. These ten signs are told for the aspirant's study. With the help of these signs, continue your study or practice, and these signs will show up in your behavior. All is untrue in this world. How then can one thing evoke anger? Even that thing is untrue. This is the way one must think. One should recognize all the causes of anger in the mind.

2. **Detachment:** Detachment is the absence of even a single desire. This leads to fearlessness. Otherwise, there is no freedom from fear for you. One should not depend on others as in the case, "If I do not get anything to eat I will die." Desire for the bliss of Self is a desire for bliss within. People who hoard millions and then go about speaking to others about the "Knowledge of Brahman," do not do good to themselves. Instead, they commit fraud. They do not know the meaning of detachment. Absence of anger gets reinforced through detachment. Absence of anger is really inner detachment. Even if one gets something, one should renounce it. Be good to those who cause you harm. To be in one's own nature is the main indication of a realized person. Everyone should be granted freedom. One should never get angry. As we are the Inner-Self, Brahman, no one can really insult us. So, one who gives us trouble, liberates us from the ego of the body. This is what we should understand. If you put this into practice, it will become your habit. One should think for oneself why anger arises. It is not difficult to bring all these ten requisites into practice. You find them difficult because you have not formed this habit up to now. Detachment means to have no desire. A person becomes miserable because of the absence of detachment. The meaning of the word Karbhari (worldly person) is that Kar means trouble, and Bhari means a lot, plenty. We must leave off our wants through discrimination. The highest fortune of a Yogi is when detachment (the complete understanding that all this is false) gets rooted in him. This Maya or Illusion is so peculiar that it gives nothing to the one who begs and gives (all) to the one who does not ask. Everyone has developed a fondness for worldly objects, but the more detached one is, the happier he becomes.

3. **Control of the senses:** This means not to be attached to the senses. With strength, anything is possible. When one becomes dependent, then one thinks of Rama (only for some gain or benefits). If there is strength, there is less fear, and it becomes easier to think of

"Knowledge." A strong man understands Knowledge better. Virtue is indicated by control of the senses.

4. **Mercy or forgiveness:** Everyone is the Self. Therefore, we must forgive those who harass us. Never harbor hatred in the mind, because the burden of the desire to take revenge festers in the mind with the result that only enemies and misery are created. Therefore, every time there is some offense, one should be ready to forgive.

5. **Compassion:** One should be kind to all. What is compassion? Not being cruel to anybody.

6. **Peace:** Maintain peace. Do not worry, and enjoy the bliss of the Self.

7. **Complaisance to others:** Without hurting anyone, if we help others, they develop love for us. If we wish that good should not come to others, then good does not come to us either. He is a good man who becomes happy when he wishes for happiness for other people. The one who acts contrary to this, is a miser.

8. **Absence of greed:** Do not be greedy. Greed is only for objects in Illusion that are untrue.

9. **Magnanimity:** This is true nobility. To desire that all should be happy, you must learn to be magnanimous from the very core of your heart.

10. **Fearlessness:** Fear creates misery. If it is possible to be rid of misery, it is the duty of the Jnani to do so.

Start putting the above traits into practice. Through this, you will enjoy the glory of Knowledge (Jnana). These are the ten external signs of Knowledge. To be one with your Self Nature, or "Being," is true happiness. He who is happy both within and without is blissful. To behave nobly means to let each one act according to his or her desire. Otherwise, one forms a habit of censuring others. One should never speak ill of others. Also, never bother yourself with petty observations about others. Do not meddle in the affairs of others. This is called charity. Do not waste your time getting involved in others' affairs. Only the one who achieves "Self-Knowledge," is a realized person. He becomes happy if he puts the above ten requisites into practice. Lord Krishna is called a liar, yet he is a God. This is because Krishna did lie, but at the same time he was always identified with the Self.

Lecture 29 – Words About the "Wordless"

"Please explain what is meant by formless, what is meant by That which is without support, and what is meant by That which is without any concept or idea." (*Dasbodh* - Chapter 9, Sub-chapter 1)

That which has no support of any kind is Brahman. What support does it have? That which exists without any support is the Thoughtless Reality. It is not seen or felt. That it is, without any objects, implies that it cannot be an object of any of the senses. Form is the object of the eyes. Smell is the object of the nose. Taste is the object of the tongue. Sound, word, etc., is the object of the ear. Touch, hot or cold sensations, etc., is the object of the skin.

All senses are the object of the mind. Mind is the viceroy of all. All objects are understood by the mind, and it is the mind that also knows all the senses. The senses know the objects. However the objects do not see the senses. A mirror is an object to the eyes, but that which is seen within the mirror is a reflection of the object in front of the mirror. Mind cannot be an object for the senses, or an object of the senses. The mind, senses, and objects are the objects of Knowledge. But Knowledge cannot be understood by or through the mind. Knowledge is an object for Vijnana. Vijnana is not an object for anything. Actually, even the power to know, or "Awareness," is absent there (as there is no "other"). Vijnana is the Ultimate Reality. It cannot be felt or imagined. Vijnana implies "That" where perception itself ceases to exist.

Parabrahman means "That" which is prior to concept, or mind, or thought, or idea. That is why it cannot be conceived of while everything else can be. Concepts cannot arise in it because there is only "one," and no "other" to conceive of. Therefore, the one who conceives is actually without any form. Reality is "unconditioned." This implies there are no conditions like Awareness, or ignorance, jiva, Shiva, etc. It is not dependent on anything (such as fasting, austerities, etc.) That it is disinterested means that there is no expectation such as, "If you meet these conditions, I shall come to you." The word Niranjan means "without any embellishment." This means that there is no necessity for mind, intellect, eyes, nose, consciousness, etc. If it would have been possible to know Parabrahman with the help of eyes or anything else, that would mean that it would be perishable. Nirantar means eternal. This means that it exists forever in knowledge as well as ignorance. It does not have qualities of any kind. There is no forgetfulness in it. Therefore, there is no Tamo Guna there. It is not necessary to remember it, therefore there is no Sattva Guna. There is no mixture of remembrance and forgetfulness in it, so there is no Rajo Guna. Nirmala means that there is no impurity of any kind in it. Nischala means that it is steady and that it always exists. Nishabda means that it is without word and that it cannot be conceived of through words. Nivritta means there are no states of mind such as Knowledge or ignorance in it. Unblemished implies that it cannot be tarnished with Knowledge or ignorance. Nameless implies that there is not a single name or form related to it, and that it is without birth. Therefore, it can never die. It exists, but it is invisible. Such is Parabrahman. It cannot be quantified. This does not mean that it is a void, it has no conceivable measure at all. It can never be decreased or increased. Alakshaya means that it is unidentifiable, which implies that there is no symbol related to it. Such is Brahman, all symbols come to an end. Whatever can be known is Maya, Illusion. Brahman can never be destroyed by anything. Nothing can make it disappear. Apar means that none can cross it or go beyond it. This means that it is all pervasive. Atarkya means that it is unimaginable and that logic fails in respect to it. Advaita, means that it is without duality. This means that you are alone, there is nothing else. You are beyond all. What pervades all, and yet remains, is Parabrahman. "Para" means beyond. One who has been initiated by a Master understands this secret.

Lecture 30 – Reality is Bodiless

"Whatever is visible ultimately gets destroyed, but the True Nature of the Self exists eternally." (*Dasbodh* - Chapter 9, Sub-chapter 2)

Whatever is seen or felt ultimately gets destroyed. Because we conceive, or imagine, all is visible. However, whatever exists is only memory. At night, when memory is held in abeyance, everything is erased. Dates, or days, are not absolute. At night, as soon as we forget ourselves, everything disappears. Sleep is a state where the world is forgotten. If one is worried about something, he will suffer from insomnia. The Self never disappears. All that comes from remembrance and disappears through forgetfulness is not true. Concepts, or to conceive, implies remembrance. The Self exists regardless of the existence of concepts. The Self is the essence, it is eternal. It is true. It is factual. There is no difference between you and the Self. God's own nature, is God's own "Being."

The Self is given many names in order to facilitate understanding. In reality, however, it has no name. It is present within and without. One who gets carried away by worldly affairs does not understand it. We ourselves are That, yet we do not understand it. The scriptures say that, "This God is within all," so people try to see Him within. Trying to see in this way, one feels only darkness all around because there is no sunlight within us. The scriptures say that whatever is visible is perishable. One's own Self cannot be perceived. One who does not have a realized Master sees only that which is visible. One should gain a proper understanding of one's own Self through the Master's teachings. Everything is seen in one's own Self, only by virtue of the Self.

Your form is like space. It is all-pervading. It cannot be grasped. The ego only proliferates when one tries to create divisions in the divine Self, which is in fact completely indivisible. The ego produces all distortions, such as, "I am a man, I am a woman, I am rich, I am poor, I am happy, I am miserable." The feeling of "I Am" has its source in one's own Self, but this subtle Illusion makes one feel that one is the body. Illusion has its beginning there. If I call myself "I" then there is no Illusion. "I am that 'I.' I am That." Maya is ignorance, delusion. You are the source of "OM." OM indicates Brahman. Maruti (Hanuman) is the mind. One who functions behind the mind is Rama, the Self.

I will now tell you the sign of ego. To say, "I am the body," is bondage. To say, "I am not the body," is liberation. "I" and "mine" means bondage, and "This is not mine. I am not," is liberation" (From *Sadachara* of Adi Shankaracharya)

Ego, is the Hari (or God) who resides inside the four bodies. In the state of wakefulness, all that is seen through the gross body vanishes when the "gross body" disappears. Once the gross body disappears, there is no experience for Him. In Hindu scriptures, there are four bodies, or bodies of the individual being, and four bodies of the universe. The first body of man is called "gross body," the second is the "subtle body," (subtle means mind, intellect, senses, etc.), the third is the "causal body," and the "great-causal" is the fourth body. The four bodies of the universe are called Virata or huge, Hiranyagarbha or golden womb, Avyakruta or ignorance, and Moola Prakriti or Knowledge. "Gross" and "Virata" correspond to each other, etc.

In the *Deepa Ratnakara*, it is said that the disciple prayed to his Master. "Tell me about that Knowledge by which a man becomes Parabrahman (the Absolute Reality)." The Master said, "If you come with me, I shall make you Parabrahman." (I shall take you to that point beyond Knowledge.) You climb the four mountains (the four bodies), or what are also called the seven heavens. The gross body is the state of wakefulness. You discard that body and that state because you are not the body. If you consider the body as yourself, then you are bound. The body is mortal. If you call the body as your own, then who are you? Know your Self. In the gross body, every organ has its own name. None of that is you. The intellect is Brahma (the Creator). That this body is created by Brahma implies that it is created by the intellect. So Brahma is the creator. So let the intellect remain with Brahma.

Next comes the subtle body. The consciousness, mind, intellect, eyes, ears, etc., are not you. They are yours. Possessiveness is the feeling that they belong to me. From the consciousness means from Vishnu. They belong to Lord Vishnu. Give them back to Lord Vishnu. The state of the subtle is the dream state. The temptation of worldly objects brings your downfall. If you leave this mundane world, there is nothingness. Yet something remains. That is the void, which is ignorance, or the causal body. The state of the causal body is sleep. There all is destroyed. Its deity is Rudra. It is all dark there. Even though Shiva is the embodiment of Knowledge, Rudra is the aspect of ignorance (knowledge and ignorance or Shiva and Rudra are not separate, but co-existent opposite aspects like two sides of one coin). Rudra is Shiva invaded by the night. To dispel Rudra, you have to awaken yourself and remove ignorance. Return this ignorance that, "There is nothing," to Rudra. This is the third mountainous step of deep-sleep, which is now left behind.

Now, there remains nothing. Only He who has transcended the three bodies remains. This is Awareness or Consciousness. In other words, "I" remains. Give up this "I" as well. "I" cannot be given up. He is always there in the three states described above. "I" is the essence of Existence, Consciousness and Bliss (Sat-Chit-Ananda). In the state of wakefulness, there is both happiness and misery, as this state is the state of duality. But in the state of sleep, there is pure joy (bliss). Thus, bliss is present only in the causal body.

The great-causal body is called Shiva. It is also called Brahman. When Shivaratri (night of Shiva) finishes and Shivadini (day of Shiva) begins, what is implied is that one has discovered one's true Self. In the great-causal body, you realize that "I am Shiva" (God as Pure Knowledge). The jiva who is an ignorant being is present in the three bodies, therefore those who are Jnanis say, "I am Knowledge," which means, "I am He," or "I am That," and "I am the one who makes all the three bodies work." The one who practices Aham Brahmasmi (I am Brahman) diligently gets such an experience. One who says that he is the body, has the desire for the body while dying, therefore, he takes birth again. The mind is the cause of both bondage and liberation. One does not become the body if this desire for embodiment is hazy. The desire has to be very strong.

The subtle body made of Rajoguna faces God on the one side, and the demon (ignorance), on the other. Say "Na Aham" (I am not) at least once. Then you will be liberated. This has been misunderstood as "chant the name" (Naam), or chant "Rama." Keshava is who is present in this "Shava" (dead body). This "I Am" is the fourth body. Go beyond this body as well. This subtle ego or "I Am" which is the same as God is also destined to perish. Beyond this "I Am" is Parabrahman, where there is neither bondage nor liberation. Sadashiva (Absolute Reality) has neither bondage nor liberation.

When you cross the four mountainous states (four bodies) you are Parabrahman. To say, "I am Knowledge" is also a state of mind. Without saying anything or remembering anything, you exist. In order that you understand the Self properly, you were told to say, "I am Knowledge." To say "I am Brahman" is also ultimately egoistic. Therefore give it up. "I am jiva," "I am Brahman," "I am a Jnani," is all delusion. Parabrahman is neither Knowledge nor ignorance. It is beyond both. I shall tell you something more to make you even more aware of this ego. The night which has befallen Shiva is this ego. "I" or ego has been created from ignorance. (One should awaken from both Knowledge and ignorance). To say, "I am of the nature of knowledge, I am Consciousness," is egoism. "I am Brahman" is also egoism. True aspirants understand this ego. There is no need to say, "I am Brahman." The moment one says it he is separated from the Self, as he has created duality. Instead of saying "I am Brahman" in words, imbibe it's meaning. Then you abide in Parabrahman. When one abides in the Self, without duality, it is called "Experience."

All actions and rituals are meaningless unless one gets Self-Knowledge. The knowledge "I Am That" is Self-realization. The name and form of an object are not the object itself. For example, a wall which is really nothing but bricks and clay, is still called a wall. All of the objects, which are not our Self, are untrue. They are mere words. "Experience" means "I am That," and "That" is Brahman." To understand or realize "That," is the experience.

When desire is overcome, only the Self remains. Then, there is no need to say, "I am Brahman." For example, the eyes will see only if there is something to be seen, and if there is nothing to be seen, the eyes will still exist. Similarly, Brahman exists even if it is not seen. This Self is ever-existent, without attachment, and without either Knowledge or ignorance. This science has to be experienced by oneself. Leave off talk and try to gain experience.

Vedanta means direct proof, or the facts as they really are. They are to be known or read only with direct experience. You have to experience "That" yourself. To know what is indicated is to know it through experience. "Indicated" implies to give up the expression of words. Experience the Self according to what the Master has told you, by thinking of the four "Great Statements" (Mahavakyas): "I am Brahman" (Aham Brahmasmi), "You are That" (Tat Tvam Asi), "All this is Brahman" (Sarvam Khalu Idam Brahman), and "Supreme Knowledge is Brahman" (Pradyanam Brahman). The Master explains these tenets for the disciple to gain the ultimate understanding.

Analysis of the basic principles implies giving deep thought to the gross and the subtle bodies and discarding them. One should use the correct method to clearly understand and realize Brahman. A man who goes to see God eventually becomes God himself. No one can go to heaven by means of the gross body. The Self is beyond the four bodies and the three Gunas. Analyze within yourself without any need for talk. Maintain silence. Understand what the scriptures cannot say and keep silent. All words become silent before the Self. What is Knowledge? It is that which is "not." What is ignorance? It is that which does not exist. It is not a ghost. It is not a demon. All words are in the negative. Brahman is really "nothing" (it exists only in concepts). That which remains, without thought, is Parabrahman. Where the scriptures turn back saying, "not this, not this" that is Parabrahman. If after "experience," one still tries to infer it, he is obstinate.

Lecture 31 – True Renunciation

"Regardless of whether or not birth is imagined for the attributeless, or its existence is denied, it is He himself who denies or takes birth." (*Dasbodh* Chapter 9, Sub-chapter 3)

Prakriti means the three bodies, the perishable. Purusha, the Self, is imperishable. Where nothing remains how can "I" remain? "I" also disappears. The Self remains after "killing" death itself. There is no objection at all if you first renounce and then take part in worldly existence. Merely wearing monastic robes and carrying a begging bowl is not renunciation. Renunciation of all the bodies is true renunciation.

Lecture 32 – Like Reflects Like

"In the world there are so many people. Someone is powerful, and someone happens to be weak. One is very clean, and the other is dirty. What is the reason for this?" (*Dasbodh* - Chapter 9, Sub-chapter 4)

The reason that one is poor, and the other is rich, is because of the three gunas; Sattva, Rajas, and Tamas. If we are happy, our face reflects joy. Therefore, it depends on one's qualities and the mind. If we take up good qualities we become happy. Live with an open and clear mind without retaining irrelevant thoughts. If anyone talks ill of you, do not hear it. It is the nature of the jiva, the individual, to find fault with others. If you have a perverted outlook then only bad will accumulate around you. Saints (sadhus) are pure minded. We go to them after leaving behind what is impure or bad in us, thus they are surrounded by good.

The Self gives good results to those who are good, and gives bad results to those who are bad. This can be seen. The Self is all-pervading. The Self is of the nature of Parabrahman (Absolute Reality). The jiva (gross body) is because of the desire to be. People often have the desire, "Let me be happy. It does not matter even if all the others die." Negative desires such as these will yield only negative results. As is the desire, so is the result. If we are good then the world is certainly good. Otherwise it is the opposite.

Lecture 33 – Knowledge is the Primal Illusion

"The structure of the universe is like that of man. This is not just imagination, but if we try to find out the truth, there are so many opinions that people don't get the experience and become confused." (*Dasbodh* - Chapter 9, Sub-chapter 5)

The questioner asked, "Is that which is in the universe (macrocosm) the same as that which is in man (microcosm)?" The macrocosm is nothing but our own concepts and thoughts which are visualized externally. Understanding this thoroughly is called Vijnana, or direct and correct Supreme Knowledge.

Just as the sky is without shape, Brahman is also without shape. Just as there is air in the sky, Consciousness exist in Brahman. Our natural "Being" contains this Awareness, which is also known as Moolamaya, the original Illusion, in much the same way as there is air or wind in the sky. Like the sky, our original nature remains ever the same. There is no distortion in the sky even if darkness or light pervade it. The Pure Consciousness (Awareness) that arises in Being is called the "Shuddha Sattva Guna." This awareness is also called the "Mahakarana Deha" or the great-causal body. This is the all-knowing, all-witnessing state.

The arising of "Shuddha Sattva," or Pure Consciousness, was followed by the simultaneous arising of the three attributes (gunas) of Maya; Sattva, Rajas and Tamas. Once awareness, or remembrance, arises, forgetfulness must also arise. The juxtaposition of remembrance and forgetfulness is called Maya (Illusion). This means that which is known and that which is unknown are both Maya. Remaining silent is Brahman, the Reality. Discard the states of what is and what is not. The visible is something you can talk about, or that which is seen. Give up all this. Observing silence is the best. Where even Awareness cannot reach, that alone is Parabrahman, the Absolute Reality. By giving up "I know, and I know not," one attains the natural state. In this state if the "I" arises, the natural state vanishes. No thoughts of country, time, objects, nor the thoughts of small or big exist in the natural state. When the natural state subsides and Awareness arises, it is known as "vikshepa," which means arousal from the natural state. The natural state is thus attained upon "laya" (dissolution) of vikshepa (arousal).

In the scriptures this is known as Purusha/Prakriti. Prakriti is the objectiveness, or power (Shakti). Awareness, or Consciousness, is called Purusha. In this Moolamaya (Primordial Illusion) are contained the impulse of "I Am," and the five elements, and the three gunas or attributes. Forgetfulness and remembrance are always in juxtaposition with each other. Space, where there arose an impulse or movement (which is the characteristic of wind), along with the five elements and the three attributes in a subtle form, forms the Moolamaya (or Vidyamaya, Illusion of Knowledge). When these attributes are in equal proportion it is a state of perfect balance. But when the Moolamaya (Primordial Illusion) becomes manifest, (when this balance is disturbed), it is known as Gunakshobhini, the stirring or arousal of the gunas. When Awareness looks externally (towards objects), one forgets oneself completely and that is ignorance. When one starts knowing oneself, one is God, Ishwara. When one starts knowing the outside, one becomes Vishnu (the Inner-Self) and then later the elements arise (space, wind, etc.).

In the Moolamaya (Primordial Illusion), one is Shiva, and when one looks outside towards the world, one is a jiva, the individual. When one makes a decision, one is the intellect. When one starts thinking "something like that exists," one becomes the mind. Pure Awareness is Shiva, but when one starts looking at the individual consciousness, one is a jiva. It is the jiva who moves around in the three worlds. The more powerfully one looks outside (lending reality to the external world), the more forcibly and completely one forgets oneself. All so-called worldly wisdom is foolishness. Forgetting one's own nature is called tamoguna, ignorance. When a bag containing gas is opened, the entire gas is diffused, in the same way the latent gunas or attributes spread outward when they are excited or disturbed. As is your conviction ("I am the body," or "I am the Self"), so will be your experience. Being bound by a concept means that one takes as truth all that exists in the conceptual world, and the world expands limitlessly if one proceeds in such direction. If you give it up as untrue, then all, is of course, untrue. Whatever is "practical" or worldly is false. The seer is Brahman, and all that is visible or seen is Maya, Illusion. Purifying one's own mind is Knowledge. As are the thoughts, so is the result. Moolamaya is Knowledge. Brahman is like space, and Moolamaya (Primordial Illusion) is like wind. Just as wind can be felt, but cannot be seen, Gunakshobhini Maya is experienced when the gunas are excited or disturbed. It is the way of the world to forget the Self and focus on the external world. To know the world is ignorance.

Moolamaya (Primordial Illusion) is of the nature of wind. When the three attributes manifest themselves, it (Maya) is called Gunakshobhini. Maya's nature is such that it tries to know what lies ahead and forgets what remains behind. Forgetfulness and Awareness (remembrance) go hand-in-hand. When the Self is forgotten, space arises. Arising of space means that even your own Self is not felt. This means there is nothing, the void. Why is it seen? Because we are not in our own Self. Because nothing is felt, there is no time, no fixed hour, no place. Nothing is perceived in Brahman. This implies that there are no objects. When perception arose, concepts of space, time, and objects were created. In the beginning of creation, three things were created; (1) Space, (2) Time, and (3) Objects. And then the world came into being. When did it appear? When you saw it. In reality, there is nothing.

Space is desire, or a component of the eye. Then from that "word" (AUM) came knowledge. The *Vedas* and scriptures (*Shastras*) were founded on that word. But the *Vedas* and scriptures are all worldly knowledge. It is only the end of *Vedas* (Vedanta) that gives us Direct Knowledge. The end of knowledge is called Vedanta. Veda means misery. When one gets knowledge, he becomes miserable. In deep-sleep, there is no awareness of anything so there is no misery either. There is no differentiation in deep-sleep. How can there be differentiation in Brahman. One who is worldly wise is less happy than the one who is not.

Vedanta is like a book that puts an end to unhappiness. The word (AUM) arose from the Inner-Self. So the *Vedas* were created by Vishnu. The four kinds of speech (Para, Pashyanti, Madhyama, Vaikhari) are the four hands of Vishnu. Knowledge can be acquired or imparted by all the four kinds of speech. How was anything about creation written in the *Vedas*? When there was no matter, on what basis were the *Vedas* written? Matruka means vowels and alphabets. As soon as a child is born, it starts screaming, "Aa" or "Aai" (which means mother in Marathi). Mother is the same as Maya (Illusion). She makes the child stay in this world.

The five elements are the original elements that already exist. When the Self is forgotten, the three gunas (attributes) come into being. All these changes or distortions are just like air bubbles. In the original impulse of "I" the three gunas and five elements exist in a subtle form. If there is no impulse there is no Knowledge in the Absolute. There is no movement, so accordingly there is neither ignorance nor Knowledge. For the purpose of understanding, in the scriptures it has been stated that the three attributes and five elements were created one after the other but the faculty of knowing and the three attributes and the five elements are present simultaneously in that impulse. In the Hindu tradition when a woman gets married she gets the blessing, "Ashta putra saubhagyavati bhava," "May you be prosperous and blessed with eight sons." Because Maya produced eight sons (five elements and three attributes) she prospered, or became manifest. The gross elements were produced from each other. What came first in this world, the seed or the tree? The tree is potentially present(in a subtle form) in a seed. A man's sperm is a blueprint of the man himself. These five elements and three gunas proliferated everywhere, therefore you see them as distinct, saying only the earth has smell, only water has taste, etc. They became distinct due to tamoguna (ignorance). They got separated by being assigned to the five sense objects. These five elements are compounded in every being. If pungent, sour, sweet and salty foods are mixed and eaten, the mixture will taste like mud. The seven seas, of seven types of taste arise from the earth. There is only one earth, but different types of grain can be reaped here and their taste is different in each case. Every being is the product of myriad permutations and combinations of the three gunas. However, their proportion differs in each and every being.

In Moolamaya (Primal Illusion) there is the faculty of Knowledge, where is this faculty in the senses? Awareness or Consciousness means movement. Since the Inner-Self is pure, there this faculty of Knowledge can be observed. It is not so in other places. But the faculty of Knowledge is of course there in subtle form. The gross form of impulse is wind. Therefore Awareness is present in the wind. Although it may not be always perceived by everyone, Awareness is ever-existent. One who has a discriminating intellect can experience this. The Primordial Illusion is subtle, while the Illusion which excites the attributes is manifest and gross. Awareness exists in sleep, but it is not noticed. The air in a room is invisible, but it still exists. The fire in wood cannot be observed, but it exists in potential form. In deep-sleep you experience your existence beyond doubt and objects.

Lecture 34 – Drink the Nectar of Soham

"The listener said, First there is the gross body. Then come the five aspects of the inner-mind. It is because of the gross body that discrimination is possible." (*Dasbodh* - Chapter 9, Sub-chapter 7)

The listener asked, "Initially, there was the gross body. Then came the five aspects of the inner-mind such as mind, intellect, etc. I feel such a sequential manifestation is the rule of the process of creation. But you tell us that first there was Brahman, Moolamaya (the Primal Illusion) then came Guna Maya (Illusion with attributes), then came the five aspects of the inner-mind, etc."

In the beginning, the owner needs to be present, then he builds a house and lives in it. Thus, the being is created first, and then the house he lives in. First there is "Being," or Awareness, then comes the Inner-Self, the body, etc. The subtle body appears first, then later the gross appears, and finally, the world appears. This is the way a realized person understands the process of creation. A realized person knows that the Self is first, whereas an ignorant person believes that the world comes first. In a dream, one leaves this body and takes up another body. In this same manner, countless bodies are taken by the Self. If you say, the world comes first, then there is no end to the diversity of the process.

The gross body is in this gross world, but the subtle body is present since time immemorial. Bodies do change, but "we" do not change. The mind and the intellect have always existed. An illustration is provided in the Yoga Vasishtha. When a woman's husband passed away, she wailed and cried and would not permit anyone to remove the corpse. Her maid servant then informed her that God helps in times of such adversity and one should therefore try to attain Him. Accordingly, she asked the woman to worship a particular goddess. Her ceaseless worship resulted in a dream of the Self, which appeared before her in the form of the goddess. As one conceives, so does one see (the form). In the hearts of all, there is the same impulse of Awareness. It is this conviction that one should constantly hold in one's heart. Finally, the woman became Brahman.

This jiva (the individual) is my own concept, said Lord Krishna. There is no rebirth for the one who understands that the world is created from one's own Self. In the world of "Soham" (I Am That) lives Narayana. This means that the drink of "Soham" is the nectar by which birth and death are eliminated. That one should drink this nectar implies that one should continuously practice the truth of "I am that which never dies."

"Drink, drink until you fall down drunk. When you rise, again drink some more. Drink so much that you are never born again." (Take in the Master's teachings and analyze ceaselessly. Keep analyzing until ultimately thinking itself ceases and you go beyond all thought (Thoughtless Reality). The meaning of the above statement is that if one dies knowing that one is not this body and is thus reborn as Knowledge, and yet "drinks again," one transcends even Knowledge (I Am Brahman), and there is no rebirth.

Narada is the mind which roams around in the three bodies and finally merges in Parabrahman (Absolute Reality). You are the Absolute Reality. It is necessary to imprint this knowledge in you with the aid of a million devices (arguments). AtmaRama lost his wife Sita (or peace) to the ten-headed Ravanna (the ten senses). Rama then killed Ravanna and brought Sita back. This Knowledge brings one back to one's original abode (Ayodhya). Ayodhya is the place where there is no war ("yudha" means war). One is brought back to this original holy place. Rama thus returns to his own kingdom after handing over Ravanna's kingdom to his younger brother, Vibheeshana.

Lecture 35 – Self-Knowledge is Liberation

"The Jnani is liberated due to Knowledge, but how does one who is bound take birth? At the time of death, what is it which belongs to the bound one that takes birth?" (*Dasbodh* - Chapter 9, Sub-chapter 8)

The questioner asked, "Who gives birth to whom (who creates whom?), and what is this bother of Brahmadeva (the Creator, the God who has created the world according to Hindu mythology)? No one has seen Brahmadeva creating the world. And neither has anyone seen Lord Vishnu guarding or looking after it, nor Lord Rudra (Shiva) destroying it. Who creates Brahma? Who looks after Vishnu, and who destroys Rudra? How is desire born? Desire is remembrance, or memory. Desires are modifications of the mind. The mind means remembrance. At the time of death, this memory disappears, but there is no forgetfulness either. Where and how can desire survive? There is no birth. There is no sin and no virtue. The man who is dead is not reborn again, said the listener.

When the mind dies, the breath leaves the body, then remembrance or desire goes along with the breath (prana) and is later reborn. The pitcher breaks, but the clay still exists. In the same way, if the mind says, "I am the body," it gets a body, but if it says "I am the Self," it becomes one with the Self. All cannot cross the river, only the swimmers can go across. Similarly, only a realized person can cross the river of mundane existence. He knows that, "I am not the gross, subtle, or causal body, etc.," and through this realization he knows his own Self. The one who understands that he is the Self, different from the four bodies, is free. The reason that you have taken birth is due to ignorance. When this ignorance disappears, birth and death also disappear. All others will experience birth and death. Because of this, the *Vedas*, scriptures (*Shastras*), mythological books (*Puranas*), Knowledge (Jnana), etc. have survived as traditions. They declare that the cause of birth is sin and to be free from birth is virtue. Ignorance is sin, and Self-Knowledge is virtue.

To live in the mother's womb is a term in hell, in that there is no place to escape. For nine months, the excrement and urine of the fetus is linked to it's mouth and nose. This is what is meant by a term in hell. When the desires and prana (breath) flow out of the body, they have to settle somewhere. They cannot remain without a body. There is an intense desire to acquire a body and therefore one acquires a body. If one gives up love for the body and adopts love of the Self, one gets rid of the body. It is this desire which makes one take on an endless number of births. In the human birth, one is aware of the knowledge "I Am," therefore, human birth is considered to be the highest or most evolved. There is no greater bondage for any creature other than a human being. And there is no meaner species than the human anywhere. Further, there is no creature who worries and frets like a human being. But despite all this, the human being is the pinnacle of creation. This is because only the human being has self-awareness and therefore the power to discriminate between the "real" and "unreal."

If this discrimination is not practiced to attain Knowledge, it brings about downfall. Failure to gain Self-Knowledge is what is considered the greatest sin. The realized ones wrote the *Vedas*, scriptures, etc. If you claim they are wrong, how can you guarantee that only you are right? The realized have said that the Self is not bound. The one who has Self-Knowledge sees all this world appearance as false. The one who has no Knowledge is maddened by the world and goes about taking everything to be true. An ignorant one binds himself with his own concepts. As soon as you abandon the pride of the body, you are free. Go on and continue your worldly duties, but with the firm conviction that you are the Self. It is true that Vijnana (Supreme Knowledge) is like ignorance, but ignorance is not Vijnana. Really there is no bondage. Because of ignorance, it is believed that there is bondage. When ignorance vanishes due to Self-Knowledge, bondage also vanishes.

Instead of finding a method to achieve real Knowledge, some people unnecessarily go on pilgrimages, others practice yoga, etc. In fact, there is no bondage. But still all these pursuits have driven people crazy. A realized person will say one should not go after all this. One who discriminates between "nitya" and "anitya," the permanent and impermanent, will say that those who are bound will be reborn. Give up everything and say just once that all this (Illusion) is untrue. This world has become divided because of the delusion of Maya, however, it is all pervaded by Brahman. When one starts searching for a needle, one forgets the house. When one searches for a pair of shoes in the temple, one forgets God. In the same way, one who pays attention to this world forgets one's own Self. If one becomes aware of Brahman (the Self), the world disappears. This world is like a small grain of sand in Brahman. Whatever uneasiness or conflict you experience will make you forget Brahman. Give up unnecessary conflicts and pay total attention to Brahman, then you are nothing but Brahman.

Lecture 36 – Brahman is Unaffected by Maya

"Brahman (Self) cannot be pushed away. Brahman cannot be collected. Brahman cannot be put aside. It is ever present in it's place." (*Dasbodh* Chapter 9, Sub-chapter 9)

Truth cannot be avoided. It cannot be distorted or changed in any way. Such is Parabrahman (Absolute Reality). Opposite to this, Maya (Illusion) is that which can be manipulated or changed. Both entities (Brahman and Maya) are present. Hence, you have to find them out for yourself. Try to realize that all external objects can be moved or pushed. The earth both rotates and revolves. Wind, fire, and water, are also movable. The sky (space) however, cannot be pushed even if one tries to. However, if the eyes are closed, even the sky disappears. Sky is the mother of all objects. All objects (the manifest world) are untrue. There is no object in this world that does not disappear if one tries to ignore it's existence. Now, look within. The gross body disappears, and mind is merely thoughts and speech.

If one keeps quiet (if the mind is at rest), dreams, doubts, intellect, thoughts, etc. disappear. Then, what remains, is nothing. This "nothing" can also be given up, but the one who gives it up remains. "I" am the one who transcends everything. So, "I" remain as a witness. Finally, leave even this "I." Now there remains just Truth, which is beyond knowledge and ignorance. One who has forgotten all still exists. "One who comes shall go, whether he is a king, a poor man, or a beggar." One who renounces everything is no longer in the thrall of change. This is to be understood as Brahman (Self). Everything is in Brahman and Brahman is in everything.

If there is bread in the mouth, then a certain amount of space is occupied in the mouth by the bread. However, if two hundred camels are seen in the mirror, the weight of the mirror will not change as the camels seen in the mirror are merely a reflection. Similarly, although the phenomenal world is in Brahman, it does not affect or distort Brahman in any way. Therefore, once you abide in your own Self, all these external objects disappear. All of this is Maya, mere delusion. The Self remains untainted by Maya. One's birth acquires true meaning only when one realizes the Self. From the Self have arisen intellect, knowledge, ignorance etc. Therefore, "you" are the precursor of all. Lord Brahma, Vishnu, and Mahesh (Shiva) owe their existence to you. During sleep, all these disappear, but you still exist.

Lecture 37 – You Are That

"How does one worship the one devoid of attributes? By becoming one-pointed and without attributes oneself. Blessed is the one who achieves this Oneness. (*Dasbodh* Chapter 9, Sub-chapter 10)

A brahmin is mindful of the caste of a person, but a fly does not discriminate like this. Just because a fly does not discriminate between feces and sweets, it does not mean that it is more knowledgeable than the brahmin. You must know what you really are. One who does not know the Inner-Self, may do a lot, but it will all be in vain. One who has not known the Self destroys himself. One who devotes himself to the Self ultimately becomes the Self. If this body is provided for, until it's death, then another body is ready for the next birth. All the four bodies are untrue. Be aware of these and contemplate on the Self. Then you become Nirguna Atman, the Attributeless Self.

You have to become one with the Self. This means you should worship the Self by becoming the Self. Renunciation does not simply mean abandonment of worldly life. Who are you? Know this. One who knows oneself becomes the Self. If lust, anger, temptation, etc., arise, let them arise. They will eventually subside. How do they affect you? Know that you are quite different from all these. Knowing that, "I am beyond knowledge and ignorance, different from all," remain steady, at peace like a king. Know that God, your Self, is without shape, without attribute. Then you become free. Nobody can worship Nirguna (the attributeless) by remaining a separate entity. You have to become one with Nirguna. Being "That" is worshipping Him. The devotee has the right to worship God. This means you have to become God and then worship Him. Bhakta (devotee) means Oneness, to become one with Him. To become Lord Shiva is his worship. To be natural, as you are, is your true Self. Such a state is called the "mindless state" (unmani). Even if one is accustomed to running a long distance, he has to eventually stop. That state which is without any activity is God. To know this is Knowledge. Thus, nothing is required to be done to achieve Him. This state is also called "Kevalam" (Absolute) or "Jnanamurti" (the embodiment of Knowledge). You are "That" from the beginning, but you do not realize it. If you take the body as yourself, if you think that "I am the body," you become a jiva. To think "I am the Self," is being Shiva.

In fact, there is neither jiva nor Shiva. Jiva is ignorance and Shiva is Knowledge. You are Parabrahman (Absolute Reality) when you realize that both are false. The devotee is a concept, and Shiva is also a concept. When the difference between jiva and the Self ends, Absolute Reality is there. The same "you," on knowing "You Are That" is truly blessed. One who says "I Am," is the Self. Until now you were calling this body of flesh and bones as yourself. This was a mistake.

"One who does not realize the subtle Brahman, is no brahmin, even if he is a brahmin by caste."

To consider the gross as "I" is delusion. The body itself is delusion, so accordingly, all actions done through it are delusion. Delusion will only increase through attachment to the body. Knowledge is necessary to wash away this delusion.

What we light is a "diva" (lamp), and the sun is "Divakara" (one who lights up the whole world). The one who is not visible either by the lamp or the sun is God. He knows all, that is why He is the greatest of all. Can anyone say what He is like? He who is within is the true Lord, and no deceit is possible in His presence. To achieve what is not, requires some method, but God is always present. No effort is necessary to achieve Him. To recognize God is the ultimate aim in life. He has no shape, color or form. Although He is different from all the colors, He is the one who knows them all, that is why He is called "RangaNath" (Lord of Color; "Ranga" is color and "Nath" is Lord). The most profound understanding is that I am beyond sound, space and time, I am the Self. Why should one need to take up some method or practice when one is always a Siddha (realized)? You are already That which you seek through various methods. One who knows this becomes fearless. All the scriptures, and Lord Krishna say "You Are That." In Hindu worship we offer only a small piece of thread to God in the household temple in place of cloth, or we offer only a spoonful of water for His bath. This type of worship will not do for the Self. "You" need a to have a proper bath and a proper garment to wear. Understand the Self as that which is without quality, and without shape. The Self is there as the Self, and the body remains due to body-consciousness. This body-consciousness is our illusory thought (that the body, mind, intellect etc., together is myself). "I" does not exist. You are Brahman beyond knowledge and ignorance. There is no reason to try to deduce it with logic. When it is confirmed that we are Brahman, then there is no place for doubt. (One who is "Shanka-Rahita," is "Shankar." "Shanka" is doubt and "rahita" means without). The Self should be as obvious as the thumb of your hand. There is only one Truth. The body, mind, etc., all exist in "That" (Brahman). When the stomach is full, is there any point in cooking? When the Truth is self-evident, there is no need to practice anything. If anyone thinks of some method (for understanding It), it implies that he still has some room for doubt. "What shall I do, where shall I go?" There is nothing to be done, nowhere to go. One who was trying some method to achieve realization has taken for granted "I am the body," and now he has become God. After becoming a king, why should one live as a beggar? All methods should cease once it is understood that "I am Brahman."

That which was to be achieved through (different) methods has been achieved. After becoming "That," where is the necessity of rules, regulations and routine? The body is made of five elements. Bones, flesh, skin, nerves, and hair all are created out of earth. Jiva is none other than Brahman. The body is like an actor on a stage who changes his costume for every play. When one gets "real" Knowledge, he has no birth, and he abides in his own Self. One which eternally exists will never disappear, and that which does not exist will never appear. The body is made up of five elements, but the Self is Brahman. The jiva is a unit of Brahman. One needlessly feels that God is separate. However, with discrimination one realizes that there is no "I" or "you." There is nothing.

Lecture 38 – Know the Self

"If one looks casually, the ego seems to exist, but upon careful examination, it becomes evident that there is nothing at all. When all the elements are dissolved, one into another, only the steady Self remains." (*Dasbodh* - Chapter 9, Sub-chapter 10)

When the elements dissolve, only Knowledge remains. What is untrue is Maya, Illusion. If one tries to search for Maya, Atman, and jiva, then the world calls him a saint. It is the way of the world to know others, but to not know oneself. "You have become learned, and you expound the *Puranas* (mythological books), yet, you do not know who you are." After careful thought, nothing was left. Having forgotten the senses, etc., only "I" remained. What does it mean when it is said, "Sweep the house and then sit"? It means that knowing this body to be a compound of the five elements, and thus analyzing it, what remained was the "One" who always exists. The Self resides in the heart. Once you know Him, everything is over. "Those who know the Self know Me with very little effort and those who do not know the Self, cannot know Me even with great effort." This shows that knowing Him is effortless. Lord Krishna told Arjuna, "Why should one beg after he becomes a king?" We are that which the *Vedas*, *Shastras*, *Puranas*, and yogis struggle to realize. When we become the Self, what else remains to be known? Does a holy place go for pilgrimage? Just as God meditating on God is illogical, the Self cannot meditate on itself. If the aspirant is asked to engage in any practice or method, it is like asking water to take a bath.

Lecture 39 – The Inner-Mind of All is One

"The aspirant asked, "Is the inner-mind of all one, or is it separate?" Everyone must hear the answer to this must be comprehensively explained." (*Dasbodh* - Chapter 10, Sub-chapter 1)

The aspirant asked, "The scriptures say that everyone's inner-mind (antahkarana) is one. Is this true or false? "Inner-mind" means the knowledge, or awareness. The snake "knows," and rushes to bite a man, and the man also "knows," so he runs away. If someone comes to kill it, the snake runs away. The knowing faculty is similar in both creatures. So for both, the inner-mind is the same. Even if water is poured in a hundred vessels, the water is the same. This is a known fact. The knowing Self is the same in all. The senses such as hearing, smell, etc., are the same in all (the faculty of knowing through the specific sense organs is common to all).

Likes and dislikes may be dependent on the individual, but the inner-mind is the same. All beings knowingly eat, knowingly fear, hide, and experience this phenomenal existence. Awareness is the same in all creatures, whether big or small. There is not a single being that exists without awareness (the sense of being conscious). The Inner-Self sustains all. Thus in Hindu mythology, Lord Vishnu (who symbolizes the Inner-Self) is the protector of all creatures.

The ignorant being, or one without awareness, perishes. Rudra (the destructive aspect of Shiva in Hindu mythology) is the destroyer. Because the correct remedy is not found, death occurs. Those who put it down as fate are absolute fools. If you do not eat, you will die. This is a self-evident fact. If you get tired of eating the same food, and eat only a small quantity, the growth of the body will be stunted. If you know the correct remedy, you can avoid a hundred deaths. Not thinking of the correct remedy is ignorance. This is why it is said that ignorance causes death. With knowledge, one has a clear idea of what to do, and the work is well accomplished, whereas ignorance only causes destruction. You do not die of thirst because you know that you should drink water when you are thirsty. Otherwise, you would have died. As soon as knowledge ends, death must come. Thus in mythology there is a dispute between Vishnu and Rudra.

Creation is because of the rajoguna (mixture of knowledge and ignorance) One becomes miserable if one does not know the Self. All worldly affairs are managed with the intellect. This is what is meant by saying Lord Brahma is the creator. This is how Brahma, Vishnu and Shiva reside in the body. They all appear to exist only because of the Self.

Lecture 40 - Only the Self Remains

"The listeners should know that when the three deities, Brahma, Vishnu, and Shiva go to sleep, that is what is called the dissolution of the universe through sleep." (*Dasbodh* Chapter 10, Sub-chapter 5)

Do not think that there is actually some entity that creates, protects or destroys. Brahma, Vishnu, and Shiva seem to exist only because of the Self. As long as the Self is present, knowledge and ignorance (lack of knowledge) are present in the body. Once the Self leaves (the body), both knowledge and ignorance disappear. Thus Brahman is the natural state where there is no knowledge, no remembrance, no forgetfulness. Remembering the Self without any conscious perception is called the impulse of knowledge or awareness. Arousal of "I Am" implies "I am all." When awareness becomes aware of itself, it gives rise to the impulse of "aham," or "I." At the source of this impulse is Maya (Illusion). That which is not, was never there. In the beginning there is a disturbance in the Self. We call a small part in our Self as "I" and that which remains, we call a "dream." The impulse to know is vayu or willpower. That alone is the Primal Illusion. That is of the nature of vayu, or wind. The root of all, however, is the Essence (Brahman). Later come the Gods, Narayana, etc. These are only names.

The disciple then asked, "Tell us again how the world was created?" The faculty of awareness, or knowing "I Am," is Ishwara or God. When the same faculty of awareness is used for seeing the external world, the jiva (individual) comes to exist. First comes ignorance of the Self. This is Rudra. Vishnu is none other than the Inner-Self, Consciousness. "To know" is Vishnu. When Vishnu looks at the external world, He becomes a jiva, thus falling into bondage. Therefore, he gets engrossed in worldly affairs.. He becomes Maya in the form of Lakshmi.

The jiva accepts the three gods, Brahma, Vishnu, and Shiva, by it's own imagination. Prior to these gods is God, Ishwara, Brahman. All the three gods are without any physical body, just as the beings in a dream are conceptual. Hiranyagarbha means one without body. This is the creation coming from the original concept (the first principle, "I Am"). When a concept becomes gross, it becomes this gross creation. The creation we see is objective, gross. When a concept or feeling becomes ingrained, the five elements also become firm. If the concept is taken as untrue and is analyzed properly, then all is like dust. This dust is caused by wind and wind (vayu) is Consciousness, or movement.

When we sleep, the world perishes (dissolution through sleep) in the same way that it perishes when we die (dissolution through death). However, the dissolution of the world through discrimination is called the fifth dissolution. If the five elements are dissolved through discrimination, the dissolution is instantaneous. The one who dissolves everything with discrimination is a realized person. When all is dissolved by discrimination, only the Self remains. As long as we take the world to be true, the five elements are like ghosts in the dark. When we think of Knowledge ("I Am"), only the Self remains. This can be experienced. Four of the kinds of dissolution are according to the rules of creation, but the fifth dissolution is through discrimination. When one discriminates, gods, deities, and ghosts all disappear. You are the Self that remains, and all the rest is untrue. All these ghosts run away via the twelve outlets. Twelve outlets means the ten senses, the mind, and the intellect. All the senses can experience this dissolution. This phenomenal world has come into being because of thoughtlessness, and you have believed it to be real. Accordingly, its destruction will come through proper thoughtfulness, or discrimination.

It is a wrong concept that there is punishment after death. In Hindu mythology, Vishnu is in the seven seas, implying thereby that this body is composed of seven entities called "Dhatus" (covers or layers), and within these layers is present Vishnu in the form of the Self. One who does not believe that all this as true is "Agasti." (Agasti; "gasti" means true.) Until you meet a realized person, and he eradicates the fear in you, you will feel all of this to be true. There is no sin or virtue that is not known to the mind. Sin is ignorance, and virtue is Knowledge, arrived at by inquiry into "Who am I?" To think of what this world is, and to analyze our existence, is Knowledge.

Lecture 41 – Know the Self

"The processes of creation, sustenance, and destruction have been explained. The Supreme Self, Paramatman, is without attributes, and without form. It is as it is." (*Dasbodh* - Chapter 10, Sub-chapter 6)

What do we mean by the creation, sustenance, and destruction of the world? What do we mean by spiritual understanding? The fourteen streams of learning, and the sixty four types of arts, are all for the sake of earning one's livelihood, for worldly existence. When we do not know the remedy for our pain, out of fear, we take medicine from the doctor. Doctors have learned about medicine for their livelihood. This is worldly knowledge. The foolishness of fools benefits the wise. The learning meant to earn money by hook or by crook for livelihood is called avidya (not real knowledge). The motivation for both the teacher and the student while imparting such type of learning is to get some benefit.

What does the understanding of the Self, or true knowledge mean? It is about how this world is created, how it works, and its future condition. Who is the one God who is prior to everything. (A worldly man has nothing to do with this type of learning.) True knowledge deals with the condition of all beings, and the creator of all the beings. To spend one's life caring only for the stomach is behaving like a beast, and is for low-minded people. You people do not think. To think about great things such as spiritual knowledge is for great-minded people. In spiritual learning, knowledge about the Self and the cosmos is taught, and is called "true knowledge" (Sadvidya).

Here the aspirant asks the Master about his own identity, and that of God. The Master starts explaining to the aspirant as follows: "You are not outside of the body. Therefore, discriminate between that which is Self and that which is not Self, and discard all those things that you are not. Then you will understand who I am, and who you are." In school we are taught addition and subtraction. Here also, you should learn to subtract. Subtract the mind and intellect, and other components of the subtle body, and then only ignorance (the causal body) remains. Are you that? If you leave aside that as well, what remains? If you leave aside that "nothingness," or ignorance, the One who leaves aside everything remains, and that is the real "you." You are the Pure Knowledge that witnesses everything, and who says "I." You are "That." The nature of that "You" is Absolute Knowledge, or "Kevala Jnana." One who knows this, is a Jnani, a realized one, and one who identifies himself with the body is ignorant. Our Being is the embodiment of Knowledge. "That Thou Art." Call it "I," call it "God" or call it "Shiva." The one who says that he is Knowledge is Shiva, and the one who says he is the body is jiva (ignorant being). I am the "Awareness," or Consciousness that pervades the background of one's thought, and when this disappears for a while, that state is called deep-sleep. This Awareness is called God, as in it is all the possible greatness. Because I exist, other objects appear real, otherwise everything is worthless.

The One who gives godliness to the worldly "god" resides in the heart. It is this God who should be dressed up, worshipped, and given offerings. "I am God," and it is to me that the world owes it's greatness. If the one who says "I," quits the body, then life loses it's meaning. In the Sanskrit language "Omkar" means "I Am." The whole world is created out of this "AUM," or "I Am-ness." The origin of words, or sound, is called "AUM." Brahman is the one from whom the "I Am-ness" has emerged. "AUM" is of the nature of Knowledge, and "aham" (ego), or "I am an individual," is ignorance. Absolute Reality is where both "Knowledge" and its opposite "ignorance" are absent. Where both Knowledge and ignorance are absent, that is my Self.

Knowledge or ignorance can never be part of Absolute Reality. Do we need a lamp in order to see ourselves? Only when we have to talk to others, do we have to say "I am." We do not ever tell ourselves "I am." When one wakes up from sleep the "I Am-ness" gets fully exposed. When even this "I Am" is given up, the result is called Absolute Reality. The fourth state, or Turya, is the state in which one says "I am Knowledge." "Tu" means "you," and "rahya" means "to remain." In deep-sleep one is not conscious of anything, including the moment when sleep overtakes you. Absolute Reality is beyond the state of deep-sleep. In our natural existence, there is neither "Awareness" nor "ignorance." There is neither space, nor any other concept in our natural state. The Pure Awareness, the knowledge "I Am," appears, and this is called the God. To know means to become God. When that awareness conceptualizes, all of manifestation becomes perceptible, and when all concepts are given up, all of manifestation perishes.

As long as you hold on to manifestation, it exists. Once you leave it, it just vanishes. During sleep you leave all the senses, objects, mind, intellect, etc., and upon waking up again, you seize them. The body may be termed as the incarnation (Avatar; coming down) of God. In this way creation, sustenance and destruction come upon you. Nothing has happened to you. By eating tamarind, did you turn sour, or by eating sugar, did you turn sweet? The sugar tasted sweet and has disappeared. You remain as you were.

All bodies have come upon the Pure Knowledge of "I Am," like scenes on a screen and have eventually vanished. What can they do to you? Even though digested food in the form of feces is inside the body, has it ever bothered you? Attributes (gunas) means that which is not. If the feces in your body does not affect you, what can the attributes of the body do to you? Since the mind, intellect, etc., which are present in the body cannot affect you, there is no question of qualities such as sin and merit affecting you.

The mind has created concepts such as Brahma, Vishnu, and Shiva, and allotted the duties of creation, sustenance and destruction to them respectively. The mind gave Lord Vishnu four hands, and Lord Shiva a naked appearance with ashes on his forehead. Finally, when the mind tried to contemplate on who is the Self, the Lord of all, it failed. The attributeless Self can never accrue any sin or merit, which are but attributes labeled by the mind. Since the mind cannot grasp the Self, the Self that is "I," is called "Kailasa Loka," the place where all bodies end. ("Kai" means body, "la" means "laya" or dissolution, and "asti" means existence. Hence, "Kailasa" means that which remains after the dissolution of all the bodies.) The gross body, which has to die, is the world of mortality. The subtle body, which enjoys pleasure, is "heaven." The causal body, where there is darkness (ignorance), is the nether world. And the great-causal body is the world of "Knowledge." Beyond these four bodies are you, the Absolute Reality.

You are always as you are, without any change. Whether the states of wakefulness, deep-sleep, or any other things come upon you, it does not matter to you. You are always original thing, prior to anything. Creation and destruction do not affect you. The "awareness" in you disappears just as the wind disappears in space. You (the Absolute Reality) are always without any distortion, and you have no dissolution at any time. Even an ignorant person inquires about his previous birth. This proves that you existed before. Whatever appears, eventually disappears. In the end everything is dissolved, but you exist eternally. The one who has understood this is the realized one. The deluded one cannot understand this. Only if one seeks knowledge from the Master, can one understand. One has to recognize Him who has no such delusion. I will tell you a "sign" to recognize Him. He is the one who has undergone no change or distortion. Whatever appears is only delusion. Where all concepts are discarded, that is the end of the universe.

It is all delusion to say I, you, god, demon, etc. Even prayer is a delusion. If the "knowing faculty" conceptualizes, then everything appears good. If one conceptualizes through ignorance then bad things (such as ghosts) are seen. The seer belongs to the party of the five Pandavas and the seen belongs to the party of the Kauravas (of the Mahabharata). Kaurava means those who thrive ("Ravanna") in the body Kaya". In what is seen, there appear human beings, animals, gods, demons, I, you, worshipper, worshipped, etc. All this is delusion. When this delusion disappears, only the Self remains. As the Illusion has grown very thick over the Self, one cannot realize it. He who understands that all this is delusion is the realized one. The deluded take the world to be true and therefore go about seeking only, food and material satisfaction. They fail to realize that in this is delusion. Even God and his worship are delusion.

Until one gets knowledge of the Self, one cannot predict in what way he will be deluded. The mind conceives many things and various gimmicks are employed. If the mind makes one an ascetic, then one feels like growing the nails, going about naked, feeding only on leaves or resorting to starvation, repressing the senses, etc. Such concepts arise in the mind. One from whose mind all concepts about good and bad have lost their meaning, is the real ascetic. If one gives importance to any particular thing, then one is pushed away from one's real nature. To the one who knows his true nature, there is no difference whether he eats several times a day or fasts, whether he sleeps on a royal bed or in a gutter. He knows that all these are merely bodily affairs.

One who knows the Self, is the truly "realized one." You have to recognize the one who has no delusion. A realized person is one who knows that his Self is the only truth, and that everything else is a just a play of thoughts. It is delusion to search for a thing (outside) when it is within ourselves. It is delusion either to think of a good or a bad omen, or to pray for a dead man's soul to rest in peace. Sometimes, the one who is involved in various rituals prescribed by religion deludes himself, and believing that he is a realized person, instead of imparting knowledge, does quite the opposite. To impart knowledge without experience is also delusion. One who performs yoga without knowing the Self suffers needlessly for what he did in a past life. Unless he wanted to perform yoga in his previous life, he will not get such desires. All these are delusions. What should you select from the Illusion? Everything except your real Self, which is without attributes, everything else is delusion.

People feel that if one worships the samadhi shrine (mausoleum) of a realized person that miracles occur and one's desires are fulfilled. Only the one who is free from all such thoughts realizes the Self. One who has no delusion is indeed a rarity. The one who realizes is wise, and all others are insane. Having taken a human birth, one who has not gained the ultimate experience has wasted his life.

Experience of the Truth is the final proof. If you go only by logical inference, it will only hinder you. Ignorance binds all human beings. Some want to realize the Absolute Reality by rituals and various other techniques of punishing the body. They are in turmoil due to their own grievances and they pine away, never satisfied. Everyone in the world is suffering from misery, even though they do not show it externally. The world suffers from a malady which no one can identify. One who is shy to admit it is committing suicide. Even if you take it for granted that the manifest world is true, nature teaches you that you are wrong. The right approach is to sincerely seek and obtain knowledge from the Master. Otherwise, one who has lost the delusion of remaining clothed, then suffers from the delusion of remaining naked. In short, delusions of all types affect one or the other. Only the one whose mind is rid of all delusions is free from doubt.

Abhimanyu (son of Arjuna, one of the Pandavas) means pride (Abhimaan). One can enter the circle of this mundane existence through pride (ego), but one cannot come out of it through ego. (In the Mahabharata war Abhimanyu enters the circular military formation created by the Kaurava army, but does not know how to come out of it.) Only a true disciple of the Master can emerge from the cycle of worldly as well as spiritual ideas. One who sticks to the Self achieves realization. One should sincerely do as the Master says. After being established in Pure Awareness, if pride sets in, one sinks in ignorance. It is good to know the Self and the creator of this manifestation. If one only infers about the Self, without practice and experience, then all his spiritual knowledge is a waste. In the absence of experience about the Self, and beset with all kinds of doubts about the Self, one struggles to save oneself from the trappings of this mundane existence. A firm conviction about one's real nature is best. One who has doubts is a fallen person.

I have imparted this knowledge so that people might get enlightened. Find out who the "doer" is. One who has not understood from where Illusion arises should contemplate about it with an alert mind.

Lecture 42 – Relinquish Pride and Gain Self-Knowledge

"Parabrahman is eternal. Illusion only appears to exist in it, and as such it is experienced. But even though it appears to exist, in the course of time it perishes." (*Dasbodh* - Chapter 10, Sub-chapter 6)

All that is not our own Self, like worship, the thought of God's existence, this mundane existence, etc., is delusion. Illusion does not permit Knowledge of the Self. It is not possible to predict in what type of delusion one may get trapped. When the Self gets eclipsed, the mind starts conceptualizing. With ideas of actions, God, heaven, sin, merit, karma, various religions, aspirants, conditionings, sacrifices, etc., the mind drifts. These delusional ideas impel some people to wander about as ascetics. Others are deluded into thinking that growing one's nails will take one near God. Some become mute, some wander about naked and live on neem leaves, or live as celibates, and in this way their minds become senile. With a lot of food in the house, some people fast. The mind engages in ideas of fasting or other methods to torture the body, in the hope of achieving God.

One is called a renunciate (sanyasi) only when all these delusions have disappeared from the mind. For the true sanyasi all of the above concepts have disappeared from the mind. These concepts, which are symbolized as hair, will disappear when the hair is shaved off. One who has banished the good and the bad from his mind is the real renunciate. The rest, because of the above prejudices, forgot their own Self. One who realizes the Absolute Reality, "Vijnana," who has known his Self and rests with the understanding that everything else is only concepts of Self, is the true Vijnani. The firm conviction "I am the Self" is the sign of liberation. Never forget "I am the Self." If you starve, it is the stomach that starves. The subtle actions of the mind and the actions of the body do not affect the Self. The Self, one's True Nature" (Swaroopa), is forever the same. Nothing changes "That." One is a true Jnani if he is indifferent to whether the body sits in a palanquin (a platform carried by others) or falls in garbage.

Recognize the one who has no Illusion. One who imparts this Reality to others, is the "Brahmajnani." The rest are all enmeshed in Illusion. Is it not delusion to forget and lose the Truth that resides in us? One who feels afraid, when witnessing a dream in the form of this world, is deluded. The thought of bad or good omens is also a delusion. A dry tree trunk was seen, and the mind took it as a ghost. This is also delusion. Pride (egoism), pride of the body, pride of one's caste, pride of good actions, pride of the family, pride of Knowledge, and pride of liberation are all delusion. To practice yoga without Knowledge is to needlessly make the body suffer. Artwork done without Self-Knowledge is not art.

For realizing one's "True Nature," it is not necessary to have matted hair, perform sacrifices, etc. King Janaka (Sita's father in the Ramayana) continually abided in his True Nature. And even though he was seated on the throne, he was "videhi," free from body-consciousness. All concepts are delusion. Everybody has their own ego, or pride. All is Illusion except Brahman (Self) which is without attributes. Knowledge does not take note of "samsara," the mundane worldly existence. One with Knowledge is liberated even while living in this mortal form.

When you worship a saint's "samadhi" (memorial shrine), you may get some spiritual experience. But is that a miracle performed by the saint who has left the body? Do saints die with desires? No. So the answer is that such experiences are only due to one's faith. Miracles or experiences fructify in accordance with the faith of the aspirant No saint comes to eat sweets in the shrine. Those who are liberated are forever liberated. All the rest is delusion. Out of a hundred persons, only one person's faith may result in such an experience. Just as the coincidental breaking of a branch when a crow happens to sit on it. (An allusion to the Yoga Vasishtha) Yet the delusion endures. I have told you about faith and its effect, A Jnani(realized person) is one who is indifferent to both faith and delusion. "I Am" is delusion. Similarly, "You are" is also delusion.

Both belief in God and worship are also delusion. Finally, the world is rooted in delusion. Every one gets bound by one's own concepts. Listen to the "Master Key." I shall tell you what Knowledge is in one sentence. One in whom conceptualization has ceased is the Jnani.

It is wise to get gold or gems verified and appraised. Otherwise, you may run the risk of being cheated. In the same way, this human birth is wasted without the "experience" of the Self. Experience of the Self is the only proof. All the rest is delusion. There are many who have assumed different guises. There is no contentment or peace in knowledge that is without experience. Only when you know its effectiveness do you take the medicine. So experience the Self. There are as many techniques and methods as there are gods. If an inexperienced doctor is consulted, the child will lose its life. One who broods if he cannot experience the

Self, and yet does not want to go to another Master, is the killer of his own Self. If one is shy to tell the doctor everything, what happens? The lack of accurate information will ultimately result in death. Do not let your ego get in the way like this in pursuit of Reality. What can a knowledgeable person do? Maya (Illusion) can reveal Truth to the True one, and it can also teach falsehood to the deluded one. Surrender to the Jnani who is free of all delusion and gain True Knowledge.

If you leave one concept, another will chase you automatically. If you renounce eating onions then you become a victim of the delusion of not eating the onion. Abhimanyu (ego), Arjuna's son, entered into the circular military formation, but he could not return. It is possible to enter into the wheel of mundane existence but one cannot come out of it with the aid of the ego. Only Arjuna (a true disciple) could return. Worldly existence and spirituality are two wheels of a grinding stone. One must get out of both. Only a "guruputra," a son of the Master can do this.

Saint Kabir and his disciple Kamal were walking along. When Kabir saw a turning flour mill he said that no one who was caught up between the two wheels could come out safely. A Jnani will confirm this. If you hold on to your pride or ego, you will drown. What has the Jnani lost? The ignorant one is drowned due to pride. A woman was unhappy with lamp oil so she had to sit in the dark. If you do not like oil, sit down in darkness. What has the oil lost? One who has been performing rituals to gain spiritual Knowledge has wasted his life. If doubt is not eradicated, and if delusion has not disappeared, one's life is fruitless. The whole world is drowned in doubt. Only the saints have conquered doubt. The sign of true spiritual Knowledge is that one is free of all doubt. If people think that God will grant them salvation, then they do not know God, and they do not have true realization. Thus when one dies, only the five elements are liberated, and not your Self. If you do not know who you are, or who is God, then why did you take birth at all? If you do not understand Illusion, what is the use of having a body?

Lecture 43 – Only Brahman Exists

"As one's conviction gets firmly fixed in the realization of Truth, one's Power increases on the path of Knowledge. Then one must take care that the state of Oneness is never disturbed." (*Dasbodh* - Chapter 10, Sub-chapter 7)

Indeed, all is Brahman. Name and form are false. The numerous beings, houses, etc. that are seen, are all transitory. Wind, fire, water, etc., exist due to Consciousness, the Life-Energy. All beings arise from the earth and ultimately return to earth. Everything is created from the five elements, and back into them, everything finally gets dissolved. Consciousness is wind. Water and fire and earth are all also created out of Consciousness or Life-Energy. Consciousness is all. "Sarvam Khalvidam Brahman," everything is Brahman (one of the Mahavakyas of the Vedas). If one out of the five elements is absent, no being can live. The five elements and Consciousness (the Self), make six ingredients which are necessary to make the body work. This is all a bundle of those six ingredients. Who then is the "I" that has come in as the seventh? His name is ignorance, concept, Maya. Maya or Illusion means that everything is false. That which is "not" must be false. Once this is understood, duality vanishes.

Brahman is non-dual. "Only One exists, there is no other." The Supreme Self, Paramatman, is a singular whole, and without His presence, no object can exist. All is Brahman. If there were any principle other than Him, God would be imperfect. The imperfect is perishable. That which is imperfect is not the Lord. The Lord of the world is only One. "You" are nobody. To feel you are, is delusion, ignorance. If you are not, neither is anyone else. These bodies are temples made up of bones and flesh, and the one who resides within is God. He who has understood that there is nothing except the One is a Jnani.

To perceive an object as something other than what it actually is leads to a wrong concept of that object. When we are Brahman, to think of ourselves as a jiva (individual) is a wrong concept. Why does Knowledge elude us? It is because of the strong conviction of its impossibility. If the Guru says, "You are Brahman, You are That," initially a doubt presents itself. "When I am a man, how can I be Brahman, and how is it possible that all is Brahman?" Maya itself is false, so one who says, "I am speaking the truth," is also false. One who speaks the truth says, "There is only One without a second." The one who is without doubts and wrong concepts is a "Yogi" (one in union with God). He alone has known the Self because he understands that there is nothing that exists apart from the One. When one gets such a firm conviction, he becomes free of all sins. When one thus becomes the Lord, one becomes all powerful. One who has Brahmajnana (Knowledge of Brahman) perceives wife, house, world, etc. as Brahman, because no object can exist without Brahman. Only such a person has truly understood the scriptures and is the recipient of the Master's grace.

The greater your doubts and concepts, the farther you go away from Reality. If you do not get rid of the conviction that it is impossible to get rid of doubt, you will labor mindlessly. Brahmavidya (Knowledge of Self) is the knowledge of oneself, one's True Nature, devoid of doubts. Study or practice is the means for getting rid of the conviction of "impossibility" of becoming free of doubt, and attaining Knowledge. When you are convinced of Truth, the Master's sermons have born fruit. "When the conviction gets firm, one achieves greatness through Knowledge." We attain the Knowledge that we are God.

Lecture 44 – The Knowledge of Brahman

"As one's conviction gets firmly fixed in the realization of Truth, one's Power increases on the path of Knowledge. Then one must take care that the state of Oneness is never disturbed." (*Dasbodh* - Chapter 10, Sub-chapter 7)

All is Brahman (Reality) and that alone is our true "Self Form" (Swaroopa). The world is our own Self. All the joy or happiness in the world is for Him, and whatever He says, happens because He is God. Why are Rama and Krishna considered Gods? Because they saw nothing in the world except their own Self. Only one who knows one's own True Nature becomes God. All beings are just One. This oneness is the prerequisite for "godliness." The cause of jivahood (individual consciousness) is the feeling "I am the body." There is no other object except the One. This is the very reason that there is godliness. As is your faith so is your God. When one purchases a cow, it's milk, urine and droppings will all come along with her. In the same way, the glory of success, prosperity, bravery, etc., all emerge with the "Knowledge of the Self." The body of the Jnani is the entire universe.

The gross and subtle bodies are your creation. When you become a jiva due to identification with the body, you become limited. When you become Shiva (the Self), you become vast, and all-pervading. Then it is not necessary to search for happiness, it just naturally is. When there is only One, the whole world exists for His service. How did the god in the temple come to be called "God"? The answer is that he understood that all manifestation is His own form. With this, came all of the offerings. One becomes the incarnation of God when one gets the knowledge that "This world is mine, I am everywhere." Brahma Vidya (Knowledge of Brahman) converts the jiva into Shiva. One with the Knowledge of the Self is God incarnate.

Krishna says, "Whatever the caste (or creed or sex), and whatever knowledge is established in the body, I serve the disciples of that Realized One birth after birth."

In the Kali Avatara (the tenth and final incarnation of Lord Vishnu), I become "Knowledge" itself, and I alone spread the message through the medium of Knowledge. It is this that I have come to tell you. I have now given you the "Ultimate Knowledge." This is the "Knowledge of Brahman." Conduct yourself in accordance with this Knowledge. You are Paramatman, the Supreme Self. If one's tongue is diseased, he cannot taste the mango. Japa (repetition of mantra), austerities, and other such remedies are not required. If the cloth is clean, no soap is needed. He is God, how can He purify Himself? His worship consists in knowing that He is always present eternally. Then there is bliss, "Diwali," pleasure and joy wherever He is. The power of the Master is greater than destiny.

Once you become God, sin and virtue will not hold any sway over you. A king remains a king regardless of whether he sits on the throne. Similarly, this "God of Gods" is the supreme in any situation, there is nothing auspicious or inauspicious for Him. This world is created for His pleasure. For instance, when one builds a house, it is for one's own pleasure. Because He has created the world, there are no laws for Him. He has complete freedom. When the world is created out of this Lord, it exists for Him. All the happiness is for Shiva (Self) and all the unhappiness is for the jiva (one who identifies with the body).

No one can approach the Lord. The Lord creates bliss, wherever He is. The conviction that one is a jiva creates misery. Conviction that one is the Lord creates bliss. Wherever Lord Krishna is present, victory is assured. What can this world of objects do? The whole universe and all gods are in the service of this one Lord. All glory is for that Lord. The extent of one's faith determines the results. If I am the Lord, whatever I do is right. Insofar as there is a king (or head of government) in place, governance proceeds automatically.

Do not forget your Self. Do not descend from the position, "I am the Lord. All of this works through My power." In absence of such conviction, everything is useless. Has God created this world? Is there any law without the Lord? There is no law for the One who is beyond all laws. There is no bondage either. Whatever He says, happens. The more you nourish the conviction that you are the Self, the more powerful you become. One should always have implicit faith in the Master, in the Self. Then one is automatically free. These are two powers. The Master is the father and the disciple is the child. When they become one, they become greater than the whole universe. After understanding the Knowledge of the Self, if one worships the Master, he is greater than the person of highest realization. My words will be as useful as the wish-fulfilling tree. For those disciples of the Master who absorb my sermons as nectar, fate will ensure their well-being. Upon them, fate will bestow auspiciousness. When the "Ocean of Knowledge" is churned, the nectar of immortality is imbibed by the true disciples of the Master who have complete faith in Him. (A reference to Hindu mythology, where it is said that when the Ocean of Knowledge is churned, the "nectar of immortality" is produced from it.) This Knowledge will bear fruit only for those who are faithful dedicated devotees of the Master.

Lecture 45 – Devotion to the Master

"If after having realized That which is without attributes, if one abandons worship of the One with attributes, then such a knowledgeable one loses out on both sides." (*Dasbodh* - Chapter 10, Sub-chapter 7)

"Nirguna Jnana" (Knowledge of the attributeless Self) means "I am That," Brahman. Once one realizes that there is no one else in the world except the Self, that conviction must be sustained. After complete and clear understanding, the intellect becomes irreversibly rooted in Absolute Reality. If one sits for a meal, then one only thinks of eating. The intellect has the inherent property of becoming one with whatever action it performs. When it thinks of crying, it will cry. If it listens to stories of saints, worship of the Master, or Self-Knowledge, then it becomes engrossed in that. If it thinks of worldly objects, then jivatva (I am the individual) is the result. If it discards objects, it becomes Paramatman.

Hence the need to keep the intellect immersed in the realm of Reality. One should not abandon worship. Serve the Master, and worship him with intense devotion. Have sweetness in your speech, respect even for an enemy, and consideration for others' feelings. Such an attitude is necessary. The Guru (Master) is Brahma, and the Guru is Vishnu. "He is the Highest of all, Paramatman incarnate." With steadfast devotion, this understanding grows within. Only such a person will get Self-Knowledge. A corn plant can never bear pearls. A woman cannot deliver a child unless she becomes pregnant. Unless you eat, you will not get energy. Without absolute faith in the Master, the aspirant can never acquire Knowledge.

All pride must vanish. As long as the ideas, "I am the body, my wealth, my son, I am a person with status, my wife, my relatives, etc.," exist, there cannot be "real" Knowledge. After realization of the Self, the aspirant regards his Master as the greatest of all. He feels that he belongs to the Master. Lord Krishna has said in the Bhagavad Gita, "Whatever the caste (or creed or sex), whatever knowledge is established in the body, I serve the disciples of that Realized One birth after birth." Everything belongs to the Master. For the realized person, there is nothing greater than his Guru, just as for a householder there is no one more important than his wife.

"Spiritual Knowledge unsupported by worship is baseless." If there is no Devotion (Bhakti) there is no Knowledge (Jnana). Devotion is the mother of Knowledge. Without the Master's grace, there is no Knowledge. When will the Master's grace flow? Only through steadfast devotion. Then, even mud will turn into gold. The Sadguru is the protector. "Why bother about others when the Sadguru is your guardian?" You thank someone even if he gives you a cup of tea, then how can you ever lose faith in that Sadguru who has enabled you to transcend birth and death, and thereby made you immortal? Even a dog belonging to the king is respected by all. Success, fame, achievement are all dependent on devotion to the Master. So keep up the worship without expecting anything in return. This worship without any expectation is ideal for the exaltation of the soul. Who is really powerful? One who asks for nothing. Look up to Lord Mahadeva (Lord of Lords). The rest of them, Lord Vishnu, Brahma and the whole world are slaves. Power, prosperity, and liberation are His servants.

Where there is ability, there will be absolute devotion to the Master. The Sadguru will make you Parabrahman after making you transcend this Maya. Sit in a temple if you think God gives you everything. Why work or engage in service at all? Those who worship delusion will never be free of want. Those who are deluded can never worship without expecting something in return. If you worship with desire you become a slave. Desireless worship will give you a king's status, it makes you Paramatman (the Supreme Soul). You become the Master and your rule prevails. One becomes free from lust, anger, desire, envy, etc., One transcends birth and death, becomes pure, all-pervading and immortal. Only good is thus achieved. When you buy a bull, his horns, his tail, etc., all come together with it. Similarly, those who worship without any desire, attain the status of the Master. If you serve the Master without expectation, you will get true satisfaction.

Lecture 46 – Saguna Worship

"Even though one may be knowledgeable, by giving up the worship of God with attributes, one becomes unsuccessful in realizing Brahman. Therefore, one should never abandon saguna worship, the worship of God with attributes)." (*Dasbodh* - Chapter 10, Sub-chapter 7)

Be engaged in Saguna worship. The Sadguru resides in the heart of the one who worships him, and becomes his guardian. Fortune and misfortune depend on you. If you behave according to what the Master has told you, you will always have his blessings. Just as the child does not need to ask its mother to breast-feed it, it is not necessary to ask the Sadguru to bless you. Wherever you go, he is your eternal guardian. But if you neglect his instruction, your own curse befalls you. Therefore, everything depends upon what you do. He knows how strong your faith is. If your actions are correct, then what can God do to you? The boy who studies well in the school does not need to plead for a passing grade on the examination. If Self-Knowledge is practiced, misery, death, sin, virtue, will not dare to come your way. For a realized person, there can be no evil. No danger can approach a lion. One who abandons worship of the Master is a failure. At a wedding feast it is not necessary to tell anyone to serve the bridegroom. Similarly, a realized person does not need to pray for his own well-being.

Abandon all desire and carry on with your worship. Do not worship with the expectation of the power that Knowledge can yield. "We are servants of our Master. Nothing happens according to what we say." Then even before you ask for something, it will happen. You get good results even if you do not ask for them. If one goes out to beg, he does not even get alms. Our only duty is worship of the Sadguru. Good results will surely follow. Only do not become anxious for them. Siddhis (occult powers) or miracles come automatically. "Ramaa (Goddess of wealth) serves the one who does not ask for anything." He enjoys limitless power. The angels serve those who do not crave power. Why should one who has become God worry about his next meal? Your conviction that you are as big as the world should continue strengthening. Limitless power will be felt. If you worship the Sadguru, he fulfills all your dreams. As the mother is worried about the child, so is the Master worried about the disciple. Do not become impatient. Worship the Sadguru without desire. Do not wait in expectation of any power to come. Otherwise, it will be like decorating an adolescent who is impatient to get married.

When Hanuman asked Rama for the boon of immortality, Rama gave it to him. But even that was only a state, not Absolute Reality. When you are the king, what do you need to ask for? Let there be no desire for anything. Stay put with the firm conviction, "I am Paramatman (Absolute Reality)." This is called desireless worship. Then, whatever comes to the mind of the devotee is immediately fulfilled. God (Supreme Power) grants even before a desire arises in the devotee. God and devotee are one and the same. He is the doer. So continue the worship of the Master. Then, the Master becomes your protector. One cannot imagine the power the devotee gets if he continues worship of the Master after Self-realization. "You are the Self," you are One without duality. There is no liberation without a Sadguru (Master). The doer of all is that Lord, your own Self. "You cleansed me and gave me the status of Brahman. The eclipse of the sun and the moon (desire and senses) is over."

Lord Hari (the Self) is the enjoyer of everything. It is He who eats. It is He who bathes. Whatever had to be told has been told. Now the enlightenment (of your intellect) depends upon you. Your boat will surely reach the shore beyond this world. Each one will achieve the status he deserves. As is your faith, so will your Knowledge of the Self come to fruition. Glory, success and fame will be accrued according to your faith, and all of these will be accrued effortlessly to those who worship the Master. This is indisputable, just as light and heat are naturally present in the sun.

Lecture 47 – Desireless Worship

"Even though one may be knowledgeable, by giving up the worship of God with attributes, one becomes unsuccessful in realizing Brahman. Therefore, one should never abandon saguna worship, the worship of God with attributes." (*Dasbodh* - Chapter 10, Sub-chapter 7)

If saguna worship is given up, the mind only indulges in worldly pursuits. If one goes to the temple of a saint, one becomes free from desires. If one abandons saguna worship, Knowledge becomes impure. Thereby, one becomes a failure. This means that saguna worship is the food for Knowledge. There is nothing in all the three worlds to equal desireless worship. Desireless worship thus calls for extraordinary ability. It is service without payment. Only then does one's nature become truly desireless. Bhajan (worship) is to be done without any motive. If the Bhajan is desireless, Self-Knowledge results. Such a one is greater than even God. Only the knowledgeable person can worship without desire. The ignorant person worships with some motive. One who realizes the Self and still worships without desire is indeed the greatest.

If the jiva is told to do a certain thing, he will not do it. He always wants some benefit or gain. Desireless worship is the only way to achieve greatness. Through desireless worship, one becomes the Lord. See for yourself the difference between worldly benefits and Godhood. It is indeed great to attain Godhood. Therefore, never abandon saguna worship. Only by worshipping the Master can one realize the Self. Only the Sadguru (Master) is the doer, the non-doer, and the extraordinary doer. The power of God is beyond words. He can do things that nobody can ever imagine. All this power is achieved by desireless worship. Attainment of Self-Knowledge depends upon you. It is mainly nourished by devotion to the Master and saguna worship. Then, automatically the light of the Self shines forth.

The sun never leaves the earth in darkness. The sun nurtures the earth. Thus, you should enhance your Knowledge of Brahman. It will then automatically be strengthened. If someone gives you respect, assign it to the Sadguru. If some one bows down to you, understand that it is for the Sadguru. People are always ready to fool you. A diamond can only be set in gold. It is never set in iron. God (the Self) has reserved a safe and comfortable place for those who are devotees of the Master.

Lecture 48 – Knowledge is the Primal Illusion

"Just as wind arose in space, Moolamaya (Primal Illusion) arose in Brahman. In this wind, the Primal Illusion arose as the three attributes (gunas) and the five elements." (*Dasbodh* - Chapter 10, Sub-chapter 9)

Your Self is clean, pure like the sky. But just as air was created in the sky, the Primal Illusion (Moolamaya), or "Awareness," arose in the Self. Know yourself as Purusha/Prakriti, Shiva/Shakti, Consciousness, the Seer, the Witness, etc. The natural state is like space. This is the contention of the scriptures. Shankaracharya calls this natural state as Moolamaya. Parabrahman (Absolute Reality) has no name. Brahman means the Life-Energy, and "Brahmatita" means beyond Brahman. Those objects which have name and form are perishable. They actually do not exist at all. All objects exist only in name (as concepts). Parabrahman has no name. All objects with names are essentially concepts, and hence false. The natural Self is Parabrahman (Absolute Reality). Whatever is created will die. Because "Awareness" has appeared (upon the Self) it will not remain eternally.

"Whoever comes has to go, whether he be a king, a poor man, or a wandering ascetic." Even if one reaches godhood, one will perish. Whatever is created will be destroyed. Parabrahman has never been created, so no one can ever destroy it. It is eternal and self-evident. There is no awareness, yet it seems to appear. The source alone is Moolamaya (Primal Illusion). Some people call the same as "Mother," or "Devi" (Goddess). Whatever has been produced out of this Illusion is all untrue. Do not think that it is some female figure. The Illusion which appears in the beginning, which is variously referred to as "Prakriti," the impulse of "I," or the knowledge "I Am," in the form of Awareness, is the Omkar (the first word according to Indian philosophy) or Shiva/Shakti

(Knowledge and Power). Awareness is Ishwara (God), and the impulse of energy" or power is Prakriti or Maya.

Consciousness (Knowledge) is called Vishnu by Vaishnavas (followers of Lord Vishnu), and Shiva by followers of Lord Shiva. When the "I Am" appeared in Consciousness, it became Laxmi, the consort of Lord Vishnu. When it is said that Laxmi has come home, it means that the impulse "I Am" has arisen. It is said that Laxmi serves Lord Vishnu. Vishnu implies "Pure Knowledge" or Pure Awareness, and the impulse of "I Am," or "awareness" appearing in this Pure Knowledge is Laxmi who is thus always at His service. All of the gods have come from that Parabrahman. Govinda means "the One who makes the senses work" (Go means senses, and vinda means to drive). The entire world came to exist in the Awareness that vitalizes all the senses. God thus has a thousand names, such as the "Life-Energy" of the world, Consciousness, the Witness, the Doer, etc. He is the foundation on which Maya arises. Maya exists only as long as He remains. If Awareness vanishes, Maya disappears. Then the body "dies," and people say, "Take it quickly to the crematorium." Suppose someone says "Keep the corpse for a few days, after all you loved him so much for all these years." "Never!" says the family. When life stops, Maya also vanishes. While one is alive, even his smallest ailment is treated, but as soon as one is gone people, rush to cremate him. Not only this, but if a deceased person appears in a dream, it causes great fear.

Thus, Moolamaya is the same as "Awareness," (Knowledge) and in it exists the whole world that is in the form of the five elements and the three attributes. Just as in a seed, the entire tree is present (in a subtle form), the whole world exists in "Awareness." Trees proliferate from the seed. Similarly this Maya, or Awareness, is the seed from which this world has proliferated. Understand the true nature of this Maya. Consider your experience during the night in deep-sleep. You do not have the slightest perception of the existence of the world, your wife, your own body, and everything that is near you. The world exists only as long as you perceive it. When the word is forgotten, that state is called deep-sleep. In a dream the same "Awareness" projects another world. When space and bodies are created in the dream, is there actually any space? No. The one who "makes place" for space (creates space) is Awareness. It is the support of the whole world. In this dream you create countless worlds. Then why can you not create another world in this world? The reason is your own resolution, "I am a body with 1imited power," comes in the way. You say you cannot do anything. But, in reality, whatever you think will definitely happen.

You are the wish fulfilling tree. This Awareness (Knowledge) is itself the Moolamaya. It is God, Ishwara, due to which the whole world exists. If there is no Awareness, there is total destruction. Whatever dreams come upon you, go away, they get completely destroyed. You have a firm belief that this world is true, so destroy this belief. When Awareness projects the dream world, this waking world is completely destroyed. Gods, demons, wife, children, everything is destroyed. Whenever Awareness projects another world, it is accompanied by the destruction of the previous world. But if it merges into the Self, only Parabrahman remains. If there is a master of these infinite worlds it is this Awareness. Once it merges into the Self, all the universes perish.

In the Self arose the impulse "I Am." This impulse is called "Prakriti" and Knowledge is Purusha. These are two forms of the one Self, just as heat and light are two attributes of the sun. But the sun is only one. When a man is young, he is called a boy, when he becomes older he is called a man. The man is the same, he only gets different names due to the different stages in his life.

The Primordial Illusion is nothing but Knowledge. Do not think that it is some woman goddess. After all, what is the river Ganga? Only water. Thus Purusha is Knowledge and Prakriti is Vayu, wind. The subtle awareness in this wind is the sign of the Creator. If something is known, it can also be forgotten. Thus, awareness is accompanied by ignorance. The three attributes and five elements are a mixture of awareness and ignorance. Vishnu is Knowledge. Without Knowledge, no action can be performed. If one looks inwards, one sees the Self, if one looks outwards, "awareness" arises and one identifies with the body. In a dream, all that exists is only awareness, and this awareness becomes a king, a bull, a cart, etc. When the awareness vanishes, life is over. It is because of this awareness that a bull is called a bull, or Krishna is called Krishna. When it vanishes, everything comes to an end. All beings die. All phenomenal existence is due to awareness. This awareness grants godhood to God, and ghost-hood to a ghost. The ghost affects only those who believe in their existence. Likewise, the planets affect only those who have a belief in astrology. One who says (without realization) that all this is false accrues sin. A dog who raises his leg and urinates on the idol of God does not invite his wrath, and does God do anything to the mice who eat his prasad (offerings)? The mind, our own concepts, lead to bondage. The Jnani is never possessed by ghosts, spirits, etc. This is because he is devoid of concepts. Only an ignorant person nourishes various concepts and superstitions about bad and good omens. If you want to get out of this nonsense, you have to study Self-Knowledge. Then, all this seeming reality is destroyed, and you acquire solid proof that your Self is Parabrahman, the Absolute Reality.

If you practice virtue then you will have to take up a body to enjoy its fruits, and if you sin, you will have to take up a body to suffer for your sins. "It is impossible to eliminate one's karma (actions) without Knowledge." Only one who realizes Brahman is liberated. Liberation is impossible without Knowledge, and one can never gain Knowledge without the Sadguru (Master). That is why one should remain in the company of saints, and surrender oneself to the Master. The analysis of the "principles" should be firmly established in the heart. Then You alone remain. You become "That," Sat-Chit-Ananda. All that is done without understanding leads to birth. To understand this, one must think. Lord Krishna said, "One who thinks is a Purusha, a man. One who does not think is but a beast."

To expound the Final Conclusion (Siddhanta), the primary premise of the *Vedas* has to be discarded. The primary instructions are given so that the aspirant can understand the basis of spirituality. Listen to the Master's teachings, reflect on them, and verify them for yourself, and automatically the Truth will arise within you, and ultimately you will receive the experience "I am the Self." Therefore, the only methods required for Self-realization are thoughtfulness (vichara) and listening to the Master's teachings (shRavanna). No sacrifices, austerities, pilgrimages or fasts are needed. One who does not listen to the Master will never be liberated. One who follows the Master's teachings will surely attain Absolute Reality. "Do not bother with incantations or austerities, do not go for pilgrimages. Do not go anywhere, except to listen to the Master's teachings." Experience for yourself whatever the Master teaches.

Samartha Ramdas therefore asserts that it is only thought that is the Self, that is awareness, that is the objective body, that is the subtle body, etc. You must experience all this for yourself. Otherwise, the entire process of listening is like a mere recording. Examine and analyze the Master's sermons. This will lead to true understanding. One must acquire true "Knowledge." It is you who should experience whether or not what I say is true. My philosophy turns jiva into Brahman. Only the realized ones are able to vanquish Maya. I can impart this Self-Knowledge. Then, the jiva finishes its term in the world and becomes the creator of God himself. One who listens earnestly surely becomes Brahman.

Lecture 49 – Awareness is Illusion

"Brahman is empty like space. Like space it is vast and limitless. It is pure, attributeless, steady and eternal." (*Dasbodh* - Chapter 10, Sub-chapter 10)

Space is motionless, pure, and clean. In the same way, Parabrahman (Absolute Reality) is clean, pure and motionless. In this Parabrahman was born the power "to know." Brahman, or Atman, means knowing oneself. Moolamaya (Primordial Illusion), etc., are merely names. Some say that space is Brahman. Awareness has many names like Ishwara, Atman, Shiva etc. But its true nature is Parabrahman. It has no name. That is why it is said to be beyond Brahman (Para means beyond). The impulse of Awareness is the Primordial Illusion. Everything except Parabrahman has names, and everything that has a name, perishes. Whatever has a name does not have a permanent existence, and therefore, it is absolutely false. Names and forms are completely unreal. The natural state, which is like space, is Parabrahman. That which did not exist originally but appeared (within Parabrahman) is called Moolamaya. One who is born shall die. One who comes must go. Awareness, which was not always present, but which happened, is the Moolamaya (Primordial Illusion). It is called Maya or God. Maya is Awareness. The (river) Ganga is not a female, but because she has a feminine name she is considered to be a woman. The Moolamaya (Primordial Illusion) is Ishwara, also known as "Ardhanari Nateshwara" (half-woman/half-man) because Awareness is God (male) and the impulse, "I am," is Prakriti (female). It is but one entity with two sides. "Laxmi" is the awareness "I Am" (Laksha is awareness, mi is "I"). The body is a temple and the idols of Laxmi-Narayana are within. Govinda is the one who drives the senses. He is called the "Life of the World." And wherever He is, there is Maya. Once Awareness vanishes, He does not remain. This mundane existence is because of this Awareness.

Within Awareness are present Rajoguna, Tamoguna, and Sattvaguna, the three attributes. When breaking open a seed, the tree (which is present in the seed in a subtle form) can never be seen. Similarly, the three attributes and the five elements are present in Moolamaya (Primordial Illusion) but are not seen. All has come to be because of this Awareness. Because Awareness is not perceived during sleep, we do not experience anything. When Awareness is lost, nothing is seen because the whole world is only a memory. When Awareness moves in another direction (as in a dream), another world is created. Thus a new body along with its related activities comes into being.

Awareness thus creates a world that does not have any real existence at all. You make a firm resolve that you cannot change anything. This is why you fail to understand Reality. Whatever Awareness conceives comes to existence. "Satyanash" (Satya means truth, and nash means destruction) means the total destruction of whatever was felt to be true. Wherever there is Awareness, the world appears to exist.. Where there is no Awareness, everything disappears. When Awareness merges into the Self, it is the end of the world and only Absolute Reality remains. That alone is the Lord of infinite universes.

In the motionless space there are two divisions, Awareness and your natural Self. Awareness is called the "Light of the World," or Ishwara. There is only one sun, but it has two qualities, light and heat. The impulse "I Am," and the faculty of knowing, are the two divisions of this Awareness. They are the power of action and the power of will. Whenever any action is performed, various concepts such as the power of action, the form of the object, the power of wealth, etc., arise due to the different kinds of actions performed.

Awareness is Sattva Guna, the spiritual attribute. Together with awareness there is ignorance. Ignorance is forgetfulness. To forget is Tamo Guna. Awareness is always followed by forgetfulness. Can any action be performed without you? The inner-mind is the form of Lord Vishnu in the body, and it is due to this part of Vishnu that the world functions. Everything works only due to the power of this awareness. When a single lamp is surrounded on all sides by glass, you see many lamps. Many images are seen only because of that one lamp. If the pride of the objective body is given up, you can take up another form merely with the aid of another concept.

The realized one does not have any concepts or thoughts. That is why ghosts (of doubt) never possess him. One realizes that in order to free oneself from all this, Self-Knowledge should be acquired. Without Self-Knowledge, it is impossible for all actions (karma) to be nullified. Without Knowledge, liberation can never be achieved. And without the Master, Knowledge is impossible. Analyze these principles in your mind, ultimately you will experience "I Am That." To achieve this, one must utilize the power of discrimination.

The primary teachings were given to enable the aspirant to imbibe the theory. Later, this theory has to be discarded. You should listen and contemplate. Only then will you truly understand that you are the Self. To realize that the Self is Brahman, one has to think deeply. Then no other methods such as charity, rituals, etc., are required. One who does not listen to the Master's teachings will never escape misery. If you listen to the Master, you become liberated. Faith comes by gaining experience. What is meant by listening? Experiencing the One Principle, means that one must analyze and examine the objective body, the subtle body, the causal body, and the great-causal body. Examine and experience. Experience for yourself whatever I tell you. Then Self-realization is not far off. I am telling you the Purana (sacred story) of the Atman. I am telling you the Purana of how to turn the jiva into Brahman. Maya has enslaved Brahman, Vishnu and Shiva. That slave has to be transformed into Absolute Reality. So, one has to listen to the Master and experience Truth for oneself. You always were, and continue to be, the creator of all. Nothing can be achieved by merely reading or hearing about it.

Brahman is like space. Brahman means your natural state which is pure and eternal. That which is beyond Brahman is known as Paramatman (Absolute Reality). It is beyond or detached from the Self (Atman). In all the four states (wakefulness, dream, deep-sleep, and Turya or pure consciousness) it is present as the "Eternal Truth." If you try to know what it is, it will seem like a void. It cannot be seen, and it cannot be perceived. It "begins" when all

concepts end. Absolute Reality is present even when concepts are present. This subtle movement which is sensed in the motionless Self is called "Awareness" or "I." The unsteadiness in the Self is symbolic of Maya. The Atman (Self) has many masculine, feminine and neuter names. It cannot be seen, and yet all these names exist. Why do they exist? For what purpose? Because the Self is invisible. These different names, therefore, are pointers. Self is not seen, but pointed to by names such as Moolamaya (Primordial Illusion), Moola Prakriti or the impulse "I Am."

The experience "I Am" always exists. This is why it is called "Sat" (Existence). It is known consciously, which is why it is called "Chit" (Consciousness). And it is due to this Knowledge that there arises joy, thus it is called "Ananda." It is known by countless other names such as Knowledge, Brahman, etc. That which eternally exists without expression or manifestation is Parabrahman, and saying "I Am" is "Sat-Chit-Ananda." OM (the first word) is the cause of all "japa" (incantation). OM means "I Am." Without this OM all other mantras are meaningless. OM symbolizes Brahma, the Creator. "I Am" is the Moolamaya (Primordial Illusion).

The Vedas have given us thousands of signs so that we do not lose our way. Awareness was created first. Then came thoughts, words, letters, etc. The aggregation of letters and words came to be called as (worldly) knowledge. The Moola Purusha (the Primordial Being) is so called because creation started with Him. "I" am the one for whom the names Shiva, the "Auspicious One," etc., are used.

Examine and experience for yourself whether you are the state of Consciousness or Awareness. The knowledge expounded by the scriptures, the Master's teachings, and verification in one's own experience is called the threefold verification, the complete understanding. In the absence of actual experience, what is the use of mere empty talk? Know your True Self. The ten organs, five pranas (vital airs), mind, intellect, the inner-mind, etc. comprise the subtle body. Wind flows in the motionless sky. Both are not visible, yet there is a difference between the two. Similarly, there is a difference between Parabrahman and Awareness. The natural state is not a state of mind. It is actually a "stateless" state, the absence of any state. Movement, Maya, Consciousness, are all nothing but delusion. To enhance or magnify this delusion, it has been given names such as desire, impulse, power, etc.

If someone suddenly calls out to you while you are asleep, you wake up startled. Thus arises Moola Prakriti (the Primordial Nature). It is also known as Mahakarana, or the great-causal body. Moolamaya (Primordial Illusion) is Moola Prakriti. The causal body of the microcosm (the living being) is the same as the Avyakrut (not manifest) body of the macrocosm (the universe), while the subtle body is the same as Hiranyagarbha (invisible power) at the level of the universe. Avyakrut implies space (Vyakrut means manifest). What is not manifest (space) can however be perceived (like objects). This world appearance is called Virat (huge). Krishna is nothing but "Pure Awareness" or "Awareness in the form of Knowledge" (Pradnyanam Brahman). Whatever is in the body is small, whatever is in the cosmos is huge, Virat. In the Virat form (revealed by Lord Krishna to Arjuna in the Mahabharata) Lord Krishna had the face of every being. Many were being born, and many were dying, just as it happens daily in the world. Ishwaratanuchatushya implies the four bodies (Virat, Hiranyagarbha, Avyakrut, and Moolamaya) of God. Dualists consider Awareness to be Paramatman (Absolute Reality), just as an average working man is respectfully called "Sir" by a sweeper or person from a lower class. Whatever is distinct, hence giving rise to duality, should be destroyed. This is known as Aparoksha Jnana, Direct Knowledge, or Paramatman (Absolute Reality). It is also known as the embodiment of Knowledge. That through which all this is realized is called Ishwara Jnana (Knowledge of God). Om, the first word, originates from Ishwara. The "I," or ego present in the world is known as the aham (aham means ego). These are masculine names. It also has feminine names such as, mother of the three worlds, inner-consciousness, etc. Eternal Knowledge is the Knowledge that exists for all time; the past, present, and future. "He" is ruthless as well as kind-hearted at the same time. For instance, a robber mercilessly steals from some, but shares the loot with his dear ones. The latter is a sign of kindness. One who understands this gets liberated. Bondage has come due to ignorance, and liberation will come with Knowledge. In Vijnana (Supreme Knowledge) both bondage and liberation are merely a childish game.

The impulse of Knowledge is called Sayujya Mukti, liberation through "Oneness" (considered by many to be final liberation). All these are merely names of the unsteady. The "Steady One" has neither name nor form. The "Luminous One" is the One who makes everything manifest. He is known as Jyotirupa (Jyoti means Light, rupa means form) because all this is visible due to His power. "Awareness" (Shakti, power) always runs rampant like a tiger. Hence, She is depicted with the tiger as her mount. Yama, the God of death is shown riding a buffalo. Those who wallow in this world (like a buffalo does in the mud), fear Yama (death). The realized one does not have any fear of death.

Lecture 50 - "I Am" is the Original Illusion

"Brahman is empty like space. Like space it is vast and limitless. It is pure, attributeless, steady and eternal." (*Dasbodh* - Chapter 10, Sub-chapter 10)

He is called Paramatman and there are many more names for Him. Yet He has no name. Know that He is eternally the same. Brahman is empty like the sky, as if there is nothing at all. So, it seems it is like vacuum, pure, as always, eternal. It is there for all time. This is called Paramatman. It is present in the beginning, at the end, before concepts are formed, and even when they arise. Whether one is asleep or awake, the perception of one's Self is always there. It is natural. It is not felt nor seen, but it is there. It is present prior to, during, and after the arising of a concept. It is motionless and steady. In this motionless nature, some movement is felt. This is called Illusion, Awareness, or Maya. When the transient is felt, it is called Ishwara (God) or Maya. There are countless names, masculine, feminine, and neuter in gender that are given to the One. It is neither seen, nor felt, yet many names have been given. A symbol is used to identify an object or idea which cannot be directly seen. Likewise, various names are used to identify this nameless Paramatman. Names are merely pointers, not the objects themselves. Similarly, names have been given to Brahman for the purpose of identification. These names are for understanding the "Awareness," the impulse of "I Am."

What are we? We are the embodiment of Existence-Knowledge-Bliss (Sat-Chit-Ananda), hence we have known Existence, and therefore there is Consciousness followed by Joy or "Contentment." There is only the impulse of "I Am." It is for this "I" that the names Awareness, Moolamaya, etc., exist. Existence alone is Parabrahman, so why then use the names of Satchitananda, Awareness, Moolamaya, Knowledge, or Consciousness, for the "I Am"? Only to help us "know" Reality.

You exist unconditionally, effortlessly. Upon you arises Awareness. This is Moolamaya (Primordial Illusion), or all those names that were mentioned earlier. Upon that Awareness, arose letters, words, thoughts, mind, intellect, etc. Letters and words come together, thereby giving rise to speech. This is called Vidyadevi (Goddess of Knowledge), or Shiva. Many such names are given to Him. So, all that is necessary is to recognize Him. "Purushartha" implies the process of recognizing Him. What is Awareness? It is Consciousness. Once you know this "I Am," you can describe it. Of what use is this litany of names without knowing the Self? Therefore, try to examine it within yourself. Confirm what the scriptures and the Guru have told you with the proof in your own experience. One will progress if one understands what is gross, and what is subtle. All the visible is gross. Then arise the ten senses, and five pranas (Prana, Apana, Vyana, Udana, and Samana), the mind, intellect, etc.

If you proceed without understanding, then nothing will be understood for millions of births. In the steady motionless space, there is wind, but there is a subtle difference between wind and space. This is not detected by the naked eye but there is a difference between the two. Wind can be felt but space is just a void. Similarly, there are subtle differences between the Self and Awareness, just as there are subtle differences between brass and gold. There is no modification of any kind in the Self, hence, it is unconditioned. This is called steadiness. Thus, Chaitanya (Life-Energy), or Maya, is delusion and there is only Brahman in the Self. As there is wind in the sky, so is there the impulse "I Am" in Awareness, which itself is called Power or Life-Energy. It is also called desire. The impulse "I Am" is called Moola Prakriti. It is also called Mahakarana Deha, the great-causal body. In it arose the other three bodies. The one sitting within this four legged table is Parabrahman, Parameshwar. He is eternal and unmoving, like space. Awareness pervades all. Thus, Atman, the Self has a thousand faces, forms and shapes. This has to be understood. Understanding that there is only "Oneness" in this panorama of apparent existence is called "Adhyatma Vidya" or Spiritual Knowledge.

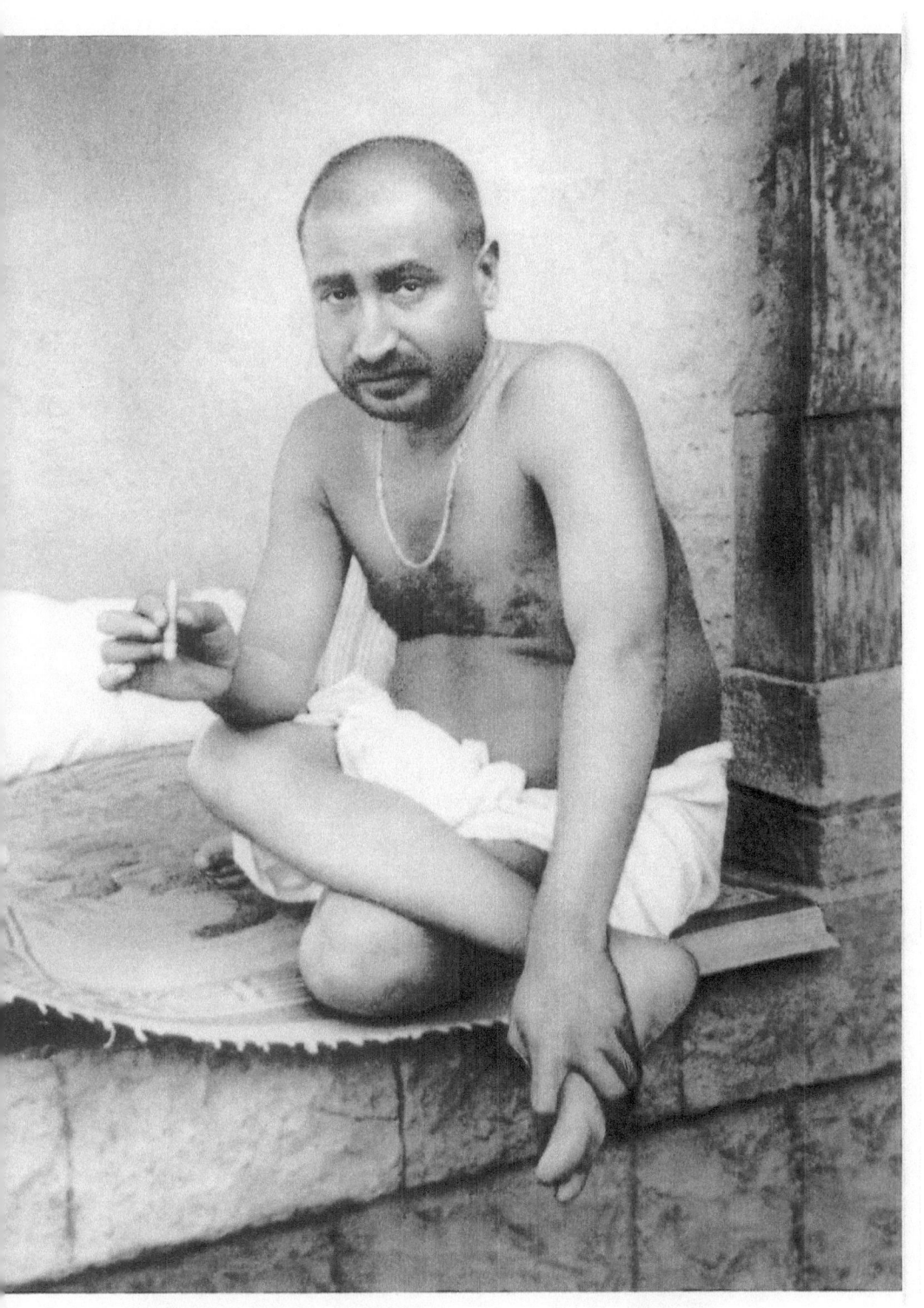
Shri Sadguru Siddharameshwar Maharaj

Amrut Laya II
The Stateless State

Spiritual Discourses of His Holiness

Shri Sadguru Siddharameshwar Maharaj

Lecture 1 - The Sadguru, the Greatest Illuminator

God is the "Divine Illuminant" who gives light to all. He is the divine light, which illuminates and expresses everything. No thing can illuminate Him, not the sun, the moon, nor fire, nor wind. It is only the "True Master" (Sadguru), who illuminates "The Illuminator." The Sadguru is "The Greatest Illuminator."

Just as the power behind the lamp destroys darkness, the Sadguru reveals that which is hidden. He introduces us to our Self (Atman) and helps us to understand it. He destroys the darkness of Ignorance, and unveils God. He illuminates God, therefore, we bow to the Master in reverence. No one can bring God into existence. He is self-established, self-existent, self-luminous, and self-evident.

Even if one happens to be in darkness, no light or other instrument is required to see one's Self. All practices and contrivances employed for this purpose only lead one off the track. This goes to prove that we ourselves are God. We are the Truth (Paramartha), and it is Truth alone, that can never be destroyed. We are Consciousness (Chit) itself.

God lends light even to the Sun. Only the Sadguru, and no one else, can reveal the Truth. The realized person (Jnani), or Saint, is in the form of Reality. It is only the one who approaches a Saint, and experiences His bliss, who becomes happy. Merely looking at a Saint cannot grant happiness. The purpose for which we have come into this world is fulfilled, and we attain liberation, when we find a true Saint. Liberation is the adornment of a Saint. One who seeks and expects happiness from others, is but a beggar. Only one who is completely devoid of desire, is truly wealthy.

Spiritual Science (Adhyatma) is the science where the Self (Atman) is considered to be first, and foremost. A yogi is one who acquires that which is relevant, that which is essential, the Truth. One who has washed off the dirt of Illusion (Maya), and has become peacefully steady in the Self after attaining the clean and pure Truth, is a Saint. Only the Saints have given up this material world and regard it as a mere Illusion. This world is a battlefield where a struggle for survival goes on perpetually. A Saint is the one who chooses not to reside in this battlefield of the objective world.

07/01/1933

Lecture 2 - The Four Bodies and Five Sheaths

It is said that Saint Tukaram went to the abode of Lord Vishnu (Vaikuntha) along with his body. This indicates a bodiless state. "Along with his body" means while he was still alive. To put it in simple words, although Saint Tukaram possessed a body, he had abandoned "body-consciousness," so it is said that he had become bodiless (Videhi). The body is but one sheath, or covering on the Self. There are five sheaths, and there are four bodies.

The four bodies are:

1. The physical, or gross body, which has the waking state as its main attribute. It is visible to the physical eye and possesses a definite shape.

2. The subtle body, which is characterized by the dream state. It is not visible to the eye, yet it functions in a manner similar to the gross body. It consists of the mind, the intellect, the thinking, the vital breaths or energies (pranas), and the ego or identification as "I."

3. The causal body is Ignorance, and is characterized by deep-sleep. It is this dreamless deep-sleep itself, which is the state of the causal body. It is a state of forgetfulness, where "nothing" is experienced.

4. The fourth body is the great-causal body and does not represent any kind of world. It exists as the fourth state, the Turya state. It is the "I Am" or "I Am He" (Soham) state. As long as one feels limited or bound by the previously mentioned three bodies, he is called the individual (jiva), and when one transcends them, one is transformed into God (Shiva).

The five sheaths are:

The gross body which is the sheath of food (Annamaya), the three sheaths associated with the subtle body which are, the sheath of the pranas or vital breaths (Pranamaya), the sheath of mind (Manomaya), and the sheath of intellect (Buddhimaya). The fifth sheath is associated with the causal body and is called the sheath of bliss (Anandamaya).

The three worlds; 1) heaven, 2) the world we live in, sometimes called the world of death, as death is inevitable, and 3) what is called the netherworld, are none other than the gross (characterized by waking state), the subtle (characterized by dreaming state), and the causal bodies (characterized by the deep-sleep state) respectively.

Everyone naturally possesses a depth that is deeper than the nethermost world. This is why it is said that the proper utilization of the human body can help bring about the transformation of the ordinary human being (Nara) into the Lord (Narayana).

21/01/1933

Lecture 3 - Vidyamaya, Avidyamaya, and Moolamaya

The mortal individual (jiva) is hounded by Illusion (Maya), due to doubt (vikalpa). It is illusory appearances that delude him. An ordinary human being who is ignorant of his true nature continues to exist as an individual, and is remains oblivious to the fact that he is immortal (Shiva). The notion that he is mortal, is itself delusion. This delusion, or Maya, is of two types. The delusion that pertains to the mundane transient world, is called Avidyamaya, and the delusion which is beyond the appearance of the world and is directed towards one's "Divine Nature" is called Vidyamaya. That which is nonexistent, that which is untrue, appears to exist due to Avidyamaya, and when everything that appears in the world is seen to be untrue, it is Vidyamaya. Both Avidyamaya and Vidyamaya are derived from the "Primal Illusion," or Moolamaya, which is Consciousness itself. Our "True Self" (Paramatman), is prior to, and beyond, even this Consciousness.

When speaking about the Self and Consciousness, it is like a river compared to an ocean. Consciousness is like a river, or "Nadi." Nadi is the Marathi word for river. Nadi is the words "na" and "adhi" together. Na means not, and adhi means prior. Therefore in this example, Consciousness as the word nadi suggests, is not prior to the Self. On the contrary, the Self is prior to Consciousness. Both Avidyamaya and Vidyamaya constitute the ocean of mundane existence. This ocean has come into existence after the appearance of Consciousness. He who is disinterested, detached from, unaffected, and untouched by Illusion, is truly powerful. He who has truly renounced Illusion has long since renounced desires, too. He is purged of both sorrows and joys. A devotee is the one who serves and honors the Saints. The one who feels honored and achieves a sense of complete fulfillment while serving a Saint, is the true humble servant. One should be detached from Illusion, disenchanted by it, and should understand Brahman through discrimination. Detachment is indeed the "True Essence."

26/01/1933

Lecture 4 - One's Primary Duty

The Ultimate Truth (Paramartha) means the attainment of Paramatman, the one beyond the Self (Atman). One attains the form of that which is worshipped. If you worship the body, you are the body, and if you worship Paramatman, you attain that state. When Paramatman is attained, the worshipper is transformed into the object of worship.

One who has sought and attained Paramatman, is the true seeker, or achiever. He is the true Saint. The primary duty of each individual is to remain immersed in his own "True Nature" (Swaroopa). This duty is the most important duty and it should be duly executed, setting aside every other duty.

28/01/1933

Lecture 5 - The Consciousness of All is the Same

When a snake approaches a man in order to bite him, the man tries to get away from it in fear. This is because it is Consciousness that prompts the snake to bite the man, and it is Consciousness again, that prompts the man to run away. Everyone functions through Consciousness, so it follows that the inner-consciousness, or inner-mind (Antahkarana[1]) of all, is the same, while their minds (manas) are different.

Lord Brahma is the "Lord of Intellect," which is the origin of desires. Desire is the cause of birth, therefore, we say that Lord Brahma is the Creator.

Lord Vishnu governs the inner-mind (Antahkarana). This is the faculty that every living being uses to look after oneself. Therefore, it is

---

[1] Antahkarana is a word that has no English equivalent, and is difficult to define. It is generally considered to be the consciousness, or sense of being conscious that is common to all beings. It is characterized by the motion of the attributes arising out of the attributeless Consciousness. One could say it is the source of the mind, or that it is one's innermost mind, or innermost heart. It is the origination of, or assertion of, objectivity. It is the mind at its most subtle. "The inner-mind of all is the same, while their minds are different." Throughout this text, it will be translated as "inner-mind" for consistency.

said that Lord Vishnu, in the form of Consciousness, takes care of all, sustains all.

Lord Shiva represents the Tamo quality, or Ignorance. It is due to Ignorance that man incurs a loss, or is destroyed. This simply means that Lord Shiva, in the form of Ignorance, destroys everything.

The desires of one who is ignorant are very strong. It is due to lack of Knowledge that his desires remain intact and grow stronger. When one who is ignorant dies, his desires along with the vital breath (prana) wander in space and eventually enter another body.

29/01/1933

Lecture 6 - The 3 Gunas, the 4 Geneses, and 5 Dissolutions

The Primal Illusion (Moolamaya), Consciousness, has arisen due to the power and existence of Brahman. It has neither come into existence of its own volition, nor has it been created by anyone else. It can be realized but cannot be talked about. The three cosmic qualities (gunas), Sattva, Rajas, and Tamas have originated in Consciousness. Consciousness or Knowledge, is related to the Sattva quality and Ignorance or oblivion, is related to the Tamo quality. The Raja quality is associated with both Knowledge and Ignorance. Those who are Self-realized (Jnanis), are the incarnations of Lord Vishnu, and those who do not have Self-Knowledge, who are ignorant, are equated with demons.

Lord Vishnu is described as the one with four hands (Chaturbhuja). The mind (manas), the intellect (buddhi), the ego (aham), and the thinking (chitta) symbolize the four hands of Lord Vishnu. The ten incarnations (Avataras) of Lord Vishnu represent the ten senses.

The four faces of Lord Brahma represent the four geneses, or origins of all living beings. These living beings are classified as:

a) Andaja - Beings that have originated from eggs.

b) Jaraja - Beings brought forth from the womb by live birth.

c) Swedaja - Beings brought into existence the mixture of moisture and heat (bacteria, etc.)[2]

d) Udbhija - Beings that sprout from seeds.

---

[2] In the past Hindus used to believe that certain creatures such as lice were born from sweat. Modern science has since proven otherwise, but has also discovered a different type of generation, in which bacteria and single celled creatures arise from the combination of heat and moisture.

Mortal individuals (jivas), come into being when the vital "Life-Energy" (Chaitanya), and the five elements come together and unite in different proportions for creating females and males. Knowledge of the Self eradicates the fear of the world of death (Yamaloka).

The dissolution of the individual, the jiva, comes in five different ways:

1. Dissolution through death(when death comes, the world disappears).
2. Dissolution through sleep(in deep-sleep, the entire world disappears).
3. The Sleep of Brahma(when the physical world disappears).
4. Dissolution of Brahma(when the cycles of Brahma disappear)
5. Dissolution through discrimination (when the Real is discerned from the unreal, the world disappears).

The Self, or Consciousness, is not the Ultimate Truth (Paramartha).

30/01/1933

Lecture 7 - Elements of the Subtle Body

Twenty-five elements constitute the subtle body. They are classified into five sets, each containing five elements.

a) The inner-mind or consciousness set which consists of 1) the mind (manas), 2) the intellect (buddhi), 3) the thinking (chitta), 4) the ego (aham), and 5) the inner-consciousness, or inner-mind (antahkarana)which sees the other four arise.

b) The set of 5 vital winds, or breaths, which consists of, 1) that which supplies liquid food material to the entire body (vyana vayu), 2) that which is found in the navel (samana vayu), 3) that which occurs in the throat (udana vayu), 4) flatulence which occurs in the bowels (apana vayu), and 5) that which we breathe in and out (prana vayu).

c) The set of 5 sensory organs which includes, 1) the eyes, 2) the ears, 3) the nose, 4) the tongue, 5) and the skin.

d) The set of the 5 organs of action which consists of, 1) the hands, 2) the feet, 3) the mouth, 4) the genitals, and 5) the anus.

e) The set of the objects of desire, or material sensual pleasures, which consists of, 1) the desire for speech or sound, 2) the desire for touch, 3) the desire for seeing, 4) the desire for taste, and 5) the desire for smell.

The ultimate goal is to understand who we truly are. One who has accomplished this, enjoys the sense of fulfillment. It is the one who stands beyond the subtle body, who attains liberation (Moksha), and is free from bondage.

04/02/1933

Lecture 8 - Discrimination Between True and Untrue

One who thinks and discriminates properly becomes free and the one who does not, is but a beast in bondage. The Ultimate Truth (Paramartha) is the discrimination between the "True" and the "untrue." The Self alone is True and everything other than the Self is untrue.

"Brahman alone is True. The world is untrue. The jiva and Brahman are one." - Shri Shankaracharya

The individual (jiva) itself is only Brahman. It is the Self in the form of Reality, in the form of the "Supreme Truth," that is truly Brahman. The one who experiences the Illusion, is the "True," whereas the experience itself is "untrue." That which is hidden, or latent, is the essence, the Truth, and that which is manifest is untrue. After renouncing all pride, He who remains, is the Reality, the underlying support of all (Shesh). To give up all untrue concepts and bondage is itself the Ultimate Truth.

That which is secret and hidden is of essence, and that which is open and seen is nonsense. You are not the body, nor the senses, nor prana, nor mind, nor intellect. All of these are prone to change and doomed to destruction. Using discrimination, understand that you are apart from the four bodies.

The four bodies are; 1) the physical, Gross body, 2) the Subtle body, 3) the Causal body, and 4) the Great-causal body (Consciousness). The gross body is constituted of the Five Elements, Space, Air, Fire (Light), Water and Earth.

22/02/1933

Lecture 9 - The Steady and the Unsteady

The Primordial Illusion (Moola Maya) possesses shape and qualities, whereas Brahman is devoid of them. Qualities indicate unsteadiness, and bring Illusion to the forefront. Unsteadiness is an inspiration (an arising movement), a mere concept. A concept means that it is only a thought. We forget our "Self" because we get engrossed and absorbed in thoughts.

We are steady by nature. Unsteadiness comes later, and then goes. We resemble the sea in this respect. The sea is inherently calm and quiet, but appears agitated due to waves. The sea represents Brahman, the steady, while the waves represent the Illusion, which is unsteady.

The fourth body, the great-causal body, is that Consciousness wherein you are conscious only of "I Am." Ignorance comes into existence when you are unaware of it. Pay close attention to Consciousness, and notice that everything is Ignorance in the form of mind. The mind has limitations, whereas the Self is all-pervading and boundless. The individual (jiva) is the one who is governed by the mind and who tries to understand the minds of others. When you focus on the mind, all that you see is unsteadiness. This is called inaccurate vision (Vikalpa Drishti). At most, you could say that it is a perverted way of seeing. The subtle body is full of inaccurate and perverted knowledge. This means that the activities of the mind as well as those of the intellect are unsteady and ever-changing. These ever-changing, unsteady activities flow downwards into a relative inertia and take the form of the gross body. "As the Self is in all beings, God exists in all." This should be our attitude. The Ultimate Truth resides in the fact that we are formless by nature.

18/03/1933

Lecture 10 - Keeping the Company of Saints

From a talk on the Eknathi Bhagwat of Saint Eknath

The association with Saints helps destroys all doubts, along with one's established mindsets, etc. Self-realization is thereby attained directly. Just as a cocooned caterpillar is transformed into a butterfly, so it is with a devotee. The devotee, by virtue of association with Saints assumes his "True Form" (Swaroopa) and reaches the state of the Sadguru. The association with Saints elevates devotees to such a status that they are worthy of worship even by the Guru. To reach the Self, there is no other means but to keep the company of Saints.

Renunciation (sanyasa) alone, does not drive away the pride associated with the body. It is your duty as a devotee to sacrifice everything that you think belongs to you at the feet of the Master. Give up all of your belongings, give up the desire for everything, and strive hard for Self-Knowledge. Do not simply give things up in charity, as charity brings nothing but pride.

The whole world is lost in empty rituals and superstition. Nothing is achieved by all the various rituals involving mantra and tantra.

02/06/1933

Lecture 11 - The Power of the Saint

The Inner-Self residing in all is my own reflection. Yet, I cannot be achieved even with the help of innumerable practices. Only when one associates with Saints, do I myself go and meet the devotee. It is then that one can reach the ultimate state of the self-existent Paramatman. Even those who have fallen integrate into my nature when they join in the company of Saints. Those who do not have faith in the words of the Saints, are prescribed various rituals and charities in order to cleanse their chitta (make the mind more subtle). It is the Saints alone, who have set the gods, humans, and even demons, on the right track. It is they alone who make Paramatman, the "Sublime Truth," steady in its status. It is the aspirants who need to make their minds more subtle, who are initially prescribed various practices, such as meditation, mantra, etc. by the Saints.

03/06/1933

Lecture 12 - Spiritual Practice and the Gunas

Although the female companions of Lord Krishna (gopis), came to Him with lust on their minds, He purged their minds of lust, and helped them to attain to the highest state. Fire consumes all kinds of wood. It equally turns coal, as well as sandalwood, into burning embers. It converts them into its own nature and form. In the same way, the virtuous company of a Saint transforms one's nature and form.

One can attain the nature and form of Parabrahman only by associating with Saints. Saints are the guides who can lead you to your "True Nature" (Swaroopa). As soon as an aspirant meets a Saint, he gets inspired and is filled with the thoughts of the Supreme Self. The Reality is without attributes, whereas the *Vedas* are bound by the three attributes (Rajas, Tamas, and Sattva). The *Vedas* initially coerce and lead an individual (jiva) into practices (actions, karmas), and ritualistic worship. These ignorant deeds are indeed mysterious, as Ignorance itself is untrue.

In relation to spiritual practice, the Rajas quality manifests itself through worship, Tamas quality manifests itself through rituals, and Sattva quality manifests through Knowledge. What then, is Ignorance (Avidya)? All of our concepts constitute Ignorance. Nothing can be distinguished as good or bad in Ignorance. The rules and regulations regarding what is to be done and what is forbidden are all nothing but concepts of good and bad. When concepts are renounced completely, one attains the state of Brahman.

04/06/1933

Lecture 13 - Renunciation of Pride and Desire

Knowledge derived with the aid of concepts is Ignorance (Avidya), whereas that which "is" without concepts, is Brahman. That, which cannot be perceived with the aid of the mind, the eye, or anything else, is Brahman. Knowledge derived without the aid of concepts or any other mental constructs is one's own True Form. It is "Samadhi without concepts," or Nirvikalpa Samadhi. "Dos" and "don'ts" have been set up for the ignorant. The "dos" (vidhi) means to accept, and the "don'ts" (nishedha), means to renounce. After renouncing Ignorance, that which remains is Brahman. Once it is understood, that "I am not the body," Ignorance automatically becomes eliminated. Vedanta helps us attain Knowledge, as listening to it helps us to destroy Ignorance. To completely destroy Ignorance, surrender to the Sadguru.

Give up the pride of practical wisdom, the ego, the attachment to wife, children, etc., and surrender to the Master. Renounce the pride of that which is good, as well as bad. Give up even the study of the *Vedas* and other scriptures. Renounce continued activity (pravritti), as well as liberation from worldly existence (nivritti). Renounce the importance of, and pride in the mind, of practical wisdom, and of wealth. In short, give up desire in general and surrender to the Master. After surrendering to Him, you will acquire His blissful state. To unite with Him, one has to sacrifice even one's religion.

He is in every heart. Words cannot describe Him. Faith without delusion is the only requisite to realize Him. The understanding that "I Am He, and not the body," can only be gained with the help of the guidance given by the Master. Saints always consider themselves to be the Self and behave accordingly. Every human being should think and find out whether anything has held him as a slave. One should think of what he has been doing and where he has been led by his desires. Abandon all desires and surrender to the Master. Renounce the pride for the body and surrender to He who resides in your heart. Abide in the feeling "I am present in all," and behave accordingly.

05/06/1933

Lecture 14 - Pride is Ego

One's "True Form" (Swaroopa) cannot be understood due to the presence of pride, or ego. Pride has turned Paramatman into an ignorant individual (jiva). OM means, "I am present in every heart." OM (AUM) is the statement of Brahman. It is the name of Brahman. Name means speech. Renounce your pride for the body and surrender to the Master. The agent, or the doer, who is in the body and who claims to have done everything is called "I," yet it is truly the Self alone that is one's "True Form."

Do not consider the objects in the mundane world that may come your way, to belong to you. Do not shower your love on material objects. Give up the pride associated with all of these objects. The predator "time" stalks every mind and every body, but it does not trouble the Self (Atman). The Self is unaffected by time. The state of beings is itself the "Power" (Chaitanya). It is the "Original Object." It is that which remains after all names, forms, qualities, and doership are given up.

After realizing the Self, wherever you look you will feel "I am there in all beings." In every body, it is the Self, which is named as "I." It is that "I" which is the essential principle of the *Vedas*, the scriptures, and the yogas. The ultimate bliss is to identify yourself with Brahman, to be one with it. As long as the concept "I am the body" persists, the Self is believed to be an individual (jiva), and is considered to be the doer, or the agent of all actions. In that state, the "I" is affected by joys and sorrows. It is in this state that the "do" and "don't" statements in the *Vedas* become applicable to one. All these statements become redundant after the ego of the body leaves. Only the Master can explain this. Rituals can be followed only until the Master's arrival.

Tuesday 05/06/1933

Lecture 15 - The Self is Not the Body

It is the individual, who grants God his god-like qualities. It is only God (Shiva) himself, who is the individual (jiva). It is because of the identification with, or pride for the body, that God has turned into the individual. Let the Self (Atman) dwell in any kind of body, it is none other than Shiva. The Self is the reflection in the mirror of the body. It is the body that has the attributes of birth and death, yet it is mistakenly believed that it is the Self that is born. The Self is subtle and agile, while the body is inert. The Self has no attributes and cannot be described. It is neither large nor small, neither great nor insignificant. It is huge while being subtle. It is so huge that the entire universe is contained in it. It is from the Self, that the universe has originated.

The appearance of the Life-Energy (Chaitanya) in the senses, is called the "reflection," whereas that which dwells in the inner-mind (antahkarana), is the Life-Energy itself. It is this Life-Energy, which casts its own reflection. That which is steady is the Life-Energy in its purest form. It is the Self in the form of the notion of "individual consciousness" (jiva) which associates itself with body, yet it's nature remains pristine and uncorrupted, as it is unblemished and untouched by the faults or misdeeds of the body. If the Self were truly the body, then there would be no death for the body. The Self merely imagines that it is the body. Upon attaining Knowledge, it understands that it is not.

The reflections of the Sun and Moon appear and disappear on the water while the Sun and the Moon themselves are unaffected. Just as the appearance and disappearance of the reflections are brought about with the aid of water, the comings and the goings on the Self (Atman) are seen with the aid of the body. The absence of water puts an end to the reflections, but does not put an end to the Sun or Moon. Similarly, the Self does not come to an end with the destruction of the body.

Actions (karmas) cannot bind the Self, on the contrary they only disappear. The Self is as pure as Fire. Whether we are asleep or in darkness we are accompanied by the feeling "I Am." This inner "I Am" is the nature of the Self. It is called the "unbeaten sound" (anahat) that originates from within, as it is not produced externally. The "I Am" feeling itself is "Soham." This unbeaten, internal chanting of "Soham" goes on all throughout one's life in the form of the breath, over 20,000 times a day. Although the individual seems to be the body, it is the Self that truly identifies with the body. This is the power of Illusion.

07/06/1933

Lecture 16 - The Inner-Mind, and the Five Elements

That which is very subtle, resembling and accompanying the ever-flowing, unnoticed prana is the feeling "I Am" embedded in our inner-mind. The origination of the words, "I Am" is the mind in its most subtle extreme. It is called the speech which is well formed yet not distinctly pronounced (Pashyanti speech). It resembles the prana which is unnoticed, yet circulates in every limb and every organ of the body (Vyana Vayu). The practice of hatha yoga indicates affecting the union of the breath (Prana Vayu) with the intestinal eliminative gases (Apana Vayu). The True Yogis, or Jnanis, have no attachment to anything. When they are at peace, their Prana and Apana naturally slow down and join together. Joining together simply means that the Prana and the Apana are balanced and maintain equanimity.

The Self is the origin of, and permeates the inner-mind. It also conducts and manages all three worlds; the waking state, the dream state, and the deep-sleep state. These are symbolized by the world of truth, the mundane human world, and the nether-world. These transient worlds all reside in the Self. There exists nothing but the "I Am." If there is no thread, there is no cloth. By the same principle, if "I don't exist," then the world consisting of the five elements also does not exist. This world of five elements revolves around the "I Am." Worldly pleasures and pains do not exist in the absence of the "I Am." Wherever "I Am," bliss exists there, in its true form. "I Am," is omnipresent and all-pervading. However, due to delusion, people deny the very existence of the Self.

Dust particles in their most subtle form constitute the wind, which is not visible. Wind is the manifest form of Life-Energy (Chaitanya). When Life-Energy flows freely, it is called wind or air. The slowing down of wind is the source of water. The earth is brought forth from water. The speeding up of air constitutes fire. When the Life-Energy calms down the "I Am" is brought to the forefront. Air, water, earth, and fire (light), are names of the elements given according to their characteristics. Though the world has been so named, it is this "I Am" which is the source of this world. For one who has realized Me, "I am everything," whereas one who has not realized Me, is involved only in worldly life and conceives of sins and virtue. The one who has not realized Me, finds that which he conceives, believes in it, and gets carried away by it. Sins and virtues are like seeds, which sprout and strike roots in the form of infinite desires in the soil of delusion and ignorance. The tree of worldly life grows watered by deeds and non-deeds and their resulting joys and sorrows.

08/06/1933

Lecture 17 - Worship of the Master

Two birds representing two kinds of intellect, live on the tree of worldly existence:
1. One takes pride in the body.
2. The other says, "I am not the body."

Everything in this mundane world comes into existence as a result of a subtle stirring within the Self.

All living beings depend on the Sun. It is due to the Sun that all living beings are created, sustained, and are destroyed. It is the individual (jiva) that experiences all that lies between the Earth and Sun, whereas it is God (Shiva) who experiences the feeling "I am not the body." Those who are lustful and long for all sorts of worldly pleasures are nothing but vultures living in houses. Worldly life is the "be all, and end all" of their existence. An aspirant should live in his own house as though he has performed a sacrifice giving up the ownership of all belongings and worldly possessions. The aspirant then becomes a mere trustee. The aspirant should serve the Master, and while doing so should remain in his "True Nature" (Swaroopa).

Desire only leads to one's deterioration and downfall. While going through the stage of domestic life, an aspirant should be constantly aware that, "I am not the body." One who hears from the Master that "I am not the body," and who realizes "I Am Brahman" is transformed into Shiva. Only such a one becomes free from worldly life. This worldly life is illusory. It is untrue. Those who have recognized that this worldly life is only Illusion are the "Truly Knowledgeable." They are called the "Paramahansa[3]." One who realizes that the world is "not," has no more longing for it. Those who want to realize this should devote themselves to following and studying the Master's teachings.

It is by virtue of satsang, the company of Saints, that all attachment towards worldly life ceases. The Master's (Sadguru) worship alone is the true satsang. Without worshipping the Sadguru, this tree of the mundane life cannot be brought down. Only complete, unswerving faith in the Master can bring down that tree. Worship of the Master puts the fear of the mundane to rest. Words fail to describe the Sadguru. He alone has realized Brahman. He can gauge the disciple's caliber, and guide him accordingly. Such a guide is the real Master, and one should surrender only to Him. Regard all rituals and religions to be untrue and completely dedicate yourself to the Master. The Master ferries you across this ocean of worldly life and helps you to realize your True Nature. He helps you avoid the cycle of birth and death. The Master should be worshipped because he is the "God of Gods." The "Wish Fulfilling Tree"

---

[3] In Hindu mythology, Paramahansa is a swan which is able to sift the milk with its beak out of the combination of water and milk in order to drink only the milk. This symbolizes the saint's ability to sift Reality from the Illusion.

(Kalpataru[4]) may grant you your worldly desires, but the Guru helps you be rid of all desires, and drives away greed.

09/06/1933

Lecture 18 - How to Worship

Previously we have seen how God should be worshipped. Now we have been asked to worship the Master. Who is God after all? God is the Self, our own Self. You cannot find God without worshipping your Master, as God is none other than the Master. However, nothing can be achieved by mere blind physical worship of the Master. You should have a thirst for the "Knowledge of Brahman."

The Bhagavadgita says, "All rituals are meaningless, without the Knowledge of the Self." Lord Rama and Lord Krishna are none but great Masters of ancient times who with the passage of time have come to be looked upon as gods. The ritual of offering money at the feet of the idol symbolizes one's intention of giving up the desire for money. One should only worship the traditional gods and gurus until he meets a "True Guru," a Sadguru, who possesses the divine "Knowledge of Brahman." It is the Sadguru alone who is Lord Brahma, Lord Vishnu and Lord Shiva.

One should be thoroughly infused with the understanding "I should be at the service of the Master at all times, and serve to the fullest." Love develops through service. While serving the Sadguru, desire, thirst, hunger, sleep, laziness, lethargy, yawning, and slothfulness should all be given up. When there is intimate affection in worshipping the Guru, one forgets oneself (jivahood). Worshipping is done through singing the praises of the Sadguru (bhajans, kirtan) and through contemplation on Him and His teaching.

Let your mind follow the Master. Let it go wherever the Master goes. Understand that "I Am Brahman, and this world is untrue." Thus, the nectar in the form of realization, is gained with the help of the Master's guidance. Through His words, one comes to understand that all mental efforts to realize Brahman are useless, and that "no effort" is the only

---

[4] In Maharashtra State in India rural village people hang pieces of clothing on a Wish-Fulfilling Tree in hopes of having their desires filled.

"effort" that is required. Ultimately, the concept "I Am Brahman," is also a delusion.

In Indian temples we generally see a tortoise carved out of marble or any other stone, placed in front of the idol, facing it. This is meant to signify that the young tortoise continuously looks to its mother. It can survive and grow only under its mother's loving gaze. The young tortoise symbolizes the disciple. The disciple should continuously look toward the Sadguru. The disciple can grow and flower into a Jnani under the loving gaze of the Master. Pray to the Sadguru that He may grant the boon of "devotion to Him."

10/06/1933

Lecture 19 – Give Up Pride for the Body

The only desire, which should be entertained, is "I should be continually in the service of the Master, and should serve him devoutly." The one who does not consider devotion to the Master to be far superior to the "Knowledge of the Self," should be dubbed a fool. He fails to put faith in the Master because he has not gotten over the pride for the body. Service to the Master helps to vanquish pride. Service to the Master is not difficult, but it seems to be, until we get started on it. One should serve the Master in order to put into practice the Knowledge that has been listened to. As body-consciousness begins diminishing, the importance of Brahman increases proportionately. Devotion to the Master helps you gladly and willingly reduce the importance given to the body. Circumstances in life should not be what compels one to lower the value of the body. Its importance should be willingly, and voluntarily, lowered. This approach of knowingly and lovingly reducing the value of the body is called devotion. Devotion or service to the Master is the first and the most important step towards attaining Knowledge.

Devotion is the mother of Knowledge, as it brings forth Knowledge. He alone who fully devotes himself to the Master's service, dedicating his body, mind and speech, together with his life, acquires the "Knowledge of Brahman." The more easily and naturally disposed one is towards worldly pleasures, the more anxious one is to acquire them. You should be equally anxious to serve the Master. In this fashion, one who willingly and happily serves the Master, lays his hands on the treasure, in the form of the "Knowledge of the Master." As one gives increasing importance and value to the body, the value of the Self decreases. Thus, the body appears to diminish the power of the Self. One who has lowered the importance of the body is rightfully the Master's son. Those who are the sons of the Master, bravely assert the value the Self. One should go even so far as to cultivate the habit of doing menial tasks in order to drive away the pride for the body. Devotion to the Master is not always easy. Immense efforts, along with an intense desire for realization are required. One should solidify one's resolve for giving up the pride for the body. Attempts at giving up the pride for the body should be made as often as possible. Don't forget that the remarkable and rare can be accomplished only by doing something rare, and remarkably different from what others do.

11/06/1933

Lecture 20 - Spiritual Science and Eliminating Pride

The word "pradnyavritti" means "the concept in the mind which urges one to gain experience and learn." We are the Self (Atman). This means that "We are Brahman" and should behave accordingly. "Spiritual science" (Shaastra) and the weapon (shastra) holder should be treated as the same. The one who takes up spiritual science is himself the weapon holder. This is because the weapon holder holds the weapon of spiritual science. Spiritual science is the ceaseless study of "I Am Brahman." The weapon holder himself is Brahman.

It is because we draw distinctions in Brahman that the Self seems to have descended to the state of an individual (jiva). This notion of individual consciousness can come to an end if we put an end to it by striking it down. Every moment presents an opportunity. Seizing opportunity, one has to strike. Striking down the tree of the state of the mortal means to give up the concepts that one so deeply loves. A True Master (Sadguru) is required in order to gain experiential Knowledge. This Knowledge should be brought into practice in everyday life. After practicing in this way, the ultimate state is reached, and the various practices prescribed by the *Vedas* are no longer required.

Spiritual practices only serve the purpose of purifying the thinking (chitta), thereby making the mind more subtle. Give up those mental habits that increase your tendency towards making distinctions, which in turn nourish body-consciousness. The various practices and rituals in the *Vedas* have been set up for those who identify themselves with the body. When it is understood that the body itself is Brahman, all of the precepts of the *Vedas* become false. He who has recognized that he himself is Brahman need not follow any specific practices or take refuge in any religion. The struggle of the individual to follow innumerable practices is futile. Just as a plough is of no use to a farm ripe with corn, likewise, all such practices are worthless to one who is realized. He ultimately gives up even saying "I Am Brahman."

Mundane existence (samsara) is the thorn of Ignorance, and you have to rid yourself of it. While it is true that Ignorance must be eliminated, it is even more important to give up the pride of Knowledge. Only then can full contentment be reached. The shackles of Ignorance are like iron shackles, while those of Knowledge are as if made of gold. Still, both are shackles, and must be removed. Do not be proud even of the fact that you are Brahman.

The vain pride arising out of Ignorance dies down easily and quickly, but it is much more difficult to get over the pride of Knowledge. The pride of Knowledge is worse than the pride generated due to Ignorance. It is as exasperating and irritating as a biting bed bug. The pride of Knowledge is wickedly obstinate and subtle. Its presence is never felt and even if it appears to have been completely wiped off, traces of it continue to persist. Moreover, pride, or ego, as long as it persists, it will continue to create distinctions. "Good aspiration" is to believe that "Everything is Brahman," without entertaining any element of doubt. Of all the known practices, devotion to the Master is the most valuable practice to a disciple, for it is by virtue of such devotion that one humbles oneself and attains the state of Brahman without pride.

12/06/1933

Lecture 21 - Description of the Master

From a talk on the Eknathi Bhagwat of Saint Eknath

The Master is Anaadi. Anaadi means "nothing is prior to Him." If Paramatman is similar to Hansa (a swan), the Sadguru is "Paramahansa." He is the God of Gods. The Master is called Paramahansa because it is

He who has granted the quality of God (godliness) to God, and has thus established Him and honored Him. Oh Master! Your "True Form" (Swaroopa) is purer than the purest essence of Sattva. Having given up all castes and distinctions, you shine in resplendent glory. You frolic amongst the lotuses of hearts that have blossomed with Divine Love. Your play is beyond the mind. The "Love Blossomed Hearts" of devotees are invariably inclined towards Consciousness.

With a beak in the form of discriminatory power, and with the help of rational thinking, you see the distinction between the Self (Atman) and non-self. The Rajhansa (Royal Swan), a legendary bird is believed to have a keen sense of discrimination by virtue of which it can separate milk from water, sipping only the milk and leaving the water. The Master, too, in a manner similar to a Rajhansa separates the two entities, the body and the Self. He then closely scrutinizes the two, and selects the milk and discards the water. He selects the Self over the body. When the thoughts, "Am I the body?," or "Is there some owner of the body?," occur, it can be concluded that the devotee is on the path of liberation. However, when the thought "I am the body" haunts an individual, it can be said that he is destined to be affected by the cycle of births and deaths. Everyone should realize the Self. Not to know the Self is suicidal.

According to the Hindu epic, the Mahabharata, Adhogati means retrogression, and it brings about deterioration. Narakasura is the individual, the jiva, who continues to be affected by worldly life which is in the form of hell. Those who die without realizing the Self are simply reduced to the five elements. He who takes pride in the body is Dhritarashtra, the blind king who sired a hundred sons. His vices represent the one hundred sons, and desire represents Dusheela, the sister to these one hundred brothers.

It is believed that the Rajhansa, the legendary bird, feeds on pearls. The "Pearl of Liberation" is formed in the shell of detachment. Feed on this Pearl of Liberation. When you fall into the shell of the Atma-Brahman, you are converted into a "Pearl of Brahman." One who realizes the Self does not touch the earth. This means that you do not get trapped in body-consciousness. The sun does not see you, nor do you encounter supernatural elements such as spirits. You then start considering even infinite space as a trifle. As the space is embedded in Brahman you do not find a place in it, only the five elements. This path is entirely different and truly unique. The power of understanding is indeed exceptionally extraordinary.

Lecture 22 - Four Types of Speech, and "Soham"

The Sadguru is the one who grants statement to all the four types of speeches.
1. The inspiration arising in the heart (Para).
2. That which is inarticulate at the throat (Pashyanti).
3. The speech that is a whisper occurring in the mouth (Madhyama).
4. The speech that is audible and is expressed by the lips (Vaikhari).

It is the Sadguru alone who helps one acquire Knowledge. It is only because of Him that one is able to impart that Knowledge to the world, by way of speech. If not for the presence of the Sadguru, learning, penance, repetition of mantra (japa), meditation, etc., would have never existed. It is He alone, that exists uniformly in all bodies. Birth and death can be avoided by bowing to Him, identifying with Him, and surrendering exclusively to Him.

Laxmi, the goddess of wealth, takes up residence with a person who comes to know who he is. It is when you identify yourself with the body that the cycle of birth and death begins. In order to avoid this cycle, you have been endowed with the inherent memory of "Soham" (I Am He). The cycle of birth and death is afraid of the word Soham. Upon hearing it, the birth and death cycle beats a hasty retreat. Death eradicates birth, and Soham eradicates death. Birth and death will never cross one's path if one identifies with the Master, surrenders to Him, and realizes this Soham. Birth and death are only concepts that take their shelter in delusion. Soham is not a delusion, therefore the concepts of birth and death are not seen in it.

14/06/1933

Lecture 23 – The Three Gunas

The "Three Attributes" (Gunas), Sattva, Rajas, and Tamas, belong to Prakriti (manifestation, the body) and not to the Self (Atman). The Sattva guna is what arouses the desire to work towards the attainment of the Self, and in turn results in the individual (jiva) putting forth the necessary effort to attain Self-realization. Sattvaguna that is tainted with the pride of Knowledge should be given up with the help of Pure Sattva, or "Shuddha Sattva," which is untainted by pride.

Taking up residence where the Sadguru resides develops Sattvaguna. If you go to the place where there is singing of devotional songs, or where there are discussions on Knowledge, Sattva guna naturally springs forth. It is most easily developed in the company of Saints, and where there is dancing and singing of devotional songs praising the Lord or Sadguru, unaffected by pride. Intoxicants and liquor produce Tamo guna (ignorance, lethargy, inertia). Tamoguna is commonly developed in unclean places and at night. Rajoguna is produced when in the company of people constantly discussing mundane matters, such as professional topics, or in the company of traders, etc. Rajoguna commonly arises in places abounding in comforts and luxuries.

The best period of one's life is when one receives advice from the Master. During this period, Sattvaguna rises to its peak. It can be described as "The Golden Day," which is immortalized by drinking the nectar of the Guru's teachings. In worldly life one has two separate entities as parents, the father, and the mother. However, the Guru is both father and mother rolled into one, a complete parent. It is the Sadguru who helps you overcome birth and death. It is He who exorcises the spirits in the form of five elements, and who proves that you are not the body but the Self. He breaks the bonds that bind the individual.

Only a fortunate few come across this True Father." He is the father, as well as the mother, who rescues the child (the devotee) from this illusory worldly life. He nourishes the devotee with his own Self, and elevates one to the state of immortality by helping one to evade birth and death. One who surrenders to the Sadguru, far excels above everyone else, even the gods Brahma, Vishnu, and Shiva. The nature of Sadguru is the same as that of his disciple. No distinction can be drawn between the two. Initiation which helps one attain "liberation" should be sought. Meditation is sattvic when we meditate on the Self.

15/06/1933

Lecture 24 - The Mantra "I Am Brahman"

Although one may meditate upon any one of the "Four Kinds of Liberation" (Salok, Samip, Sarup and Sayujya), all that you are really doing is meditating upon Life-Energy, or Consciousness. Therefore, meditate solely upon the Life-Energy. This is the command of the Sadguru. This is the meditation that purifies the thinking (chitta) making the mind subtle. The essence of Brahman resides in this Life-Energy. The Sadguru himself is the Life-Energy. Mantra makes the mind subtle. The Gayatri Mantra[5] is considered to be the mother of all mantras. It destroys the mortality of the individual and bestows godhood, thus giving a second birth into Reality.

The Mantra "I Am Brahman" is the greatest of all. Liberation can be attained by virtue of this mantra. There are other mantras that may give one some desired worldly fruit, however it is only the devotees of the Sadguru who utter the mantra "I Am Brahman." With this mantra, Illusion beats a hasty retreat. One who has not grasped the magnitude of this mantra will not be able to realize Brahman. Realize the Self, which is Consciousness (Chit), and is in the form of the Knowledge, "I Am Brahman." Various thoughts, doubts and perverted concepts, which occur in the mind are wiped out when one repeats the mantra "I Am Brahman."

One should have complete faith that "I Am the Self." Discard all concepts and exercise control over the mind. Constantly contemplate on the Self so the mind does not stray. In this way, the mind becomes subtle and Sattvaguna is predominant. Just as a maid who is a slave to her master dares not disobey him, so should the mind be brought under the subjugation of the Self. It can be taken for granted that the thinking of one, who during his daily affairs does not like to discuss topics other than the "Knowledge of Brahman," has been purified. With each breath, keep on knowingly saying, "Soham, I Am Brahman." Everyone strives hard, putting in a lot of effort to learn worldly arts and sciences. If you were to try to gain the "Knowledge of Brahman" with just one hundredth of that effort, you are sure to attain the state of Brahman.

Active nightlife, alcoholism, sensuous pleasures, plays, dramas, cinemas, etc. are characteristics attributed to Tamoguna. Those who are prone to anger, vengefulness, vindictiveness, and who harbor enmity are the products of Tamoguna. Indulgence in charity or rituals for the sake

---

[5] The Gayatri Mantra was first recorded in the *Rig Veda* some 2500 to 3500 years ago. It is transliterated as:
om tat savitur varenyam - We meditate upon the radiant Divine Light
bhargo devasya dhîmahi - May it awaken our intuitional consciousness
dhiyo yo nah prachodayât - of that adorable Sun of Spiritual Consciousness
Translation by S. Krishnamurthy

of name and fame, having a strong liking for scents and fragrant materials, attraction for pleasures, greed for being acknowledged as a person of high station, intense longing for honor, etc. are all characteristics which can be attributed to Rajoguna. The period between sunrise and sunset is when Rajoguna is at its height. It is very difficult to be rid of this guna, which endows a man with the mantra of lust for things in the world. This guna also prompts a person to take advice only for the sake of worldly gains, which is why a man "meditates" only on his wife and children. While Sattvaguna can be discarded, and Tamoguna also, will vanish, for instance when a major calamity befalls one, or in the face of crisis, Rajoguna however, try as you may, refuses to leave.

16/06/1933

Lecture 25 - The Self Does Not Die

Take it for granted that the body is perishable. However, if it is judiciously utilized, one can easily realize that the individual (jiva) is Paramatman. The intellect then undergoes a radical change. Only when one deeply contemplates "Who am I?" will one experience "I Am Paramatman." Paramatman, the Almighty, has gifted the human being with the ability to give thought to the "True Nature" (Swaroopa) of who he really is. Every living creature, with the exception of man, who has been gifted with the thinking capacity, must experience the fruits of their actions, while going through the cycle of 8.4 million births[6] in various species.

That which remains after discarding everything is untainted objectless Consciousness, Brahman. If the Self who claims this body were truly only the body, it would never leave it and accept another. Because the Self who dwells within the body has only temporarily identified with it, it is obliged to eventually vacate it. The body is gross and sluggish. The vital Life-Energy in this body is the Self, and this Life-Energy is Shiva. The Self does not die with the death of the body, nor does it take birth when the body does. The individual consciousness (jiva) which identifies with the body, has been obsessed with desires in innumerable past births, and is likewise fond of them in this birth.

---

[6] In Hindu mythology it is said that the realm of birth and death is comprised of 8.4 million creatures.

Desire is the poison of this world. One who is poisoned by it, dies 8.4 million deaths. "Soham" is the most sattvic of all foods. Besides eating your usual quota of food, you should also consume the word Soham. Understand its meaning by experiencing it. Other than Soham, everything we eat develops either the rajas or tamas guna. Soham alone is sattvic. On experiencing it, one develops sattva and turns toward the attainment of the state of Paramatman.

One is in the grip of Ignorance due to Tamoguna, identifies with the body due to Rajoguna, and identifies with the Self due to Sattvaguna. Instead of realizing, "I Am the Self," people give in to desires. When one claims to be the doer, one gives in to the temptations of desires. Ignorance prevails and one becomes identified as a mere possessor of the body, seemingly trapped within it. In this way, one becomes unable to reside in the Ultimate Truth, and instead dwells in the world of birth and death.   17/06/1933

Lecture 26 - There is Only One Self

The subtle body is comprised of the sensory organs, the five vital breaths (pranas), the mind, the intellect, the inner-mind, and the "I" sense (aham). The one who, in deep-sleep, knows that there exists nothing but Consciousness, is the Fourth body, or the great-causal body (mahakarana deha). This Consciousness is itself Brahman.

God with attributes, who sees all, is in the form of Consciousness, and Brahman without attributes, is also in the form of Consciousness. The vitality that animates all, is the Life-Energy, Chaitanya, and it is distinctly apart from the gross, subtle and causal bodies. When this Life-Energy separates out from the living gross body, the one who realizes, "I am not the body" stands as the "Almighty." After giving up the body, the notion of individual consciousness (jiva) departs, and one is thereby transformed into God (Shiva).

Intellect itself is the Creator, Lord Brahma. The body is perishable, and all actions performed with the help of the body are also perishable. Despite the fact that Lord Brahma has created this universe and has done many deeds, he stands distinctly apart from the resulting sins and merits. The Knowledge that reveals this secret is the most superior and ancient Knowledge, and it happens with the aid of Lord Vishnu. It is also called "Eternal Knowledge." The general question "Who are you?" is often asked. This question cannot be answered. This is because the two worldly entities, "I," and "you," are both untrue. There is only one entity, the Self (Atman). It exists in one and all. There is no distinction in it whatsoever. It is futile to ask, "Who are you?" If "you" and "I" do not exist, how can an answer to this question ever exist?

Living beings may possess different names, looks, and belong to the same or different castes, but still all have only one form. Had they been different, then the questions "Who are you"" or "Who am I?" would have been relevant. The Self, the very basic factor present in all, is only one, and there can be no distinction. The bodies of all beings from Lord Brahma to a mosquito are composed of five elements, therefore you cannot address the question "Who are you?" even to the body. As far as the essence is concerned, it exists equally in everything, and the five elements are distributed equally in all. There is no discrimination. Therefore, asking someone "Who are you?" is like addressing the question to oneself. In this universe, the Self is the only entity. The one Self singularly pervades the entire universe. 19/06/1933

Lecture 27 - The Self is the Only Experiencer

In the world, there is nothing but the Self. "I Am" the only entity. The Self in everyone is one. Just as the water held by a container continues to be water and is nothing but water irrespective of the shape of the container, so it is with the Self. Irrespective of the shape of the body it resides in, the Self continues to be the Self, and nothing but the Self.

The bodies of all living beings are made up of the five elements, and after death, all bodies turn to dust. When the body dies, it mingles with dust until the last subtle particle is eventually blown away by the wind showing that even this transient dust is not true. However, all objects are brimming with Life-Energy.

Mind is the Self saying something, but mind is only Consciousness. Mind is similar to the "inner-mind" (antahkarana) and Parabrahman, in that it cannot be indicated by any description. The bodies, minds and the Self of all living beings, are one. Mind, is the Self, in the form of Consciousness. When the Self conceives something, or says something, it is called the mind. Similarly, if it is called the body, it appears to turn into the body. However, even after calling the Self "mind," it does not really turn into the mind. No one can utter a word without Consciousness, as

Consciousness is Brahman, the Self, who is the knower of *Vedas* and their content. It is Self-enlightened.

OM (AUM) is in the form of Consciousness, and is called "Pranava." The various organs of the body carry out various functions, such as sight, hearing, etc., but their principal function is to be conscious, and this Consciousness is of the Self. In fact, this Consciousness is One and only One. Seeing Consciousness is like seeing the "eye of the eye." The Self is the eye of the eye. It is the one who sees, as well as what is seen. This situation is best explained by the analogy of offering sugar to an idol of God that is made of sugar.

The Self is full of Knowledge. Wherever Consciousness exists, the Self exists. It is the speaker, as well as the listener, and it is the one who understands the meaning. The Self is the doer of everything. The Sun owes its status and light to the Self. If not for the Self, the Sun would not even be called the Sun. The Self is the creator of the universe, as well as the one who labels everything as untrue. One who realizes this can reach the state of one's "True Nature" (Swaroopa). The transient world, which is based on good and bad concepts, continues to pass away. The "Knowledgeable" (Jnanis) know that it is the Self (Lord Hari, Vishnu the sustainer), who is the doer of everything, and that it is only He who gets everything done. The one who experiences everything is only He, the Self, the only true experiencer.

20/06/1933

Lecture 28 - Renunciation of Desires and Pride

Worldly desires have crept into the thinking, and have inter-mingled with the thoughts. It is in the company of the body that the thinking has shaped itself with the mold of desires. So, the question arises, "How can they be separated?" The "Knowledge of Brahman," can never be acquired unless desires are given up. Due to the habitual notion of "doing something" and reaping the fruits, our "inner-mind" (antahkarana) is inclined toward the fulfillment of desires, and this has given rise to ego.

It is in the forgetting of one's "True Nature" (Swaroopa), that one clings to the concept of "I am the body," and the mind becomes identified with the individual consciousness (jiva). This body-consciousness is the reason one becomes fascinated with worldly desires, and fond of sensuous pleasures.

Had thoughts ever been the true nature of the individual, they would have gravitated only towards the individual consciousness, and would have never become involved with desires. The individual consciousness, while forgetting its "True Nature," strives to satisfy the thinking. As the thinking has become infatuated with desires, the individual consciousness has accordingly become obsessed with them.

The individual consciousness is truly eternally free, and is only in the form of Life-Energy. The pride for the body, the pride of the mind, along with the pride in ones thinking have all snow-balled into a rigid, yet untrue, pride. It is due to this pride, that the individual consciousness (jiva) seems to have become the body, and in its constant company, has yielded to desires. One who gives up all pride, attains freedom from bondage and comes out from the ocean of worldly existence.

As all objects are only Paramatman, nothing can be claimed as one's own. One should have the attitude that "All of this belongs to Paramatman. Let things take their own course, what is it to me? Whatever happens, whatever is lost, it is none of my concern." One who behaves in this manner is transformed into Paramatman.

It is said that "intense detachment" is total renunciation, that "pure detachment" is to live in this world as we would in a guesthouse, and "moderate detachment" is to gradually draw apart from the worldly affairs. When none of these three is possible, service to the saints and sages with a total dedication of body, mind and wealth can help generate detachment.

A yogi's fortune is truly great when detachment from the body is established. One should renounce all desires. The pride associated with one's house, wife, children and wealth, all should be given up. This helps one break free of bondage. In order to give up pride, one should worship. One should know and say, "I am not the body, I am the Self." One should say, "I Am He, who is in all." After expelling desire, one comes to know that all beings are Paramatman. This is when the individual consciousness attains the state of Paramatman. Since desires and thoughts are both untrue, how can they ever really affect an individual?

The individual consciousness, with the help of the body has fulfilled many desires in this transient world. Thoughts (chitta), in the company of desires have turned passionate. Day and night, the intellect (buddhi) thinks of sensual desires that are dear to it. This is why the pride associated with desires has come into being. Strong ties have been developed with worldly desires, and one's concepts have become an obstruction.

Due to the pride associated with the body, the individual consciousness considers all things related to the body, whether good or bad, as its own. The individual has thus forgotten it's own "True Nature" (Swaroopa) and instead has focused on desires. Knowledge is nothing but radical change in the intellect. The moment one is truly initiated, or starts behaving according to the advice of the Master, one can immediately attain liberation. Listening to, and reflection on spiritual discourse, is the only method to arrive at the "Ultimate Truth" (Paramartha).

21/06/1933

Lecture 29 - Abandoning Pride

The individual consciousness (jiva) has no bondage, as the Self has neither birth nor death. Yet, because it has identified with the body, it has to suffer births and deaths. The Self is bound only by the concept of being an individual. Only with the aid of the human body can this Knowledge be understood. It is this Knowledge that can bring about liberation. If the individual consciousness, with the aid of its own determination, realizes that it is not the body, but the Self, then it stands liberated.

One should come to despise desires, and give up all pride associated with desires. All pride associated with the body should be abandoned in order to help one break free from bondage. One who has given up the pride for the body is ever free and attains the bliss of the Self. He is purged of all worries. The passionate attachment to the body has to be given up. He alone, who casts away the ego associated with the body is fortunate, and is the instrument of ultimate happiness. After forsaking pride, the individual consciousness attains the form of the Self. Thoughts and desires then stand renounced.

In this world existence, everyone leads a life guided by the dictates of destiny. No one really looks after anyone else. Whatever happens to someone is according to destiny. In order to abandon the ego, discard all passionate attachments and surrender everything at the feet of the

Master. Once this is achieved, one comes to know that everything is but a mirage, and it is the Self alone that exists. One will even come to know that "I am not related to anyone, I belong to no one."

As pride is cast away, one is transformed into the "True Nature" of Paramatman, and remains so in all the three states; the waking, dreaming, and the deep-sleep states. All of these states are the characteristics of the intellect, the play of the intellect. The fourth state, the Turya state helps one relinquish the pride of the other three states. That which brings about the relinquishment of pride, is Knowledge (Jnana). The dreaming state is dismissed as untrue while one is in the waking state and vice-versa. In the deep-sleep state, both the dreaming and the waking states are untrue. Finally, it is in the state of "Knowledge" that the pride (ego) associated with the other three states is cast away, and these states become untrue. This itself is the fourth state, Turya. All of the states, other than the Turya state, exist solely in the intellect.

22/06/1933

Lecture 30 - The Self is not Affected by the Body

A man traveling in a train may cover a considerable distance, yet he does not walk that distance himself. The train goes the distance, yet the man claims that he has covered it. In the same fashion, the individual consciousness (jiva), without doing a single thing, says that it has done everything.

You cannot strike a blow to fire, yet as soon as the fire mingles with iron, it has to suffer repeated blows from a sledgehammer. Similarly, when the Self associates with the body, it suffers sorrows and miseries. Iron derives considerable benefit in association with fire. It cannot be given a desired shape without the help of the fire, but the fire itself remains unaffected. Much in a similar fashion, the body can be fruitfully employed in association with the Self, but the deeds of the body do not affect it.

When water breaks into ripples, the reflection cast in it by the Sun moves. It appears as if the Sun has moved and rendered the water turbulent. Similarly, the Self seems to have become turbulent due to concepts. Everything that seems to exist in this universe is based only on concepts and is therefore untrue. Hence, one should give up all concepts dismissing them as untrue.

One who has intense faith in his Master is blessed with the Master's grace, which is true understanding. The Master's grace depends upon the intensity of faith that one has in Him. Love for the Master helps us to get over the passionate attachment to desires. Loyalty to the "Ultimate Truth" leads to Self-realization, whereas loyalty to desires leads only to the generation of more desires. The Self is present everywhere, even present even in desires, but desires have blinded the Self into believing that "I am male, female, etc."

The Master weans his disciples from desires and reveals their True Nature to them. To get rid of the inclination towards desires, it is necessary not only to say that the desires are untrue, but also to bring this understanding directly into practice. The attitude of the individual consciousness, is that of both a slave, and a Master. Although one may say that desires are untrue and that the world is untrue, still this attitude is not put into practice.

One who has intense faith in his Master, and who follows the Master's teachings completely, is one who is bereft of name and form. Such a one turns into the Ultimate Truth, and once he attains the Ultimate Truth, he denies the ownership of even his own relatives.

23/06/1933

Lecture 31 - Renunciation of Passionate Attachment

The path of Knowledge should be understood by employing great skill. Desires may or may not be obstructive. They are not obstructions for one who gets them when they do not particularly like them or long for them. However, the one who has strong likes and dislikes and cravings, and then gets desires, becomes displaced from his True Nature (Swaroopa). It is in this way that one takes oneself to be an individual (jiva), and is thereby deprived of the bliss of their True Nature.

Understand that everything is made up of your "Swaroopa" and behave accordingly. Nothing remains there. The Ganges River is said to descend from the head of Lord Shiva because He has realized that everything is in the form of the Self, God. Hence, He is known as Shiva. The individual consciousness (jiva) says that the Self (Shiva) is everywhere, and yet continues to draw distinctions such as, "This is my mother. This is my wife," etc., because the passionate attachment to desires has not been completely overcome.

In other words, one has not gotten over worldly ties and relations. Besides this, one does not give up pride, and therefore continues to suffer from the same old miseries and joys. Desires are related to the body, the mind and wealth, and pride has to be forcibly relinquished. It does not go easily. However, once we make up our mind, we can get rid of it immediately.

Illusion should be renounced fully, willfully resorting to any method necessary. Objects of worldly desire, even if acquired by virtue of destiny, cease to be attractive when one is no longer passionately attached to them. Passionate attachment relegates one from the status of the Self, or God (Shiva), to the status of an individual (jiva). This body is eventually relinquished like garbage, and whatever we do for this body is a mere addition to the garbage heap. In this dreamy transient world, the state of highest pleasure can only be reached if you attend to your Self. As soon as you come to know that everything in this world is transient, you are called "detached." Just as the mice are not bothered about anything that may be in the house, so should it be with you.

One can be considered to be endowed with the Self-Knowledge when one no longer weighs the pros and cons of all actions. Even if one merely sits at a particular place for a short while, one gets flushed with sense of pride for that place. If one is stricken with the same pride for the body, it coerces us to forget the Self and destroys the inspiration of attaining the state of Paramatman. Once the individual consciousness comes to know that it is Brahman, it drinks nectar. If not, it sinks in the mire of desires.

24/06/1933

Lecture 32 - Relinquishing "I" and "Mine"

The distinctions such as "I am a separate entity," "You exist separately," and "The world stands distinctly apart from me," have been drawn and maintained by all. These distinctions persist because the feeling on which they are based is not easily snapped off. What is discrimination after all? We say that there is one Self existing in everyone, and still we continue to make distinctions. This is called discrimination and it exists solely in the mind.

The waking state is so named because in it attributes, or qualities are kindled, or "awake." This itself is called the world, as the whole world revolves around these attributes. Give up all previous traditions and prior practices, thereby stamping out the ego born of them. Only then is the waking state destroyed.

All that happens according to our wishes is termed good, and that which is against our wishes is termed bad. Good and bad are only concepts. In order to root out the ego, one must enlist the help of the intellect, and dedicate everything at the feet of the Master. Surrender yourself along with the body, mind and wealth at the Master's feet. When "I" do not exist, the question of "mine" does not arise. If we claim that all this is mine, body-consciousness comes to the forefront. If we rest for awhile at an inn, does any pride for the inn haunt us? No, never, we feel that it is "not mine," and that "I am only a temporary visitor." One should behave in a similar fashion with regard to the body and everyday life.

"I" (ego) and "mine" (attachment) are two demons that haunt us in this world. They have smothered the Self. He alone who has freed himself from the clutches of "I" and "mine," is truly fortunate. To achieve this, one should behave as if the Sadguru is the owner of all. It is very difficult to give up I and mine, as it requires gigantic effort. To get rid of I and mine, say that, "I am everywhere, in all." By behaving in this manner, one will give up the attachment to the body. If one cannot do this, then one should surrender everything to the Master. It should be understood that one who is prone to discrimination (differentiation) is not truly devoted to his Master, or rather has not yet gained Knowledge.

For the one who has become conversant with the "Knowledge of Brahman," but has not yet gotten over the habit of discriminating, his deeds are futile, and all of his "knowledge" is in vain. One who is not over pride may appear to be in the waking state, but in reality, he is fast asleep in Ignorance. Everybody strives to inflate pride. Nobody ever tries to be rid of it. One who is swollen with pride raves on like a madman in a manner similar to a person who has consumed the datura seed[7].

One who is not over the habit of drawing distinctions, does not derive the real benefit from the *Vedas* and various other scriptures. One should carefully consider how far he has succeeded in giving up pride and curbing body awareness. You cannot acquire the Ultimate Truth unless you give up your habit of differentiating. Full faith in the Master helps

---

[7] Datura seed is a strong intoxicant which causes the person who has consumed it to rant and rave like a madman.

one break down the bonds and ties that have risen as a result of pride. It is only when one surrenders at the feet of the Master that one is blessed with grace, or true understanding, and it is this understanding that helps one to be rid of pride. Complete devotion to the Master puts one on the right path. The main point is that discrimination along with pride is totally wiped off only when one surrenders entirely to the Master. I bow to the Master who is fully realized. "OM Namah Siddham."

25/06/1933

Lecture 33 - The Objective World is Like a Dream

A golden ring is so called because it is made up of gold. We look at it and call it a ring but never call it gold. Similarly, one gets carried away by outer forms and names, never bothering to find out the basic ingredient, the Self. When one holds the thought "I am great," the "Knowledge of Brahman" can never be gained.

He alone is a valiant warrior who kills the ego and continues to live in this world. It is said that, "I should follow the precepts of the *Vedas*, when it is myself, who has brought forth the *Vedas*." In other words, it is the water itself, which is thirsty. Those who are ignorant and follow rituals are advised to follow the dictates of the *Vedas*. This is because they are saddled with the sluggish and inert body (body-consciousness) and are prone to differentiation, making duality out of Oneness. It is for them that the *Vedas* have been compiled.

One who knows that "I am in everyone," and who does not draw distinctions, need not be governed by the precepts of the *Vedas*. For example, a woman, with respect for social graces, may keep her opinions to herself when she is with her husband out in public, but does not feel the need when she is at home alone with him. Where greed, affection, passionate attachments, desires, etc. exist, that is objective knowledge. When they are discarded, objective knowledge stands eradicated and the dictates of the *Vedas* are not required. The stars shine only at night, and once the sun rises, they become lusterless. In this example, the sunrise means Knowledge, and the stars, are the precepts of *Vedas*.

Just as children play "house," so should we treat our domestic life. Vedic precepts are like old newspaper wrappers for the one who goes about his life in an unaffected and unattached way. Vedic precepts are to help one realize their "True Nature" (Swaroopa). Once one's True Nature is understood, these vedic principles lose their significance. So long as there is the bondage of objective knowledge, the bondage of the *Vedas* persists. Once Self-Knowledge is attained, all objective things turn out to be as untrue as a dream. Although a "Realized One" (Jnani) remembers his former domestic life, he knows that it is untrue, just as children feel it is untrue when they play house. The understanding of the oneness with all helps one to acquire the "Knowledge of Brahman" (Brahmadnyana).

This transient world is like a feeling that one experiences in a dream. Such a feeling is taken as true only in the dream. Once one wakes up, even if the dream is remembered, the entire experience is known to be unreal.

26/06/1933

Lecture 34 - The Self is Consciousness

What is the difference between the mind and the Self (Atman)? That which is laden with curiosity and which is occupied with classifications of objects, is the mind. That which says something, is called the mind. Whereas, that which is "Conscious" of everything, is the Self.

Existing quietly on its own, the Self alone is "Conscious" of everything. No entity other than the Self ever exists. When the Self approves of the existence of something, it becomes our concept, and when it denies, or disapproves of it, it turns into a doubt. It is the mind that conceives all doubts and concepts. The mind is full of concepts, whereas the Self is free from them. The Self is the ultimate "resting place." What is this "rest"? That which remains after forgetting everything is called rest. There is bliss in the forgetting of everything. That which remains, after giving up the distinctions such as "I" and "you," is bliss. After giving up pride, one can enjoy undifferentiated happiness.

Why do we find happiness in deep-sleep? Because the feeling of "I" (ego) and "mine" (attachment), is absent in sleep. All pride is given up while going to sleep, and then we can get rest. While we are asleep we repose in our "True Nature" (Swaroopa) and bask in happiness. However, due to Ignorance, we cannot appreciate the bliss, and we call it sleep.

It is the Self who sees through all of the happenings in all the three states (the waking, the dreaming, and deep-sleep), and so it is called the "Lord of the Three Worlds" (Trailokyanath). The waking world is called the "World of Truth" (Satyaloka[8]), and the intellect (Lord Brahma) is the creator of this world. At night, the intellect takes leave of the waking world, and the three worlds are destroyed (disappear). However, Consciousness remains, due to which, we dream. Desire is the creator of the dream world. The deep-sleep world can be identified with the "nether world," or Ignorance.

The one who has realized the Self stands beyond all activity and consequences. The "inner-mind" has three attributes (gunas). It tends to be peaceful when governed by Sattvaguna, it is inclined towards worldly enjoyment when influenced by Rajoguna, and is possessed by anger when stricken with Tamoguna. All of the three attributes are characterized by objective knowledge. They sprout from the conceptual pride "I am a body." This pride associated with the body is the generator of the transient world and it is due to this pride that we are oblivious of the Self.

The illusory transient world, which has been brought forth by the Self, has proliferated to such an extent that it has pushed the Self out of sight. All have become fascinated with this material world. Lord Vishnu, the sustainer of this world, has thus acquired the form of a temptress. Our inner-mind has become mesmerized. The Self that resides in the body has been fascinated by the temptress "Objectivity." Just as the earth casts a shadow on the moon, making the disc of the moon appear dark, so does the Illusion shadow the Self. However, the moon is still there above, unaffected. Similarly, the Self always remains unaffected by Illusion.

27/06/1933

---

[8] In Hindu mythology, Satyaloka is the said to be the world, or "loka," where the "Creator," Brahma resides. It is also called the "World of Truth," because we take it to be true and believe in it. It is also call Brahmaloka.

Lecture 35 - The Self is the Real "I"

The Self is apart from any deed, yet no deed can be accomplished without it. It is the Self (Atman), which animates all of the organs, yet is far above the work of the body, or manifestation (Prakriti). All of the senses are limited to their particular field, but the Self excels in all fields. Even Ignorance itself is only pure Consciousness. It is called Ignorance only because the true form of Knowledge, Pure Consciousness, is not known. The Self is far superior to the work of the body (Prakriti; manifestation). It is the "Illuminator" of the state of the body, and the "Controller" of the attributes and organs associated with it. The ties, or bonds, with objective knowledge are the ties of the "nonexistent."

The chief qualities of a good disciple are faith in the Master and detachment. What is detachment? Detachment is to be aware of the fact that there is nothing worth having or achieving other than the Self. The absence of desire is conducive to the gaining of Knowledge. Together, detachment and lack of desire help one to gain the wealth of Knowledge.

"I Am Brahman" (Ahambrahmasmi) is a science, and Knowledge of the Self is the only Truth. Nothing here is based on emotions. That we are not the body, is an open fact. Just as the owner of a house is distinctly apart from the house, and walks in and out of it, so is the Self apart from this body. Some day it will discard this body and leave it. From this, it can be concluded that the body and the owner of the body are entirely different. When one says, "This body is mine," it proves that the Self is distinctly apart from the body.

Who then, resides in this body? "You." The one who you address as "Me" is you. The one who is named as "I," is "I." All of the various body organs are not named "I." The "I" who resides in this body is the real "I." When everything is eliminated, there remains nothing. Then, when even that nothing, the Ignorance (causal body), is given up, the one who says "Nothing is left," still remains. He who remains, when nothing is left, is the Self. The Self can never be eliminated. You are the Self. "Tatvamasi" means "You are He," "You are That."

The gross body is not the real "I." It is the "Awareness" of Ahambrahmasmi, "I Am Brahman," that is the real "I." Tatvamasi, "I Am That" is the weapon granted to you by the Master. The sage Vasishtha, the Master of Lord Rama told him, "Do whatever you want, but engrave the advice that I am not the body, I Am Brahman, on the mind." We are the pure, ever free Paramatman, yet we call this bag of flesh and bones, which is the doer of all actions, as "I." What an amazing thing! The one who holds the weapon of "Tatvamasi" and is well conversant with "Ahambrahmasmi" is one and the same. Thinking used in this way eradicates the pride associated the body.

In Ignorance one clings to the belief that "I am the body." Give it up. Abandon it. It is this belief that paves the way for all doubts. Influenced by it, we remain oblivious of the fact that we are the Self (Shiva), and start believing that we are the individual (jiva). This belief fuels lust and anger (by-products of an external search for happiness). It is because of this belief that the individual is hounded by bad thoughts, and birth and death. The belief that "I am the body" is the mother (origin) of all disasters, with "attachment" is its daughter, and "Illusion," the governess who looks after this daughter. This belief and all that accompanies it, must be brought down with a blow of the weapon, "I Am Brahman."

To sum it up, the threesome "I am the body," her daughter "attachment," along with "Illusion," the governess of "attachment," should all be destroyed with the help of knowledge.

28/06/1933

Lecture 36 - The Knowledge "I Am Brahman"

The notion, "I am not yet endowed with Knowledge," is the root of doubt, and should be weeded out. It is from this bulb of doubt that all sorrows sprout forth. It is due to this doubt that one is hounded by births and deaths, and the results of one's searching for happiness externally such as lust, anger, etc. are nourished. This bulb of doubt should be destroyed with the single stroke of the lustrous weapon of Self-Knowledge acquired from the Master.

The meaning of "Soham" should be studied in detail. The word "aham" means "I am," "koham" means "Who am I?," and "Soham" means "I Am He." To take shelter in one's Self means to understand "Who am I?" This itself is the shelter, so take shelter in "Who am I?" The "Knowledge of Brahman" is the understanding of the knowledge "I Am Brahman, I am the Self, that is Brahman." The mere oral repetition of this is called verbal knowledge, and is of no use. Ego cannot be wiped off by merely saying or thinking that the Self is present in everyone. The ego, or pride, torments us secretly and cannot so easily be vanquished. It is not possible to transform oneself into Brahman with mere words. Not a vestige of pride can be found when one thoroughly understands the Knowledge that "I Am Brahman, and I alone am present in one and all," and puts it into practice.

All is nothing but Paramatman. One should practice this in a quiet and contented manner for the ego to be wiped off. One who practices this becomes worthy of adoration. The Master is Parabrahman, and ego can be wiped out by completely surrendering to the Master. "Ananya" means "exclusively singular, allowing no other feeling." Knowing that the Master is Parabrahman, one should relinquish the ego, and surrender to Him. Those who are inspired by this feeling and behave accordingly, easily acquire Self-Knowledge.

Knowledge is easily achieved if the Master is looked upon as Paramatman and worshipped. One who worships the Master and conducts himself with the understanding that Paramatman exists in everyone, can be called a "Jnani." Just as darkness vanishes when one holds a lighted torch in one's hand, so do Illusion, affection, ego and the concept "I am the body," vanish when one worships the Master. One should worship the Master with the pure feeling of taking the Master to be Paramatman. The Self which is present in all, and which gives pleasure to all, should be worshipped by renouncing ego, attachment, and Illusion. The Self is best worshipped by worshipping the Master.

If you want to sing, sing the hymns of a Saint. If you want to travel, visit the towns of a Saint. Worship by bowing your head low, at the feet of a Saint. Dispose of the rubbish of ego by surrendering to the Master.
29/06/1933

Lecture 37 - Non-Conceptual Knowledge

From a talk on *Dasbodh* - Chapter 1, Sub-chapter 10

The human body with its unique characteristics, is sacred and blessed, and is obtained by rare chance. The one who utilizes this great fortune of the human body and follows the path of the Ultimate Truth (Paramartha) is sure to be crowned with success.

The human body has an auspicious aspiration, the aspiration for that which is most auspicious, the Self. It is a very big aspiration indeed. It is the aspiration of Brahman. The Sadguru is who leads you to Reality. Why is he called a Sadguru? He introduces us to the only "True Thing," Sadvastu (Reality). One should behave according to the advice of the Sadguru with exclusive, uninterrupted faith in Him. This is what is necessary. Only if the body is utilized for spiritual pursuits, does this life prove to be fruitful.

What is it that existed prior to the universe? It is "I." It may be possible that one can see all of the gods while meditating, but it is Mahadeva (Shiva), the Greatest of all Gods, who is supreme above them all. Who is He? He is "I," the Self. This "I," the Consciousness which resides in the body, is not a concept. That which remains after relinquishing everything, is Consciousness, and that alone, is Brahman. The state of Ignorance can best be described as the feeling that nothing remains after everything is forgotten. Yet, it is the one who forgets, who remains, and "He" alone who is real. That is our very own nature, our "True Form" (Swaroopa). That which is called by the name "You" is you, and "That" alone is your "True Form." You are "That" from which the sound "I" emanates.

The "non-conceptual" (Nirvikalpa) state is that which remains after all concepts are given up. Knowledge devoid of any concept is called Nirvikalpa Knowledge. The "Realized-one," the Jnani, possesses this Non-conceptual Knowledge whereas the individual (jiva) possesses conceptual, or Savikalpa Knowledge. Unlike that of an individual, who possesses objective knowledge, the Knowledge of the Jnani is not contaminated by any specialized objective knowledge. The Jnani possesses the "Knowledge of Brahman," while the individual possesses worldly knowledge. The Jnani always lives in a spontaneous and natural state, but the individual is always affected by the material world and lives in a specialized, particularized state. The knowledge of the individual is motivated by desires, whereas the Knowledge of a Jnani is devoid of them. The Knowledge of a Jnani is the Consciousness common to all living beings, while that of the individual is tinged with some particular objects. He who is prior to the universe, is steady, ever present, ever manifest, ever shining, and radiantly brilliant. He is pure, enlightened, and beyond the realms of meditation. He, who is "Conscious of All," is the only "True God."

All objects can be seen with the help of a lamp, and this is how the lamp acquires the status of greatness. Likewise, it is due to the light of the sun that all objects including with the lamp are visible, and in turn it is the sun, which has a status greater than all objects including the lamp. Furthermore, it is Consciousness that helps to see not only all objects and the lamp, but also the sun. Hence, it is Consciousness, which ultimately has the greatest status of all.

Consciousness is aware of all, but no one is aware of this Consciousness. Consciousness is "He" who resides within the hearts of all beings, and is called the brilliance behind the "inner-mind" (antahkarana).

Saint Dnyaneshwar says, "The sun can only shine. It is God who endows the sun with luminosity."

The one who is beyond the inner-mind is God. He quietly exists in all. Existence itself is His true form. He is devoid of delusions. In fact, His existence is characterized by the absence of delusion. He who forms the base of the stateless state most certainly exists. His existence is beyond all doubt.

01/07/1933

Lecture 38 - Attainment of Knowledge

The aspirant acquires the "Knowledge of Brahman" through the understanding given by the Master. A ripe aspirant is one who is unaffected by any sort of pride, who takes the Self alone to be true and treats all else as untrue. Only such a ripe aspirant understands and is aware of this principle. His entire attention is focused on the Self (Atman), which resides within all hearts.

For attainment of that which is unchanging and steady, one may resort to looking to that which is transient, but instead, you should be indifferent to the world, just as you have no attachments to the dead. Although the Self is clearly evident, and even lends brightness to the sun, it is of no use to a person whose thoughts (chitta) are tainted with worldly attachments. Anything that Illusion presents is untrue. Those who do not accept the existence of the Self are truly miserable beings. A swan does not care for, nor does it think about frogs, or household pests such as mice, rats, etc. In a similar manner, a true aspirant does not think about those who do not accept the Self. A man is known by the company he keeps. The "Knowledge of Brahman" is attained in the company of Saints. When you go out for a walk, you hear the sparrows chirp, but do you ever try to figure out what they say? Are you really interested in what they do? Do you ever really care? In a similar manner, you should be unconcerned about all that is said or done by nonbelievers. Remember that an elephant is carefree and majestic, and just keeps on walking, even as barking dogs follow it.

It is Knowledge alone that exists in all three states, the waking, the dreaming, and the deep-sleep states. That Knowledge is Brahman, just as the waves, bubbles, and foam are all nothing but water. These three states of the water are characterized by distinctions, while the water itself is characterized by the lack of distinction, or Oneness. Similarly, the three states of waking, dreaming, deep-sleep are characterized by distinction, whereas Knowledge is characterized by Oneness. The aspirant should keep in mind "I Am That Knowledge." The inherent nature of "wrong knowledge" is that it makes a thing seem to be something quite different from what it actually is.

That which is seen in the mirror of Knowledge is mere appearance and is untrue because it inevitably vanishes after it is seen. It is with the help of Knowledge that we become aware of things gained, known, or experienced. When both Knowledge and Ignorance are renounced, what remains is "Absolute Knowledge" (Vijnana). One who realizes that he is not the body but the Self, is pure and clean. One should realize that their true identity is the Self.

The Self is ever present in the space between two successive thoughts. Laya is the end, or absorption, of a thought, while vikshepa is the origination of another. Just as water in its true, unqualified form, is present between two successive waves, so is the Self present, as the base, for the origination and absorption of thoughts. Knowledge is brilliant like the sun and it is the only "Truth." Everything should be offered to it. Here, everything means the senses. When the senses turn towards Knowledge, they are satisfied.

Those who know that the Self is a fire and all else is untrue are the true "fire worshippers." The thoughts (chitta) should be offered unto the blaze of the Self, which is the "Self-luminant Fire." The body is a temple, and the one who resides in it is none other than the "Almighty."

In the classic spiritual text **Dasbodh** Chapter 8, Sub-chapter 9, it is asked, "How does one recognize that the Knowledge of the Inner-Self has been attained?"

How could it be evident that the "Knowledge of the Self" has been well assimilated? One who has accomplished his mission in life is called "Siddhapurusha." He has the distinct proof that his "True Nature," Swaroopa, the nature of the Self, is Aroopa, formless. Swaroopa is "self-evident" as it is neither seen, nor shown, by anyone. One who realizes this "True Nature," or "True Form," is a true sage. It is like this: "I set out in quest of God, to seek Him, but I could never find Him. I now realize that I am He."

Accomplishment befits only the accomplished. Just as a nose can never turn into an eye, the "accomplished," or realized one, can never become unaccomplished, or ignorant. All that is seen in a dream is untrue. This material world is also dreamlike and untrue. Knowing fully well that everything here is untrue, the accomplished do their work happily.

For example, a man was once told that his cattle were impounded. Upon hearing this, he was unperturbed. Later, another man came along and informed him that his cattle were to be freed, and that no fine was going to be slapped on him, and he remained just as calm as before. This was because the cattle were not his. As he was not the owner of the cattle, he was not affected by the news. He became neither happy nor sad. You also, should behave in a similar fashion, and lead your life as if nothing in this world belongs to you.

Detachment is the "True Essence," and freedom from thoughts should be continual. The "Knowledge of Brahman" is not child's play, and the inner experience of it is essential. Just as one does not have attachment to the dead, one should also be disinterested in the world.

05/07/1933

Lecture 39 - The Pride of Ignorance and Knowledge

Q: How can Brahman, which is intellectually understood, be truly experienced?

SM: Brahman is not new. It has always existed. It is "Self-existent." You are that Brahman. It is due to Ignorance that one becomes deluded by worldly life. You must get over this delusion. In order to remove delusion, one can take help of the pride "I Am Brahman." Although you may have understood about Brahman, you remain proud of domestic life. To destroy the pride associated with the body, you can take the help of the pride of "I Am Brahman." However, if you can succeed in getting over pride without the help of the pride of Brahman, then it is preferable that you proceed without it.

Q: What is non-conceptual happiness?

SM: One may have a tendency to believe that once Brahman is understood, concepts are eliminated. This is untrue because there is no relation between Brahman and concepts. They are distinctly apart. It entirely depends upon an individual whether or not to form concepts. Whatever may be the nature of the concept, it can either bind or liberate. It is equally untrue to believe that once Brahman is understood, concepts are formed. It is up to the aspirant to get the clear understanding of Brahman, therefore, Brahman is described as non-conceptual. The Master says, "The state of Brahman is a non-conceptual state." If you follow the advice of the Master and put this concept into practice, you can easily be in the state of Spontaneous Samadhi. Those who know that the Self is neither bound nor liberated, are truly liberated, while those who claim superiority due to pride, effectively kill their own Self.

A person once unknowingly imprisoned a man, thinking that he was his enemy. He later came to know that the man was his father. After realizing his mistake, he got him released, honored him by offering him a seat, and then begged forgiveness and worshipped him. This pleased his father. Another person similarly imprisoned his father and later, he too, released and honored him. Up to this point, his behavior resembled that of the person mentioned previously, but later he exhibited strange behavior. He once again arrested his father with the help of a servant and established that he was deceitful. He then ordered his servants to severely punish the father after imprisoning him. The act of the first man seems natural, while that of the latter seems peculiar. Yet, whether natural or peculiar, they are both unreal. Even to label things as untrue, is untrue.

Once it is understood that the pride of Ignorance, as well as that of Knowledge, is untrue, everything is seen as untrue. It is all only Illusion. The one who realizes this, is no longer affected by it. As is our pride, so are our actions. The feelings of bondage and liberation are associated only with the gross body and not with one's "True Nature" (Swaroopa). One's "True Nature" alone is pure and untainted. The feeling "I Am" arises in it. This feeling of "I Am" is ego in it's first and purest form. Later, it is tainted with the pride associated with the body, "I am so-and-so." Understand that these are both only different forms of ego.

Liberation and bondage are both expressions of the ego. Only one who recognizes this ego can be truly realized. Saying that "I am liberated" is to remain in bondage. One can drown even in the shallowest water of Illusion by tying on an anchor in the form of the pride of liberation.

23/09/1933 - Morning Lecture

Lecture 40 - Be God to Know God

Reality is non-dual. One who strives to understand it, becomes non-dual. How does this occur? In order to worship God (Shiva), one must become God. This is known as "scriptural knowledge," which reveals how to worship, whereas worldly knowledge simply tells one how to behave in this world.

The many various types of chanting, austerities, and practices only generate duality. In order to recognize God, assume the characteristics of God. Be like him. Be quiet. In this way, one can aspire to acquire the "Knowledge of Brahman," a truly auspicious aspiration. This can be achieved by sitting peacefully with concentrated mind. He, who illuminates all, is the true God. Just as you use an eye to see your eye, recognize the Self, using the Self. If you try to meditate upon the Self, duality is generated. Be aware of the fact that the five elements are apart from you, the Self. Understand that the Self is beyond, or prior to, the five elements. In this way, the misidentification with the five elements is given up. This can be achieved only with the help of Knowledge.

23/09/1933 - Evening Lecture

Lecture 41 - Salutations to Ganesha

From a talk on the *Yogavasishtha* - Chapter 1

Shri Ganeshaya Namah - Salutation to Lord Ganesha

All of the classic spiritual texts deal with only one theme, that of the Self, and they all begin with a salutation to Lord Ganesha. In the salutation, the word "Shri" indicates affluence, or wealth. The word Shri is associated with Paramatman. We must turn ourselves into Paramatman to attain true prosperity, as true prosperity is closely associated with Paramatman. The word "Gana" means the origin of all. He who is the originator of the world is Ganapati (Ganesha). Birth is the origin, the foundation, and the motive of all sorrows. It is the mine of poverty. One can attain wealth and prosperity, unblemished by birth and poverty, by worshipping Him, the originator. To worship Ganapati, means to be Ganapati. The word "namah" includes three actions "salute," "praise" and "worship." Paramatman is spontaneous and is in the form of bliss, spontaneous bliss. He who feels that he is himself the origin of all (Ganapati), or Paramatman, is full of bliss, is himself the spontaneous, "self-existing" Paramatman. All that is remembered during the day is forgotten while we sleep at night. Yet, Paramatman, which helps us remember, remains ever present, never erased, beyond forgetfulness.

Sweetness, sourness, spiciness, etc. are considered pleasurable. What is pleasure after all, other than an experience that can be likened to a favorable transient tingling sensation? However, the bliss of our "True Nature" is neither merely pleasure, nor a transient favorable tingling sensation. It is only experienced spontaneously. It is that which is spontaneous, or "self-generated," which is full of bliss. What does this bliss resemble? It resembles the Self. After giving up everything, it is the one who renounces that remains, and that is your "Self." This bliss is devoid of all pleasure and pain. He who is blissful, is Paramatman, and that all-pervading, blissful Paramatman is your Self. Individuals (jivas) suffer from two basic feelings; 1) they find it impossible to believe that they are Paramatman, the Supreme Self, and 2) they believe themselves to be something other than Paramatman such as the body, or mind, personality, etc.

If you regard your guest, friend, wife or any other person, as your Self, then this is the true sign of magnanimity, enabling one to approach all situations with calmness.

24/09/1933

Lecture 42 - The Self is Beyond Concepts

From a talk on the *Eknathi Bhagwat* of Saint Eknath

That which is in the form of Consciousness, is the Self (Atman), and it is like a mirror. There arises a spontaneous feeling of "I Am" in the Self. This is ego, and is itself the sense of "individual consciousness" (jiva). On the advice of the Master, this ego starts referring to itself as

Brahman. It is the ego that says "I am so-and-so." Jnanis give up the ego, which is merely conceptual. A dream is short-lived, while the concepts made by the mind in the waking state constitute a long dream. The Self is the original deity of both of these two dreams (waking and sleeping). Just as a man walking in the desert takes the mirage to be true, similarly the Self takes the concept of the worldly life to be true, and fails to see through it. Generally it is the nose ring that is admired and valued, and not the nose. Similarly, it is that which is visible that is valued, and not the Self. The deity of the world is the Self, and all else is projected on it. Like a firebrand, Brahman is a stark truth, and worldly life is untrue. One should understand that the realm of the five elements is an untrue appearance and only the Self is "True."

If we are involved only in worldly life, we become entangled in it as an insect would in a spider's web. One should ask oneself the important question, "Can daily tasks be carried out more successfully by identifying with the body, or can one be more successful in performing them by identifying as the Self, and considering all else as untrue?" We believe in this worldly life only because of the delusion of the concept "I am the body." Therefore, this delusion should be destroyed.

The pure, or divine "sight" is acquired when one begins to feel that only the Self is present in everything and everyone. Living a merely worldly life then seems futile. The "discriminating sight" which makes distinctions, disappears only if you behave as though you exist in everyone. Mental peace is then achieved. Both, auspicious as well as inauspicious deeds were done only by the Self, and the deed of classifying them as auspicious or inauspicious, is itself inauspicious.

24/09/1933

Lecture 43 - The Nature of the Mind

From a talk on the *Yogavasishtha*

Lord Rama told his guru, the Sage Vasishtha that worldly life had become excessively dear to him. Although he should not be attached to it, his love for the Illusion has compelled him to cling to it. If this love pulls his thoughts (chitta) towards distress like a magnet, how can he safely overcome this worldly life? What could be the remedy to destroy this Illusion?

It is the mind itself, which is the cause of delusion. The mind means saying something. It is the arising of, or assertion of, a thought. When the mind comes into being, worldly life originates, and when the mind is destroyed, worldly life comes to an end. When the mind arises, one's "True Nature" (Swaroopa) is forgotten. Destruction of the mind means the remembrance of one's True Nature. The individual (jiva) has entered the cycle of 8.4 million births, because it has forgotten it's True Nature. The more one develops a dislike for mere worldly existence, the closer one gets to one's True Nature. Just as adults treat a child's pride of leadership as unimportant while the children are at play, Jnanis treat worldly life as insignificant, and refrain from attaching any importance to it. If one wants to break free from the web of Illusion, there are a number of remedies available to be rid of this worldly life, if one has the strong desire to do so.

The mind runs rampant in the company of desires. Although the mind may become steady, desire arouses it. How does desire arouse the steady mind? What is desire after all? The memory of all that which has been done, heard, seen, or experienced in the past with a wish to experience it again, is called desire. The mind is defined as the memory of this desire. The vital breath (prana) in combination with desires lends the mind its ever-changing, fickle characteristic. Desires should be given up, as it is because of desires, that objects seem dear. Desires are cultivated by former influence. The pleasure that one finds in desires, is the joy derived from objects. Desires perpetuate the enjoyment of the material world. The presence of desires explains our love for the world, and lends vitality to the mind.

25/09/1933

Lecture 44 - Giving up Body-Consciousness

From a talk on the *Eknathi Bhagwat* of Saint Eknath

The leaving behind of misidentification with the body, followed by dispassion from worldly life, should be obtained with the aid of the body, mind, and speech. By constantly thinking of the Self, the passionate attachment for worldly life begins to fade, and one's True Nature comes into focus and is realized. The mind then gives up the ego and forgets the body.

When the mind is directed towards the Self, it discovers that the Self is omnipresent. Aspirants who want to experience the Self are required to give up any thought of the body and focus exclusively on the Self. Body-consciousness must be vanquished, and then the aspirant is left with no other motives or impulses. Such a person may carry out their daily routine, but their actions do not reveal bodily awareness. While going through their bodily actions and routines, they never consider themselves to be the doer.

Just as a dry leaf is easily blown away by the wind, body-consciousness should also be blown away. One should give up being obsessed with the body. Only then, does one discover one's true Self. We can elevate ourselves, and bring about our own upliftment, but while we remain engrossed solely in worldly affairs, it is we who are responsible for our own sorry state. Procrastination is a common habit that should be discarded. If one always puts off giving up body-consciousness until tomorrow, it will never be done at all. Tomorrow never comes. In this way, we bring about our own destruction. If you have ever attempted to sit on your own shadow, you see that the moment you try to do so, your shadow disappears. In a similar manner, the moment you overcome body-consciousness, Illusion is destroyed.

A Jnani understands and experiences that the body is untrue. Even if a Jnani says "I have done this, I have done that," he remains unaffected by any outcome, as his body identification no longer exists. He has understood everything clearly. His ego is wiped out, and he is unaffected by pride. Body-consciousness influences one's behavior, so as one increasingly identifies with body-consciousness the result is that one becomes swollen with pride. One should investigate and find out how much body-consciousness, and how much consciousness of the Self one possesses, and in what proportion.

25/09/1933

Lecture 45 - Destroying Illusion with "Right Thought"

From a talk on the *Yogavasishtha*

The Self is beyond concept, and is ever free and ever pure. All else (the world, Illusion) is conceptual. It is a mere concept, our own concept to be precise, but the origin of this concept is Brahman. The "Ultimate Truth," (Paramartha), is also a concept. To say "I am good," or "I am bad," are also only concepts. The scriptures have put forth the concepts of good and bad only for the sake of the ignorant. The "good" and the "bad" together constitute worldly life. What is this worldly life all about? Sansar (Samsara) is the Marathi for "the world," or "mundane worldly life," and it indicates that it is only oneself that gives rise to "ego." All that is done with the aid of the ego is worldly life. In short, worldly life means to take pride in just about everything. Complete renunciation of pride is true liberation. It is not enough to have a merely intellectual understanding of the concepts of the Self, humility, etc. Putting this teaching into practice is what really matters, and is truly beneficial.

Worldly life ceases to exist when one's wrong notions about life and one's "True Self Nature" (Atma Swaroopa) are wiped off, and it comes into being when thoughts (chitta) stray away from the Self and become externalized. Thoughts are adept at making something out of nothing and it is the creation of this "space," that leads to the appearance of the world. It is in this manner that one becomes awakened to, or aware of the non-existent world appearance. The generation of non-existent matter is the characteristic of thoughts. By close examination of this process one can see that the world appearance comes into being by way of thought, and that it is in its entirety only the product of the wild imaginings of straying thoughts. Paying heed to stray thoughts leads to a slight deviation from one's "True Nature," and gives rise to the world, which then proliferates and appears to go on for countless years. The delusion of the world lasts only as long as we want it to. Once one's thinking is turned towards the Self, all opposing thoughts stand eradicated, and this worldly life is destroyed, like bamboo trees get destroyed when brushing up against each other.

The house, the body and prosperity are all products of desire, our own desire. Only if we think along the right lines, does worldly life come crumbling down. Ignorance of one's True Nature is a fascination, or infatuation with that which is objective, and this fascination generates the world. In a similar manner to a child who is overwhelmed by the fear of the "boogie-man," who actually exists as far as the child is concerned, the individual (jiva) is concerned with fears in this worldly life, which appear to be true. Sorrows have descended upon us from the day that we have forgotten the Self, and we are destined to suffer so long as our concepts of the world persist.

"Chase away the dark with a burning torch."

You discover the non-existence of the world when you look for it with the torch of "right thought." What is right thought? To examine what the world is, is what is meant by right thought. To take this worldly life to be true, or to believe in it, is what is called Illusion. The destruction of Illusion brings untold joys, while belief in its existence proves to be a source of unending sorrows. As long as one assumes the existence of Illusion, one is thereby affected by its aftereffects, which are sorrows. Illusion persists only as long as it remains unexamined, and it is difficult to focus on until one looks upon it with right thought. Once we watch it closely and think it over carefully, it exists no more. For the individual, the thought of worldly life is at the forefront of the mind and in this state, all that is done is "thoughtless." It is such thoughtlessness that perpetuates the Illusion, and it is only right thought that can put an end to it.

26/09/1933

Lecture 46 - Right Thinking Brings Liberation

From a talk on the *Eknathi Bhagwat* of Saint Eknath

How long does it take to attain liberation when one is in the company of Saints? People do not know what liberation is, yet they would like to attain it. "Liberation" means to become free, and "bondage" means to be bound. It is a state of slavery. The concept "I am the body," or "I am an individual (jiva)," is what holds one in bondage. The Self resembles the boundless sky, yet when it is restricted by the identification with the body, it assumes the role of the individual and in the process brings upon itself many limitations.

By "right thinking" alone one can attain liberation, otherwise, one continues to remain in bondage. Only one who thinks, proves to be a human being, all the rest are but beasts. By listening to religious discourses often and contemplating upon them continuously, one cultivates the idea "I am not the body, I am the Self." Such constant churning of the teaching while eating, working, and in general going through daily routines, culminates in the establishment in the Self. This itself is spontaneous (sahaja) samadhi.

Once you return home on a hired horse, do you ever bother to find out its whereabouts, or do you even stop to think about it? Treat the body in a similar way. Let the body live or die, it is in the Supreme Self that one should firmly be settled. Like a young bride who gives up her parents house and settles down to enjoy a life of marital bliss, similarly, the individual (jiva) turns into God (Shiva) and gets absorbed into one's "Self Nature." The world can only provide the joys and sorrows of worldly knowledge and desires.

The "Turya State" (the fourth body) is realized when pride is relinquished. Just as one does not take care for the mice that may live in one's house, and does not constantly think about what they do or what they eat, similarly, a sage does not care for his body. Truly great are they who merge with the Master completely. The one who knows that he is not the body but the Self, is a Jnani, full of Knowledge. There is no difference between a young child and a yogi, except for a fact that the yogi possesses Knowledge and the child does not.

From a talk on the *Yogavasishtha*

The waters in a river continually flow away, and their place is taken up by fresh water, but every time we look at the river, we feel that it is the same water that has been seen earlier. Like this, day in and day out, the world also continually changes. Old things are destroyed and are replaced by new things, but we feel that they are the same as that which was seen previously. This is because we never "think." Every time we see the world, we see it only as it appears at that particular point in time, but it seems to be just as it was before. It is only through proper thinking, that you will come to know that the world is but a representation of Brahman, otherwise, all that is seen, is Illusion (Maya). To exist as a mere image of flesh and blood (the body), and to be related to someone as his or her father, son, mother, etc. is indeed shameful as all of these are but wrong concepts. However, no one feels ashamed to claim possession of such a body, which is only full of dirt.

The origination of Illusion brings infinite sorrows, and its destruction brings untold joy. Illusion helps the world go on, as it veils the Self. How can it be destroyed? Just as one who is fat and huge is sure to die early, so is it with Illusion. Although it is huge, it is destroyed easily by "right thought." This is because it is only wrong thinking which has brought it into existence.

Accurate Knowledge helps one acknowledge and think about that which truly exists. If you view with accurate Knowledge, you will not see the universe at all. The moment you are armed with accurate Knowledge, you will witness that the universe is destroyed. With the help of accurate Knowledge, Illusion is wiped out and the Self is attained. In the same way that fuel makes a fire burn vigorously, so does "wrong thought" give rise to Illusion. Repetition of mantras, rituals, etc. only serve to support the Illusion. Delusion cannot be wiped out without right thought. There is no remedy that can prove a dream untrue. It only becomes untrue when you wake up. It is only by correct seeing, and then understanding, that the Illusion can be destroyed. All other attempted methods are useless. Just as the delusion that turns a rope into a snake is destroyed by correct seeing, so is the illusory world destroyed by understanding.

Joys and sorrows in this world do not actually depend on material objects, they depend upon one's thoughts. All objects are constantly subject to innumerable changes and therefore untrue, whereas that which is true never changes or gets destroyed. The true is unaffected by the past, present, and the future, while Illusion can be destroyed by thought and is thereby proved to be untrue.

Brahman is obvious and apparent. It shines forever. It is eternal. It is infinite. This is not so with Illusion, as accurate Knowledge can destroy Illusion and at the same instant reveal Brahman. Illusion is not true, however it appears to exist, and therefore one hesitates to dismiss it outright. Its nature is dreamlike and cannot be easily described by words.

In speech, we use words to tell us whether a thing "is" or "is not," saying that something is "true" or "not true." But what can be said about Illusion? Illusion is that which from the beginning was not, that which never came to be, and that which is untrue. Nevertheless, it is seen, just as a mirage is seen. In this world, an object cannot simultaneously be and not be, or in other words, it cannot be true as well as untrue. Truth can never be untrue, yet Illusion is strangely unique as it can neither be true or completely dismissed as untrue, while by nature it is untrue. It is indescribable, while you need not try to describe it either. Its nature is like a dream. The moment you say that a dream is untrue, it vanishes. Yet, all the same, it still appears.

26/09/1933

Lecture 47 - Give up Body-Consciousness

From a talk on the *Eknathi Bhagwat* of Saint Eknath

The long forgotten "Self Nature" (Swaroopa) and the consequent ever increasing body-consciousness have made spiritual advice absolutely necessary. The moment that you realize that the praise of your body makes you angry, it indicates that you have understood Brahman. When dissolved in water, salt no longer maintains its identity and it becomes a part of the solution. Similarly, those who have understood Brahman exist in the form of "Life-Energy" (Chaitanya). The rope, which is mistaken for a snake is not aware of the existence of a snake. In a similar way, a true devotee is no longer conscious of the body. He stops making distinctions such as "you" and "I," and is no longer inflicted with ego.

The one Self assumes many different forms because of body-consciousness. Though the Self is manifest as the form of "OM," it appears to lead multiple existences. When limited by the body, it is tame like a dog, and when devoid of the body, it is as majestic as a lion. One may say that giving up body-consciousness is easy but it is not so. One cannot so easily be rid of it. Even though "wrong knowledge" (Avidya) is given up, the misidentification with the actions of the body does not vanish. Here the question may arise, if one who possesses the body gives up body-consciousness, how will the body survive? In response, it may be asked, can we prevent the body from ever contracting a disease, even if we take extremely good care of it? In order to thoroughly understand disassociation from the body, one must study and understand the science of the five elements that make up the body. Without this study, the "Knowledge of Brahman" cannot be attained.

27/09/33

Lecture 48 - Three Types of Differentiation

From a talk on the *Yogavasishtha*

The Saint is one who has realized the Truth, "Reality." One who is not a Saint, is always affected by Illusion and does not approach Reality. Illusion flees from the discrimination between truth and untruth.

Illusion requires neither speech nor silence to be expressed, and there is no need to establish that it is false. The belief that Illusion exists should be wiped out with the right thought generated by the Master's advice. The thought of the separate existence of two objects is called differentiation. Illusion exists only because of the existence of Brahman, which has no beginning, and no end. It is timeless. The objective world by nature can never be timeless. The notion of an individual (jiva) is instability personified. Nothing exists independently from Brahman.

"Brahman is singularly unique, only one, and incomparable, one of its kind."

We see all objects with the help of three types of differentiation.

1) Differentiation applied to dissimilar species, such as "this is a man, that is a dog, that is tree, stone, etc."

2) Differentiation applied to the same species such as "this is my son, this is someone else's son, my wife, etc."

3) Egotistical Differentiation such as "I am so-and-so, my status is this, these are my possessions." This is the making of distinctions that go into what makes up the "individual" with its qualities that revolve around "me" and "mine."

In the above quote from the *Yogavasishtha*, "singularly unique" negates differentiation applied to dissimilar species. "Only one" nullifies the differentiation applied to the same species, and "incomparable; one if its kind," negates the egotistical "me" and "mine" differentiation.

28/09/33

Lecture 49 - The Jnani is Beyond Karma and Death

From a talk on the *Eknathi Bhagwat* of Saint Eknath

Many people are under the Illusion that a Jnani possesses a lot of power. Power is not desirable, since it is only an Illusion. The one who desires to attain power can not be a Jnani, nor can he attain power. How does the body of a Jnani function? The Jnani attributes the actions (karma) and functions of his body to its destiny, and stands indifferent towards it.

In the past, powerful kings would renounce their empires and go to the forests, not in search of power, but in search of the "Bliss of the Self." A real Jnani abandons all power in his possession for the bliss of the Self. For example, one who spends his money on wine chooses willingly to get intoxicated. In spite of possessing a body, such a person is indifferent to the state of his body, and towards its status. Similarly, a Jnani, who is intoxicated with the "Knowledge of Brahman," is also indifferent towards his body. Pleasures and pains of the body are totally dependent on destiny. As evidence of this, it can be demonstrated that one may strive hard the whole life, yet still remain a pauper, whereas another may effortlessly acquire riches.

If we have troubled others in the past, we will surely have to reap the fruits. As is your wish, so is the fruit. People wish ill of others, and suffer accordingly. A Jnani says that the body will have to bear the fruits of its actions. One who wishes for the well being of others, is always happy. He says, "All are equivalent to God" and treats them accordingly. If one develops this attitude, he will be infinitely happy. If we are good to others, they will in turn, be good to us.

To get pleasures or pain in this world lies exclusively in our hands. As you sow, so shall you reap, is the rule of thumb in this world. The ignorant enjoy their deeds, yet are very much reluctant to face the aftermath. This is because they possess pride for the body. The ignorant have to pay a price for identification with the body. Knowing that the worldly life is untrue, a Jnani is indifferent towards it and stands unaffected by consequences. In spite of living in the body, one who does not take pride in it, is truly "Knowledgeable." However, it should be recognized, that mere mental indifference is not synonymous with samadhi (absorption in Reality). The indifference of the Jnani is the behavior that arises out of the feeling that "I Am the Self, and I and only I, exist in all." This is the true samadhi.

The individual consciousness (jiva) only exists within the bounds of the waking, sleeping and dreaming states. To think of all this worldly life as untrue implies transcending the boundaries of all three states. In this manner, one achieves victory over the ten sensory organs. One who stands beyond these boundaries, is victorious. The "Victory" (Jai), which is everlasting and imperishable, is "Ultimate Victory" (Vijay). A Jnani does not become entangled in the body, or its functions. He gains victory over his body, and is ever victorious.

28/09/33

Lecture 50 - The Nature of the Body

From at talk on the *Yogavasishtha*

"There is nothing that exists other than Brahman. The existence of Illusion is out of the question."

Driven by excessive affection towards the five desires (wealth, sex, food and drink, fame, and sleep) we remain passionately attached to the body. As long as this affection lasts, attachment continues to exist. The body then becomes a necessity. It is a medium to enjoy desires, and thus arises the need for births and deaths.

The wind blows because it is governed by the Life-Energy, and Life-Energy is a very subtle form of wind. The whole world is in the form of a wind. This is because this world is a dream and wind (breath) forms the base on which dreams are built. Though we are not in the shape of a body, we assume that we exist in that shape, and perceive everything in relation to that shape. This is because we use the body as the medium through which to perceive everything.

29/09/33

Lecture 51 - The Jnani is Reality

From a talk on the *Eknathi Bhagwat* of Saint Eknath

Having cast off bodily pride, the Jnani exists in his original state, "Reality." He is Reality. He is the one who performs all the bodily functions. Samadhi (absorption) is to know that everything other than one's "True Nature" (Swaroopa) is untrue. To live a life of mere indifference (a passive existence) is not samadhi.

"Pridelessness" together with "Timelessness" is called "Uninterrupted Eternal Absorption." The one who says that simple indifference is absorption, knows nothing about their True Nature. To say that samadhi has been attained through indifference, is as good as comparing samadhi with passing time in sleep. Indifference is not samadhi, knowing one's True Nature, is samadhi. A man once dreamt that he went into samadhi and assumed an attitude of indifference. Later he woke up and remembered his dream. As it was a dream, he knew that the samadhi was unreal. Similarly, one who has realized their True Nature knows that indifference is not samadhi.

A Jnani leaves all the functions of his body in charge of destiny. He then never cares for his body. That which remains after all of the "me" and "mine" is left behind, when the obstructed and obstruction are both cleared away, is called "spontaneous samadhi," unrestrained samadhi. He who attains such a samadhi remains unattached even as he undergoes various experiences, and remains untouched even though he does everything. The Self is not attached to any actions (karma). We are what we say we are. If we say we are the doer, we become responsible for the actions, if we don't, we aren't. All beings are non-doers. They are not really linked with their actions. Yet, they say that "I am the doer of the action." Therefore, the actions seem to affect them. Those who realize this truth, are the non-doers, and those who do not know this, are also non-doers, however, they are unaware of the truth. We are bound only by our very own concepts, otherwise, we are absolutely free.

The more we are affected with pride, the more we are bound. If we gain a little knowledge, we are bound to a slightly lesser degree, but bound nonetheless. The body is governed by bodily duties. It functions through habit, but one's Self is apart from the body. The Jnanis not only think in this way, but behave accordingly. Wood catches fire and keeps the fire burning, but can the wood say that "I can go on holding the fire indefinitely"? No, it is not possible. You are born with a body. A Jnani also has been born with a body, and He has attained the state of "Self-Knowledge" with its help. He is now devoid of the body. After having understood his True Nature, a Jnani carries out his worldly activities, but these activities now take on a new dimension, and turn beautiful. A king is a king, whether he lives in a forest or in a palace. Attaining samadhi (absorption), and then coming out of it is the sign of an incomplete man, and not that of a Jnani. In the olden days, men played female roles in stage plays for the sake of entertainment. A yogi leads his domestic life in a similar fashion.

After waking up from sleep, we do not treat the actions that we performed in our dreams as true. It is in this way that the Jnanis treat the world. They consider it to be a dream. True yogis treat worldly pleasures as the pleasures that only a dead body enjoys. All that happens in our dream no longer affects us when we awaken. It no longer affects this waking dream, so it does not affect the Self.

29/09/33

Lecture 52 - Illusion is That Which is Not

From at talk on the *Yogavasishtha*

If you say that Maya does not exist, it seems to be there in front of you, and if you say that it exists, it is untrue. It is neither Brahman, nor is it distinctly apart from Brahman. It is neither true, nor untrue. The word Maya literally means that which is not (Ma is not, and ya means that). The word "not" always indicates the absence of the Truth. It is not true, and is therefore indescribable. An indescribable object is only a passing appearance. Maya is illusory in nature. All the objects in it are phantasmal. They exist only in your imagination. Objects that change every minute are illusory. That which is true, can never be false and that which is false, can never become true. Indescribable objects are illusory, illusory objects are perishable, and perishable objects are subject to change.

These perceivable objects are all similar to the fallacy of the "boogie-man." They are the cause of joys and sorrows. They are ephemeral. Maya appears when we are not aware of her (as Maya), and upon knowing her, she is destroyed. Without pondering over Maya, she can never be destroyed. This is because we foolishly take pride in our body, without recognizing our true Self. She does not require even the support of thoughts to appear before us. She has begun to appear just because we have assumed that she exists.

Not only is Maya untrue, but she is not worth being pondered over even for the sake of proving that she is untrue. We have to "think," because all along we have assumed her to be present. Hence take the help of your thought in order to destroy her. Illusion is called the five-streamed flow. It veils the individual consciousness (jiva), and envelops the Self with its five-streamed flow. Some call it the five afflictions. The five-streamed flow is ignorance, egotism, anger, hatred, and greed (insatiable desire), and is only the sentiments of our inner-mind.

Ignorance is amnesia. It is being oblivious to one's True Nature. It is the condition wherein we forget our Self, and concentrate elsewhere. It is the delusion which makes one forget the Self, our own existence. One forgets the Self due to this Ignorance, yet nonetheless remains only that Self.

Pride represents a contrary feeling, the opposite of what actually is. It is when something is interpreted as being something quite different from what it actually is. It is out of this feeling that one may do something as strange as calling a chair a donkey. It is the condition of the mind wherein one never acknowledges "That" which truly is. It is when something exists in one form but is assumed to be in another. The idea that "I am the body" is itself pride. It is because of this feeling that one is oblivious of the true "Self," and possessed by body awareness. This is because we identify ourselves with the body. This is because of the belief that we are the body.

30/09/33, Morning Lecture

Lecture 53 - Knowledge and Worship

From a talk on the *Eknathi Bhagwat* of Saint Eknath

Included within the traditional knowledge that has been handed down from ancient times, is the "knowledge of qualities." It is not included in the teachings comprising karma yoga, but is the treasure house of advice. This "Spiritual Knowledge" is prevalent only in India, and even in India not all gain access to it, and most people do not avail themselves of it. It is told that as Lord Brahma was so engrossed in the work of creation, He could not deliver this ancient Spiritual Knowledge. Therefore, it was Lord Vishnu, who took over this responsibility.

The advice of the Master begins with the fact that the body is untrue. Those who behave according to the advice of the Master become proficient in the "Knowledge of Brahman." The Saints acquire their "saintliness," only after they imbibe this Knowledge. Those who do not know the Self, are not "well known." In fact they are infamous. Even those who are predisposed to evil ways, have acquired their "evilness" only because of the Self, but they have failed to recognize It. The Self is truly selfless and qualityless.

Association and disassociation are the changing states of qualities. Darkness has never confronted the Sun in order to fight a duel, and yet the Sun has acquired the title, "the killer of darkness." Recognize that steadiness and unsteadiness are the qualities of the body. Understand that a river does not have this side or that. The bank of the river is only in relation to position. It is the property (qualities) of light, that makes this bank, or that bank, of the river apparent. No quality ever reaches the Self. Those who worship with great love, and listen to and reflect upon spiritual discourse untiringly, embrace their True Nature. When the seer, the seeing and the seen merge into one, the trio vanish, and the stateless state, Parabrahman, is acquired.

Treat both reverence and being revered as characteristics associated only with the body. While all are one with respect to the Self, being civil towards all, respecting elders, etc., are still the duties and customs of the body. A human being should definitely be well behaved. The Self is Brahman but the body can never be so.

"In principle, now that you are Brahman, who will worship whom is the question?"

When notions of separateness such as "reverence," and "the revered," exist no longer for one, the worship of the Master becomes even more important as a gesture of gratitude. This is because without worshipping the Master, a disciple cannot be rid of the pride for the body. It is because of the pride for the body, that one harbors thoughts such as "that which is mine, will always remain mine," and "that which belongs to others, will always remain theirs." So long as the feeling of "mine" (attachment) exists, ego persists.

In spite of being a Jnani, a "Knower of Brahman," worships his Master. This is because although a disciple becomes proficient in the "Knowledge of Brahman," the Master is still held in highest reverence by him ("I" don't exist, nothing is "mine").

It is worship that tears open the nets of Illusion and puts a final end to Ignorance. Become very happy, not only worshipping Him, but also singing His praises (bhajans). He who wears the ornament of Consciousness is adorned by worship.

30/09/33

Lecture 54 - Only Brahman Exists

From a talk on the *Yogavasishtha*

The word "asmita" means a "contrary" or "reverse" feeling. It is because of this feeling that a certain thing is interpreted as being something quite different. The body is full of nothing but our own foolishness. From head to toe, the body is full of nothing but germs. The germs consider this body to be their house. We eat food not for our own survival, but for theirs. Yet, constantly all we do is harp on the tune of "I." After understanding this, if you call your body "I," it is only because of delusion. It is far more preferable to call yourself a germ, but never identify yourself with this abode of germs called the body. Identifying yourself with the body is what is called a delusion, a contrary feeling, a perverse concept.

Anger is a perverse concept that comes from investing too much love in the body and the ego. It is similar to "hate," which is what happens when someone or something tries to get in the way of this love. Identification with the body itself is a perverse concept, saying, "I will die," when it is the body that dies, or "I have grown old," when it is the body that grows old. Or, to say, "I am fair or dark, male or female," when it is only the body, which is fair or dark in color, and that is in the shape of a male or a female. It is all only wrong concepts to consider the state of the body as one's own state, or to try to measure oneself with the yardstick of the body.

Just as a bead belonging to a strand of beads thinks that it is the strand itself, one refers to the body as "I" and conveniently forgets the Self that resides in all. The Self is omnipresent. All have forgotten the

Self and have identified with the body. The body is taken to be "I," and this is Illusion. Illusion induces the oblivion of the Self. We forget the thread, which is woven into a garment and see only the garment. In this way, we bestow a false identity upon the thread as "garment." Can the garment continue to exist if we separate the thread from it? Just as a woven thread is accused of being a fabric, in that it takes on the identity of "fabric," so is the Self accused of being a body.

The Self is the only Truth, yet people have cultivated the habit of looking at it in completely the wrong way. All have conceived an incorrect perspective on it. Accepting the existence of Illusion forces us to deny the existence of Brahman which is eternal, and compels us to treat the ephemeral "I," as the only truth. Under the influence of this Illusion, we treat whatever is untrue as the "truth." If you want this delusion to vanish, be thoroughly acquainted with the fact that whatever is seen, conceived, or felt through the senses, is untrue, a mere appearance.

A camel kept in a small box can never be a real camel. Similarly, all that is perceived by the eye is untrue. This worldly life is untrue. Hence, "That" which is invisible and not perceived is the Truth, and that which is visible and perceived, is untrue.

That which is external, which is apparent, should be destroyed with inner thought. Only then can birth and death be avoided. Death does not affect the Self. It is a time of conversion for all, back to dust. On thinking, it will be found that all objects are nothing but dust. The worldly art that converts one into many is called jugglery, an act of a conjurer. Similarly, one individual is addressed as uncle, brother, father, husband, etc., and he responds to all these labels as well. It is due to thoughtlessness (lack of investigation) that all objects appear to be true. Although gold may be shaped into any variety of ornaments, there is one and only one basic ingredient in all of the objects, gold. Brahman is similar to gold, as it is the basic ingredient of all objects.

01/10/33

Lecture 55 - Knowledge, or Jnana

From a talk on the *Eknathi Bhagwat* of Saint Eknath

The Master's advice clears away the Ignorance of the individual (jiva). The common man has not understood what the "Ultimate Truth"

(Paramartha) is, nor what mundane worldly life (samsara) is. The Jnanis come into this world and spread Knowledge. They have united the two paths, that of Knowledge (Jnana) and that of Devotion (Bhakta). Jnanis like Gurulingam Jangam Maharaj and Bhausaheb Maharaj, have imparted experiential Knowledge to the world, and thus have brought on the dawn of this Knowledge.

We have received this Knowledge by the grace of Bhausaheb Maharaj. We are greatly indebted to him. This debt can only be repaid by putting this Knowledge into practice. The preaching of the ancient Jnanis lacked preciseness whereas Bhausaheb Maharaj's teachings were direct, straightforward, precise, brief, and to the point. The Knowledge imparted by him is based on firm determination and resolve. For example, in the olden days, great effort was required to reach the hill station Matheran, In those times, it was practically inaccessible, but now we can get there easily. Similarly, the modern man has been immensely benefited from the ancient Knowledge, which he now finds easy to understand. Moreover, he has made improvements in it. It is easy to improve upon previous experience or Knowledge. Jnanis can now impart and explain Knowledge using simpler methods.

Lord Vishnu has made the preliminary preparations, Lord Krishna has cooked, Eknath Maharaj has served, and Bhausaheb Maharaj has fed us this Knowledge. Eknath Maharaj constitutes the pinnacle of devotion to the Master. Eknath Maharaj having transcended the bounds of intellect, has conceived the holy text the *Eknathi Bhagwat*.

Shri Samarth Ramdas in *Dasbodh* has described the Master in the following words, "Oh Master, forever be as you are." He also says that "Just as the moon feeds the chakora (a legendary bird) with nectar, so does the Sadguru hand out nectar in the form of Self-Knowledge."

What does it mean by granting the state of immortality? Contrary to the usual meaning of living forever, all that it means is going beyond birth and death. Lord Rama (the Self) helped Hanuman (the mind) overcome the cycle of birth and death by making him drink the nectar of Knowledge. Presented here is the same Knowledge, and no instrument other than this Knowledge can help you join the rank of such immortals. Why would Lord Rama himself die, if he could help Hanuman become immortal in the worldly sense? Remember, becoming immortal means becoming free from the cycle of births and deaths. The true meaning of many words in these ancient stories is quite different from their current meaning.

Sage Vyasa and the Sage Vasishtha are two sages who labored and brought forward this Knowledge. This was possible only with the help of Knowledge. Just as it is the nose that helps one smell fragrance as well as stench, so does Knowledge help the sage attain sagehood. Sages have put up intense and unsparing work in order to attain sagehood and make Knowledge easy to understand. Hence, in present times it has become easy to acquire Knowledge.

In the past, the muslin fabric from Dacca was very expensive, and it found a place only in a royal wardrobe, but these days it has become cheaper, and as a result, even the poor can afford it. So it is with Knowledge. It has now become easily available. No longer are hardships required to achieve it. It is ironic that therefore, its importance has been greatly diminished. This Knowledge bears the same fruit today as it would in the ancient times, but with much less effort. What can be said about this? Others can serve and feed you, but to digest is your own responsibility.

"A person was once, by God's grace,
visited by Kamadhenu (the wish fulfilling cow).
He could find no place to stake her down,
So unfortunately, he had to drive her away."

Only one who strives to attain this Knowledge gets it. There is no discrimination such as young or old, rich or poor, or male or female for attaining Knowledge. Peace, having prostrated itself with adoration and in submission, enters the house of a person who gives up all pride and lovingly immerses himself in the nature of the Self. One who considers oneself to be present in one and all, and who therefore loves everyone, is truly superior to all. Just as darkness vanishes with sunrise, so are all vices wiped out with the rise of Knowledge, and everything is experienced as pleasurable.

01/10/1933

Lecture 56 - Names Are Untrue

From a talk on the *Yogavasishtha*

Objects that can be destroyed by right thought are not only insubstantial, but were non-existent to begin with. All objects that possess name and form are destroyed by proper thought (vichara, inquiry into the true and the untrue). Names are untrue, and hence all objects that possess names are untrue and doomed to destruction. All that arises from dust is nothing but dust. What is food? It is only dust originating from the earth. All objects including our bodies are made up of dust. Metals, again, are variations of the same dust. The same object (dust) has been invested with a host of different names, just for the sake of facilitating practical life. These names are nothing but man-made concepts. All of the eight worlds, that of words, that of imagination, that of the thoughts, etc., are all untrue. They are all only concepts. Once you become aware of this, your "so-called" world collapses like a house of cards.

It's told in the ancient mythological books (*Puranas*) that upon attaining Self-realization, Bhasmasura, a devotee of Lord Shiva, set everyone and everything on fire, turned it into ashes, and rubbed the ashes on Lord Shiva. In simple words, after realizing that everything is dust and nothing but dust, he turned everything into the form of Shiva. The *Puranas* were written in order to help us find out whether Knowledge has been correctly understood. Brahman is also known as "the Visionary," "the Witness," "the Life-Energy," "the Power," etc. All of these are only names, and hence untrue.

What then is Parabrahman? Parabrahman is That which extends beyond Brahman and is the one and only Truth. It has no name, and therefore is true. All those pleasures and pains, which have been experienced by us so far, were nothing but concepts. Just as the shadow cast by a moving cloud does not last at a particular place for long, so is this transient world, ever-changing, passing like a motion picture on the Self. One who realizes this dreamlike quality of the world, attains Parabrahman.

02/10/1933

Lecture 57 - Renunciation is True Happiness

From a talk on the *Eknathi Bhagwat* of Saint Eknath

The meanderings of the thoughts vanish in the "Bliss of the Self." In the pleasure stimulated by objects and in the fulfillment of desires, arise the numerous meanderings of thought. In this world, all material pleasures are enjoyed only through the medium of thought and its meanderings. The Bliss of the Self is attained only after the meanderings of thought are given up and consequently left off without a trace to be found. This itself is true Yoga.

Renunciation is the only true source of happiness. Considering the world to be untrue, the one who calms the thoughts attains the Bliss of the Self. If a person undertakes a certain business transaction, it follows that he has to face a series of complications and it requires him to adopt various strenuous efforts to fulfill his desire. This "extraneous worldly covering" (appearance of various circumstances on the Self) only torments and creates more stimulation for the thoughts. Understand that the fulfillment of worldly desires can never provide as much happiness as their renunciation.

A person who goes to watch a drama has to spend money for a ticket, and has to sit upright, even uncomfortably at times, for hours. He also has to stay up late, even well past midnight. On the whole, he suffers more, and enjoys less. So much for objective happiness! On the contrary, the person who does not go to watch the drama is spared of all the trouble. He sits back, relaxes and enjoys a peaceful evening and a good night's sleep. The more that one renounces appearances, the greater is the "Bliss of the Self."

He alone who finds this extraneous world appearance distasteful can be called the true devotee of the Master. No other bliss, or joy, is as great as the "Bliss of the Self." The Bliss of the Self is also known as the "Bliss devoid of desires." The fleas on the udders of a cow do not drink milk. They enjoy blood instead. Similarly, those who are not true devotees do not attain the Bliss of the Self. They don't know any better, so they drink of the world, and not of the Self. However, one can never really develop an aversion towards the Bliss of the Self, as this bliss is not experienced through the sensory organs.

The bliss or pleasure that is enjoyed through the sensory organs in the fulfillment of desires only serves to tire and weaken the body. Eventually one develops an aversion towards such joys, because they are based in desire. Those who lovingly keep the company of the Saints may experience desires, yet will never be troubled by them. Saint Tukaram was broke in worldly life, yet in the company of Saints, he became a devotee and reached the pinnacle of devotion. Devotion should be practiced in various ways. If one keeps up the practice of devotion, detachment is sure to follow.

A lamp is not lit in order to set the house on fire, but if the lamp flares up and catches something on fire, it burns down not only the house, but even the entire village. Similarly, when the fire of Knowledge lights up one's heart full of faith, it flares up and burns down all desires, and detachment is born. Many people may listen to discourses, but without faith in the Saints, it does nothing but provide them with expertise in debate. They may become unyielding like a tree, or bloated with conceit and pride like a bull, but their faith in the Master is not firm. If there is humility, modesty and equanimity in one's behavior, and if one invests tremendous faith in the Master, then the residue of former concepts is washed away, and one becomes detached from desires.

One who is in the company of true Saints, indeed speaks like a Saint. Devotion to the Self can turn a servant into a Master. Infinite is the range of devotion. The power of devotion is such that it makes the devotee superior even to a king. One who worries over the returns which devotion is likely to bring can never attain the bliss of devotion. Lord Krishna in the Bhagavad Gita says, "I myself am unable to describe the importance of devotion to Me." It was devotion that enabled Saint Tukaram, a small-time shopkeeper to say, "The Saints are prior even to God." Devotion can bring about immense change in the devotee. Such is the greatness of devotion.

02/10/1933, Evening Lecture

Lecture 58 - Ignorance Vanishes with "Right Thought"

From a talk on the *Yogavasishtha*

Any object that appears to exist, but vanishes with the application of "right thought," (inquiry into the true and untrue), is untrue. All visible objects possessing names and forms are untrue. All that is visible and conceivable is perishable. All that is perceivable through the senses is perishable. When the cause is perishable, its effect is also perishable. As the sensory organs themselves are untrue, accordingly, the experiences derived through them are untrue. This magnificent spectacle called Illusion, is the magic of the eye. It is plain trickery. All of this Illusion is the product of the combination of the sense organs and thoughts.

The wonders of thought are many. When we see a shapely idol or a beautiful picture, our thoughts are pleased, yet animals are unable to recognize or appreciate the significance of it, and perhaps may even trample on it. It is told of how one man broke and desecrated many idols of God without so much as the slightest bit of remorse. Was he punished by God for that? No, yet it is common to see people refrain from even stretching out their feet in the direction of an idol[9]. Many would flinch if such a thought even occurred to them.

Why is this? It is only thoughts, which are responsible for this. For example, with love, the husband's love for his wife, is entirely different from the father's love for his daughter, or the wife's love towards her husband. All of this is just the mire of thoughts. Know for certain that this untrue world undergoes continuous destruction just as a camphor pellet undergoes continuous burning[10], until it disappears.

One may ask, "How can the Illusion be called untrue, when it is openly seen and readily apparent?" Understand that all perceivable objects are perishable. By nature, the inherent characteristic feature of delusion is to be visible. It's similar to how an image in the mirror is visible, although it is changeful by nature, and bound to disappear. Or, like how a mirage is clearly seen, yet is really untrue and sure to perish. In the same way, the entire world appearance is based only on delusion. By the application of "right thought" this entire universe gets destroyed.

Ignorance brings the world to the forefront. However, just as a dream vanishes upon awakening, so does this world vanish, with right thinking. Know that the body is your archenemy, and that it always only troubles you with disease, discomfort, etc. If this body had truly ever been who we are, or truly belonged to us, it would never give us any trouble. Take it for granted that the body, and the mistaken identification with it as "I," which everyone so lovingly calls it, is your enemy. In this Illusion, relatives coax and cajole you before beginning in with their harassment. In spite of the fact that our body torments us, and even though our relatives harass us, we continue to harbor a deep love for the Illusion. This is due to ignorance. Upon awakening, after attaining Self-Knowledge, a Jnani sincerely repents for calling the body as "I," and from then on begins to consider the body as an enemy, or as a dead body.

---

[9] In Indian custom it is considered a sign of disrespect to point ones feet and legs in the direction of an idol of God or in the direction of a highly respected person or Guru.

[10] When a camphor pellet is burned it burns continuously until nothing remains, like the world continually disappears.

Although one may be awakened by Knowledge, one must still get over the waves of dreams (desires and imaginings). Thoughts are constantly changing, and illusory. They are so fickle that they can turn your best friends into sworn enemies, or can turn your enemies into friends. The Self however, is neither seen, nor is it illusory. Thought can bring the Self to life, and also lends to it the quality of "Truth." Not only this, but proper use of thought can bring one to the experience that "I Am He."

Morning 03/10/1933

Lecture 59 - Primal Illusion and Destruction

"The sky (space) gives rise to wind, this is what is actually experienced. Wind brings forth fire, this should be listened to carefully and understood." (*Dasbodh* - Chapter 11, Sub-chapter 1)

The more we let the "original concept" (I Am) take firm root, the more it grows and finally takes on a manifest form. This basic concept is the "Primal Illusion" (MoolaMaya, the original Illusion with the potential for attributes). When this Primal Illusion is made firm with determination it is called "Illusion with Attributes" (GunaMaya). The subtle elements and the subtle qualities are primal in nature, while the gross or inert elements come into existence later. If consciousness (collectively the mind, thoughts, intelligence, etc.) is subtle, its functioning is also subtle. As thoughts about the gross become determinedly more fixed, concepts continue increasing.

That which has come into existence initially has been termed the "Primal Illusion." This is the most subtle form of Illusion, Illusion without attributes. From this comes "Illusion with Attributes" or Gunamaya, where the three qualities (gunas) of Raja, Tamas, and Sattva co-exist and intermingle in their respective proportions. From these arises the gross form of Illusion or "Ignorance" (Avidya). This gross form of Illusion is called "Avidyamaya.

The Consciousness which is the substance of the Primal Illusion is the fourth body, or the "Great-causal Body" (Knowledge, or "I Am"). It is the Tamoguna quality (Ignorance) that makes us forget our True Nature, while the Rajoguna quality (objective focus) makes us think of activity in the Illusion. The "subtle" lies in the Sattvaguna (turning ones focus towards Reality). That which assumes all of these types of gross characteristics is the Avidyamaya.

It is not enough merely to know all of this intellectually. That is not the goal. To truly understand and realize "I Am Brahman" is what is all-important. All that is required is firm determination, and it is "right thought" (vichara) that brings forth this determination.

"That" which is as spontaneous and natural as the sky, is our own nature, while Consciousness is in the form of concepts. This Consciousness has conceived infinite concepts. If the Lord conceives "Himself," He is God (Shiva), and if He conceives the world, He appears to turn into an individual (jiva). Having no memory indicates having no sorrow. It is said that it is the Lord who enjoys pleasures. This simply means that if we concentrate on and understand ourselves fully, without giving any thought for anything objective, we are in the form of Bliss (Ananda).

It is when we start transacting with the objective world, that joys and sorrows come into being. The Lord is sitting alone in the shrine, devoid of joys and sorrows. When the Lord begins to focus on external objects, He seemingly turns into an individual. It is like when a man leaves his house and goes to serve others, he turns into a servant, similarly, when one turns into an individual, it's as if one's home has been abandoned. When you assume external objects to be true, you remain as an individual (jiva) and when you start treating the objective world as untrue, and you are the Lord (Shiva).

Now I will explain the process of destruction. The ancient scriptures have predicted that the doom (Kalpanta, end of the world, or literally the end of concepts) will begin with a drought, which will last for a hundred years and dry up this entire earth. The parched earth will crumble down to a powdery mass. Large fissures will appear on the surface of the sun-scorched earth. This period of drought will be followed by a spell of heavy rains, which will melt away the powered earth.

Fire is an element, which consumes all that is in its vicinity. If all other things are absent, it completely burns itself up. It then turns into only a passing wind, and then even this wind dies down into space. With the study of the five elements, we come to know that if the elements cease to function, all that is bound to remain is space. This space also vanishes eventually, and it is Knowledge alone that remains. This Knowledge ultimately merges into Absolute Knowledge (Vijnana; what remains after the destruction of both Ignorance and Knowledge).

The word "paaoos" is Marathi for rains, and is the combination of the words paha and haus. Paha means "to see," and haus means "a desire." Put together, the word paaoos means "a desire to see." In light of this explanation, let us see what is actually meant by "one hundred years of drought." The "drought" means a condition generated by the lack of rains, which indicates the absence of the "desire to see." To see what? To see the world of course! If one proceeds to repeat a hundred times that the world that is seen is untrue, then the desire to see the world fades away. This is the inner meaning of what is meant by a hundred years of draught.

Make a firm determination, a hundred times if required, that the world is nothing but dust, and watch the world gradually turn to dust. Everyone is always looking externally. The aspirant should stop doing this. All that one needs to do is sit to quietly and stop all of the mental constructs. Wipe one concept away with the help of another. Just as an ailment afflicting one in a dream can only be cured by medicine that is available in that dream, likewise, it is by using a concept, that one can bring down another concept. This world appearance is just like a dream.

In Marathi, the word for dream is "swapan." Swapan is the two words "swa" and "pan" put together. Swa means "one's own," and pan means "determination." Hence, in accordance with this explanation, a dream, is merely one's own determination. Give up the world, which is the outcome of your own determination, using the help of concepts. This is what is called "The end of concepts," or "kalpanta." Kalpanta is comprised of the two words kalpa, meaning "concept," and the word anta, meaning "end." The world Kalpanta is considered as "the destruction," or the "end of the universe," which occurs through the destruction of concepts. Giving up the world by using concepts brings about the destruction of the universe, as the universe is only the creation of our own concepts.

Give up all desire for the Illusion. In Marathi, "Maya Nirase" means giving up the Illusion. The word Maya means "that which is not." Although it appears, "that which is not" is still only Illusion. The word Nirase is the two words Nir, which means "not," and aasha, which means "desire." Put together "Maya Nirase" indicates the state of no desire for the Illusion. It simply means giving up desire for the Illusion, the desire for illusory objects.

The "clarification" of Illusion, or making Illusion clear, similar to how one would clarify butter, is possible only if the desire for the Illusion is given up. Once this desire is given up, the knowledge of objects no longer exists. How can desire spring up where there is no knowledge of objects? This simply means that the knowledge of objects should vanish. It is because of this knowledge that worldly desire springs forth. Once you say that objects do not exist, you are bound to lose interest in them. It is with the aim of becoming desireless that objects are denied any existence. Desires should be made to subside in order to attain that state wherein you remain established in your "True Nature" (Swaroopa). The existence of something is due only to concepts. When you use the help of concepts to see that something is untrue, it is then known to be untrue. Proliferation of the objective world has been caused by concepts, and concepts alone will dissolve it. When the world is dissolved, it is then revealed that the only thing that remains is one's True Nature.

Once one gives up drawing distinctions such as "you" and "I," etc., the concept of God also vanishes. The plot will be over. The Illusion and ignorance will stop running riot. Thought, when used correctly helps to make the objective world subside, and hence it is called the dissolution through thought (Kalpanta, the end of concepts).

Parabrahman is steady, whereas the Self is ever-changing (Atman, in this context means Consciousness with attributes. In other talks, Parabrahman, or Paramatman, is referred to as the True Self). The world is ever-changing, just as its creator, the Self, is ever-changing. That which performs all duties and deeds is the ever-changing Self. That Consciousness is also called "the non-doer, even after doing." This Self, or Consciousness, exists in a king as well as in a beggar. The ignorant call it Parabrahman, but the knowledgeable call it the "Inner-Self" (AntarAtman) that pervades everything. This Inner-Self, alone has built up all of this appearance. The Inner-Self alone, is the creator of this Illusion, which by nature is destined to disappear.

With "Life-Energy" and "Knowledge" as its nature, Consciousness is the single light of the universe. The pious call this the Inner-Self, or God. The Inner-Self animates and stimulates all of the senses. It is this Consciousness alone which pervades one and all. Everyone and everything is full with this consciousness. It is what functions in all. The Jnani is one who is aware of this. There are many different names it is called by, but they are all applicable to the one Inner-Self alone. It lies below the seven layers of blood, flesh, nerves, veins, sweat pores, skin and bones. These seven layers are referred to as the seven seas. Thus, it is said that the Inner-Self is beyond the seven seas.

In Hindu mythology, Rama (the Self) has three brothers. Shatrughna (the destroyer of enemies) is the one who destroys the six vikaras (existence, birth, growth, modification, decay and death) and the three qualities (gunas). Bharata (to be filled), which means that all are filled with Paramatman. And, Laxmana (Laxa is goal, and mana is mind), which means the mind is set on the goal of attaining the state of Paramatman.

The Inner-Self is the Lord of all. How can it be said that the Self has passed away? When the eternal and perishable part ways (upon death of the body), the objective world turns rancid. When you say that the Lord is watching, it means that it is the Lord alone, who is Conscious of everything. Herein lies the whole trick. One who discerns this is a Jnani. By analogy, the Inner-Self is the King, whereas the mind is the Prime Minister. You can gauge the importance of the Inner-Self from this. Although the Inner-Self is not visible, it can be realized. The eyes can see colored objects, but they cannot see "That" which has no color. The mind can see all of the objects that lie in front of it, but it cannot see that which lies hidden behind the objects. It is the Inner-Self which lies hidden behind everything.

No one is aware of the One who is aware of all. He who lights up the world is infinitely superior to the light, as He possesses consciousness. It is because of this consciousness that He becomes apparent. He is Self-luminous. He possesses light. Light means being conscious. With the help of His own light, He is aware of Himself, and is aware of others too. He is beyond everything and everyone. He can be experienced but cannot be seen or felt. He cannot be discerned without the help of the Master. He is in the form of Knowledge (Jnana). He subtly but completely pervades the sky.

How is someone visible? It is due to consciousness. Unless consciousness reaches you, you will not be visible. Consciousness is knowledge and what you are conscious of, is the object. The knowledge in which objects and consciousness both exist, is known as "objective knowledge." The knowledge in which you can exist, but due to the hollow mortal eye, you are not conscious of the space that extends between you and the Sun, is known as objectless knowledge. The knowledge, which calls an object by a specific name, is conceptual knowledge, or the mind. The Knowledge, which does not have consciousness of objects, is non-conceptual Knowledge. Whatever you grasp is applicable to you.

In Marathi, the word for moon is Chandra. Chandra is "Cha" and "Indra" together. The word Cha means "desire" and Indra means "the mind." Therefore, the word Chandra means desire, as well as the mind. If one observes subtly, one can see the subtle. If one has not cultivated the habit of subtle observation, then you cannot see subtly. When an object is seen, we continue to exist without destroying the object. On the contrary, we protect it. Objects mix all of their fractional parts in Him, but He does not mix with anything.

The eyes cannot see darkness, but darkness is seen by the Inner-Self. An object, the light of the sun, and the eyes, form an inseparable trinity (Seen, Seeing, and Seer). If any one of them is missing, functioning of the world appearance ceases. At night when sunlight is absent, the eyes do not function. The eyes do not function, yet the Self can see the darkness. This darkness covers the entire earth, while the sun can light up only half of the earth at a time.

Krishna means darkness. This darkness is full of knowledge, theft, dishonesty, etc. When the sun rises, there is incarnation of Rama. And with this incarnation of Lord Rama, the senses (Ravanna) start functioning. It is Ravanna who rules the empire which comprises the fourteen realms, which are the ten sensory organs (The five organs of perception - the tongue, the nose, the eyes, the ears, and the skin. The five organs of action - the hands, the feet, the organ of speech, the organs of evacuation, and the organ of generation), and the four types of speech (See lecture 22). He who has given life to Ravanna is the Self, and He who has incarnated as Rama, is also the Self. It is Ravanna, the senses, who has exiled the Self. It is said that it is Ravanna, who has imprisoned God. It means that the senses have sent the Lord, the Self, the doer of everything, into exile. Ravanna has also imprisoned the gods governing the senses.

When we say that Ravanna has lost his kingdom, all that is meant is that the senses have stopped functioning properly. When it is known that the Self is the doer, it means that God is the doer, and this is the dawn of the empire of Lord Rama. When it is said that the Inner-Self perceives all objects, it only means that it is our own quality of consciousness becomes one with the object. Thereby it identifies the object as a specific object. Though consciousness is singular, various functions are performed by the sensory organs. That which enables the nose to smell, the eyes to see, the ears to hear, etc. is consciousness. He who dwells deep within and is conscious of everything is the "non-doer in spite of doing." All of the four bodies should subside. In other words, you should be devoid of all of the four bodies. You should consider these bodies to be untrue and refrain from identifying with them. Doing this is as good as giving them up.

The Great-causal Body (Consciousness) vanishes with the body, and it is the unmoving Parabrahman alone, which lasts. The discriminating person should avail oneself of this experience. Paramatman is unchanging, the Self alone is ever-changing, and the world is gross. The ever-changing is without substance. When you go beyond the Self and give up this gross world, you gain "Absolute Knowledge." You become "without mind," or unmana (Un means without, mana means mind). You yourself have to experience the state beyond the mind. Your existence, the state of being alone exists without any prop, without being impinged upon you by some external factor. The body-consciousness, mind, etc., has come into existence because of you. You and you alone are responsible for the existence of this whole universe. The Self, in spite of being the source of this universe is devoid of body (videhi). To live without realizing Him is sin itself. To realize Him is a virtuous act by which all sins are annihilated. Only the one who realizes this is contented. Parabrahman is the only "Truth." The visible (sin) subsides, and only boundless merit (Parabrahman) remains. On discerning and consequently realizing "I am the Self," one attains the "Truth" beyond words and form.

The causal body is the state of nothingness, which represents Kailasa, the abode of Lord Shiva. The merits and sins of the waking state do not, and cannot extend beyond the four bodies. What is the difference between the waking and the dreaming state? This could be best explained thus: Try to go back to a dream that you had yesterday, or more specifically, try to retrieve one of the articles that had appeared in that dream. It is impossible, as the dream is related to the dream body. Similarly sins and merits of the worldly state vanish with the gross body. It is not at all related to the Self. Without the Knowledge of Brahman, all other actions and knowledge prove to be futile. In spite of all the resolve that you make, the body can never be purified.

Lecture 60 - Brahman, Five Sheaths, Four Bodies of Ishwara

"Brahman is formless. Its nature is similar to that of space, yet Brahman is flawless, there are flaws in space." (*Dasbodh* - Chapter 11, Sub-chapter 4)

What is Brahman? Brahman is the spontaneous and natural state, which remains when the four bodies reach their end. The causal body, the third body, is called Ignorance (causal as it is the source of the world). After having given up this Ignorance, the one who does so, remains in the form of "Knowledge," the Great-causal body (Consciousness). Even this Knowledge should be given up. Knowledge is called AUM, which means Aham or "I." A person who realizes up to this point is termed as Self-Realized, or God. Beyond this, lies the shapeless, qualityless, and unchangeable Brahman. There is no activity, no movement, no entry and no exit in Brahman. The Inner-Self is ever-changing and unsteady. It is conscious of the mind, the concept, and the object. The Self, is the "seer," that is conscious of all, even while you sit quietly, or even if you are unconscious.

The mind, the intellect, speech, etc. do not exist in Brahman. By way of example, it is told that a woman's nose ring fell into a well. She asked a man to help her look for it. He entered the well, and the woman asked him to let her know as soon as the ring was found. He agreed to do so, yet he could not tell her the moment that he found the ring, because he was under the water. In order to let the woman know about the ring he would have to use his speech but he was under the water. The deity of speech is fire and as fire does not get along with water, it did not come to the aid of the man when he was under the water. As long as the man was under water, he could not convey the message to her.

The point of this is that we cannot recall or reproduce work that is done without applying our mind. On whom would the samadhi, or the spiritual ecstasy, work, if you had no existence. This is how the Inner-Self is. He is referred to as the seer, or the witness. That Self, by its nature is the original animating factor. The Self dwells in the hearts of all and looks after everything and everyone. Therefore, it called the Inner-Self. Everything turns inert in its absence. All prosperity and all grandeur exist because of the Self. The "Supreme Truth" (Paramartha) is attained only by virtue of the Inner-Self. If that Inner-Self were absent, who would even acquaint us with the concepts of good and bad deeds?

The Inner-Self alone composed the *Vedas*. The one who worries over worldly concepts such as earning a living, is the individual (jiva), and the one who builds the concept of the Ultimate Truth is God, Shiva. Parabrahman (Supreme Reality) is apart from all this. "God in the heavens" is the God beyond space. God is nothing but the Knowledge beyond the void of Ignorance. It is the Inner-Self alone, that is worshipped by the entire world. The Lord is called Keshava. What does Keshava mean? Keshava is He who abides in the body purely in the form of one's "True Nature" (Swaroopa). Although people employ various methods to worship this one God, who resides in every heart, they are not conscious of Him. Worship of the Lord with complete understanding brings about one's true welfare.

The sages recognize this God as one who walks and talks. People set up images of gods and worship the true God through them, without being aware of the fact that images cannot be a substitute for God. The true God possesses Life-Energy, Consciousness, etc. Those who have not been shown the "Knowledge of the Ultimate Truth" act foolishly, and continue to visit many different temples and worship idols. There are millions of such temples built in order to worship so many deities, yet indirectly they unknowingly worship none other than the Inner-Self. What is "Knowledge"? Knowledge (Jnana) is to recognize the one God who is symbolized by all of the idols. Followers of Vedanta refer to the Inner-Self as "Sat-Chit-Ananda," while Shri Shankaracharya regards the Inner-Self as Maya. The various paths leading to Self-realization, such as the path of actions (karma yoga), and that of devotion (bhakti yoga), exist only by virtue of this Inner-Self. The "Supreme God" (Parameshwara) can be realized only with the help of the Inner-Self (Ishwara) that resides within.

There are four powers in this world appearance, 1.) the power of action, 2.) the power of will, 3.) the power of wealth, and 4.) the power of Knowledge. He who possesses all the four powers is omnipotent. To incarnate (Avatar) means to come down. The ten senses represent the ten incarnations (of Vishnu). When you forget your Self, you turn into Rudra (the ignorant destructive aspect of Shiva). When you are in the state of Knowledge, you turn into Lord Vishnu, and when you form various concepts, you create this universe, and you become Lord Brahma. The Supreme Self (Paramatman) always remains steady. The bridge between the "ever-changing" and the "unchanging" is Knowledge. In the Supreme Reality (Parabrahman), even the Knowledge derived from the Vedanta falls short. People make the mistake of becoming entangled in Knowledge.

Often people gain some understanding of Self-Knowledge and become convinced about following the path of actions (karma). While it is true that Consciousness is the root of everything, the Supreme Self, Paramatman, has neither root nor branches. The Inner-Self (Atman) vanishes as soon as one's true "Self Nature" (Swaroopa) is realized. It is the ever-changing Self that carries out all worldly affairs. Ultimately, it must be seen that the Self is also perishable. The Self brings about so many various transformations. There are many people who say that the changeful and the changeless are the same, but this is ignorant talk. This is because they have not come across anyone who could endow them with Knowledge.

What is Parabrahman? That natural, spontaneous (stateless) state, which remains after the inspiration "I Am" is cast off, is called Parabrahman. Whatever may be called Consciousness ultimately has to be given up. This is because Consciousness and Ignorance are both concepts. Only the one who practices this with determination, understands Parabrahman. The basis of arriving at the Supreme Truth (Paramartha) is the understanding of the "Science of the Five Elements" (Panchikarana Science), and the fundamental principle behind this science, which is "I Am He" (I Am That). Parabrahman has been proved again, and again, by adopting many skillful measures.

The Self is covered by five sheaths (pancha kosha), or coverings:

1. The Sheath of the Food: This is the gross body, the material elements.
2. The Sheath of Pranas: The energy of the five pranas.
3. The Sheath of Manas (mind): The sheath of intelligence and cognition
4. The Sheath of Vijnana (higher aspects of intelligence): abstract concepts and subtle functioning, etc.
5. The Sheath of Bliss: The causal body. Forgetfulness of objectivity that brings in bliss whether done consciously, or in deep-sleep.

The mind is similar to the Saint Narada who would traverse the three worlds and play tricks on people in order to help them take up the path of devotion. Everyone's mind is limited to the three states of waking, dreaming, and deep-sleep.

Wandering through the five sheaths, one must go on a pilgrimage to Lord Vishnu, the Lord of the Universe, the Inner-Self. The five sheaths are rooted in the interplay of the five elements constituting the body. The Self is the description of the three hundred and thirty million deities of Hindu mythology, and the body is the "Place of Realization," Kashi. Whatever is in the microcosm is included in the macrocosm. What does it mean to go Rameshwar? Rameshwar (a Hindu pilgrimage place) means "Rama is Ishwara," the "Self is God." To visit Rameshwar means to be conscious of Him, the Inner-Self.

What is the difference between a jiva (the individual) and Ishwara (God)? The jiva is similar to the expressed meaning (the visible), whereas Ishwara is the meaning derived from signs and indications (the invisible). The jiva is the expressed form (Vaachya) while Ishwara is the indication (Lakshya).

Like the jiva, Ishwara also has four bodies.

1. The Gross Body, which is the physical universe.

2. The Subtle Body which is represented by Brahma, Vishnu and Shiva, and consists of the three hundred and thirty million deities that represent all of the animation of manifestation.

3. The Causal Body, which is the most subtle expressed form, the space from which the world appears.

4. The Great-Causal Body, the original, primordial body or *Moola Prakriti*; the "Original Illusion," Sat-Chit-Ananda, which can only be indicated.

The gross, the subtle, and the causal are the expressed form of the jiva. Ultimately, the expressed form and the indicated form of the jiva are one.

Wind is one of the five constituent elements of the body. This winds is the same as that in the macrocosm. This explains that the world appearance of the Lord and the gross body of the individual are the same. Both possess the same five elements.

The Sun represent the eyes, and the Moon represents the mind (Chandra), the wishes for sense pleasures. The mind is not loyal to the Master. Hence, we say that the Moon is blemished. What is meant by this is that the mind has been tainted by disloyalty to the Master.

It is said that the some rituals such as ceremonies and sacrifices (yagnas) can bring rain. In Hinduism, having a sumptuous meal is treated as performing a yagna. This only means that when the body has a hearty meal, its senses are satiated. Rains require heat, so do our senses. When the body is well fed and well nourished, heat is generated which in turn sets the senses in motion.

The word Gautam means "Go" and "Uttama" together. (Go, means senses, and Uttama means best). Hence, Gautam is the one who makes the best use of the senses. Ahilya is the wife of this Gautam, but she loves the senses (Indriya; the sensory organs). She is engrossed in gratifying the desires of these sensory organs. On being touched by the Self (Lord Rama), she is delivered from this wretched state and purified.

The subtle body of the jiva and that of the Ishwara are the same. Hence, the three bodies, which can be expressed in words, are the same in the jiva, as they are for Ishwara. The indicated form of the great-causal body are the same as well. That is Sat-Chit-Ananda. The "expressed form" of jiva and Shiva, and "the indicated form" of jiva and Shiva, are the same. The "True Form," or Swaroopa, of both jiva and Shiva is the same.

Those who say that the jiva and Shiva are distinctly apart, do not know their true nature at all. The first body is the gross body and the eighth body is the Primordial Illusion (Moolamaya, Sat-Chit-Ananda). That which remains when the four bodies of both jiva and Ishwara are put aside, is beyond imagination. It is steady. It cannot be expressed in words. A Jnani should not get carried away by the individual, "jiva," or God, "Ishwara." Both are untrue. Do not get carried away by Knowledge born of Ignorance (Vidya) or by Ignorance (Avidya) itself, and recognize the eternal Supreme Self, "Paramatman."

Lecture 61 - The Secret Ganga Revealed

"The secret ever-flowing Ganga purifies the world when we think of her. Verify and actually experience this, as it is not false." (*Dasbodh* - Chapter 11, Sub-chapter 7)

Why was *Dasbodh* composed in the first place? Many people mistake the Self (Atman) for Parabrahman (also called Paramatman). This is where the holy text *Dasbodh* comes in handy. It clearly defines not only Parabrahman, which is beyond name and form, but also the Self, and draws a distinction between the two.

The Self, Atman, which is the seer, the witness and the doer, and the "Supreme Self," Paramatman, which is known by many different names, and is yet beyond all names and forms have been clearly explained here. This is what sets *Dasbodh* apart from all other religious texts. *Dasbodh* says that Paramatman can neither be defined by any of the several thousand names assigned to Him, nor can He be described by any of the signs attributed to Him.

The Shruti (the *Vedas*) says that Paramatman is neither Knowledge nor Ignorance. The difference between Paramatman, who as per the Shruti is described by negation (not this, not this), and the Self (Atman), which is described by many different names, has been explained in the first ten chapters of *Dasbodh*. Paramatman is your spontaneous and natural Self, devoid of all concepts of Knowledge and Ignorance.

Beyond the first body, the physical, gross body lies the second body, the subtle body (comprising the pranas, the mind, the intellect, inner-mind and the ego) which possesses untrue objective knowledge. Paramatman resides beyond the realm of the bodily senses, the prana, the mind and the intellect, where speech and imagination cannot reach. Lord Krishna says in the Bhagavad Gita, "Where speech cannot reach, That is my eternal abode."

The mind is a collection of determinations and doubts, as to whether a particular thing "is" or "is not." The mind means "to say something." The "inner-mind" (antahkarana) is what sees, or becomes aware of objective things as they arise. To put an end to the mind means to keep quiet. In other words, the formation of objective concepts is stopped. When you say that a particular thing exists, the mind comes into play. This acknowledgment of objects is the mind. The one who says so, is not the mind.

Beyond the inner-mind lies the third, or causal body. This is Ignorance, meaning the void or nothingness. It is a state of "blissful forgetfulness" (as in dreamless deep-sleep) where you are neither aware of this worldly objective knowledge, nor of Reality. It all depends on where you apply your attention. Your attention turned one way sees the world, and when turned the opposite way, goes towards Reality (Parabrahman).

The fourth body, or Sat-Chit-Ananda form, knows everyone and witnesses everything. It is the Knowledge belonging to what is called the great-causal body, or "Turya" state. But this Knowledge is also Illusion. It is the "Primal Illusion" in the form of Life-Energy (Chaitanya). To be conscious of the Self (Atman) is the Turya state.

There are three things, the changeless, the ever-changing, and the gross. That which is changeless is Parabrahman, and that which is ever-changing is Consciousness. There are very few who advance from the ever-changing Self (Atman) to the changeless (Paramatman). The doer necessarily has to be animate. As soon as the deed of knowing "Who am I?" is accomplished, the work, as well as the animate ability of the doer comes to an end.

Knowledge, or Consciousness, devoid of desires is the Primal Illusion (Moolamaya). Sat-Chit-Ananda is the ever-changing subtle Illusion (Vidyamaya), and the manifestation is gross Illusion (Avidyamaya). The ever-flowing river is hidden and hence is referred to as the secret Ganga. This secret Ganga is nothing but ever-changing Knowledge in the form of Consciousness (Chit). It secretly exists within you, and is you. You are cleansed and purified merely by thinking of her.

She originates in That which is changeless (Parabrahman), and from then onward, she proceeds at a brisk pace. She takes a plunge in the downward direction (the objective world). Consciousness never flows towards the Reality (Parabrahman). This river is ever-flowing. It flows through all the four states (waking, sleeping, dreaming and Turya). She traces a winding course.

She has a continuous supply of water, but this water is not wet, it is dry, as this is the river of Knowledge (Consciousness). So swift and nimble are its waters that this river reaches the Sun within a fraction of a second. All the soft tender earth melts in it, yet the seemingly solid ego remains unaffected. However, a few have proven to be powerful enough to reach the source of this river and have been purified. One who sees this secret river, which is the originator of Brahma, Vishnu and Shiva becomes instantly purified. This river is called Aapo-Narayana (Aap means water, Narayana is the Lord who dwells in the hearts of all). This means that the water of this river is called God (Narayana). This river flows within every heart. It has occupied the Heavens, the Objective World, and the Nether World. This river itself is the "Lord of the Universe" (Jagadisha).

We are all filled with the contents of this river. Some have exhausted themselves and have eventually passed away while merely fulfilling their worldly duties. Just as we cannot estimate the value of water until we are confronted with a water shortage, we will never understand the importance of this Ganga unless we recognize our oneness with it.

If you go beyond, to its source, you will find that there exists nothing. This world is unreal. It is but the by-product of doubts and determinations (concepts). The causal body is in the form of nothingness, or Ignorance, and the great-causal body is in the form of "Knowledge." He in whom both the concepts of Ignorance and Knowledge are eliminated, is called a true Yogi.

Universal Consciousness (Chit) is itself a subtle concept. Concepts, whether in the shape of Knowledge, or that of Ignorance are both only concepts. The abandoning of these concepts is what is called the elimination of the concepts of the thinking (chitta), and this is precisely what yoga is about. Such a "Lord of Yogis" (Yogeshwar) who is devoid of concepts, is the true devotee of the Master.

Elimination of concepts is not to be confused with suppression, or reigning in of concepts. It only means that the concepts should be wiped off. Think deeply and you will find out how the devotees of the True Master (Sadguru) are the true yogis.

Lecture 62 - The Changeless and the Ever-Changing

"One is changeless, and the other is ever-changing. While the world is enmeshed in the ever-changing, the one that is changeless remains still, eternally as it is." (*Dasbodh* - Chapter 11, Sub-chapter 2)

There are two things, the "changeless" and the "ever-changing." Parabrahman is changeless and Illusion is ever-changing. The Self is Shiva. This Self is called Brahman by the Vedantins. The changeless will remain forever changeless. It is not bound by time (the past, the present or the future), hence it is "Timeless Truth." It is the only Truth, which always exists, at the beginning of creation, in the midst of it, and after its end.

Sins and merits, births and deaths, etc. are like a child's game for a person who believes in the unchanging Paramatman. Just as a small child at play takes his game seriously while the adults dismiss it as a mere game, likewise, ignorant beings take the illusory world to be true while the Jnanis treat it as untrue.

The Jnani is himself changeless. He is never affected by worldly matters. One who has given sins and merits a hard kick, just as a soccer player would kick a ball, cannot be affected by the actions of the body. Paramatman is eternally still and changeless. If you concentrate on the changeless (Paramatman) and think of Him even on your death, how could you become the ever-changing?

In the end, as is the thought, so is the fate. At night while going to sleep, determine that you are one with Brahman. If you harbor the feeling that you are the body, you will forever be limited by a body. Firmly resolve that you are Brahman and experience it. This can be at any point in your life, or it could even be right before death. Know that you are nothing but Brahman.

This Self is not a child, nor a woman or a man. Everyone talks about the "changeless," yet continue to exist as the unstable or "ever-changing" (caught in the cycle of worldly existence). The ever-changing is nothing but the cycle of worldly existence. Everyone has grown up in this Illusion and will eventually die in it. Only a few succeed in reaching the changeless. The most important thing to keep in mind is that nothing else exists in the changeless. Sins as well as merits are untrue. All desire, even the desire for merit, turns one into a "sinner," because it takes one away from one's True Nature.

"Knowledge of Brahman" helps you vanquish all actions (karma), thus eliminating your sins and merits. A total surrender of the body and mind to the one who has attained the Knowledge of Brahman can bring that Knowledge to you. Sins and merits appear only in the ever-changing and will eventually be destroyed. When people's thoughts and actions are governed by false notions such as sins and merits, their conduct no longer remains harmonious.

05/03/1931

Lecture 63 - Prologue, Procedure, and Epilogue

From a talk on *Dasbodh*

At the end of many births, by chance, the human body forms. Accordingly, live a good life, adhering to justice and morality." (*Dasbodh* - Chapter 11, Sub-chapter 3)

The gaining of Self-Knowledge requires three steps for its successful completion, the prologue, the procedure, and the epilogue. The prologue helps one develop a liking for the subject matter. In order to generate this liking, one has to prove the supremacy of Knowledge over ignorance. In order to establish the supremacy of the Self-Knowledge, you have to prove that it gives happiness, and that it brings about the welfare of all. Thus, in order to establish the supremacy of the Self, the prologue becomes necessary. The procedure explains the methodology of attaining Self-Knowledge. And, lastly, the epilogue is that one attains it.

Suppose you want to say something about water. Do not begin to describe its superiority over other things in order to establish its supremacy. Begin with its uses. Say that we get food and drink with the help of water. This is the only way you can stress its importance. Creating a recognition of the need for water constitutes the prologue for water.

First, create the need for it and then begin with the actual content. The prologue and procedure are available to you right from the beginning.

Birth after birth you wander through 8.4 million species, and it is only then that you acquire this special human body. It can be acquired only after rendering service to human beings while passing through different inferior species. All other species treat man as God. Do not become the "inferior" species. Give up the concepts of sins and merits and become the Lord of the Lords, and thus attain liberation from birth and death. Otherwise, you will become entangled in the cycle of worldly affairs.

This chance at liberation that one gets by virtue of human birth, once missed, is hard to come by again. The tree whose fruits you now eat, will some day acquire birth as a human being. You then will have to be born as a tree in order to serve it, to repay the debt that is being incurred by you. This is how one gets entangled in the cycle of worldly existence. You have to become a Jnani to break free from this cycle. The Supreme Reality (Parabrahman) is attained only after acquiring Knowledge.

Knowledge (Jnana) as a whole is One. It cannot come in bits. It cannot be described as more or less. When you acquire Knowledge, it comes as a whole, in one piece, not more, not less. The loss of this life as a human being is similar to the loss of a precious gem. The human species is the species of Knowledge. Make use of it. Do not waste it worrying over petty things like earning bread and butter, or thoughts about worldly matters. Knowledge of the Self is an utmost necessity, without which a human being is as good as an animal. Without Knowledge, one comes and goes, and it is in vain that this life is spent.

If the entire life is spent without acquiring Self-Knowledge, it is proved that you are but an animal. Acquiring Knowledge has therefore become mandatory. One who wants to see that he is a human being and not an animal should think. Try to find out who you are, from where you have come, as well as where you are destined to go, and why. It does not matter even if all other work is left unattended.

Why do we feed a horse? It is because we can mount it and reach our desired destination. Similarly, we feed our body so that we can use it to reach the goal of Self-realization. To mount this horse means to take to the path of Knowledge. If you do not acquire this Knowledge, you will have to undergo the troubles and hardships of inferior species. One should do all that is necessary to help make the "Knowledge of the Self" bear fruit. The Lord has created sorrows in order to make mankind wise enough to turn to the path of Self-Knowledge.

On what basis is it that you behave recklessly, thinking that you will be able to escape the agonies of Yamapuri, the world of the "Lord of Death"? Wake up! Knowledge alone can come to your rescue and relieve you from the miseries of this worldly life. All that you gather, hoard and stack away will one day vanish. It is Knowledge that makes one's existence fruitful. Remember that the world beyond, the Paraloka, is attained only with the help of Knowledge. One day when death comes, you have to quit everything right under the nose of your loved ones and leave. If you put in sincere efforts now you are sure to win everlasting bliss.

To attain the "Ultimate Truth" (Paramartha) you have to put in effort to attain Knowledge. Only then will you gain true happiness. Success is sweet, but the secret is perseverance. Signs of misfortune become evident with laziness. Shake off laziness. Only then will you gain contentment. All of this is the prologue.

I have to tell you that whatever you classify as excellent by worldly standards is inferior. Strictly follow the advice of the Sadguru. This is what you should do. Think it over, again and again, and you are sure to attain Knowledge. It is only because a person refrains from thinking, and subsequently implementing what has been taught to him by the Master, that one tends to forget the Master's teachings. Intense desire to attain Knowledge is called the "auspicious aspiration."

It is the desire to attain the Lord, alone, that is auspicious, and the advice given to a person harboring such a desire is sure to bear fruit. It is mentioned in the *Vedas* that Knowledge should only be imparted to a person who harbors the "auspicious aspiration." Behave according to the instructions of the Sadguru and find out for yourself whether you personally gain the experience or not. Gaining the "Knowledge of the Self" constitutes the epilogue.

Lecture 64 - Paramatman alone Exists

From a talk on *Dasbodh*

Listen seeker, with hard work, you must clear the various doubts. Have the strength to pardon injustices whether large or small. Come to know the minds of others, and develop dispassion. Bravely conduct your daily life with morality and justice. Normally the doubt arises, "The Self is said to be all-pervading, yet if the Self has to pervade an object, is it not necessary that the object should exist in the first place? And if nothing exists, what is to be seen or known?"

Paramatman does not see anything. This is because nothing exists, hence the question of pervading (seeing) does not arise. When Paramatman tries to see something and differentiate, He has to step down from the "Stateless State" and come to the state of Knowledge. When you say that "I am so-and-so," you identify with the body, and attachment is born. Attachment is what is meant by "being pervaded." Paramatman neither pervades, nor is it pervaded. The sage Agasti found the water of the entire ocean insufficient to hold in a hand. How could this be possible? This is the doubt. You have to think it over. Aspirants should know that if something exists, doubts will be raised. If there is nothing, the question of doubts will never arise.

When you think it over, you come to know that the sage Agasti had dismissed all worldly affairs as untrue. Therefore, they no longer existed for him. The ocean of the mundane was no more. Because the worldly life existed no more for him, it could not make even a handful. You should feel that there is nothing but "I." Duality is thus eliminated and the feeling of oneness dawns. Worldly matters lose their significance. The "Ultimate Truth" is noble and subtle, and thought is the only medium by which it can be grasped. The fact that worldly matters are illusory can be easily be made evident by thought alone. Then, you also find that the ocean of worldly existence is insufficient to hold in your hand. In short, this worldly existence holds no more attraction for a Jnani who has thought it over.

How to conduct oneself through such an untrue worldly existence is what is being discussed now. Offenses, whether they be grave or small should be forgiven. Never hate a person who is given to censure. Remember that he who does not point out your faults, and ignores them, is your enemy, while he who criticizes and reprimands you for them, is your friend. That is why Saint Tukaram says, "You should have your strongest critic as your neighbor." Take it for granted that the critic obliges you by helping you improve, and if you find this impossible, leave him.

The intellect of a man continues changing with respect to his surroundings and circumstances. Let people comment to their hearts content. Remain undaunted by their comments, and continue on with your affairs. Only then do you attain the state of elevation. Get rid of all malice totally. You should be forgiving, and drive lingering reminiscences out of your mind. First, you should trace out what torments you, then work towards eliminating the cause of torment.

To come to know the minds of others, means that we should find out what pleases others and strive to make them happy. One should remain detached, knowing that everything (insults or compliments) in this Illusion is untrue. You should stand apart from it. You should be eager to attain the Knowledge of the Self and be alert towards it. Do not waste a single minute without aiming at Self-Knowledge. To forget the Self is itself injustice.

The aspirant must learn to understand what an indication is. You should be able to read the Master's indication and behave accordingly. Only one whose intellect is subtle can do this. One whose mind is still functioning at the gross level will not understand, even if he is told several times. Rather than guiding a single person, explain the "Knowledge of the Self" to many people, and thus preserve and expand the Sampradaya (the way of giving explanations on the Truth).

Lecture 65 - The Self Functions in All

"Listen to the signs of experience carefully. Those who are wise see with actual experience, while all others are unfortunate." (*Dasbodh*: Chapter 10, Sub-chapter 8)

He who resides in all bodies and functions through them, is the Lord of the Lords. He by whose virtue the three bodies function is the Self (Atman) that is present in all. It is the one Self that is present in the demons as well as the gods. It is He who governs the four geneses of species. He who so remains hidden in everyone is called "Ishwara," and the one who recognizes Him turns into "Vishwambhar." As it most appropriate to identify this Ishwara (Lord) do not ever become stained by the state of samadhi.

Try to recognize Him instead. The gross body is the world of Lord Brahma, the subtle is that of Lord Vishnu, and the causal body, which is also known as Kailasa, is the world of Lord Shiva. Giving up all three worlds, establish yourself as the "Lord of the Three Worlds" (Trailokyanath). Ignoring this easily achievable treasure, people toil in vain in search of fortune. "You" yourself are Self-evident (Swayambhu means Self-evident, Shambhu, a name for Shiva, is a derivative of Swayambhu). You yourself are the Self-expressed Shambhu. You only have but to become aware of that Shiva. Be conscious of the Self. Think it over, again, and again. Turn it over and over, in your mind. This itself is the true kirtan, directing one's thinking towards the Self. A good thought serves as an instrument. The Self is as it is seen by the seer.

The individual (jiva) is a body-wielding puppet. How can it identify the Self? One who identifies with the body mistakes the body to be the Self, and focuses only on the body, whereas one who identifies with Brahman finds that the Self is Brahman. All the accusations directed towards the body, and all the limitations of the body only become applicable to the person who is identified with the body. The Self is complete but the individual is incomplete. If one continuously contemplates and analyses this, it can be understood thoroughly. One who directs his thinking towards the Self will never be separated from God. Once you become free from doubts and are certain that you are the Self, your mission in life is accomplished.

If you abide in the feeling "I am the Self," you will no longer imagine separation from God. People in the Kaliyuga are intelligent. In Hindu mythology, the entire period from the beginning to the end of this world is divided into four eras; the Satyayuga, the Dwaparyuga, the Tretayuga and the Kaliyuga. Earlier man was dull in contrast to the modern man who is quite intelligent, however, modern man is heavily absorbed in thoughts, so he is weak and short-lived. In the Kaliyuga, Knowledge can be acquired quickly. In earlier times, great effort (long arduous sadhana) and a lot of time was required to acquire Self-Knowledge.

Lecture 66 - The Jnani is Beyond Actions, Bhajans

"Recognize that Paramatman, the Supreme Self is God through inquiry and the power of discrimination. In this way, one can cross beyond the ocean of Illusion." (*Dasbodh* - Chapter 11, Sub-chapter 9)

One must come to understand how Paramatman exists within us. Realize "I Am He." It is Shri Hari (Lord Vishnu), who is the true and basic experiencer, so it follows that all we experience is ultimately dedicated to Him. Jnanis say that Knowledge is the true experiencer of everything and hence he (the Jnani) is neither the doer nor the experiencer of any action. The actions of ignorant people reflect on their gross bodies, but the Jnani is not affected by the fruits of his actions. To know accurately means to be able to see a thing as it truly is. The one who thinks that the body is the doer of actions is the individual (jiva), but the one who thinks that Lord Hari is the doer, is God (Shiva).

To sing the Bhajans of the Lord means to be conscious of Him all the while. The true meaning of Kirtan is singing the hymns of praise which depict the qualities of God. The five pranas (vital breaths), the mind, the five sensory organs, and the five organs of action add up to sixteen, and with each performing a thousand actions, the total number of actions comes to sixteen thousand. These are the sixteen thousand queen consorts of the Self, Lord Krishna.

Lord Krishna, the Self, lies here amongst actions and is yet unaffected by them. This is what is meant when it is said that Lord Krishna is a celibate despite having sixteen thousand wives. In other words, he is untouched and apart from everything. It is said that the jiva has to take birth in 8.4 million species. In Marathi it is said as "eighty-four laksha," which also means that by keeping your attention (laksha) fixed on the eight-faceted Prakriti (Five elements and three gunas), one cannot avoid birth into one of the four geneses of birth[11].

It is said that Lord Panduranga danced while Saint Namdev sang kirtans. This means that the Self that resides in every heart was readily apparent to everyone, and was clearly experienced while the kirtans were being sung. This shows that where the Shrutis (*Vedas*) have failed to describe the Self, and have preferred to resort to the negation, the "neti, neti" or the "not this, not this" method, those who are accomplished have proven that Brahman is the only existing entity and that the world is nonexistent.

Your work is done once you realize your True Nature, or Swaroopa. A hearty meal taken by the yogis is itself an offering to the Lord. Their sleep on a four poster bed itself is the elaborate puja offered to the Lord. After realizing the Self, every step is sacred. The yogis exist in the form of their own Self. One must first recognize an officer in order to offer a salute to him. This is true in the case of the Self as well. The Self must be realized first, and the inevitable offering of salutations is sure to

---

[11] The four geneses of birth are 1) birth through eggs, 2) birth through parents, 3) birth through seeds, and 4) birth through the combination of heat and moisture, such as bacteria, etc.

follow. Upon realizing the Self, one successfully crosses this ocean of mundane existence.

Lecture 67 - Spiritual Practices, Vegetarianism

"A fool has a limited perspective, while the wise man sees everything with a wide perspective, and enjoys many things in many ways." (*Dasbodh* - Chapter 11, Sub-chapter 10)

Fools concentrate only on a single thing. If a miracle occurs, they get carried away by it. Some concentrate on yoga, while some believe only in miracles. Thus, they are fools. Yoga and other methods are not the goals, but merely instruments to attain the goal, and by nature, they are sure to perish. One who is wise will give this some thought.

In the initial stage of spiritual teaching, various actions are prescribed in order to make the mind subtle. These practices also help to hold lethargy, and inertia (Tamoguna) in check. Charitable contributions help to drive out the miserliness in the mind, and the ego is sure to be diminished if one bows to God.

Eradication of all fear is true Knowledge. Delusion is eliminated with the help of Knowledge. In this world, the more we attempt to do good deeds the more we sink into confusion. Some advocate vegetarianism and prescribe it as a method for attaining Self-Realization. This is not correct, because the rule of thumb for the universe is that one life feeds on another. What you eat, and what you don't eat, hardly matters. A living being survives by devouring another. You are the Self and therefore do not eat any of the food (the food is eaten by the body).

The bag in the form of your body is full of a variety of living beings. They all use the food you eat. What is oxygen after all? It is a gas that has a life sustaining property. Whatever you may eat or inhale is in no way related to "You." You are apart from them. There is only one truth in this world and that is, "I Am the Self, Brahman." Everything else is untrue.

Lecture 68 - Domestic Life and Being Alert

"Know that the one who is free in the midst of worldly life, is the true yogi who is united with God. He sees clearly and understands what is appropriate and inappropriate." (*Dasbodh* - Chapter 12, Sub-chapter 1)

First carry out the duties and obligations of your domestic life, and while doing so, seek the "Ultimate Truth" (Paramartha). Just as one would start working after one's studies are completed, this is also when you should begin with your search for the Truth. This pattern should be followed by a person who cannot do without domestic life, and is constantly attracted towards it. One may skip domestic life and opt instead to go exclusively in search of Truth, but here a note of caution is advised. If one is unable to attain Supreme Knowledge, then that one will surely undergo a great deal of suffering in the Illusion. The suffering of hell is the suffering that you come across in this illusory world. This domestic life has never been pleasant even for Lord Indra, the King of Gods.

If you take domestic life too seriously and are attached to it, you will have to bear the sufferings of Illusion. It is for this very reason that you should worship God. One who leads a domestic life while liberated, is truly superior. One who is concerned about his spiritual welfare even while shouldering his domestic responsibilities, should be considered to be alert. We have no idea how we were previously related to our kith and kin. Domestic life means cooperation.

All of our kinsmen have gathered here and are living together, but all the same they are headed towards a certain destination in order to reap the fruits of their actions. Do not let the pride of domestic life get the better of you. That you have come into this world should prove fruitful. Everyone does nothing but nourish the body. You should remain vigilant. The one who is inattentive to his spiritual well-being while going through domestic life, is living a life of untruth. For such a person, his spiritual pursuits are for solely for enriching the quality of his domestic life. His devotion is also only for winning his bread and is short lived.

One who is attracted towards someone else's woman, brings her to his home, and is ready to give up his life for her, is lower than the inferior animals. Similarly, the one who is attracted towards domestic life, and takes up spiritual pursuits solely with the goal of making his domestic life happy, and is ready to sacrifice his entire life for it, is an inferior being. In short, when it is said that a woman considers her man to be God, it only means that she should consider the Self within to be God. Woman is Prakriti. She should not worship any other God except the Self.

Previously, you have been given instructions about what your plight would be after your breath came to an end. Only if you become conscious of your Self, will you turn to the Self. If not, you will turn to birth in some inferior species. Think about this. The one who knows this is alert, and blessed is the one who is alert. He alone looks for and finds his own satisfaction in this world. AUM is a single letter. Know that it is Brahman. Once you know your True Form you are liberated.

Lecture 69 - The Self Knows All

"Whatever the desire, whatever the concept, it is nothing but the ripples of the inner-mind, arising in different ways." (*Dasbodh* - Chapter 12, Sub-chapter 2)

You have to be wise. Oh, people obsessed with domestic life, listen! What does your desire say? What does a concept assume? All of this is known by the Self. The Self knows how you are from within. You can deceive everyone but the Self. Ask your mind how you truly are. The mind flows like a river. It can only deceive itself. The "inner-mind" (antahkarana) has many ripples but the essence of the inner-mind is the Self.

One who says that "I alone should prosper and others should be ruined," brings about his own destruction. Such a person will undergo a lot of suffering because he has failed to make a correct endeavor for happiness. If you want to prosper, continue doing only good deeds. They do pay off in the end. If you strive for happiness from the very beginning, you are bound to get it, even if you say later that you don't want it. There is a saying in Marathi:

"The one who cries, his God cries too,
The one who laughs, his God laughs too."

A Jnani does not get somebody into trouble. He does not concern himself with other peoples' affairs or indulge in worthless discussions. First, teach yourself what you want to preach to others. Be constantly aware of your primary duty to understand the nature of the Self, and remain untainted like the Self. You should find out how you are related to the world. This is what is mentioned in this chapter. Just as a lotus remains unmuddied, even though living in marshy waters, so should you remain unaffected while living through this worldly existence. Only then will Self-Knowledge bear fruit.

Lecture 70 - The Five Elements and the Mahavakyas

"First find out "Who is God?," and then ask "Who am I?" Analyze these questions with the help of the "Science of the Five Elements," and the Mahavakyas." *Dasbodh* - Chapter 12, Sub-chapter 3, Verse 5

Many people live on this earth. One should make an effort at "thinking" (vichara) in order to be elevated. One should never do wrongful deeds. Not a single minute should be wasted. Why does a snake crawl on its stomach? It is because it only crawls "for its stomach," in search of food and does nothing else. Similarly, those who chase after their stomachs can never be elevated while their focus remains on food. Ignorant people such as this have strength only to harm others, and make it a point to use their strength for that purpose. Just as the ears of a snake are useless, so are the ears of such people, as they do not pay any attention to spiritual discourses.

Everyday you should practice attaining a higher and higher state, the way in which an eagle soars higher and higher in the sky. This means that with each passing day you should try to elevate yourself. "Pragati" is the Marathi word for progress. Pragati is the two words "Pra" and "Gati" together. Pra is the word Para modified, and Gati means speed. This indicates that one should rapidly proceed towards Parabrahman. Every day think along the right lines as laid out by the Sadguru and thus proceed ahead.

To attain the "World Beyond," Paraloka, you have to be under the guidance of a Sadguru. Humbly ask him to explain "Who am I?", and "Who is God?" To understand the difference between "Who is God?" and "Who am I?," one should make use of two powerful and ancient tools, "Panchikarana," the science of five elements, and the Great Principle, "Tatvamasi" – "I Am That."

You are beyond the four bodies. You are beyond both Ignorance as well as Knowledge. That which is beyond the four bodies is Brahman. "Tatvamasi" means "He is I, and I Am He." One should fully understand that "I am the eternal and steady Brahman."

All objects, existing in various forms, are only dust and nothing but dust. Study in this manner. The Jnanis are always absorbed in the realization that "All is One." Wind is nothing but Life-Energy (Chaitanya) in its objective form. When wind solidifies, it turns into water. When water solidifies it gets converted into earth. Everything emerges from this Life-Energy, and is always only Life-Energy. Truly, everything is Brahman.

When we discard the body, the elements comprising the body melt away into Brahman. Remember, only one thing exists in this world and that is dust. It is we, who have subjected this dust to our imagination and have derived many different things from of it. Understand that even Consciousness itself does not last. Therefore, we cannot be in the form of Consciousness. Our own spontaneously existing form, free from Consciousness, is Vijnana, that which remains after the destruction of Ignorance as well as Knowledge. No concepts exist here. That alone which exists without doing anything, without any prop whatsoever, is "You."

When you say, "I Am," it indicates the Primal Illusion, Moolamaya. Looking towards the Self, is Vidyamaya, and being aware of others, looking towards the world, is Avidyamaya. Both of these are but various forms of objective knowledge. That which can be focused on is Illusion, and that which cannot be focused on is Brahman. When you become conscious of an object, the work begins (conceptualizing the world), and work inevitably leads to tiredness. That which you have forgotten is the very thing that you should remember and be conscious of. You should recognize the Self, the primal cause, the substrate of everything. Objective knowledge has come to attain importance only in this world of individuals (jivas). There are only three objects in the Illusion, the gross (Avidyamaya), the subtle (causal; Vidyamaya), and the steady (Consciousness; Moolamaya). That, which is beyond this Illusion is eternal Parabrahman.

Think along the right lines. You must learn to discriminate the gross, the subtle, and the steady, from Parabrahman and recognize it. It is eternal. Then give up untrue form and select the only "True Thing," "Paramartha." Even after the destruction of the eight bodies, (four of the jiva and four of Ishwara) our True Form (Swaroopa) lasts forever.

Illusion is the gross inert form, the Self (Atman) is ever-changing, and our "True Form" is always changeless. We should understand "That" which is eternal and shining forever, and transform ourselves into it, and remain so. The "animate" and "inanimate" are both subject to change.

The "True Form" lacks both the animate and inanimate. It exists spontaneously. You have to experience it yourself. We can either be conscious or unconscious of that which is objective, but our True Nature is always conscious.

With the help of right thought, wander through all the three worlds, the gross, the world of Brahma, the subtle, the world of Vishnu, and the causal – the world of Rudra (Shiva). According to the epic Mahabharata, Arjuna, (from the Pandava family) who was a renowned archer, made a ladder of arrows and used it to climb to heaven. This means that this teaching had entered deeply into the mind of Arjuna, and accordingly, he had attained a place in heaven. To attain a place in heaven means to attain your "True Nature," the Reality. This ladder he built has four rungs, the gross, the subtle, the causal and the great-causal.

While climbing a ladder one must place one's foot on a rung, and then lift up your foot again to give up that rung later. Only then can one proceed to climb higher. Taking the help of the ladder, give up the gross, the unsteady, and the steady, and come to rest in your Self, the Reality. Why is the gross world called the "World of Truth" (Satyaloka)? It is because you take it to be "True" and believe in it. When it is said that Lord Brahma is the creator, what is indicated is that the intellect has not only created the Illusion, but also has given everything its name.

That which is in the waking state cannot be used in the dreaming state. The activities carried out in the subtle body are of no use in the causal state of deep-sleep. Whatever is carried out in the subtle or in the causal, does not help one in the great-causal (Knowledge). People do not transcend the mind or the intellect and hence must bear the consequences of their deeds. One should constantly remember that "I am neither the doer nor the non-doer." One who comes to understand this, is unaffected by the fruits of actions (karma). Although such a one is the creator of all, He has stopped identifying with the body, and is in the form of Parabrahman.

Ignorant people take upon themselves the responsibility of all actions (karma) and pay for their worldly deeds. By analogy to the caste system, the gross body is a shudra (a menial worker), the subtle body represents the vaishya (the merchant class), the causal body, the destroyer, is called the kshatriya (the warrior), and the great-causal body, full of knowledge, is a brahmin. Our "True Nature," is beyond all classes.

This Supreme Lord who dwells in all occupies a four-legged throne, the legs of which are represented by the four bodies. When you worship Him, all of your wishes are fulfilled. Your ignorance, poverty, etc. are all eradicated. One who uses "right thought," happily reposes in the Self. Only then can it be truly said that the body has served its purpose. As long as the Self continues to live in the house in the form of the body and identifies with it, he is characterized as untrue. It is only through the advice of the Master that He, who was so far untrue and whom you are failed to recognize, becomes true.

If there is no "witness," there is no Awareness. The distinctions "You" and "I" only exist in concepts. When visible objects die away, the elements melt away, and all that remains is the Self. With the aid of the Great Statement, "Tatvamasi," (I Am That) you come to know that you are Parabrahman. Once you disassociate from worldly objects, you not only turn into the Self, you also remain in that state. Once separated from the four bodies, you attain the non-conceptual "Stateless State."

Concepts never exist in that state. You become "unmani," or "no mind." Who will meditate, and upon whom? You alone are the one to be worshipped. Therefore you not only know the object of meditation, but also you know meditation itself. You escape from the cycle of births and deaths. Sins truly never did exist in the world. The Jnani comes to "know" everything, hence "dos" and "don'ts" never bind him. He resembles an infant in that an infant is also not bound by "dos" and "don'ts." Once you know for sure that the Self is Brahman, and that everything else is worthless, the desire for the Self quickly turns into conviction, which is in turn liberation.

It is necessary to worship the Master, as it helps our Knowledge grow. Jnanis come across many obstacles or thorns while keeping up with worldly transactions. The *Vedas* have not prescribed any restrictions for a Jnani. The intellect's firm resolve that "I Am the Self," is itself the state of liberation.

Illusion is like a mirror. Although many reflections, (concepts) are seen in it, it is steady and peaceful. Whoever assumes the existence of the reflections that appear in the mirror of illusory world to be true becomes bound by the illusory world.

Lecture 71 - Renunciation and Discrimination

"It is considered a sign of great fortune when one has both Desirelessness and Renunciation together. The sages understand this properly. (*Dasbodh* - Chapter 12, Sub-chapter 4)

Even after attaining "supreme fortune," one does not know how to enjoy it. Renunciation is the greatest fortune, which when gained together with Knowledge born of discrimination, proves invaluable in the quest for Self-realization. If not accompanied by Knowledge gained through the discrimination of the real and the unreal, physical renunciation can only give rise to sorrow. Knowledge not accompanied by renunciation gives rise to pride. Such a person ties himself to domestic life and experiences passions such as anger and jealousy when he sees the worldly success of others. Knowledge and renunciation together comprise "supreme fortune." One without the other is not whole.

Renunciation is essential, and is more important than discrimination. People begrudge others for their prosperity. They feel miserable when they see others prosper. There are no trees of joy or sorrow. Joys and sorrows in this world are in fact our mental constructs. We acknowledge joys and sorrows and give them their existence. They are only characteristics or states of the mind, and are sure to vanish. If you say that you do not require anything, pains and sorrows do not affect at all.

Greed is the mother of sorrows. Discrimination eradicates sorrows of the other world, the world beyond, whereas renunciation eradicates all the sorrows that may cross your path in this world. Renunciation means detachment from material objects. You should have a desire for the joy of the Self, and have detachment towards everything in the Illusion. It means that you should wish only for the joy of the Self and consider everything else as worthless. These are the signs of renunciation. Being conscious of Brahman is what is known as discrimination.

From within, a mortal is tethered to individuality, or being the "jiva," and on the outside he is bound to worldly life. In this condition, one is tied up like a horse. However, when one understands that "I am the Self," "I Am Brahman," one breaks away from the inner bondage. When one becomes free from the desire for objects, one is freed from the outer bondage.

You have to thoroughly understand that all these things are illusory, the objects, the desires, etc. If you understand the "Knowledge of Brahman" and behave accordingly with this Knowledge, people are impressed and astonished. To imbibe this Knowledge is discrimination and to behave accordingly is renunciation. To be devoid of worry is renunciation. When this is engraved in one's mind, he turns into a sadhu, an accomplished one. He then gets absorbed in worship, singing kirtans, reading holy texts and scriptures, listening to lectures, etc. This is the interesting "kirtan" of Lord Hari. Once you know that the domestic life is untrue, live in your house as though you do not belong there.

Ultimate Truth along with worship is your only goal. The inner-mind is a theatre. The one who performs there continues to dominate the scene, and gets engrossed in his role. Similarly, if you keep thinking of the Ultimate Truth, it attains top priority and you become engrossed in "That." You then attain the state of Parabrahman.

Worship from the depths of your heart and do so with love. This will help generate love in your heart and you will immediately be on the right track. How will you know whether God is pleased or not? God is pleased when the Self is full of joy. This can only be experienced. Instead of coming to know through experiences of others, or going by the illustrations mentioned in the Abhangas (holy songs written by Saints), gaining "Self-experience" is far more important.

Lecture 72 - Swaroopa and Self-Declaration

"Objects are inert, the Self is moving, and Pure Brahman is changeless and unmoving. When this is analyzed and clearly understood, the inert and the moving become dissolved in Brahman." (*Dasbodh* - Chapter 12, Sub-chapter 5)

A note signifies sound, a point constitutes shape, and art denotes color. "A" is the first syllable and among the vowels, the sound of "A" is the first note. A point is a round shape and signifies zero. Every object can be considered to be made of points, and is therefore, zero. All objects that have shape, color and sound constitute the Illusion, and that which singularly lacks all of these qualities is Brahman. You are beyond sound, shape, and color. You are the Reality, Swaroopa. Bodies are shaped from the elements. The body is the eight-fold Prakriti (manifestation) at work. It contains eight basic components, the five elements and three gunas. Manifestation functions with the help of these eight components.

Parabrahman could have been described as space, but space can be experienced. Therefore, Parabrahman is like space, yet is not like space. How the microcosm and the macrocosm have come into existence has been explained earlier. You have also been told how destruction takes place. While the microcosm (the individual) and the macrocosm (the universe) undergo creation and destruction, it is we (the Reality, Parabrahman) who continue to exist. The Illusion may or may not exist, but the One who has understood Brahman continues to exist as Brahman.

Saying that "I am Brahman" indicates that one is still in the dream state. This macrocosm, just like a dream exists due to one's own determination. It is your own determination, a concept. The world does not exist at all for the person who uses right thought. You forget the mud that makes a wall and start thinking of it in terms of "wall." Even the concept of mud itself is a delusion. This means that you do not look at the basic thing itself, but are influenced by the shape that it takes.

Those who have a dull intellect cannot perceive Brahman. Your "True Form" that is devoid of both consciousness and unconsciousness is pure Brahman. He alone who thinks in this manner and surrenders to the Sadguru, comes to know that he is Brahman. To say that the objects, the mind, the body and the speech all belong to God and God alone, is the gross Self-declaration. This ever-changing Self that is Being, Consciousness, and Bliss (Sat-Chit-Ananda), is Jagadisha, the "Lord of the Universe." All living beings are a part of Him. It means that all beings are the Reality. Saying this, is the dynamic Self-declaration. The fact that "He is Supreme" is the dynamic Self-declaration.

The Life-Energy (Chaitanya) is also only in the form of a dream, in that it is bound to come to an end just as a dream would. God, who is eternal, is the only Truth, and saying so is the true Self-declaration. It is also called the "Eternal Self." If He is to be called "Parabrahman," you must cease to exist. Hence, "I" does not exist.

Self-Knowledge means "perfect vision." To see everything according to the already established habits of perception, is what is called "imperfect vision." Two people went to the temple of Lord Vithoba. Looking at the stone idol, one of them said "Look at Lord Vithoba." The other person said, "Where is Lord Vithoba? How can this be Lord Vithoba? This is a stone." One who analyzes while seeing, finds that all are one. You, too, will slowly draw an inference that all are one. If you think (vichara), you will come to know this. Self-declaration is the declaration of the Self, so it is your very own declaration. To date you have only concentrated upon the declaration of the Illusion. The Master has now erased it.

Lecture 73 - Primal Illusion and Death of the Ego

"Brahman is pure, unmoving, eternal untainted Essence without any blemish. Like the sky, it is clear pure vast empty space." (*Dasbodh* - Chapter 12, Sub-chapter 6)

Brahman is steady, pure, spontaneous, and most natural. We are Brahman. Deeds do not affect it. We become conscious of the Self when we think that about how there is no sky, no time, no place, no distance, etc. The One who has conceived that "I Am," is the "Lord of Attributes" (Gunas). Consciousness is called Ishwara, or Lord Shiva depicted as the half male/half female (Lingam) form. Laxmi-Narayana is Laxmi and Narayana together. Laxmi means to focus your attention (laksha) on "Who am I?" (mi), and Narayana is the Consciousness that plays in everyone.

Everything has risen from this Consciousness. Hence, Narayana is all-powerful. A place was required to accommodate Consciousness, so space was created. Later, Consciousness proliferated and countless objects came into being. With objects came the presence or absence of objects. He (Consciousness) is called "Knowledge," "The Seer," "The Witness" etc. The ignorant think of Consciousness as Paramatman (Supreme Self).

The Illusion that first came into being is called the Primal Illusion ("I Am"). This Primal Illusion is a fallacy, and whatever is created by this fallacy is untrue. It was only after the Primal Illusion that the world came into being. Just as the director of a play assigns various characters to various actors, so does Consciousness go about this play in the form of worldly existence. This play runs only on this earth. It is a grand production indeed, but it is always only the spectacle of the perishable. He who is adorned by this grandeur is called Ishwara, the Lord. This Lord Ishwara, Consciousness, has been corrupted by Illusion. Lord Ishwara has created everything. He then has to accompany (support) his creation. Ishwara has to take care of all that He has created. His grandeur lasts only as long as his creation lasts.

Consciousness arises from Reality (Parabrahman). If Consciousness plummets towards worldly matters, it is characterized by the eruption of qualities (gunas). Accordingly, it is called the exciter of the attributes (Gunakshobhini). If Consciousness is turned back towards its origin, it vanishes. When Consciousness is in the quiescent state, it is called the Gunasamya. When Consciousness is directed towards one's "True Nature" (Swaroopa), it is destroyed. If Consciousness, Lord Ishwara, is externalized, He takes interest in worldly matters. He is called Vishnu, the sustainer. This aspect of Consciousness is called Sattvaguna. However, when He forgets Himself, oblivion steps in. This aspect of consciousness is called Tamoguna. When you are conscious, Rajoguna is dominant. Belief in all that appears in this Illusion to be true, is Ignorance. Being "Consciousness" is called True Knowledge. When you are conscious of this objective worldly life, it is perverted knowledge.

First a bag of flesh and bones came into being, and then the name "Mr. So-and-so," or whatever, came later. First the body was born and then it was named "so-and-so." One lives one's life this way, having never accepted the Truth. You always say, "I am so-and-so," and you identify with the body. It is for this very reason that the authors of the ancient scriptures say that all you speak is untrue, a bunch of lies. In spite of knowing that a chair is nothing but wood, you are determined to call it a chair.

It is our intellect that is responsible for this false determination. This is because our intellect is not aware of the Truth. The intellect does not have the capacity of making a determination of the Truth and identifying the "True Nature" (Swaroopa). All determinations other than identifying the Self, are only the passing determinations of the intellect, and hence untrue. You can talk only about untrue things. The Reality is the only Truth. What can be spoken about it? Spontaneous Consciousness is the pure and absolute Sattva quality.

The seven heavens indicate the characteristic qualities of the innermind, the six urges or impulses, and Ignorance. When the "I" is born, the world comes into being. It means that ego can never reach the Reality. It has to die out. It is only the one who is under the guidance of the Sadguru, who is able to attain Reality. The ego is the one who is engrossed in the world.

Unless the thought of this world vanishes, the ego will not vanish. When the world ceases to exist, the ego dies a natural death. Therefore, do not consider this world to be true. When one considers the world to be untrue, the ego vanishes. The ideas such as "I will be consigned to hell," or that "I have merits to my credit," are only false pride for the body (ego), which must be given up.

In the Hindu epic, the Mahabharata, Arjuna is the one whose son, in the form of his pride, exists no more. (Abhimanyu, or Abhiman, is pride.) Pride is considered the son of Arjuna because Arjuna has given birth to it. This pride has pushed Krishna (Reality) and Arjuna (Atman) into the netherworlds. This illustrates how one who harbors any pride cannot attain Reality. As long as you consider this world to be true, you are full of ego, and Reality seems far away. Realizing that the Illusion is untrue and that Brahman is the only Truth, is similar to a war. Saying that this world is true is pride. You are the Reality. Your ego has taken on the seven sheaths, those of food, prana, manas (mind), Vijnana (higher mind), bliss, Ignorance and Knowledge, and has come into this world.

No one but the disciple of the Sadguru can traverse from the Reality to worldly life and return to Reality. If the Virat form (the gross body of God, the entire physical manifestation), is revealed to the ignorant, they do not understand it. To comprehend it is beyond their capacity. The Virat form could only be comprehended by Arjuna when Self-Knowledge was imparted to him by Lord Krishna. This simply means that one should take the help of Knowledge, in order to realize that the Knowledge that is prevalent in everyone is the true "I," Lord Krishna.

Search within and outside, and with the help of Knowledge realize that "I" am the only one present in one and all. That one and only Knowledge has all the eyes, hands, feet, etc. of all the individual creatures of the animal world. This universal body is in the form of Knowledge, and has thousands of faces. In his Virat form, Krishna consumed a thousand different kinds of prey with a thousand different mouths. Everyone criticizes desires, but you who do so, do you not eat or breathe? You can criticize desires only if you can live without air.

There are five types of desires, desire for words (speech), desire to feel, desire for shape (to see), desire for odor, and desire for flavor. How will your body function without these desires? Is it that people obsessed with domestic life eat, and those who seek the Ultimate Truth should go without food? If you try to seek the Ultimate Truth only after giving up desires, you will come across a great number of hurdles.

Desires are all untrue and they all serve the single purpose of protecting the body. Always bear in mind that they do not give you a sense of fulfillment. They are there for your merriment, and it is because of fondness for them, that desires have acquired great importance. Accordingly, we are having this discussion on the topic of desires. Remember that desire is not the true tool to attain happiness. Just as grass helps animals survive, similarly, keep in mind that desires merely help the body to survive. As long as domestic life runs smoothly and all one's desires are fulfilled, no one is interested in the Ultimate Truth.

It is possible to accommodate only one thing at a time in the mind. If the mind is working on one thought, it cannot accept another. Only if the mind gives up the thought, dies it become empty and then accept other thoughts. Hence, one whose goal is to acquire objects that provide fun and merriment will never be, and has never been, a true seeker of the Ultimate Truth. The Ultimate Truth can never be realized without renunciation of desires. It is only one who fulfills desires merely for the functioning of the body, and who considers the realization of the Ultimate Truth and becoming one with it, as the goal, who can attain it.

Ultimate Truth is attained only when you renounce the body that is made up of the five elements, that are alien to the Reality. After renunciation of the body, all that remains is the Self. In the past, the Jnanis who renounced in this manner made great efforts and earned great fame. People obsessed with desires feel that their domestic life alone is all-important, and remain preoccupied with only the fulfillment of their basic needs such as food, clothing and shelter. This obsession has brought about their downfall. This is because they neither possess Self-Knowledge, nor are they inclined towards renunciation (vairagya). Such people are neither pure, nor do they know how to behave properly.

Everything in the world changes, but the Reality remains unaffected by any of it. Reality is the only entity that you can be conscious of without particularly being conscious of it. It is "That" whose existence and experience persists spontaneously without being noticed, and is your own True Form. You can feel the Reality without touching. It lacks odor, both good and bad. It is the "Lord of Color," hence it is known as Ranganath (Ranga means color, nath means Lord). This Ranganath is bathed in all colors and is yet colorless. He exists within all words, and yet is not confined to words. He tastes without the help of the tongue. Enjoy Him without the knowledge of the sensory organs. Do not ever forget Him, even if the "other one" arrives on the scene. The "other one" means objective experience. Experience appears as separate from the Reality. Nonexistence of "I" (ego) is your true Existence. God is not a separate entity. You are God.

If you are wealthy, you will never befriend a beggar because he is in a different class. Such differentiation vanishes with the dawn of the thought "I Am That," and then you get independence from all differentiation. This is liberation. To experience (the objective world) means to become tiny. If some change is brought about within the changeless "True Form," experience comes into being. Experience gives rise to three entities, 1.) the experiencer, 2.) that which is being experienced, and 3.) the process of experiencing. The Swaroopa is experiencing nothing, just as silence is speaking nothing. Even on doing something, it does not become tainted. When you strike someone with your hand, you clearly experience that you have hands. Will action be possible if the doer is absent? When action is carried out, is when the Being (Sat), Consciousness (Chit), and Bliss (Ananda), become manifest.

He who brings about change, Himself remains without change. You have pushed Him aside considering desires to be good. This is sorrow. When you depend on something, sorrow is born. One who does not behave in a selfless manner is afflicted by sorrows. One who aspires after happiness should remain uninterested in desires. Take it for granted that the one who loves this Illusion is full of sorrows.

Lecture 74 - The Knowledge of Brahman

"Making us of higher intellect, understand the Reality. Become more vast than the universe by way of your understanding. How can one bring in pettiness there?" (*Dasbodh* - Chapter 12, Sub-chapter 9)

A good swimmer should not drown a sinking person. Similarly, one who has acquired the Knowledge of Brahman should save a person who is entangled in worldly affairs from drowning. What should a person do if he is alone, and has no relatives and no support? If he behaves in a manner prescribed by the Sadguru, he attains the state of Parabrahman, and is revered by all. This Knowledge of Brahman alone is sure to bear fruit.

Lecture 75 - Bhajans and the Name of Rama

"One who is adorned with the virtues of desirelessness and Knowledge is considered to be a great person in this world." (*Dasbodh* - Chapter 12, Sub-chapter 10)

If you sing early morning bhajan (Kakad Aarti) cheerfully, you remain cheerful for the rest of the day. Hence, Kakad Aarti should be sung with great joy and enthusiasm. Any spiritual act should be done with a peaceful mind. Listen to and reflect upon sermons. All of your duties should be performed regularly. Although you have acquired Knowledge, continue to worship the Master. The Knowledge that you have gained should be brought into practice. Do not hurt anyone. It is the quality of the individual (jiva) to take pleasure in the sufferings of others.

The whole world is Janardan. (Janardan is the name of Lord Krishna, who protects the people, the Jana). Accordingly, you should oblige people in various ways. Sorrows always befall the body. Keep in mind that the body is going to die some day. Submit yourself to the worship of the Lord. After the death of the body, it is this worship that will help you.

What is "Ram Naam"? Naam is Na together with Aham (Na is not, Aham means I), hence, Naam means, "I am not." "Ram Naam[12]" means "I am not the body, I am Rama." Hence Lord Mahadev (Shiva; the Self) ceaselessly repeats the name of Rama. According to the scriptures, Lord Mahadev drank visha (poison) which arose from the ocean when it was churned. When did this visha (visha in Marathi means both poison and desires) subside? His visha (desires) subsided when his attention was no more focused on them. "As is the faith, so is the God." You are the Self. All else is Illusion.

Lecture 76 - A Story

"Through discourses, the experience of Reality should be explained and various questions should be resolved. When one's understanding and realization grows, one becomes free of doubt." (*Dasbodh* - Chapter 13, Sub-chapter 5)

Two people went for a stroll on the planet Earth. In order to pass the time, one of them began to narrate a story worth thinking over. The narrator asked the listener to listen carefully as he told the story.

A man once lived with his wife (Purusha and Prakriti). Both loved each other very much and lived as a single entity. After some period of time, they were blessed with a child (Consciousness; Vishnu). This child had knowledge of everything and was well versed in all subjects. He worked sincerely, and had a son of his own (Brahma). This child was not

---

[12] Ram Naam also means "Ram Mantra," or repeating the name of Rama (Vishnu).

as intelligent as his father, and he was a workaholic, always eager to work more and more. He worked much harder than his father.

Later, the son had many children. The elder among these grandchildren was a simpleton, who was ignorant and short-tempered (Shiva). At the slightest error he would be enraged and would destroy all that went wrong. Eventually, it was the grandson (Brahma) who was hard working, who took over the work of expansion and created everything. The son (Vishnu) took over the responsibility of protecting this creation, and the ignorant great-grandson (Shiva) was the destroyer.

The creation created by the grandson proliferated to such an extent that the father (Purusha), the original founder, finally quieted down. First, the family ignored the father, then they stopped respecting each other, and finally there was chaos and anarchy. Eventually, everything was destroyed. In this story, the father represents the Self, Purusha (Pure Being), and the mother represents the Prakriti, the body (manifestation). The son is Vishnu, the Consciousness that is the sustainer. The grandson is Brahma, the Creator, and the great-grandson, Rudra (Shiva), is the Destroyer.

He who deliberates on and analyzes this story will be liberated from the cycle of births and deaths. This strange story unfolds continuously while moving forward, fading into oblivion. The moral of the story is that chaos prevailed because the Father (Purusha, the Self) was forgotten. When you focus on the creation, the worldly existence, the Self is forgotten.

Understand the shortcomings of life from this story. Only the one who uses "right thought" (vichara) can uplift the world. The more he thinks, the more he progresses. When intense thinking is done, upliftment of the world is in sight. Brahmacharya, the state of celibacy is recommended as it has the least attributes or distinguishing properties (generates less activity). Right thought is the road for those pursuing the path of Knowledge.

Worship carried out in nine different ways as prescribed in *Dasbodh* and other ancient scriptures (Navavidha Bhakti, the ninefold path of devotion), is the only job more important than what you do to earn your living. This riddle made up of many different principles must be solved, only then can peace be obtained. Contentment can be attained by continually listening to and absorbing the Masters teachings.

The man and his wife in the above story represent Purusha (the Self) and the Prakriti (body) who when taken as a single entity give rise to the Primal Illusion, "I Am." Then comes Lord Vishnu, Consciousness, which is the inner-mind. Next comes Lord Brahma, the intellect, which is made up of equal proportions of both Rajas and Tamas qualities. The eldest son of Lord Brahma is Rudra, forgetfulness, or Ignorance. It is due to this forgetfulness that a man dies without finding a solution to these riddles. It happens with all living beings. Man dies due to Ignorance. We are entangled in this cycle of births and deaths because we do not know who we are.

Destruction is brought about either with the help of Knowledge or by the lack of it. With the help of Knowledge, understand that the worldly life is merely an Illusion and watch its destruction. Concepts come to an end with the end of the search, and peace is attained. How can there be peace when there is still confusion about the five principle elements.

Lecture 77 - The Transient and the Eternal

"The expanse of the five elements is bound to perish. Only the formless Self is eternal and real." (*Dasbodh* - Chapter 13, Sub-chapter 6)

Saint Ramdas blessed Shivaji Maharaj (a king who ruled Maharashtra in the 1600's) with the "Concise Teaching," or Laghubodha (Laghu means concise, bodha is teaching). With the help of this advice, Shivaji Maharaj acquired Self-Knowledge. With this concise teaching, Saint Ramdas explained the "Knowledge of Brahman" to Shivaji Maharaj. This advice included the "Science of the Five Elements." The five elements are earth, water, fire, (light), air (wind), and sky (space).

Just as you can tell that a whole pot of rice is cooked by testing a single grain, similarly, one small experience can help you understand the illusory nature of the world. The earth vanishes, and all that is associated with it also vanishes. Water dries up, fire appears and then dies out, the wind disappears, and even space does not remain when you stop thinking of it. By thinking one can come to know that the things made up of the five elements are perishable and short-lived. Know for certain that your body, which is made up of the five elements, is perishable. When this illusory world and the body disappear, the Self alone exists. After understanding this, you will be able to understand the Self.

In order to understand this, you must look to the Saints. They say that the Illusion is perishable, and that the Self alone is eternal. You never die. It is only that you give up this body, and you keep acquiring new bodies as long as you keep yearning for them. It is when you give up this yearning that you attain your true "Self Form" (Swaroopa). You then become immortal. The Self of one who is ignorant also does not die. Nothing is destroyed in this world. The Self says that the word death does not exist in my dictionary. The five elements that have gathered in the form of the body return to their respective principles (earth to earth, air to air, etc.) Shape and form appear in Consciousness, but the Shapeless (Purusha) appears with the help of the one with shape (the body, Prakriti). This "Shapelessness" is conscious of the shape. That which possesses qualities is Brahman. Giving up all qualities, He who exists naturally and spontaneously, qualityless and beyond Brahman, is Parabrahman.

The Self can be felt in the ten organs because after occupying the whole of the universe, He is still present with qualities (saguna), which is expressed through the ten organs, five sensory and five organs of action. The one, who permeates the ten organs gets the fruits of ten million sacrifices. He can be experienced because he is intertwined in the organs. Understand the one who operates within the ten organs, and with the help of whom all of these organs function. Keep thinking of Him, meditate on Him, remember Him, and be conscious of Him.

When you know the one who operates the ten organs, you come across Lord Rama. You can be conscious of that Rama only by virtue of the ten organs. Know the one who is the shapeless, and the one who possesses shape. Brahman in the form of Consciousness, is what is called "Pradnyana Brahman." Shape is transient, whereas the shapeless is eternal. At the end of the investigation of the transient and the eternal, you find that one does not exist, while the other does. This is the investigation into the transient the eternal.

In the epic Mahabharata, it is mentioned that the Kauravas had a large army and that they refused to grant the Pandavas a place to occupy, even the space the size of the tip of a needle. The all-pervading seer is Brahman. He, who knows this, is Dharmaraja, the eldest and the most virtuous of the Pandavas (the Pandavas, are the five brothers who represent the five elements) whereas they who are engrossed in their bodies are the Kauravas. People who think only in terms of their bodies are large in number, hence the army of the Kauravas is large. Those who have attained Self-realization are few in number, hence the territory granted to the Pandavas is extremely small. The seer is all-pervading, but the father of Kauravas is blind. This blind father represents that the one who holds on to the body is ignorant. All the Kauravas vanish as soon as you are conscious of the Seer, which is Brahman.

Lecture 78 - The Self (Atman), Brahman, and Parabrahman

"Stainless, invisible, and motionless, are the indications that are used for the Sky. The Sky means Space, which is boundless, and pervades everywhere." (*Dasbodh* - Chapter 13, Sub-chapter 7)

That which is perceived without the help of the eyes does not require any rituals, rites or thoughts. It is only Brahman which remains after separating out and discarding all that is seen. The pure and steady Brahman is like the sky. Free space means empty space. Matter comes later and occupies the space. Similarly, Consciousness is like free space. Matter, or the material world is "space devoid of the Self." Whatever is projected is illusory. Consciousness is ever-changing, while the "Natural Spontaneous State" (Brahman) is changeless. The difference between Brahman and the Self (Atman) is very subtle. The entire space from the house to the sky is pervaded by Brahman, while the Self is in the form of Consciousness, and is the perceiver of the sky, the house, and the space. Just as there is a difference between the sky and the wind, so is Brahman surely different from the Self.

The past is what has already happened, and is hence proved perishable. The Self has also already come into being. It is the "changeful," which has appeared in the "changeless." This universe made up of the five elements is is full of Ignorance, and is also inert and sluggish, whereas the Self is constantly changing and unsteady. The inert universe is like a piece of camphor whereas the Self is like a flame. It burns all the "non-Self," all the gross worldly objects, and in the end is itself burnt. In this way, it is like fire. Both the camphor and the flame vanish. Similarly, the Self after having consumed everything that is non-Self, perishes (nothing objective remains).

Parabrahman is like space. Parabrahman and space are unchanging, whereas the Self (Atman) and the wind are both ever-changing. Parabrahman and the Self are entirely different. The individual (jiva) believes in the objective world and hence gets entangled with many inert objects. He clings tightly to the body, and is therefore blind and ignorant.

He is made up of only one thing, Consciousness, with which he runs the world. Truly, He is the "Lord of the World." The Self, which exists in all the bodies, is one and is and ever-changing in nature. "That" which is steady, and never changes, is Parabrahman.

Parabrahman is neither one nor can it be described as many. There are many bodies, but their governor is one. In the company of the inert (the five elements, the gross body), the Self has turned into many, but at its root, it is one. In your dreams you create many bodies, and there in addition to them, is your own body, similarly this material world, is also like a dream (the subtle body). Consciousness is "Knowledge" (the fourth body, the great-causal or Mahakarana body), and sitting there quietly, after giving up that Knowledge, is "Absolute Knowledge" (Vijnana, Parabrahman). To do something is Knowledge, and to do nothing is Absolute Knowledge. That which exists without duality, what the "not this, not this" (neti, neti) concept points to, is called the "Non-conceptual Knowledge," or Parabrahman. Although the natural state of both Ignorance and Knowledge is the same, there is also a lot of difference between the two. This is because the one who possesses Knowledge has experienced everything, but the ignorant one has not. After acquiring Knowledge, one feels that one is the same and that is true. Yet, at the same time, the feeling does differ. Even after having meals at the house of an untouchable, a Jnani's intellect does not become corrupted or defiled. The Self of a wicked person is the same as that of a realized person. There is no difference. Both notions, "I am a sinner," and "I perform pious religious duties," are only the ideas of one who is ignorant. There is no difference in their True Nature. Just as there is no difference between the gold in the hands of an untouchable and that in the hands of a brahmin, the True Nature of all is the same. There is no difference, but there is a difference in the feeling (experience) of one who is ignorant, and that of a person who has gained Knowledge.

When the Self and body come together, is when all work is possible. The body did not exist, but the Self did exist prior to the universe. The Self (Consciousness) cannot do anything, without the help of the body. The Self pervades the body. All beings are woven like flowers on the string of the Self. However, this simile does not fully apply, as the string is inert and gross. Just as there is water present in the form of sap in the various different plants, so is the Self, present in all beings. The Self is like the juice in sugarcane and the body is like the fibrous dry pulp (gross world). This is why it is said that the body is devoid of the Self. The one present in the body is the Self and the one beyond them both is the "Supreme Self," Paramatman.

The Niranjan Paramatman (the One who is seen without the aid of anything else) has no simile. Yet, I give it a simile of "the space between the juice and the pulp." The flavor of Paramatman is that of "Our Self." Parabrahman is like Space. If you manage to realize this subtle point, you will have won your own grace. From the king to the beggar, all are human beings, yet, from a worldly perspective, they cannot be regarded as equal. Though everything works by the virtue of the single source, there is variety in manifestation.

Although the inner-mind (antahkarana) within all beings is one, people are different. Sugar, mud, and gold are all One, but some ignore mud and select sugar, while others ignore sugar and choose gold. Here mud is similar to the "not Self" or gross, the sugar is similar to Self, while gold represents Paramatman. Initially one has to become acquainted with the mindset of other people. Just as you patiently teach a small child how to walk, so should you behave according to the wishes of other people. Gradually make them trust you and then teach them the "Knowledge of Brahman." If not approached in this way, you will fight ceaselessly with others all through your life, and of what use is that?

Lecture 79 - As You Conceive, So You Perceive

"The Lord of the universe is the "Primal Illusion," afterwards, the eight-fold Prakriti expanded and the structure of the universe took form." (*Dasbodh*: Chapter 12, Sub-chapter 8)

The Primal Illusion means the "Lord of the Universe," or Ishwara. From Him, has emerged the eight-fold manifestation, Prakriti (five elements and three gunas). The universe took shape later. When untainted by any objects, our nature is like empty space. There is no time or place in the formless. Place and time are associated with form. The moment one becomes aware of oneself as an individual, place and time come into existence. For example, when we are asleep we are unaffected by time and place. It is only when we become aware in Consciousness, that time and place, come into being.

As is your concept, so will you see. It is God who has conceived this world. Concept is itself the mind, "God" is your own incarnation. When you form the concept that there is nothing, everything vanishes. Birth and death are the innate qualities of the body. As the Self brings down the qualities of the body on itself, it is obliged to endure the consequences, which are inseparably linked with the qualities of the body.

Because the Self identifies with the mind, it is hounded by joys and sorrows, that really only affect the body. The Jnanis know that they are not the body, and thus do not identify with the body, so after the demise of the body, they merge into the "True Form of the Self" (AtmaSwaroopa). The yogis consider it as great fortune when detachment permeates the mind.

Birth and death, joy and sorrows, and thirst and hunger are the six urges. Devoid of these six urges, "I Am Shiva" (Shivoham). He, who is aware that God resides in the body, is free from birth and death. The concept of sins and merits was introduced to set fools on the right path. Once one has taken to treading the right path, these concepts are meaningless. You are the "Supreme Self," in the form of Parabrahman. Everything else is mere sentiment. If you remain "asleep," giving up all distinguishing properties, you are not bound by time or space.

Lecture 80 - Knowledge and Universal Compassion

"Listen to the teachings about the desireless person, and the tact, intellect, and wisdom with which you will remain forever content." (*Dasbodh* - Chapter 14, Sub-chapter 1)

A saint should never artificially take on the quality of desirelessness, but if he does acquire this quality, he should not give it up. Of what use are wealth, family, etc. to me? Thinking this way, one should break away from their spell and overcome the temptation for them. Do not lend them any importance and thereby become deliberately detached from objects.

Do not harbor too much desire for a particular thing, even if the objective is Self-realization, as this desire itself acts as a hindrance to "Absolute Knowledge." Desirelessness is the sign of a Jnani. Become acquainted with these signs, and then give them up. "I am beyond the body" is the attitude that should always be practiced. Procrastination in this regard should be avoided. Do not put this practice off until tomorrow, as you can never rely on the body.

Keep the Knowledge given by the Master glowing and shining like a newly sharpened weapon. Never let the Knowledge be contaminated with impurities. Never forget that you are beyond the body. You should adore your Master. You should have great love for worship. Sympathetic behavior towards everyone should be adopted. This is the beginning of "Universal Compassion." He, who is emblazoned with Knowledge but lacks compassion, is reckless and self-indulgent. Even after becoming a Jnani, one should have love for all.

A seeker should not be affected by envy. He should have respect for the Master. The one who shows great reverence and respect towards the Master can be regarded as a good disciple. Singing songs of praise is the love for the worship of the Master. The more you love to worship your Master, the more your inner-mind opens up, and the path becomes easy. Few disciples spread the fame of the Master far and wide. If we fail to proceed on the path of worship, it is we, who will lag behind. You should always progress on the path of devotion and never lag behind.

Lecture 81 – Kirtan Means "I Am He"

"Listen to how the stories of Lord Hari, should be made interesting with splendor and excellence so that all will be showered with the blessings of God, Lord Rama." (*Dasbodh* - Chapter 14, Sub-chapter 5)

In the present era, the Kaliyuga, kirtan (singing God's praises) is sung when you keep on repeating that "God is the seer. God is the witness," etc. Only then will you be united with the Lord. Keep saying, "I Am He." This is enough. This is because the man belonging to this Kaliyuga possesses a keen intellect. What is the story of Lord Hari (Harikatha) after all? Keep saying, "I Am He" and attain that state, this is all that matters. Neither, do you need to narrate the stories from the Puranas, nor do you need to listen to them.

Lecture 82 - Cultivating Habits

"Beauty cannot be acquired by study or practice. Everyone is born with their own natural attributes that cannot be changed. Some effort however should be made to master those qualities which can be cultivated." (*Dasbodh* Chapter 14, Sub-chapter 6)

You can develop good qualities, but beauty cannot be acquired with the help of practice. This goes to show that a natural quality can neither be altered, nor can it be given up. However, surely we can be rid of acquired qualities, as they are born of habit. Ignorance is one such acquired quality. Attain Knowledge, and Ignorance will disappear. The virtuous select good qualities and give up bad ones.

Progress is achieved by hard work. Acting itself is a courageous act. Do not be disheartened. Keep trying. Why should you not work towards your own welfare? You want to be happy, but you do not work towards happiness. As is your faith, so is your fruit. Do not ascribe the fruit to destiny. There is no such thing as destiny. The Self is God, and the one who makes a sincere attempt will surely be rewarded by the Self. If you evaluate yourself, you will come to know your shortcomings and bad qualities.

Lecture 83 - Effort and Worship

"Worship God with hands that are pure, and enjoy good fortune, Fools who are undisciplined and non-worshippers will suffer from a lack of good fortune." (*Dasbodh* - Chapter 14, Sub-chapter 8)

Destiny means action (karma). If action, whatever it may be, does not proceed in the right direction, if there is a slight mistake in it, it is bound to result in failure. Therefore, make a determined effort. Infinite is the range of action. Do not rely on God. Remember that action begets fruit. The purpose of this chapter in *Dasbodh* is to motivate people to make some endeavors. Check to see whether you possess some bad quality, and be rid of it. He who advises himself is indeed wise, whereas he who advises others is a fool. Do not laze around and waste time. No one will respect you if you do not possess Knowledge. Hence, one must gain Knowledge. Beautify yourself from within. Employ many different ways to make yourself wise.

The sun and the moon, which rise, must set, but this is not the case with Knowledge. Knowledge once gained is bound to bear fruit. Strive relentlessly to attain Knowledge. Even if you attain it at the very end of your life, the "Knowledge of Brahman" will help you evade the cycle of birth and death. Life is unreliable. You can never say when death may pounce on the body. Therefore, stick to the right path. Do not waste a single minute without the worship of Him. So far, you have wasted your life. Let it be. The past cannot be undone.

People are ignorant so they divide themselves into four classes, the Brahmins (the priests), the Kshatriyas (the warriors), the Vaishyas (the traders) and the Shudras (the laborers doing menial tasks). However, the Jnanis adopt a wider view. They think deeply and understand the true classification of all living beings. According to the Jnanis, human beings are all Brahmins, as only man can attain the "Knowledge of Brahman." The beasts of prey are the warriors (Kshatriyas), the lions, tigers, etc. The sparrows, bulls, elephants, etc. who work hard for their food are the traders (Vaishyas), and maggots, weevils, and inferior insects, etc. are all the menial laborers (Shudras).

All of you are Brahmins. Wake up in this life. Whatever has been done so far, is the past. If you do not come to understand the subtle Brahman, you are but ignorant beasts. Be thoroughly pure and devoid of all dirt of Illusion, and worship God. One who does not pay heed to his "True Nature" is ignorant. If you prefer to remain ignorant, you remain in the cycle of 8.4 million births, and suffer the sorrows of the lower species. Remember that there is no other God but you. The Inner-Self alone is God. Knowing this, worship Him. Identify with Him, and then worship Him. Worship Him with the feeling of Oneness. This is the path of non-duality.

While reading out a certain holy text, a reader came across the words "Rishin cha bhaar." A dot on the word rishi, represents a nasal sound, and when read as an "n" it is used to indicate a plural form of the word rishi. The phrase means a group of several rishis, or rishin. The reader made an error while reading. He transferred the dot from the word rishi to the word cha, and read it as "Rishi chaam bhaar." This changed the meaning entirely. It now meant that, a rishi (sage) is a cobbler or chaambhar. Now, it turned out that the one who was explaining the religious text was himself a cobbler. He elaborated on it and said, "He who is not a cobbler can never be a sage." He went on to say that a sage must necessarily be a cobbler and as the services of a sage should never be hired, the Lord (Vithoba), also had to remain barefoot. Therefore, he reasoned that a cobbler is superior even to God. That one sentence, which began as a mere group of sages, finally ended up as having rishis being cobblers. He deviated further and went to the extent of explaining why the Lord Vithoba was barefoot. This is what has happened to all of us. We are all Parabrahman, but by mere shift of a dot (emphasis) have come to the present state of being jivas.

There is another example. A brahmin, or priest, is supposed to wear a holy thread called "janave." It indicates that he is conscious (janiv) of the Knowledge of Brahman. If not, he is a worker, or shudra. As this "Knowledge of Brahman," should also eventually be given up, the "releasing" function of the thread ceremony is performed. You should first acquire Knowledge and then after giving it up, you should live in "Absolute Knowledge." Consciousness itself is Knowledge. From the ages between 8 and 12, when the mind is fresh and the intellect is tender, one should go to the house of the Guru, and be initiated into the "Knowledge of Brahman."

The thread ceremony indicates Consciousness. The thread is worn in order to indicate that the wearer of the sacred thread is a knower of Brahman. Now, times have changed, and with change the importance of the "Knowledge of Brahman" has been lost. The wearing of the thread has become a mere tradition. The inner Knowledge has been replaced by superficial formality. Hence, the brahmins have landed into a pitiable plight. This is because they have lost the Brahmavidya, the "Knowledge of Brahman."

Why is a piece of deerskin tied to the sacred thread? Because it serves as a reminder to the fact that time should not be wasted away before achieving Knowledge. In the Marathi language, the word "haran" has two meanings; 1.) deer, and 2.) is "to be snatched away." Consciousness means Knowledge, and to attain this Knowledge, certain rites are performed. These rites are called the sacred thread ceremony, or Brahma Sanskar. In the past, almost all of the accomplished ones must have belonged to castes other than the brahmin caste.

The brahmin caste is the caste which people now acquire by birth, and not by earning it through their deeds or by working towards it. Therefore comes the proverb, "Don't ever look for the source of a sage." This is said because who you are has nothing to do with ancestry. A rishi may have been born into any caste whatsoever, but after achieving the

"Knowledge of Brahman," he has become a true Brahmin. A brahmin is born through training. He is groomed to be so. Adopt the "ananya" mode (an is not, anya means different) of worship. It means worship with the feeling "I myself am not different from God." In other words become one with God, Be united with Him. Worship is the process of being one with the Lord. He, who is the best of all, should be meditated upon uninterruptedly.

Anatman (an is not, Atman is Self) is the one who is not the Self. Be aware of the fact that, you are the Self, and then worship. Practice in this way. He (the Self) who knows everyone is the witness. When you say, "I am in the form of Knowledge," it is a sign of being conscious. Later, give up that Consciousness, and be quiet and peaceful. This itself is service. Then your Ignorance will vanish and true bliss will be attained. As you are eternal, nobody can wipe you out.

Think about what your body is made up of. Look to see if you think that the human body is mightier than the Lord. Ponder over what you are, and what you are not. If you think according to the advice of the Master, and follow his instruction, you will come to the conclusion that you are the Self that is conscious of all. All else is "not Self" (Anaatman), as it is Illusion which merely appears and disappears. This is experienced with the help of the thought "I am the Self."

Only two objects exist in this world, "I" and "mine." The elephants, the horses, the wife, the son, etc. are not "I," as they are apart from me, but they are "mine." People who think in a worldly manner, identify objects with their names (labels), and consider them as mine. They are not "I," therefore they are mine. The one who is apart from the body, who has given up everything is "I," the Self, and the one who says, "this is mine," is also "I." Saying "I" is ego and saying "mine" is attachment.

Now I will tell you about the composition and arrangement of the universe. Who we are, and who we are not, should be thought over while one has the body. We should enjoy the sweetness of the Self's bliss with the help of thought (vichara). All bodies have been composed of the five elements. This world is the product of the five elements. The animals that live in it are also made up of only one thing, the body. This is because of the influence of the five principle elements. Later, all the five elements vanish in the Life-Energy, and this Life-Energy, gets absorbed into the Reality, "Swaroopa."

The sense of ego, is also untrue. Ego means "I" and attachment means "mine." Both mine and I do not exist at all. They are generated only when you think of them. Mine and I are brought into play in a pair.

Just as a father and a son come into being simultaneously, so do the seer and the seen come into existence together. When "mine" leaves, "I" automatically stands eliminated. The word "mine" is written as "mama" in Sanskrit. Here one "ma" belonging to the word "mama" represents "I," and the other represents "you." When "my mama" leaves, the "I" remains. You and I become "I." Both "you" and "I" are united. Then, "you" and "I" do not have separate entities. The distinctions such as you and I vanish. "You" are "I." You then do not notice anything other. There is no one to say that there is "so-and-so." That "so-and-so," also does not exist.

That which is seen, only appears, it does not exist. "Aadi" means that which exists prior to all. It is that which was first, the beginning. "Anaadi" on the other hand, is that which has no beginning. Nothing ever existed before it. That, which is experienced when you notice something is Illusion, and "That" which continues to exist spontaneously, even while you do not deliberately notice it, and even while you notice the Illusion, is Brahman. Brahman is Anaadi.

Maya (Illusion) means "Ma" and "Ya" together. (Ma is not, ya is this). That which is not, is Maya. Kalpanta means an "end of an era." It also means put to an end to concepts (Kalpana is concepts, Anta is end). Kalpanta means to give up concepts. That which vanishes is Maya and that which remains is God. While you are in deep-sleep, everything vanishes, that is Kalpanta, dissolution, as no concepts are there. Waking up means to remember all of this. The end of our concepts is Kalpanta, but how will you know your True Nature, while you are asleep? Give up not only your sleep, but also your waking state. That which then remains is your True Nature.

The state with no waking, no sleep, and no dream, is Turya. Turya is the state in which "You alone remain." Only then can you experience "I Am Brahman," or the "Ahambrahmasmi" state. If you look at the wall from the point of view of mud, the house will cease to exist. All that remains thereafter is mud. It is for the practical purpose of facilitating our worldly affairs that we adopt false names.

In the Mahabharata, the battle is between the hundred Kauravas, who represent the universe full of names and forms, and the five Pandava brothers, who represent the five elements. Dharma represents the space, Bhima represents the air, Arjuna represents the fire, Nakula represents the water, and Sahadeva represents the earth. When did the reign of the Kauravas begin? The moment we began to assign names and forms. The capital of the Kaurava kingdom is Asthinapur, the city of bones (death), and the body, or "Indraprastha" is the capital of King Dharma. In the end, the Kauravas were destroyed and the Pandavas survived. Later, the Pandavas, too, eventually were no more.

As long as the object exists, Life-Energy (Chaitanya) lasts. When the Life-Energy vanishes, nothing but the "True Nature," the Swaroopa, remains. What will you do after gaining Self-Knowledge? Deliver sermons, sing hymns, go on worshipping, etc. Worship the Master. Do not give up daily practices. Focus your eyes on your nose and meditate regularly. In short, practice experiencing your "True Nature." Your behavior will win you a good name. If you sit quietly and peacefully after waking up in the morning, the whole day passes peacefully.

Knowledge has been explained in the seventeenth chapter of Shrimad Eknathi Bhagwat. "I am in your heart." Now that you have recognized the Lord, who resides within you, take refuge in Him. If we are the Lord, then how are we to worship Him? You need not do anything. Just keep quiet. That is the greatest worship you can offer. Have unswerving faith in the Master, by whose grace the jiva (the individual) has not only lost his jivahood (Ignorance), and attained the status of Ishwara, but has also given it up to go beyond Ishwara, to turn into Parameshwara (Parabrahman).

One who has immense respect for his Master not only adores the Self, but also has unswerving faith in it. Such a one values Knowledge. We respect the person who gives us something. The one who feels that the Knowledge imparted by the Master is superior, has faith in Him. He who has no faith in his Master has not understood Knowledge at all. If you wish to enhance the glory of Knowledge, worship the Master. Everyone has to be independently aware of Knowledge. Worship the Master as a token of your gratitude.

Lecture 84 - The Human Body and Discrimination

"We have seen the wonder of the human body, and seen with the power of discrimination what is the Self and what is non-self. The body is the non-self, and the doer of all is the Self." (*Dasbodh* - Chapter 14, Sub-chapter 9)

It is only after discriminating (viveka) between the Self and the non-self, after discovering who we are and who we are not, after coming to know the marvels of the body, and after inquiring into That which truly exists, that one comes to know that the human body is truly superior to all others. It is even superior to God. We are not the body made up of five elements, we are the omniscient Self. With the help of Knowledge, we come to know that we are the "Witness." The Self is the doer, as well as experiencer of all. All that is seen and has an appearance is non-self. Thought (vichara) helps us to experience that we are the Self.

There are only two objects in this world. One is "I" and the other is "mine." The house, the son, elephants, etc. constitute "my" world but make no mistake, they are not "I." Saying "I" is ego, and saying "mine" is attachment, the ignorant one regards his body as "I," and calls it "mine." When asked, "Who am I?" and "What is mine?," he says, "I am I, and the body is mine. The ear, nose, etc. are mine." He does not say, "I am the nose." He says, "ear, nose, etc. are mine, but I am not the ear or nose." The nose does not say, "The nose is mine," nor does it say "I am the nose." Hence, it follows that He who calls the whole body "mine," must be someone else. He must be apart from the body. After the mind, the intellect, etc. subside (vanish) when one says that they do not exist, what remains is the real "You." That "I," is the Self. Even if you say, "The Self is mine," it means that you are the Self. You say, "The body is mine," but you still continue to identify with the body. Give some thought to this. You have already experienced that you are not the body.

Now, use thinking (vichara), and discrimination (viveka) between "the substance," and the non-substantial things existing in the universe. This radiance of Knowledge is all embracing and exists in all. This is how the sweetness of Oneness is to be relished. This Inner-Self is present in all. The bodies of all the living beings are made up of five elements. Just as ornaments are products of gold, all bodies, such as those of the trees, the elephants, the horses, men, etc. are all products of the universe. When they die, they return back into dust. That dust is blown away as the wind. The wind blends with the Life-Energy, which in dissipates into Reality. Reality is beyond Knowledge and Ignorance. It is "Absolute Knowledge" (Vijnana). There, the distinctions such as "I" and "you" disappear. These distinctions never existed in the first place. They come into play when we recall them. This itself is ego and attachment. The Reality lacks all of this.

By saying "My house," you make a distinction between you and the house. Here the word "my," becomes the cause. The seer and the seen can be clearly defined, and the seer can merge with the seen as well. The "I" and "my," simultaneously merge into oblivion. When you say that there is nothing, you still remain. Eventually, there comes a time when the one who says that there is nothing also ceases to exist. That is the true "Self Form," or Swaroopa, that is "Absolute Knowledge," or Vijnana. The "Spontaneous Natural State" is the real proof that establishes us. It is our true evidence. It is the "Truth," that is the only true state of Reality, and not a fabricated one. When you seem to make changes in it, it is all just make-believe. It is our primordial True Nature without a beginning. The moment you work on it and make slight changes in it, the untrue and nonexistent objects, though fabricated, assume a spontaneously true character. "That which can be perceived and hence concentrated on, is Illusion and that which cannot be perceived is Brahman." That which is experienced on being conscious of this world is Maya, Illusion.

In Marathi it is said that Maya Nasate. Nasate is that which is corrupt. Hence, Maya is rightfully described as that which is corrupt. Nasate is Na and Asate together. Na means not, and Asate means is. Hence, Nasate means "is not," That which is corrupt, is that which is not (Maya). Maya is non-substantial, whereas the substantial essence is Brahman. Brahman is eternal. When all else is destroyed, that which remains is Brahman. That which is destroyed is "non-substantial," and that which remains is the "essence." To sleep is to forget the memories of this world and to wake up means to remember it. When you sleep, the era (kalpa, or concept), comes to an end. When the concepts like, "inner-mind" (antahkarana), Lord Vishnu, Lord Brahma, and Lord Shiva, come to an end, you arrive at the Turya state. Turya is "Tu" and "raha" together (tu means you, and raha is remain). The state when only you remain is the Turya state. Give up that, "I Am," the Turya state, and attain the Reality (Swaroopa).

All objects originate from the dust and hence end up as dust. Yet, we lend the dust many different names. For example, we differentiate dust as wall, room for worship, living room, etc. The human body is also dust. Just as it is mud alone that is given various shapes and then called pots, pans, etc, so is this world made up of mud. If you see from the point of view of the mud, you never see the house. All names have been adopted in order to facilitate our day to day life. One who is ignorant lends names, while a Jnani realizes that all is mud. The more names, the more concepts. After all of this, you say that you are unable to give up doubts and determinations as they refuge to budge. Once you realize that everything is mud, concepts vanish. All the living beings, the universe, everything, are all products of Life-Energy and will eventually return to it.

A disciple asked. "What to do, once Knowledge is obtained?" The Master said, "Put that Knowledge into practice, and worship the Master."

Up to this point, Knowledge is elaborately explained. It is said, "In the end, giving up all the duties of the body, you take refuge in Me alone." He who resides in all hearts is "I." Doing nothing is worship, and saying nothing, is the greatest worship you can offer Him. If you try to do something, the whole process is disrupted and that which you intend to see, seems hidden. Know this and sit peacefully. This, is itself similar to worshipping Him, or singing His hymns. It is by the grace of the Master that the individual (jiva) has not only lost its jivahood (Ignorance), but has also attained Shivahood (Knowledge), and the state of Parameshwara. He has placed you under an obligation, therefore you should worship Him. The one whose thoughts hover at the feet of the Master, and who loves his Master, has faith in Him and harbors great respect for Him. This means that he loves his own Self. The one who loves his Master, values not only Knowledge, but also the Self.

If an untouchable happens to save your life, you develop love towards him. This love springs forth because he has placed you under an obligation. How does love spring? What is the measure of love? Love is measured on the scale of worship. Love is indicated by worship. Knowledge is of the utmost importance. No one besides the Guru, not even God, Lord Indra, or a King can offer you Knowledge. Therefore, you should love the Master. The more you value Knowledge, the more you will love the Master. Each of you should put your inner-mind to the test. In what does a concept deal, and what does a desire reveal? One should be earnest to know. "As is your faith, so is your God." Worship in order to enhance your own prosperity. Worship the one who has obliged you. Adopt the attitude that whatever is bound to happen, will happen. Whatever is bound to vanish, will vanish. When you are the Lord residing in the heart, what can you be lacking? The jiva has not only turned into Shiva, it has now gone beyond Brahman. He is Parabrahman.

Lecture 85 - Skillfully Eliminate Concepts

"All people have the inner feeling that they should meet God personally. However, the remedy found with the power of discrimination is something quite different from this." (*Dasbodh* - Chapter 20, Sub-chapter 9)

Why are bathing, and Sandhya (a ritual to be performed after a morning bath, by every Brahmin who has undergone a thread ceremony) prescribed? The reason is because these things help one's intellect concentrate upon the spiritual. Children are first asked to worship their slates (schoolchildren carried slates to write on), but should they carry out the same worship everyday for the rest of their lives?

Rituals are prescribed in order to make the mind more subtle, but they will not help one attain final Self-realization. Practices help us get a glimpse of God, but God is not Brahman. This is clear and needs no evidence, just as the existence of our thumb needs no evidence. A coconut is not considered to be fruit by a monkey. Similarly, Brahman is not considered important by one who is ignorant. It has to be known skillfully.

If I oppose the thinking, it may temporarily be suppressed, but it is bound to surface. Therefore, skillfully eliminate thoughts and concepts and go beyond them. You are the lone seer, and this whole world is a scene from which you now have to choose that which is beneficial to you. Moreover, this has to be done daily. Just as you clean grains by selecting the grains and discarding the husk, so should you carefully choose that which is "I" and that which is "not I." Continue the investigation saying to yourself every minute, "This is Self, and this is non-Self." This is what is called true "religious service" (Upasana). To think of Him, to get to know Him, and to surrender to Him are all various forms of Upasana.

When you take refuge in the Master with the feeling of Ananya (An is not, Anya means different), "I am not different from the Master," the Master blesses you with Knowledge. There are many theories contained in Vedanta. Deliberate over them, and then He, the eternal and substantial, can be realized with the help of your own True Nature (Swaroopa), and the "I Am He" trick. If you assume that God is apart from you and continue to worship Him, even for a thousand years, you will not be able to find Him. Never will you be able to realize God without the help of the Self. Paramatman, who can be realized by virtue of the ten organs (five sense organs and five action organs), pervades all the living and nonliving worlds and extends into, and occupies our ten organs. He is extensive, entire, and perfect. One should often give thought to this. When the Self gives up yearning for the body, it is Brahman. This is how you worship Him.

The four geneses of species denote the four methods by which living beings originate. The types of speech are also four in number, 1.) the para, 2.) the pashyanti, 3.) the madhyama and 4.) the vaikhari. The four geneses come into being because of the Prakriti, which is based on eight factors. This is what is meant by eight and 4, or eighty-four. Prakriti is based on eight factors and the four geneses of species.

When it is said that one will have to take birth in eighty-four laksha (8.4 million) species, it simply means that if your attention (laksha) remains focused on the eight-fold Prakriti, which gives rise to the four geneses (eight and four, eighty-four), you will be born again and again. In these eighty-four laksha species, you have to find out who the Self is. The eyes perform the function of looking at things around us, but the one who analyses and comprehends what the eyes see is the Self (Consciousness). Hence, it is the Self who sees with the help of the eyes, and hears with the aid of the ears. The Self is described as the eye of the eye. He alone functions through all the ten organs. Just as cream is permeating milk, so does the Self permeate all throughout the body.

It is only due to profound contemplation that our concepts lean toward the intense yearning for Self-realization. If a person beats another, we do not feel sad, because we are obsessed with ourselves. Be obsessed with the idea that the other person and I are one. Only then you will be able to feel their pain. It is you who are obsessed with the body, and therefore you feel that the Self functions through the body. Actually it is the Self who is the lone doer of all. The body is the resting place where the Self as a traveler seeks a temporary shelter. One who identifies with the body, is a mortal, jiva, and if one says that he is present in all bodies existing in the entire universe, he turns into God, Shiva.

Our Ignorance is the causal body, and the Ignorance at the level of the universe is called the Avyakrit. When the three gunas, (Sattva, Rajas and Tamas) are given up, you turn into the "Purusha/Prakriti" (Self/body) duo. From the awareness of creation, protection and destruction the Self/body duo has come into being. The one thing that is ever-changing and experienced in all bodies, is the Self. Whatever exists as the gross is ephemeral (without substance), and that which is the most subtle is eternal.

You have realized that the Self is Brahman, but in order to attain the state of "Nivritti" (elimination of concepts), you have to listen to the Master's teachings. Give up even the concept of calling yourself

Brahman. Then, "That" which remains, without saying a single word, without assuming anything, is Parabrahman. That itself is your natural, spontaneous state. Consider the Self (Atman) to be insubstantial, and give it up as well, Only then can you realize Parabrahman. Brahman is dense, as well as empty.

What does blowing of the conch indicate? The conch is blown when Lord Vishnu is held captive. It only means that when the Self enters or comes down to the inner-mind, it is held captive. Why is a lotus associated with Lord Vishnu? "Padma" means lotus, and Padmapada (lotus steps) symbolizes that Lord Vishnu has slowly descended the steps, taking a single step at a time. Take rest in Him. In the end, after giving up your ego, forget everything and remain at rest within. "That" which remains is a single entity, the one and only Parabrahman. Invocation and immersion are nothing but different modes of worship. Listen to the Knowledge, and then give it up. It is mandatory to give up the rituals and religious observances that you have adopted. First listen to Knowledge, and then give it all up. When the Self becomes completely extensive, it turns into Paramatman, and it no longer requires the body/mind combination, the individual (jiva), worship, or any other practices.

Lecture 86 - Parabrahman is "Seen" Through Merger

"If one tries to hold it, it cannot be held. If one tries to let go of it, it cannot be let go of. Parabrahman is always present everywhere." (*Dasbodh* - Chapter 20, Sub-chapter 10)

How is the Self? You cannot hold on to it. This is because it is you who would be holding yourself. Without meeting Him, you are united with Him, uninterruptedly and incessantly. In this world, you have set out on a mission to look for yourself. The entire human race has come into this world in order to seek the Self. Taking birth in various species, you have been looking for yourself since time immemorial without realizing that the destination is so very close, and you spend lives in search of it.

Your destination is found at the feet of the Sadguru. The moment you consciously attempt to experience the Self, you become small. From Parabrahman, the "Stateless State," you turn into Ishwara, the Creator and "Lord of All." It is Parabrahman that controls the mind, the intellect, the thinking, etc. Who can control Him? As soon as He is revealed, all religions and duties are laid to rest. He is called "Ananta," the endless, as He is eternal. He is imperishable. He and only He exists everywhere. Wherever you look, He is there. He faces all directions and yet does not have a face. No one is conscious of Him, but He is conscious of all. And yet, He lacks the faculty of consciousness. The moment you give up trying to be conscious of Him, you become "Conscious" of Him.

He vanishes because you try to see Him. All knowledge regarding Him is ignorance. Just as a man can never go beyond space, can you never discard Him, as He is your Self. Lord Rama was born the ninth day of the bright half of the month of Chaitra, or "Chaitra Shuddha Navami." This means that when the thinking becomes cleansed (shuddha), the Master is pleased, and the Self is realized. Rama is born. One cannot visit all of the holy places, nor can one see all of the deities representing various gods. This is not so in the case of Parabrahman. Parabrahman is empty like space. The only difference is that space has to be observed by maintaining a separate identity as an observer, whereas Parabrahman can only be "seen" by merger with it. As long as you maintain your identity, you see only empty space.

Merge with it, and you are Parabrahman. This Parabrahman includes the netherworld (Ignorance), Indraloka (the world of Indriyas, the organs), Chandraloka, the world of desires and wishes, and lastly, Vaikunthaloka the abode of Lord Vishnu, the mind. Heaven, hell, and the mortal world, all exist in the Self. This is because the intellect exists in the Self. The body is referred to as Kashi, and the Self is called Rameshwar. Kashi in the North, and Rameshwar in the South, are two of the most holy places for Hindus. This means that the heart represents the entire region between Kashi and Rameshwar covering fifty-six kingdoms. Fifty-six kingdoms means five sensory organs, and six vikaras (existence, birth, growth, modification, decay and death). The one who wins over them, is said to have control over the entire country.

Lecture 87 - Absorption of the Mind

To develop the feeling "I" in reference to one's True Nature is what called the mind. It is only Ignorance to identify different bodies as "I," my wife, etc. The relationship of "wife" does not exist in the beginning. It develops later, but one gets carried away with it. This is Ignorance.

This happens because we identify Brahman with many different bodies, although it is a single entity.

This entire world appearance is delusion. Give it up. Go about it step by step. First, get over the feelings "This is my house," "This is my village," etc. Say instead, "I am the Master's son." Why not say that? It will help you be rid yourself of delusion and gain salvation.

Although the seeker continues to be a father or a husband, he should not identify with those roles. If you identify yourself with those roles, you continue to exist as an individual (jiva). Don't do it! Do not repeat what you have done so far. Do not continue as you previously did. Help yourself attain liberation. Say, "I Exist Eternally." Do not exist as the individual, exist as Paramatman. Remember that you get what you imagine. If you think that you are the individual, you turn into the individual, and if you exist as the Paramatman, you turn into Paramatman. The concept of Paramatman should penetrate deeply. This thought process brings about the dawn of the Self. Your existence and your bliss prevail only by relinquishing the quality of individuality.

Your existence as an individual should be entirely eliminated. This is prescribed in order to attain the state of Brahman. There is no sacred hour to begin this practice. Waiting for the sacred hour to begin spiritual practice, implies that time has invaded the timeless Ultimate Truth. I prefer to preach using direct language, because I am precise and I do not beat about the bush. Where there is no sacrifice, there can be no Ultimate Truth.

Adhere to the principle, "I Am Brahman," and behave accordingly. Remaining immersed in the your True Nature is as good as singing the hymns of the Lord. One who says "I Am He," is himself Brahman. You should be enlightened with this Pure Knowledge. You will come to know this, when you worship the Master. How should you sing the bhajans (the sacred hymns) of the Lord? The scriptures have prescribed nine types of worship (Navavidha Bhakti; the nine-faceted devotion outlined in *Dasbodh*). Bhakti is a must because:

"Bhakti is the mother of Jnana (Knowledge), as it gives birth to Jnana."

If you cannot worship physically, at least do so in the mind. The Master is God, hence the glory of the Master should be extolled. Kirtan (praises put to music) means narration (of God or Guru). Chanting of "Naam" (repetition of mantra) means incessant incantation, either of the mantra given by the Master, or of "I Am He." Contemplate the mantra incessantly. Continuously recall the mantra. Keep reflection upon matters like, "I am the Self," and "What are the characteristics of the Self?," etc. This living body is a holy abode of the Almighty.

Mahadev (Shiva) is the greatest of the Gods. He is none other than the Self. He had consumed poison (poison indicates worldly desires) and digested it. It simply means that he was engrossed in fulfilling his desires. Hence, he was a poor jiva. With the aid of incessant incantation of the name of Rama, he turned into Shiva. Non-attachment, renunciation, etc. are prescribed in order to gain "experience." Once experience is gained, of what use is all of it? The "sacrifice of association" means sacrificing the association with "I" (the ego). The Sadguru (the Master) is forgiveness personified. Whatever you do, the Master ignores the misdeeds and concentrates only on the merits. The world functions on account of such merits.

That Knowledge which bears fruits at the appropriate time is the "Knowledge of Brahman." This path of Knowledge, revealed to you only by the Sadguru, is free from Illusion and delusion. One whose attention is focused on the unreal, can never turn to the Real. Regardless of the amount of effort that one has put in, and the number of practices one might have undertaken, it is difficult to find the path of Self-realization, which is known only to the Sadguru.

A Marathi proverb says, "Without a Saint in one's vicinity, you can never even think about overcoming calamity."

"Prasanga" is Marathi for calamity. Prasanga is Pra, the word para modified, and Sanga together. (Para is beyond, Sanga means company or association) All that this means is that without the association of the Saints, never will you enjoy the company of the "Para," or that which is otherwise beyond our capacity. Lord Rama and Lord Krishna who have now come to be idolized as Gods, were nothing but Masters in their times.

In reality, the one "True God" can never be worshipped, as He is not apart from you. There is not a single shrine of the True God. Therefore, you should worship only the Master, and then you are transformed into the Lord. Offer your salutations to the Sun in the form of Knowledge that lies within you. Worship that Knowledge with the help of your mind. This is called the worship (puja) done in the mind (Manas Puja). The mind becomes liberal through such worship. The Self is itself the Sadguru. To do the nine types of worship, the Navavidha worship, is the only service you can offer Him for attaining the Ultimate Truth.

There is an incident mentioned in the Hindu epic Mahabharata, that tells about how while the Pandavas were trapped in the house of shellac, the Lakshagriha (Laksha is shellac, Griha is house), it was set ablaze by their cousins, the Kauravas. The Pandavas were rescued through an underground tunnel (vivara). This means that when their house, griha, in the form of their goal, Laksha (Goal is the other meaning of Laksha), was set on fire, they were rescued and liberated by the Sadguru, who with the help of explanation, shifted their focus towards the Ultimate Truth, the Reality.

The akarma, or "non-deeds" (the things done, but not claimed by the doer as having been done by him) of the one who faithfully adheres to the advice of the Master, turn into good deeds. His deeds themselves are transformed into Brahman. He is full of purity. He is so pure that whatever the actions (karma), nothing affects him. The image of the Master should perpetually abide in your heart.

The sunlight is unbearably scorching because when the sun rises, once again the daily life, along with all its day to day transactions begins, and with it comes back all the tensions, worries and anxieties. These anxieties bring about a burning (scorching) of the mind. During the night, while you sleep, there are no anxieties. In the sleeping state, the king and the beggar are both alike. The Sadguru is compared to the Sun. The transactions of the mind are carried out in both the waking and the dreaming states. The light of the Sun, in the form of the teachings of the Sadguru, destroys the darkness of Ignorance and brings about the dawn of Knowledge. When the Sun in the form of the Sadguru arises, it destroys the night of Ignorance and with it vanishes all of the sorrows generated by Ignorance. When the Sadguru accepts you as His disciple, He convinces you that the delusion of the worldly life is untrue. Such a Master should be offered a salute (namaskar). Why? Because we need Him, as He is the Sun, in the form of Knowledge.

The Sadguru penetrates the night of Avidya (Ignorance), the objective knowledge, and brings about the dawn of a "Golden Day" in the form of advice (teachings). Night means the ignorance regarding our "True Nature," and the understanding of "Who am I?" True Knowledge cannot be realized unless worldly knowledge is proven to be untrue. The bird in the form of the individual (jiva) is given the "Eyes of Knowledge" and is divested of the feeling of "I am the body" by the Master. One becomes convinced that oneself is the Self.

The Sadguru convinces you that you are the Self by advising the intellect. He also destroys the duality that has seeped into the intellect. He eliminates the differentiating viewpoint (duality) which taints the sight of the traveler treading the path of Self-Realization. When the inspiration

Soham, "I Am He," is realized deep within, the Sun in the form of Knowledge is at its zenith. The delusion that has obscured the Self thus far vanishes. How then, can the dream in the form of this world persist? Now, the one who is the 'king of the land" in the form of our house, the Self (Atman), has dawned. He destroys both the apparent and the non-apparent.

There are two types of delusions, one is the delusion of Maya (Illusion) and the other is the delusion of Vedanta. The world is made apparent by the delusion of Maya. The delusion "I do not know the Self" is the Vedantic delusion. The Sadguru is always beyond these delusions. He may not be physically glowing but, it is as if He, that Nivrittinath (Nivrittti is devoid of concepts, nath is Lord), the Lord who is devoid of concepts has undertaken the venture of illuminating everything. I offer my namaskar (salute) to Him. When we come to know the greatness of the Lord, we can praise Him.

How do we praise the Sadguru? If we please God, he may grant us a boon or a gift, by virtue of which we will get even more entangled in the delusion of Maya. Vedanta is a marvelous invention. For the sake of the ignorant, the saints and sages of the old days have written down their direct experience as Vedanta. There are fourteen sciences and sixty-four arts. The "Science of Brahman" is the fourteenth science. Supremacy can be achieved with the aid of this science. This science which can be owned even by an individual (jiva) is called the "Science of Brahman," and it can be achieved only through the teachings of the Sadguru. Therefore, it should be learned from one who knows Brahman, and is proficient expounding upon the "Knowledge of Brahman."

Lecture 88 - Signs of a Sadguru and a Disciple

From a talk on the *Eknathi Bhagwat* of Saint Eknath

Jai, Jai, Oh Sadguru, Lord of the Lords! (Jai is a salutation meaning victory). Why is the word Jai repeated twice? The repetition suggests victory in this "mortal world," and in the "world beyond." Oh Sadguru, you lend "godliness" (the qualities of God) not only to the individual (jiva) but also to God himself. Therefore, the rank of the Sadguru has been conferred upon you when this Vishwatman (Vishwa is the world,

Atman is the Self), the Self which has come into being in this world, reaches the state of the Reality, and considers it as ones own.

Without investing full faith in the Sadguru, one can never attain "Universality." When the Self attains complete Reality, he is said to be Universal (Vishwasi). Faithful is another meaning of Vishwasi, and without faith, one can never reach Swaroopa. The one who has donned this body is not called Vishwasi. It is the Sadguru that appears in the dreaming, waking and sleeping states. Non-worshippers and the "non-faithful" have belittled the Vedanta. When shelter is taken at the Sadguru's feet, the "Tat"(That) and "Tvam" (you) both drop off, and the rank of "Asi" (are) is secured by the grace of the Sadguru. It means you come to know that "You Are That" (Tat Tvam Asi).

My parents are the father and the mother of my body, but you, the Sadguru, are my real mother, and have produced me without the help of the womb. You are my mother as well as my father. I will tell you the symptoms of the unfortunate one who does not worship such a Sadguru. One who does not worship God gets burdened with great sorrows in the form of the Illusion. Is there anyone who has taken birth in the human species who does not yet worship the Lord? No, it is when all your righteous deeds bear fruit, that you acquire a human body. You may have to take several billion births as a human being before coming in contact with a Sadguru.

You ask me to explain the *Eknathi Bhagwat* dharma (Eknathi Bhagwat is a devotional holy text describing the principles of Hindu philosophy) which will help destroy Maya (Illusion). Maya is full of the three gunas, Sattva, Rajas and Tamas. Living beings are greatly troubled by the heat of the Sun. Fire is produced by the "suryakant bead" in presence of Sunlight (like a magnifying glass). All this is done without the knowledge of the Sun (the sun is not aware of having done anything). Primal Illusion is defined as the feeling of "Existence in Nothingness." Both the body and "Swaroopa" possess neither name, nor form. The body possesses spittle, urine, sweat, etc. but does not really possess a name, because the name is untrue. In every day life, there exists an imagined person named "so-and-so," yet the Self is non-conceptual. Then who is the one saying "I"? It is the Primal Illusion.

An inspiration of existence arose in non-conceptual form. This inspiration itself is "Sat-Chit-Ananda" (Being, Consciousness, Bliss). In spite of existing in the form of Bliss, the Lord wanted to enjoy more bliss. "Let me see myself, be conscious of myself," thought the Lord. "Let me talk to myself because talking to oneself is blissful." By His own wish, the Lord created the fourfold objects such as, the four liberations, the four geneses, the four speeches, etc. He also created the three gunas, Sattva, Rajas, and Tamas, and the trinity of the observer, the observed and the observation. In spite of the existence of all this, the Lord was overwhelmed with the feeling of loneliness. For a long time, He was alone. Although He existed in many forms, He was single. He was there in all the elements, and He was all the elements. After a long time, pride came into being, and everyone named themselves. The name later became firmly affixed. Then, everyone took pride in his name, and imagined separation.

Everything that appeared, appeared in His dream, but before the dream, He was alone, and after the dream, He remains alone. When there is no knowledge of Life-Energy there is nothing, and where there is nothing there is space. When the Life-Energy (Chaitanya) blows, it is distinguished as wind and so on. This is how the Chaitanya has modified into the five principle elements. The Chaitanya is a single entity, the name is the only factor that varies. We are nothing but Chaitanya. That Chaitanya constitutes the "male" principle, and is called the Purusha (Pure Being). The source of all is the same Chaitanya, hence Ignorance and the Knowledge are the same. Maya lacks the power to know the Self. The one who knows all, who illuminates all, is the Self in the form of "Chit," Universal Consciousness.

In spite of permeating the five elements, the Self does not make its presence felt. The elements possess distinct characteristics, and the elements oppose one another, but because of the presence of the Self, they all exist in harmony. The Chaitanya in the universe is distinguished as Shiva and that in the body is known as the individual, the jiva. The Maya in the universe is termed as Yogamaya (Illusion of Oneness), and that in the body is called Avidyamaya (objective knowledge). The world of the Ishwara is in the form of Awareness, whereas the world is in the form of dream. Maya is pure delusion. As Shiva is obsessed with desires, it turns into jiva. That very jiva, which is truly only singular later turns "tenfold." In the singular phase, it turns into the "inner-mind," the antahkarana, and in the "tenfold" phase, it expresses itself through the ten organs (Five sensory organs and five organs of actions).

The one who says "O" (in response to a call from someone) is himself Omkar the form of OM. Omkar is Brahman breaking into speech. When a child is born, it only utters "O." At birth, if an infant starts laughing instead of crying, it will be said that there is certainly something wrong. When an infant cries it says "O." That "O" comprises three syllables (AUM), the "A" pronounced as "u" as in Cup, the "U" pronounced as "oo" as in Book, and the "M" pronounced as "m" as in Him. Why does an infant cry? The Lord begins to cry because He is afflicted by the state of being a jiva. That itself is the Avatar (incarnation) of "OM." Avatar or Avatarana means to come down, a downfall. He becomes captive, imprisoned in the body. If you forget the Self, the worry for the fulfillment of the needs of the body increases.

Thinking of desires is itself the mind. Afterwards, the accumulation of doubts and determinations goes on expanding. Worries, etc. are all stacked in the mind. When the mind is stable, all is well. The foolishness of saying, "I am the body" is the intellect. The intellect determines that this is the right hand, this is left, this is auspicious, this is not, etc. That which forms concepts is nothing but the mind. The mind (manas), the intellect (buddhi), the thoughts (chitta), and the ego (aham), all together have produced the worldly life. Thoughts (chitta) are in the pure form of Chit (Consciousness), but when the ego of this body and worldly life come in, the thoughts being in the form of Consciousness disappear. This is the distinctive mark of the singular phase.

Now I will tell you about the "tenfold" phase. That Lord who dwells in all, Narayana, permeates the ten organs. Specific organs perform specific functions. Hence, they are distinct. It is Narayana who functions in them all. He is simultaneously aware of the functioning of all the organs. The ego of the body says, "the tongue tastes, the eyes see," etc. He who animates the mind, the intellect, the body, the organs, the desires, etc. is the one and only Self. Because the concept "I am the body" is firmly held on to, the ignorant one considers that the organs themselves perform their respective functions. If the feeling "I am Chaitanya" is harbored, we are Shiva for sure. If no such feeling is harbored we are jiva.

As soon as we assume the body to be the doer of all actions, the organs of the body get obsessed with desires. We then become extremely small. This is how the Lord, the Almighty, is reduced to a trivial state, when imprisoned in the body. The entire world of this jiva is now the length of three arms, the length of the body. The jiva's love is restricted only to the body, in stark contrast with that of Shiva. The state of Shiva is described as "I exist in all bodies, and I enjoy and endure all experiences." As I am haunted by the concept "I am the body," the worldly life has come into being. What is pleasure, after all? Whatever gives pleasing sensations to the nerves. We first bind ourselves with our concepts and then create a false sensation of pleasure. What is true joy?

Satisfaction without concepts, is Bliss. Desires are conceptual and hence pleasure arising out of the fulfillment of desires is not true. Pleasure is a favorable sensation. Pleasures have to be enjoyed, and then forgotten, as they cannot to be stored. The ten desires of ten different organs pull the jiva in ten different directions. In a bid to fulfill ten different desires, the harmony is lost and the jiva is still further entangled in "I" and "my." Thus, though all the deeds happen due to the innate property of Prakriti (the body), the one who dons the body, says, "I have done them all" and takes pride in them. He then gets trapped. Whatever concepts he forms, his body gets adapted to them. This Self, in spite of being immortal, is afflicted by death, because it harbors the desire to reap the fruits of actions, and the cycle of death and birth continues, on and on.

The Sun is steady with respect to the earth, yet it appears to revolve around the Earth. Similarly, the Self is steady, but revolves in the cycle of 8.4 millions births and deaths, because of the identification with the body. Once one comes into contact with a Sadguru, the Sadguru helps one escape from the clutches of the cycle of death and birth, and also to cross the ocean of the worldly existence (samsara). This Self, which is indeed Paramatman, conceives that "I am the body," takes fancy to all the affections of the body, and enjoys or endures the joys and sorrows accordingly. Upon meeting the Sadguru the jiva can now opt for the path of liberation over the cycle of births and deaths.

Maya (Illusion) is nothing, and can be easily overcome by one who has given up body-consciousness. However, for the one who is body conscious, it is difficult to transcend the bounds of Maya. One who believes that the Sadguru is Paramatman, and who worships the Master, investing total faith in Him, can easily transgress the bounds of Maya. Prabuddha (Higher Intellect), the younger brother of Antariksha (the space) says, "I transgress the bounds of Maya with the aid of the advice of the Sadguru." Inspired by faith, he who seeks refuge at the feet of the Sadguru, attains liberation. What are the signs of a Sadguru? The Sadguru is He who protects the weak, and He who possesses the ability to advise disciples. He is proficient in expressing (teaching) Knowledge. He takes into account the ability of his disciples, suggests a remedy and helps them attain liberation. The Sadguru cares for his disciple as if the disciple were his son. He does not consider the disciple to be his servant, even though the disciple may serve him day and night. He does not possess the pride of being the Master. He does not depend on his disciples for his maintenance. He is unaffected by desires, as He neither entertains nor gives up desires. He is always remains immersed in His "True Form," saying that actions are the characteristic features of the body. He outwardly does as others do. He worships, remaining apart from everything. He who is adorned with peace, is a Sadguru.

The signs of a disciple will not be told. A disciple should not just merely maintain a sattvic exterior. One should not harbor doubts within one's mind. One should not be cunning, and should not cheat on Knowledge. To cheat on Knowledge means to be desirous of achieving Knowledge, but to fall short of worship. Some worship is done only to gain powers (siddhis), and some merely follow rituals, while others shun rituals. Some have their minds tainted with concepts even after receiving advice from the Master. The individual (jiva) has developed a habit of taking on the sins (activities) of others. The seekers of the Ultimate Truth are purely sattvic. One who is ever vigilant is unaffected by Maya, and considers it as non-existing. One who firmly believes the advice of the Master, and behaves accordingly, receives the support of the Master. Those who have dedicated their lives to the teachings of the Sadguru are true disciples and are unaffected by Illusion.

The conviction that the Master is Paramatman should be imbibed thoroughly.

THE END of AMRUT LAYA

www.ingramcontent.com/pod-product-compliance
Lightning Source LLC
Chambersburg PA
CBHW031056080526
44587CB00011B/705